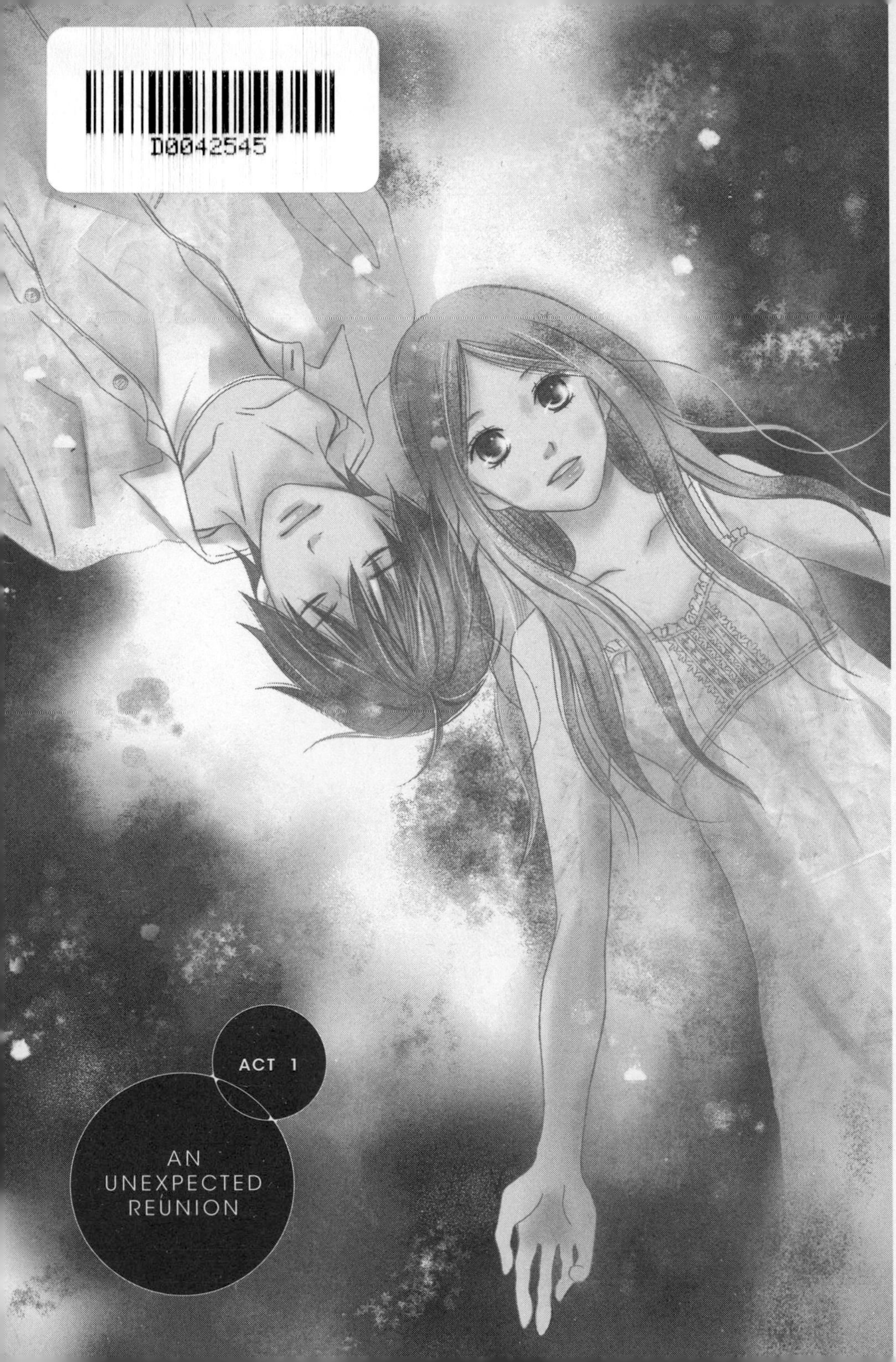
ACT 1
AN UNEXPECTED REUNION

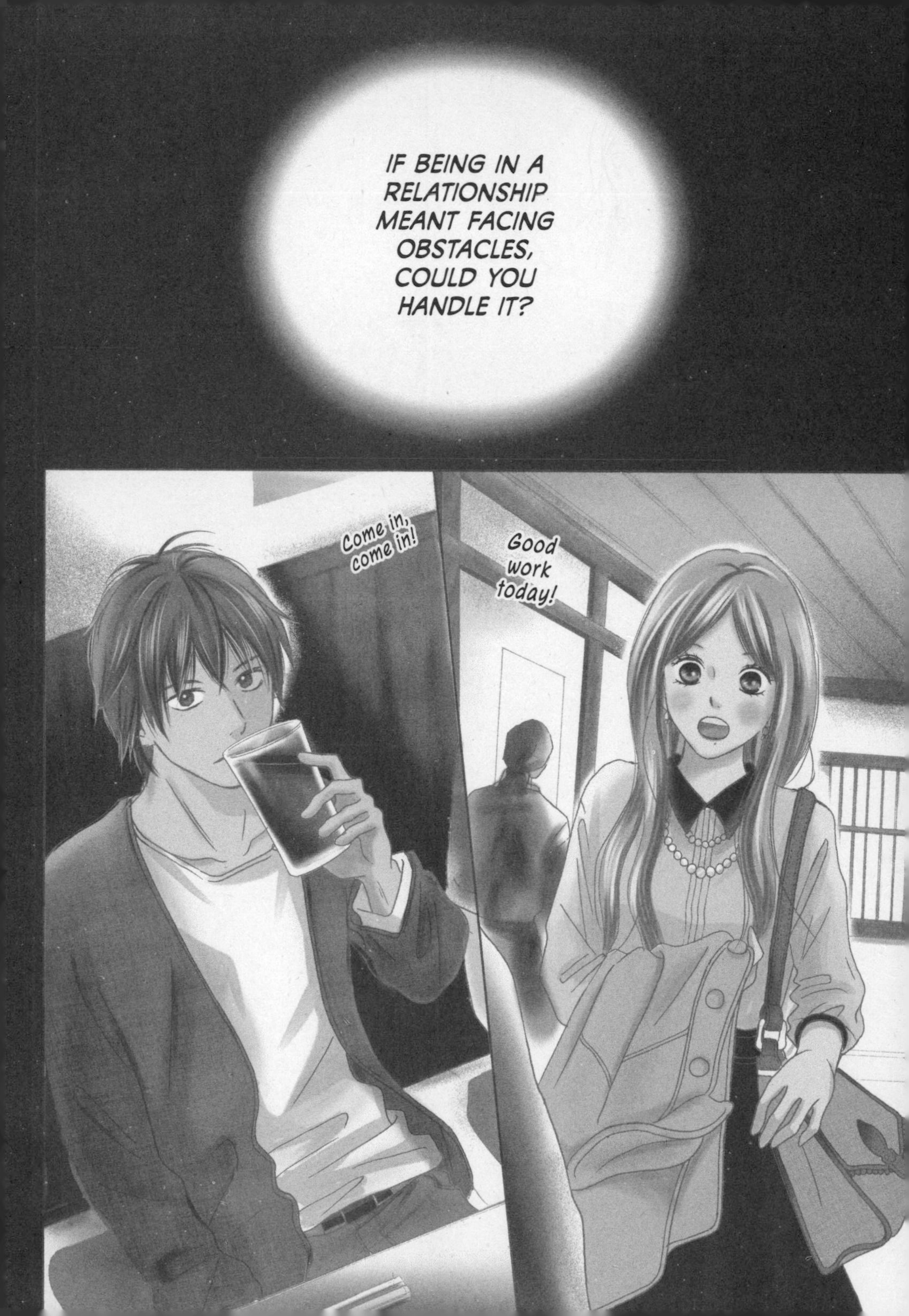
IF BEING IN A RELATIONSHIP MEANT FACING OBSTACLES, COULD YOU HANDLE IT?
Good work today!
Come in, come in!

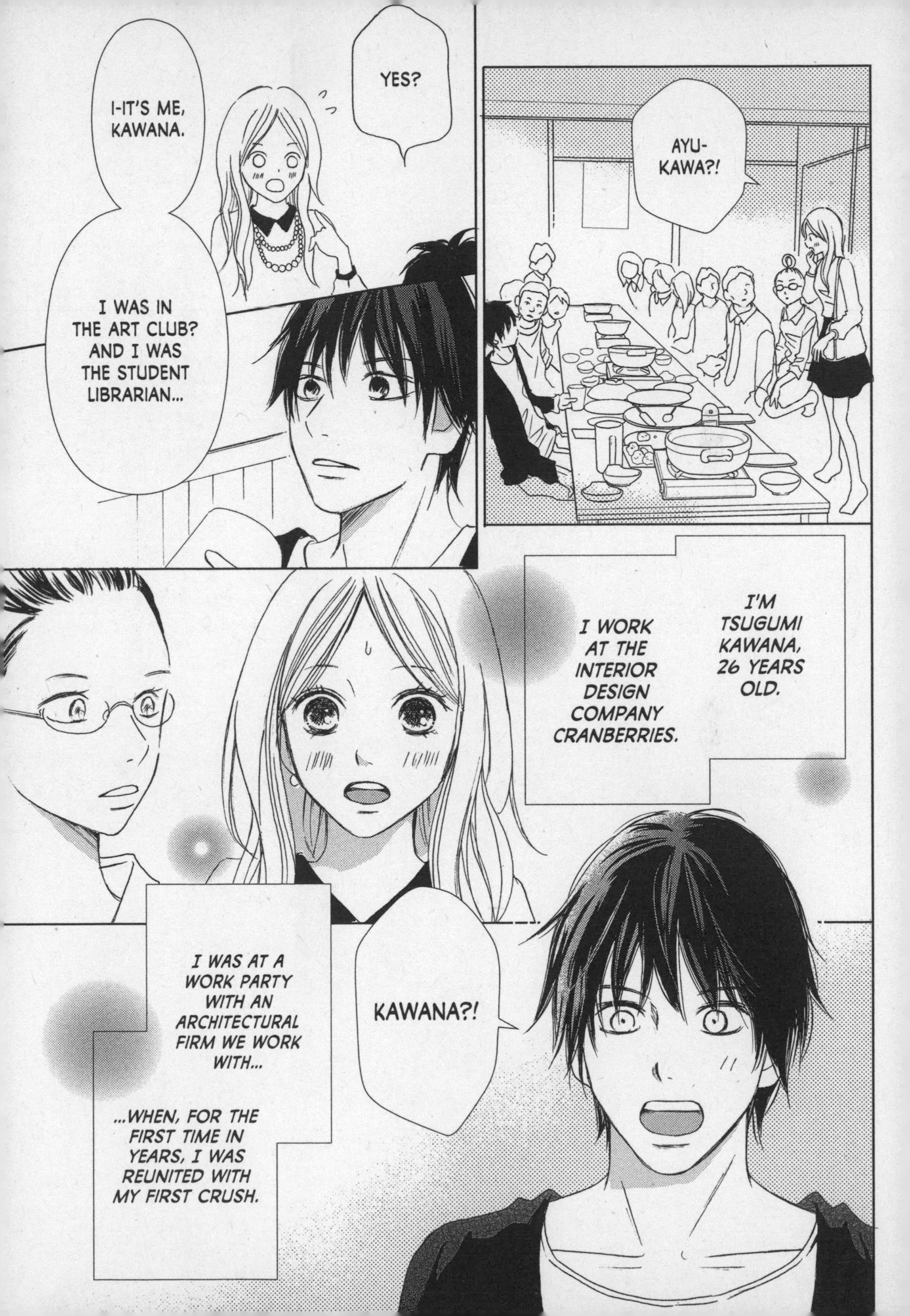
AYU-KAWA?!
YES?
I-IT'S ME, KAWANA.
I WAS IN THE ART CLUB? AND I WAS THE STUDENT LIBRARIAN...
I'M TSUGUMI KAWANA, 26 YEARS OLD.
I WORK AT THE INTERIOR DESIGN COMPANY CRANBERRIES.
KAWANA?!
I WAS AT A WORK PARTY WITH AN ARCHITECTURAL FIRM WE WORK WITH...
...WHEN, FOR THE FIRST TIME IN YEARS, I WAS REUNITED WITH MY FIRST CRUSH.

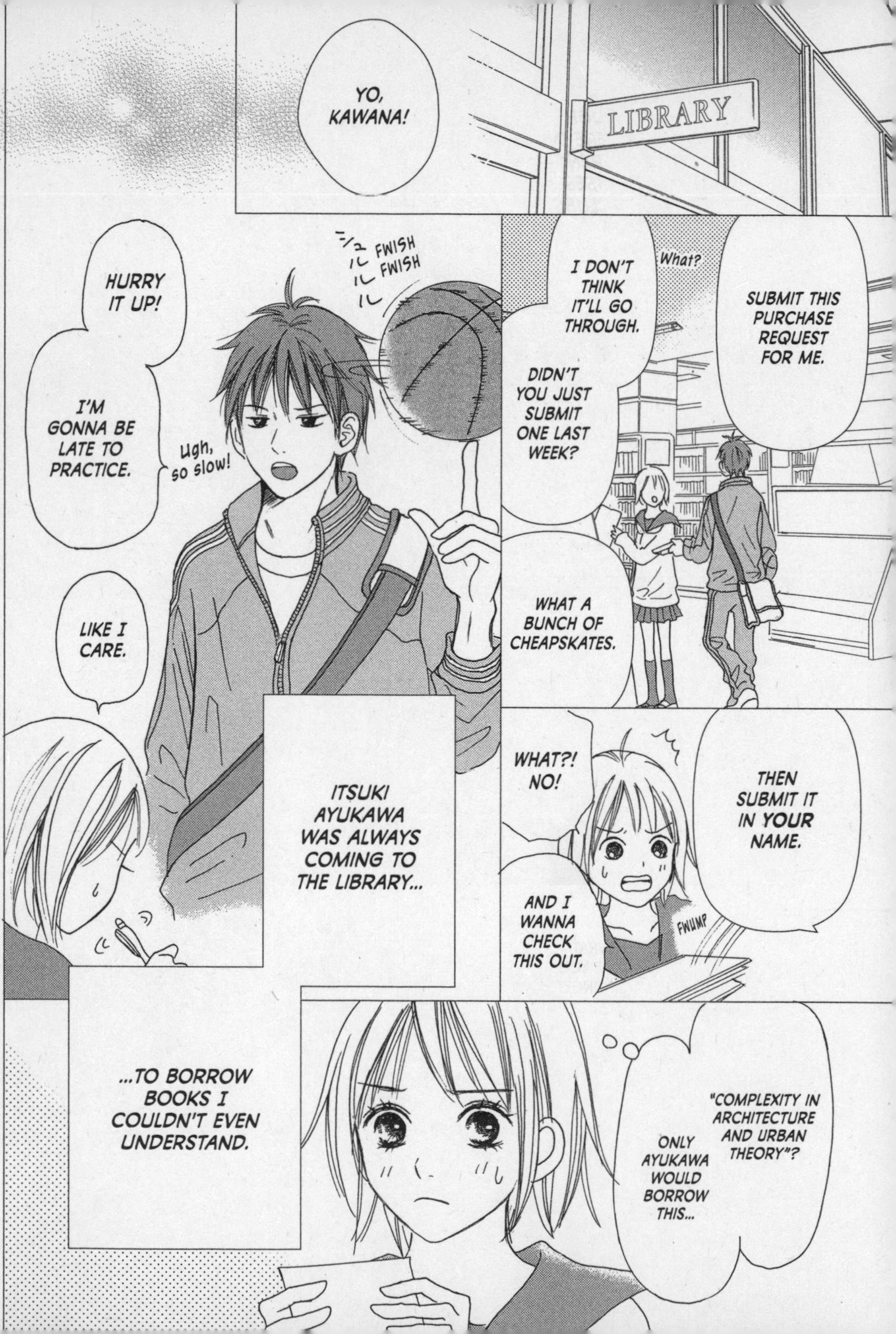
LIBRARY
YO, KAWANA!
SUBMIT THIS PURCHASE REQUEST FOR ME.
What?
I DON'T THINK IT'LL GO THROUGH.
DIDN'T YOU JUST SUBMIT ONE LAST WEEK?
WHAT A BUNCH OF CHEAPSKATES.
THEN SUBMIT IT IN YOUR NAME.
FWUMP
WHAT?! NO!
AND I WANNA CHECK THIS OUT.
FWISH FWISH
HURRY IT UP!
I'M GONNA BE LATE TO PRACTICE.
Ugh, so slow!
LIKE I CARE.
ITSUKI AYUKAWA WAS ALWAYS COMING TO THE LIBRARY...
"COMPLEXITY IN ARCHITECTURE AND URBAN THEORY"?
ONLY AYUKAWA WOULD BORROW THIS...
...TO BORROW BOOKS I COULDN'T EVEN UNDERSTAND.

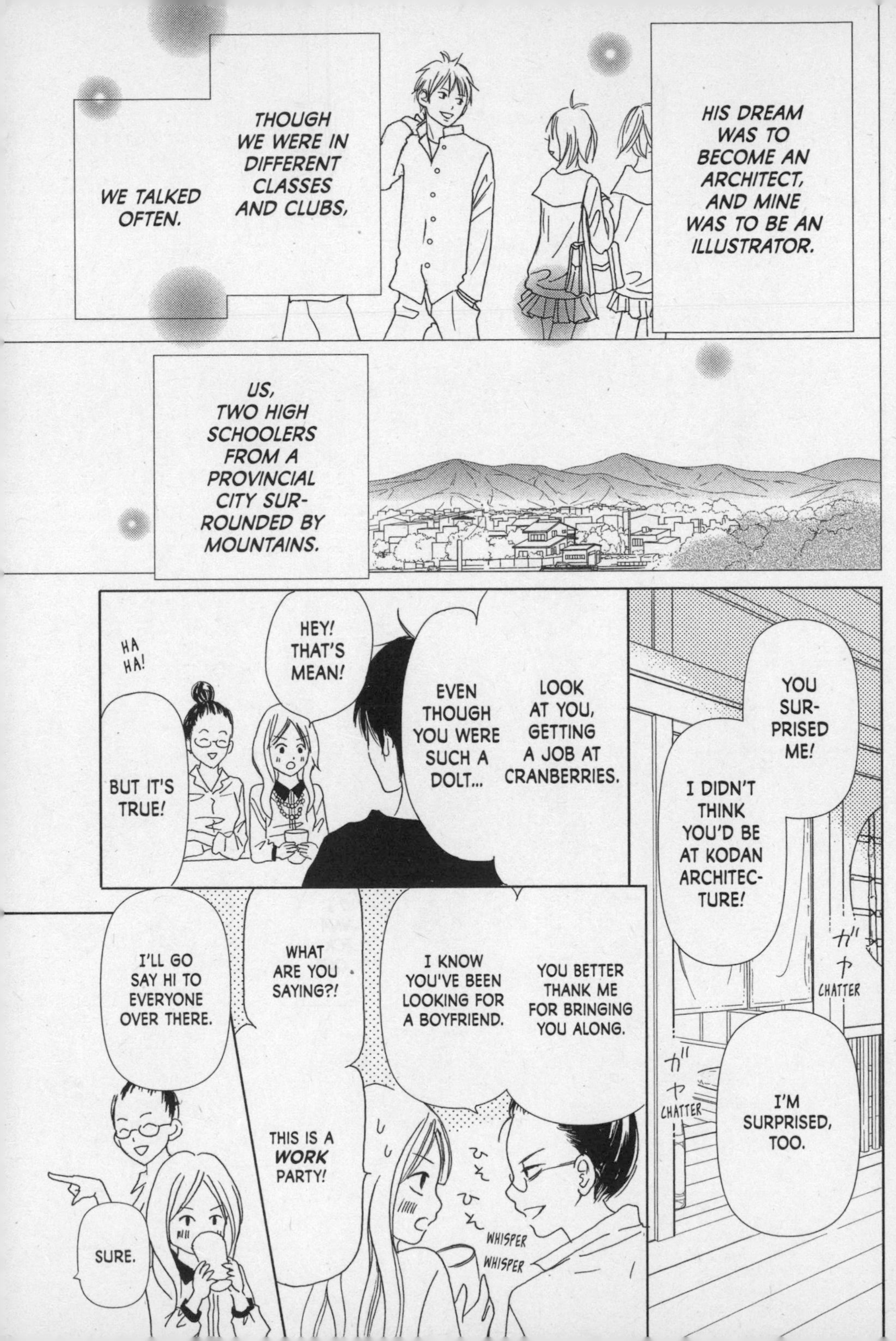
HIS DREAM WAS TO BECOME AN ARCHITECT, AND MINE WAS TO BE AN ILLUSTRATOR.
THOUGH WE WERE IN DIFFERENT CLASSES AND CLUBS,
WE TALKED OFTEN.
US, TWO HIGH SCHOOLERS FROM A PROVINCIAL CITY SUR-ROUNDED BY MOUNTAINS.
YOU SUR-PRISED ME!
I DIDN'T THINK YOU'D BE AT KODAN ARCHITEC-TURE!
ガヤ
CHATTER
ガヤ
CHATTER
I'M SURPRISED, TOO.
LOOK AT YOU, GETTING A JOB AT CRANBERRIES.
EVEN THOUGH YOU WERE SUCH A DOLT...
HEY! THAT'S MEAN!
HA HA!
BUT IT'S TRUE!
YOU BETTER THANK ME FOR BRINGING YOU ALONG.
I KNOW YOU'VE BEEN LOOKING FOR A BOYFRIEND.
WHAT ARE YOU SAYING?!
THIS IS A **WORK** PARTY!
ひそ ひそ
WHISPER WHISPER
I'LL GO SAY HI TO EVERYONE OVER THERE.
SURE.

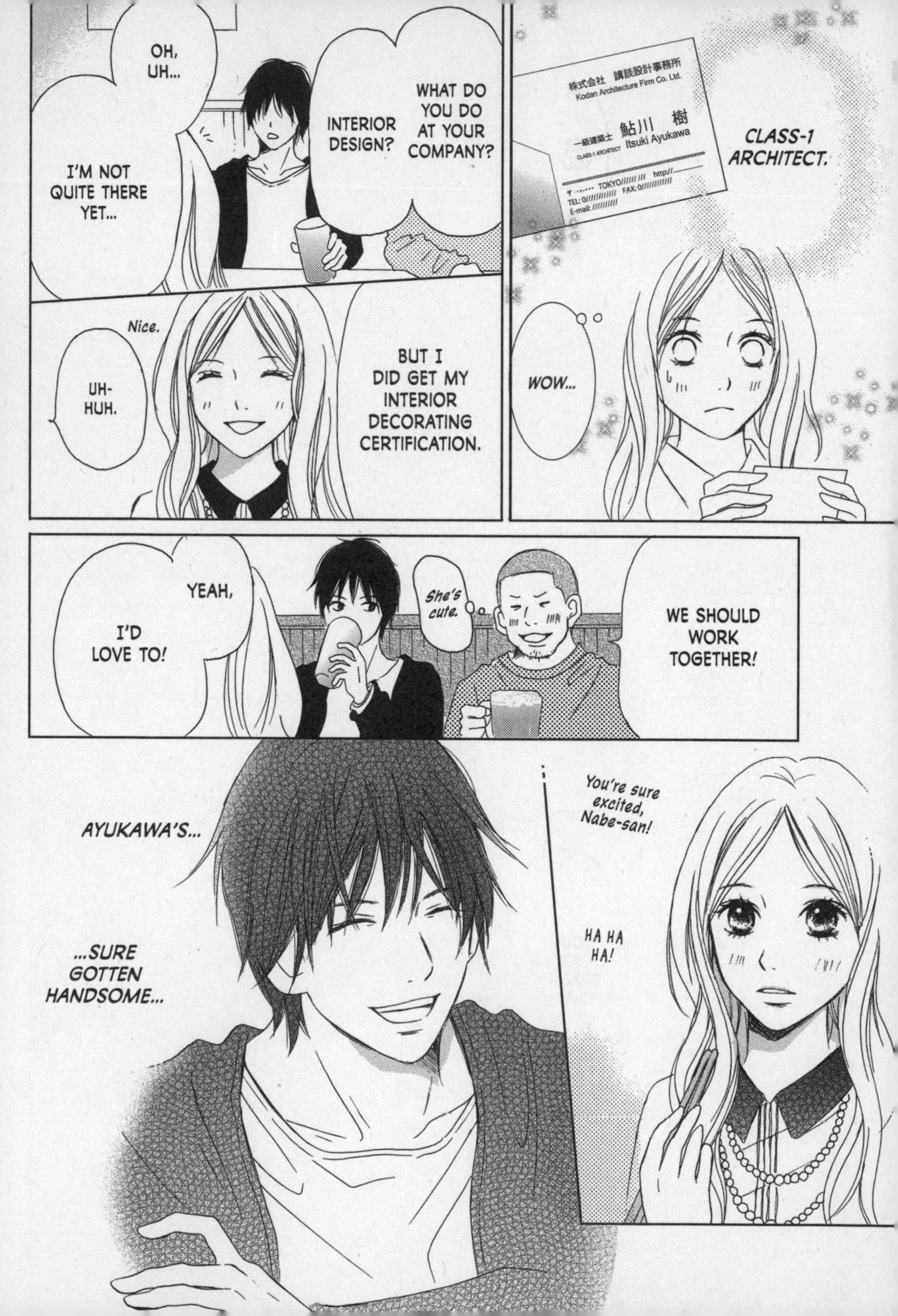

株式会社 講談設計事務所
Kodan Architecture Firm Co. Ltd.
一級建築士 鮎川 樹
CLASS-1 ARCHITECT Itsuki Ayukawa
CLASS-1 ARCHITECT.
WOW...
WHAT DO YOU DO AT YOUR COMPANY?
INTERIOR DESIGN?
OH, UH...
I'M NOT QUITE THERE YET...
BUT I DID GET MY INTERIOR DECORATING CERTIFICATION.
Nice.
UH-HUH.
WE SHOULD WORK TOGETHER!
She's cute.
YEAH,
I'D LOVE TO!
You're sure excited, Nabe-san!
HA HA HA!
AYUKAWA'S...
...SURE GOTTEN HANDSOME...

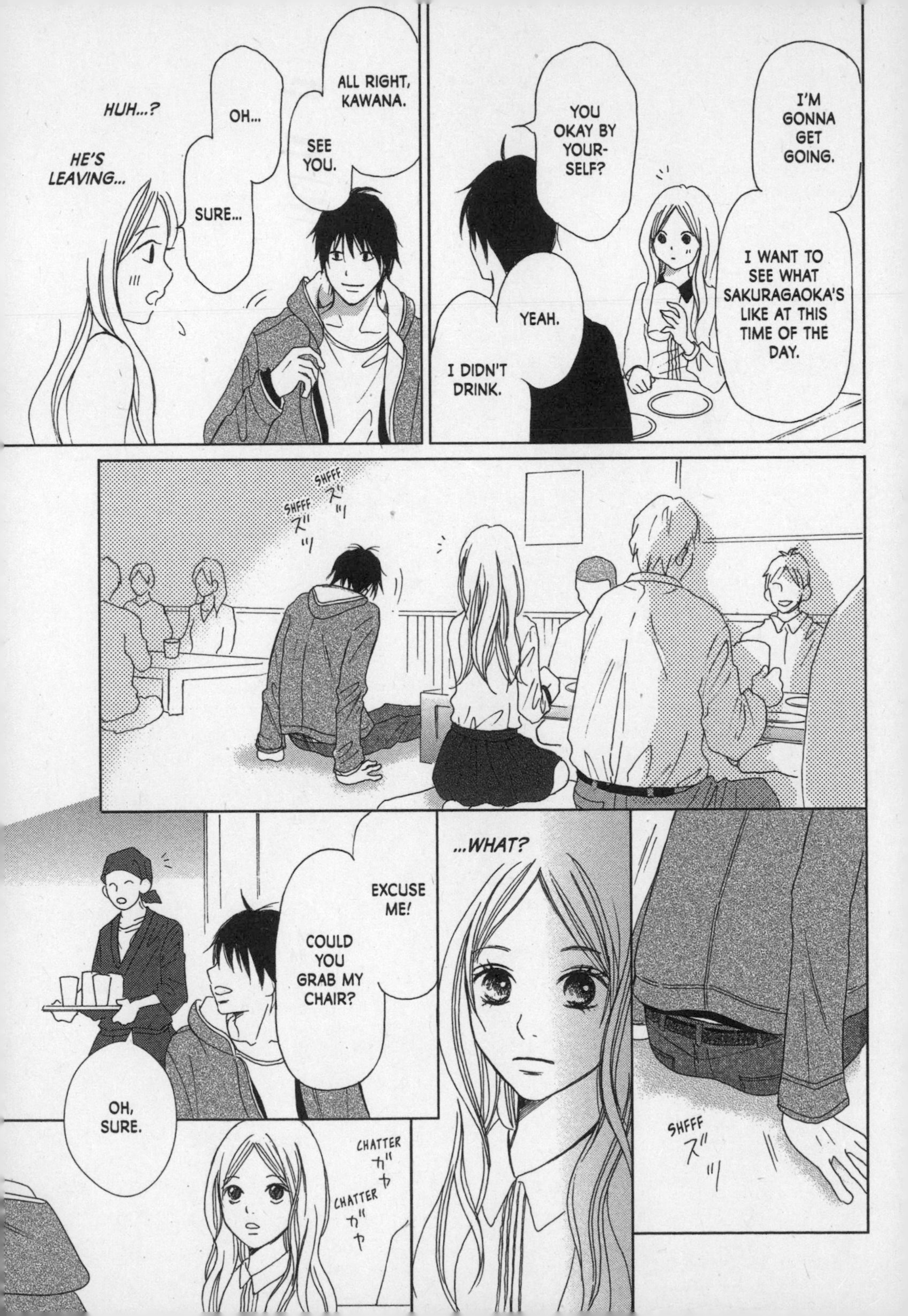
I'M GONNA GET GOING.
I WANT TO SEE WHAT SAKURAGAOKA'S LIKE AT THIS TIME OF THE DAY.
YOU OKAY BY YOUR-SELF?
YEAH.
I DIDN'T DRINK.
ALL RIGHT, KAWANA.
SEE YOU.
OH...
SURE...
HUH...?
HE'S LEAVING...
SHFFF ズリ
SHFFF ズリ
SHFFF ズリ
EXCUSE ME!
COULD YOU GRAB MY CHAIR?
OH, SURE.
...WHAT?
CHATTER ガヤ
CHATTER ガヤ

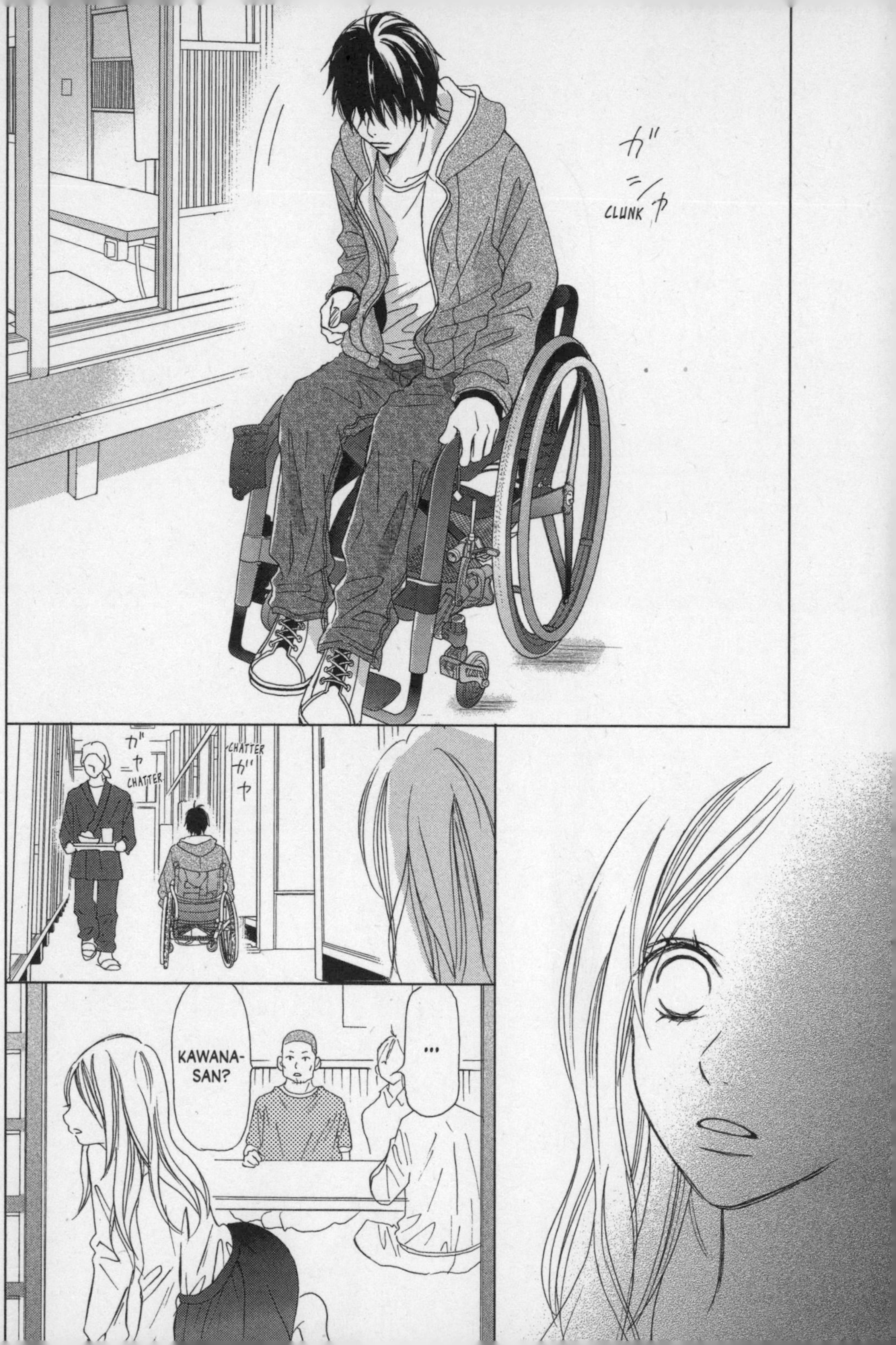
ガシャ
CLUNK
ガヤ
CHATTER
ガヤ
CHATTER
...
KAWANA-SAN?

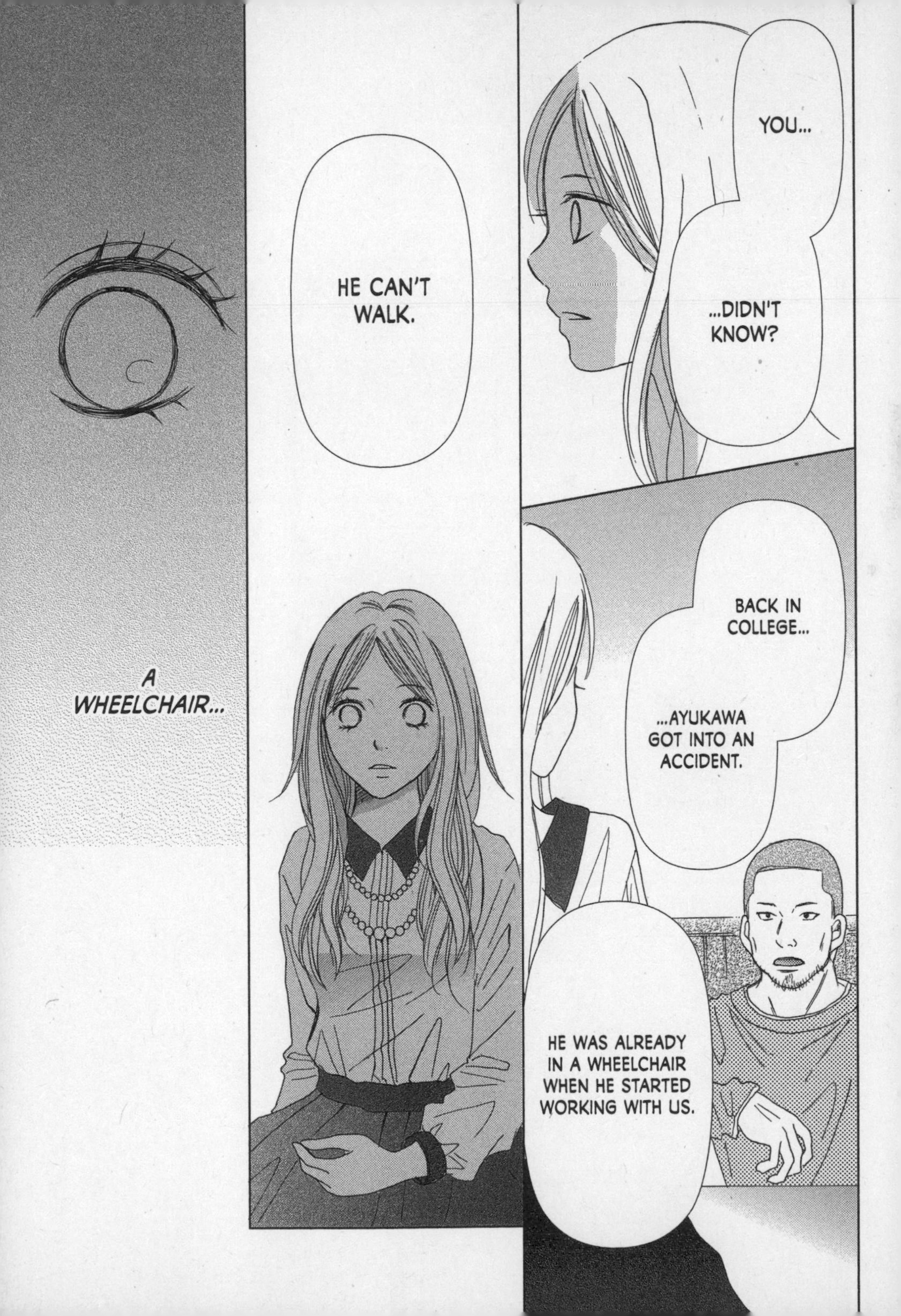
YOU...
...DIDN'T KNOW?
BACK IN COLLEGE...
...AYUKAWA GOT INTO AN ACCIDENT.
HE WAS ALREADY IN A WHEELCHAIR WHEN HE STARTED WORKING WITH US.
HE CAN'T WALK.
A WHEELCHAIR...

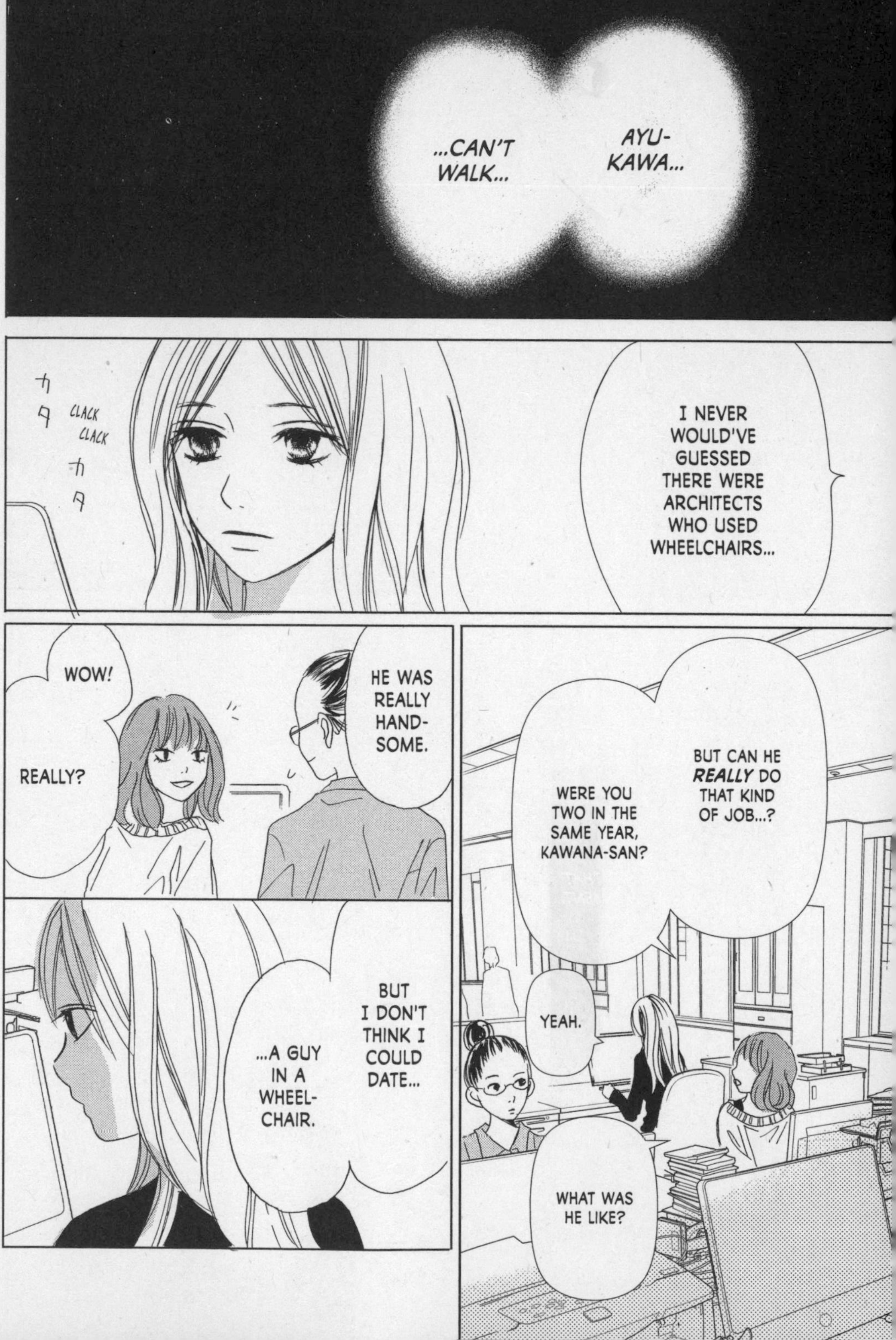
AYU-KAWA...
...CAN'T WALK...
I NEVER WOULD'VE GUESSED THERE WERE ARCHITECTS WHO USED WHEELCHAIRS...
カタ
CLACK CLACK
カタ
BUT CAN HE *REALLY* DO THAT KIND OF JOB...?
WERE YOU TWO IN THE SAME YEAR, KAWANA-SAN?
YEAH.
WHAT WAS HE LIKE?
HE WAS REALLY HAND-SOME.
WOW!
REALLY?
BUT I DON'T THINK I COULD DATE...
...A GUY IN A WHEEL-CHAIR.

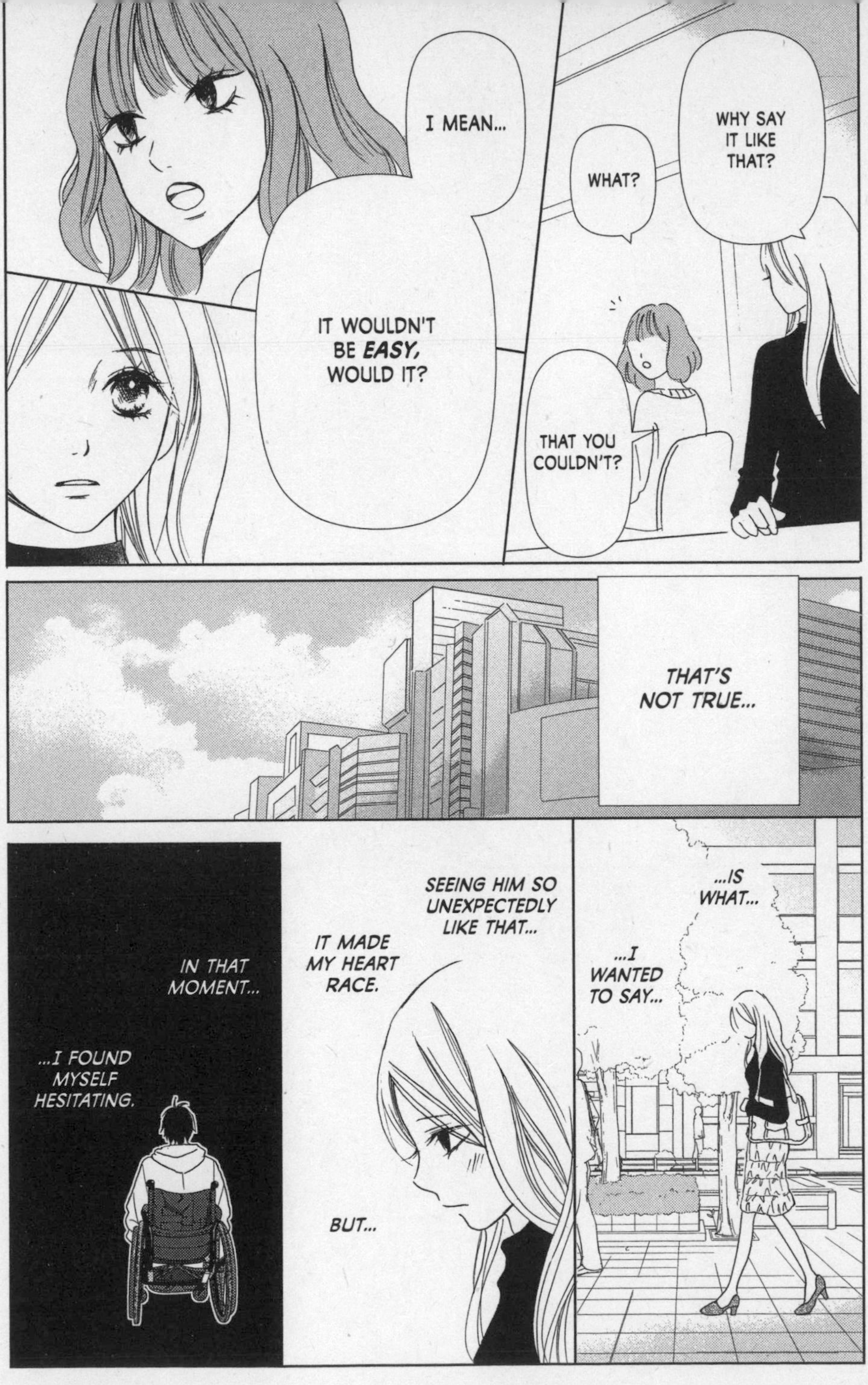
WHY SAY IT LIKE THAT?
WHAT?
THAT YOU COULDN'T?
I MEAN...
IT WOULDN'T BE EASY, WOULD IT?
THAT'S NOT TRUE...
...IS WHAT...
...I WANTED TO SAY...
SEEING HIM SO UNEXPECTEDLY LIKE THAT...
IT MADE MY HEART RACE.
BUT...
IN THAT MOMENT...
...I FOUND MYSELF HESITATING.

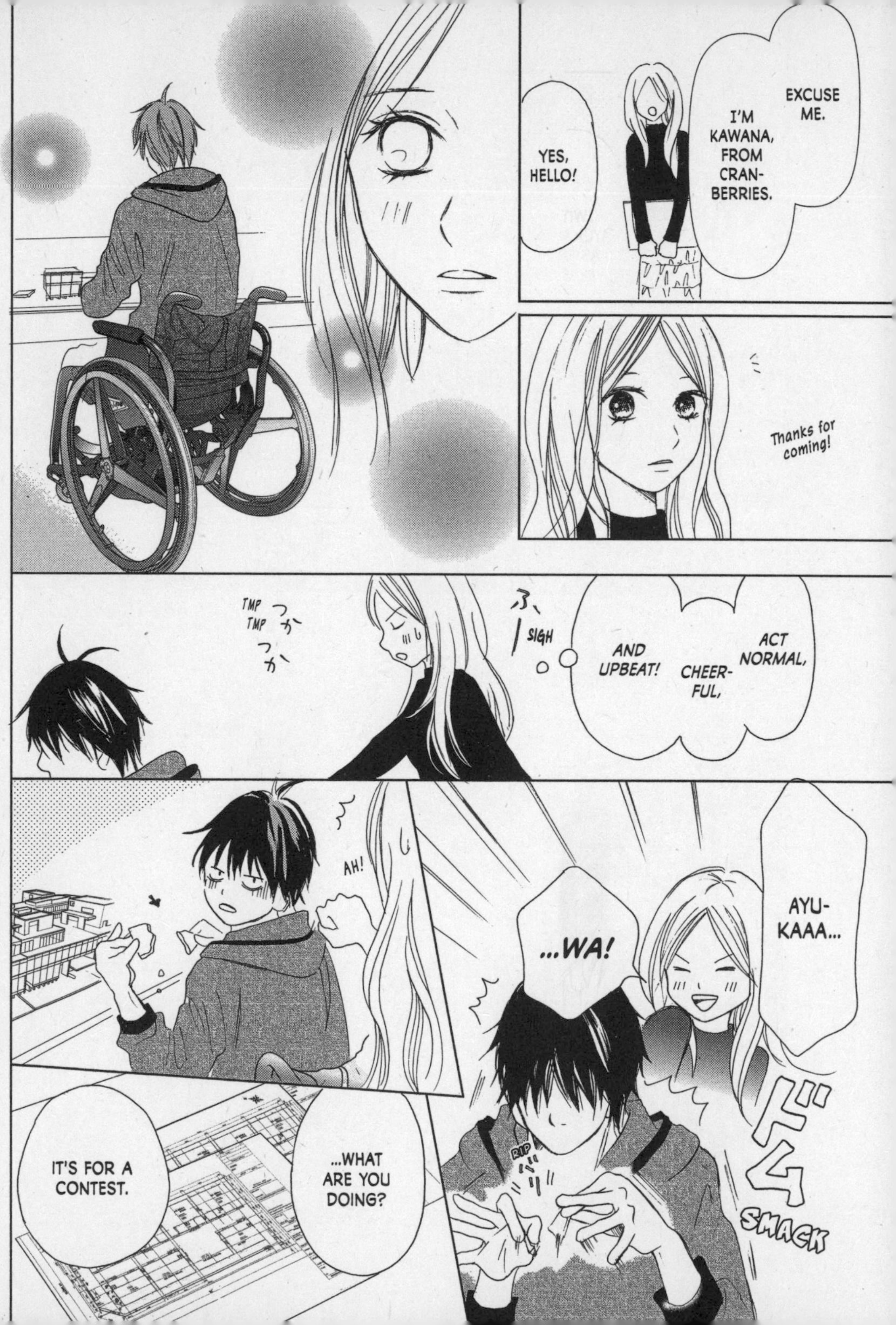
EXCUSE ME.
I'M KAWANA, FROM CRAN-BERRIES.
YES, HELLO!
Thanks for coming!
ACT NORMAL, CHEER-FUL, AND UPBEAT!
ふ SIGH
TMP TMP つかつか
AYU-KAAA...
...WA!
ドム SMACK
RIP
AH!
...WHAT ARE YOU DOING?
IT'S FOR A CONTEST.

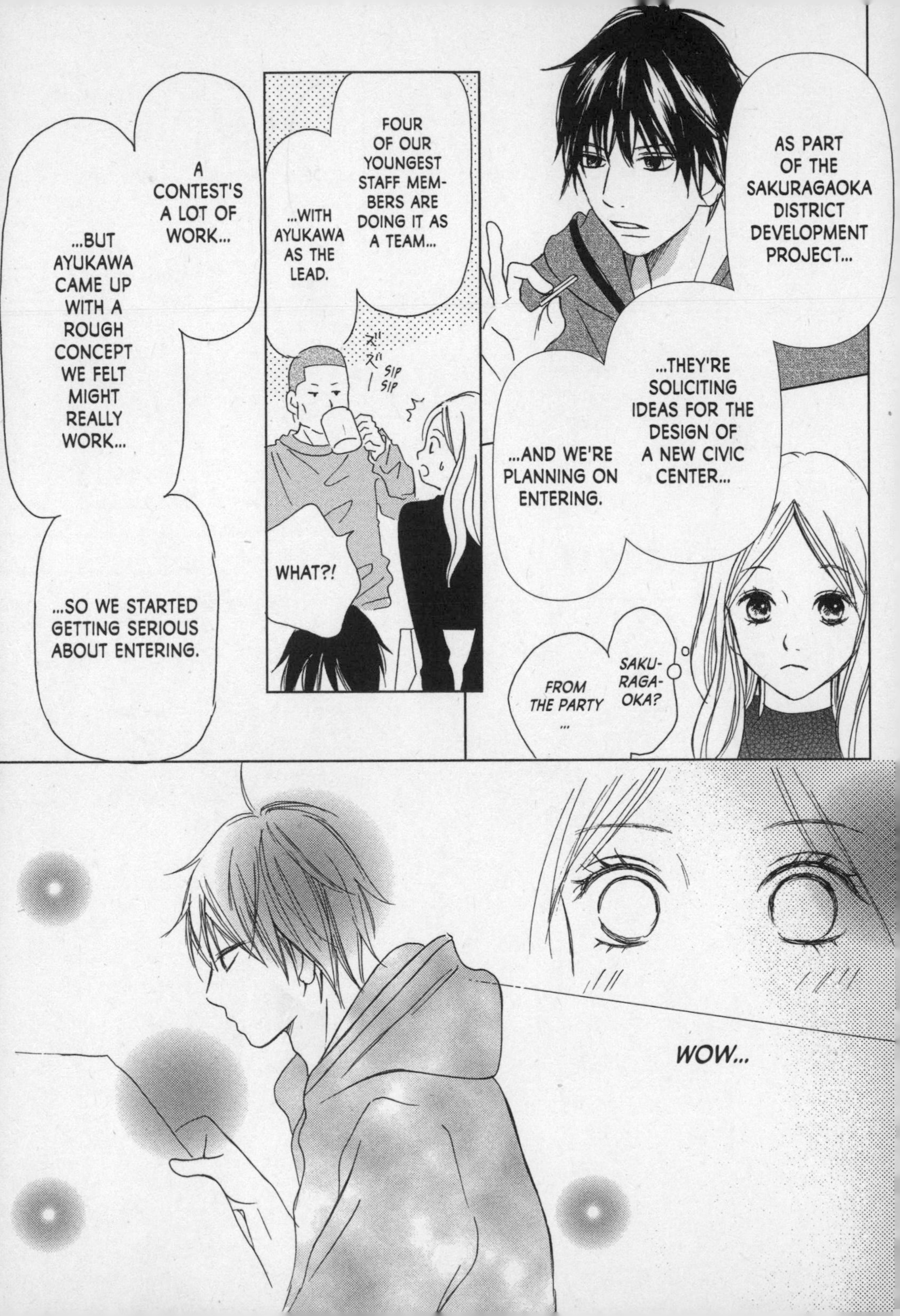
AS PART OF THE SAKURAGAOKA DISTRICT DEVELOPMENT PROJECT...
...THEY'RE SOLICITING IDEAS FOR THE DESIGN OF A NEW CIVIC CENTER...
...AND WE'RE PLANNING ON ENTERING.
SAKU-RAGA-OKA?
FROM THE PARTY...
FOUR OF OUR YOUNGEST STAFF MEM-BERS ARE DOING IT AS A TEAM...
...WITH AYUKAWA AS THE LEAD.
ズズ
SIP SIP
WHAT?!
A CONTEST'S A LOT OF WORK...
...BUT AYUKAWA CAME UP WITH A ROUGH CONCEPT WE FELT MIGHT REALLY WORK...
...SO WE STARTED GETTING SERIOUS ABOUT ENTERING.
WOW...

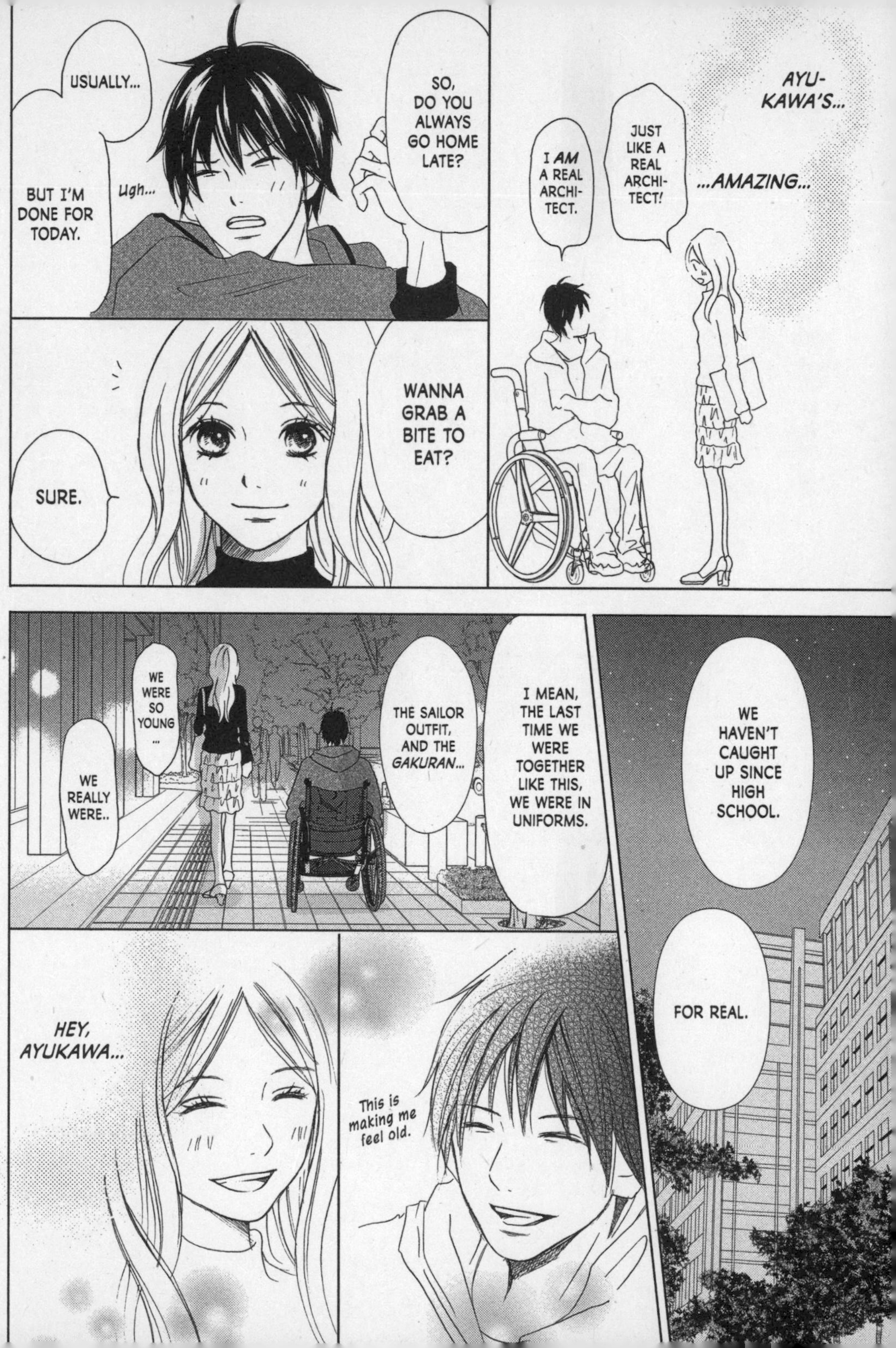
AYU-KAWA'S...
...AMAZING...
JUST LIKE A REAL ARCHITECT!
I *AM* A REAL ARCHITECT.
SO, DO YOU ALWAYS GO HOME LATE?
USUALLY...
Ugh...
BUT I'M DONE FOR TODAY.
WANNA GRAB A BITE TO EAT?
SURE.
WE HAVEN'T CAUGHT UP SINCE HIGH SCHOOL.
FOR REAL.
I MEAN, THE LAST TIME WE WERE TOGETHER LIKE THIS, WE WERE IN UNIFORMS.
THE SAILOR OUTFIT, AND THE *GAKURAN*...
WE WERE SO YOUNG ...
WE REALLY WERE..
This is making me feel old.
HEY, AYUKAWA...

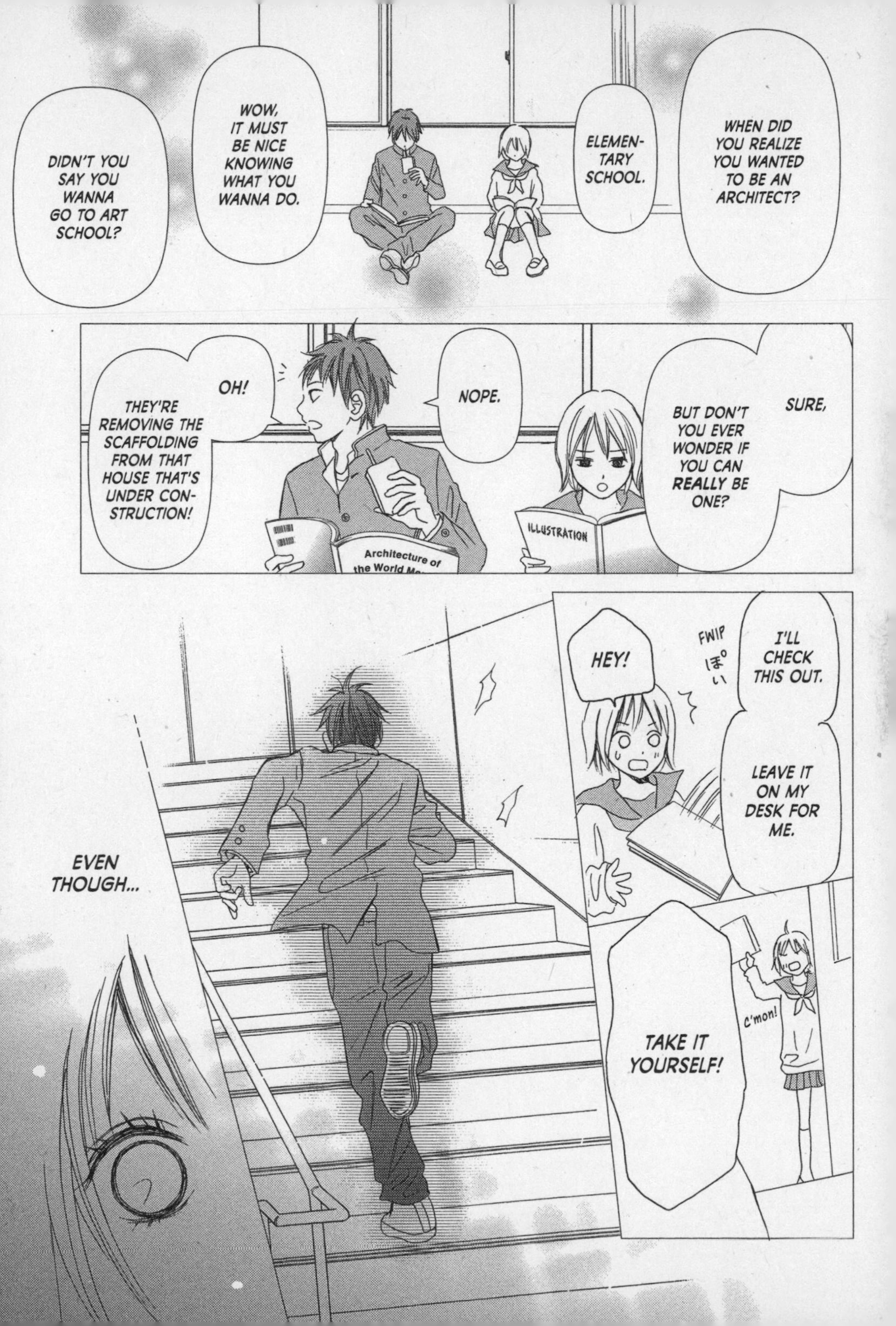
WHEN DID YOU REALIZE YOU WANTED TO BE AN ARCHITECT?
ELEMENTARY SCHOOL.
WOW, IT MUST BE NICE KNOWING WHAT YOU WANNA DO.
DIDN'T YOU SAY YOU WANNA GO TO ART SCHOOL?
SURE,
BUT DON'T YOU EVER WONDER IF YOU CAN REALLY BE ONE?
NOPE.
OH!
THEY'RE REMOVING THE SCAFFOLDING FROM THAT HOUSE THAT'S UNDER CONSTRUCTION!
ILLUSTRATION
Architecture of
the World
I'LL CHECK THIS OUT.
FWIP ぽい
HEY!
LEAVE IT ON MY DESK FOR ME.
C'mon!
TAKE IT YOURSELF!
EVEN THOUGH...

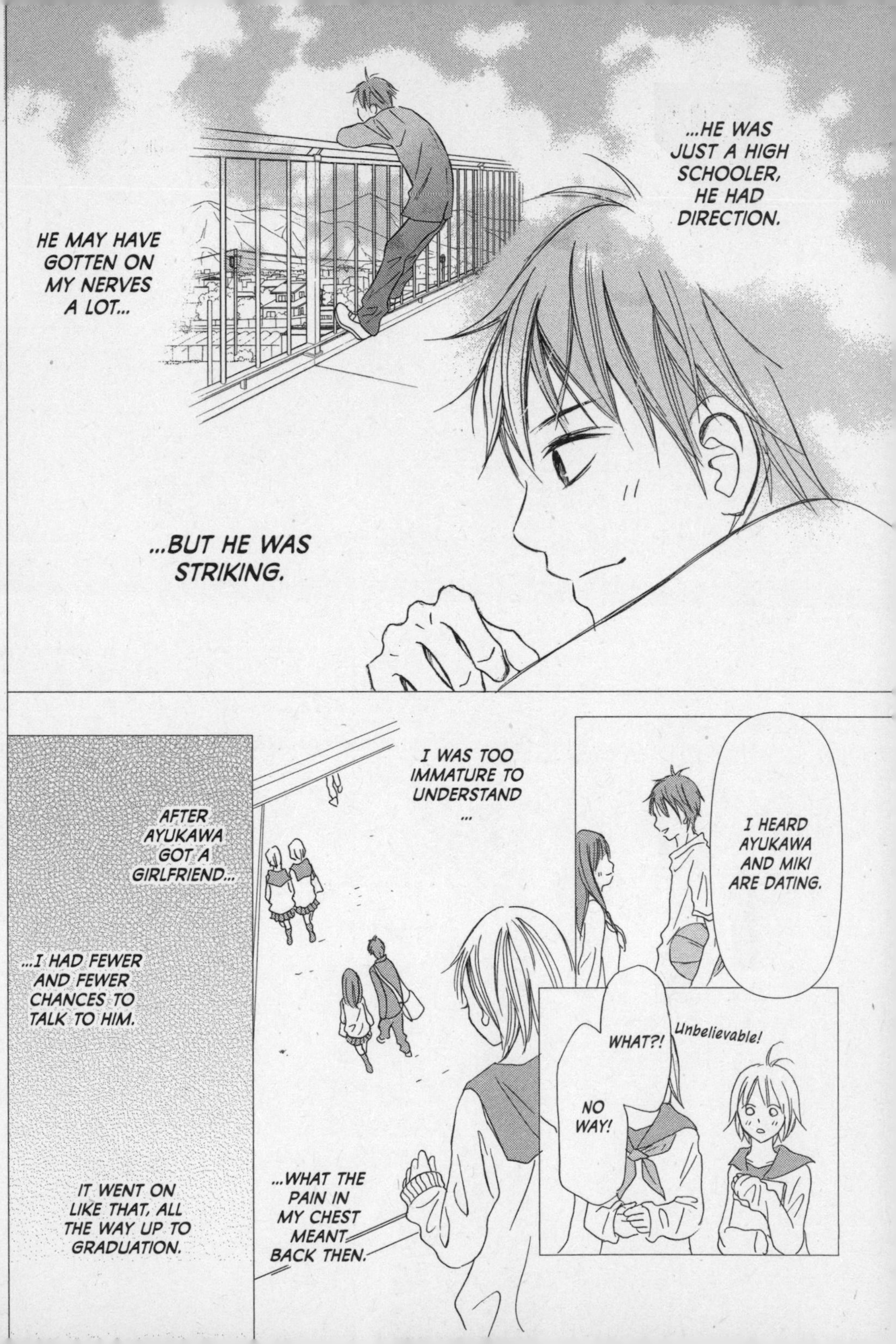
...HE WAS JUST A HIGH SCHOOLER, HE HAD DIRECTION.
HE MAY HAVE GOTTEN ON MY NERVES A LOT...
...BUT HE WAS STRIKING.
I HEARD AYUKAWA AND MIKI ARE DATING.
Unbelievable!
WHAT?!
NO WAY!
I WAS TOO IMMATURE TO UNDERSTAND ...
...WHAT THE PAIN IN MY CHEST MEANT BACK THEN.
AFTER AYUKAWA GOT A GIRLFRIEND...
...I HAD FEWER AND FEWER CHANCES TO TALK TO HIM.
IT WENT ON LIKE THAT, ALL THE WAY UP TO GRADUATION.

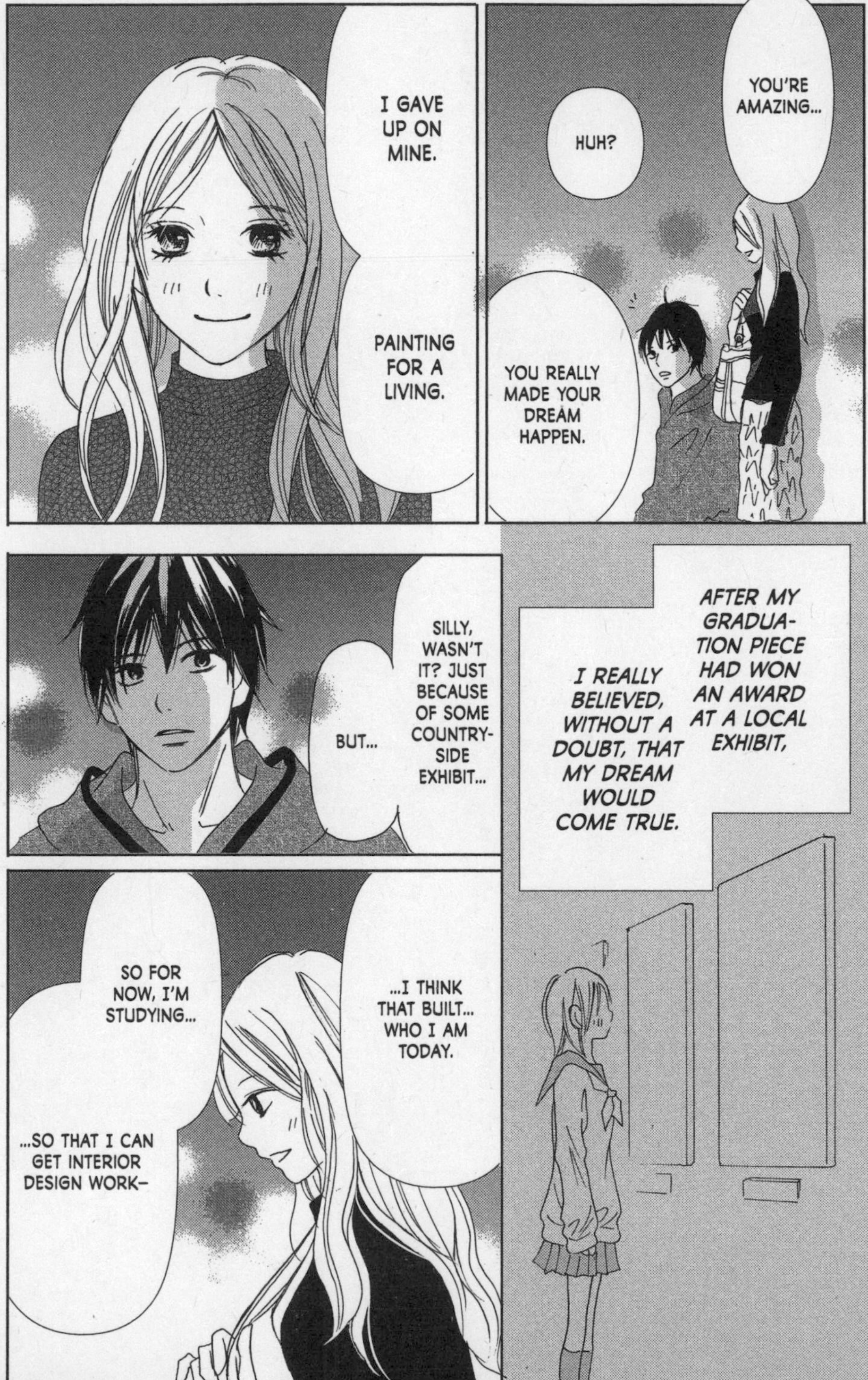
YOU'RE AMAZING...
HUH?
YOU REALLY MADE YOUR DREAM HAPPEN.
I GAVE UP ON MINE.
PAINTING FOR A LIVING.
AFTER MY GRADUATION PIECE HAD WON AN AWARD AT A LOCAL EXHIBIT,
I REALLY BELIEVED, WITHOUT A DOUBT, THAT MY DREAM WOULD COME TRUE.
SILLY, WASN'T IT? JUST BECAUSE OF SOME COUNTRYSIDE EXHIBIT...
BUT...
...I THINK THAT BUILT... WHO I AM TODAY.
SO FOR NOW, I'M STUDYING...
...SO THAT I CAN GET INTERIOR DESIGN WORK–

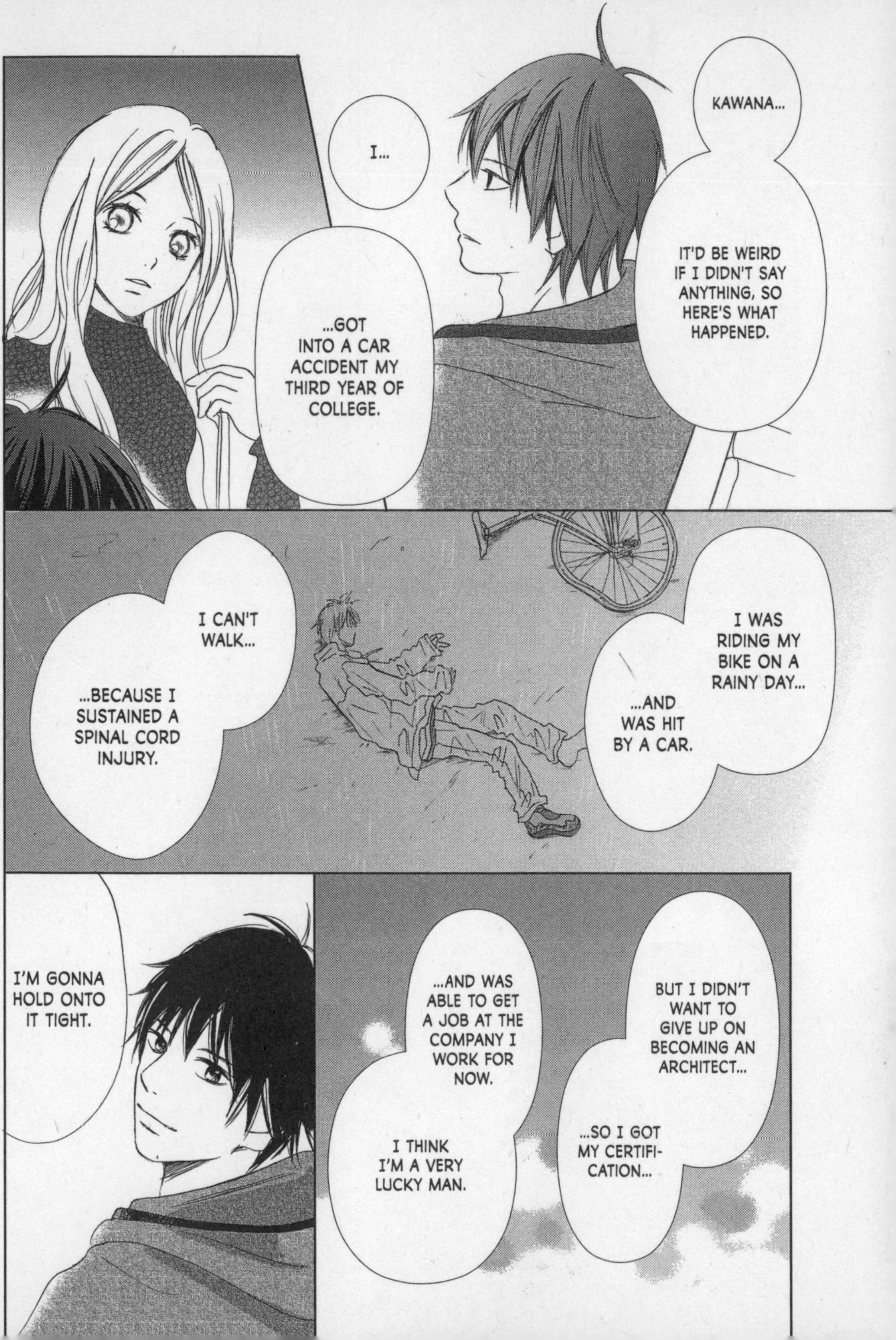
KAWANA...
IT'D BE WEIRD IF I DIDN'T SAY ANYTHING, SO HERE'S WHAT HAPPENED.
I...
...GOT INTO A CAR ACCIDENT MY THIRD YEAR OF COLLEGE.
I WAS RIDING MY BIKE ON A RAINY DAY...
...AND WAS HIT BY A CAR.
I CAN'T WALK...
...BECAUSE I SUSTAINED A SPINAL CORD INJURY.
BUT I DIDN'T WANT TO GIVE UP ON BECOMING AN ARCHITECT...
...SO I GOT MY CERTIFI-CATION...
...AND WAS ABLE TO GET A JOB AT THE COMPANY I WORK FOR NOW.
I THINK I'M A VERY LUCKY MAN.
I'M GONNA HOLD ONTO IT TIGHT.

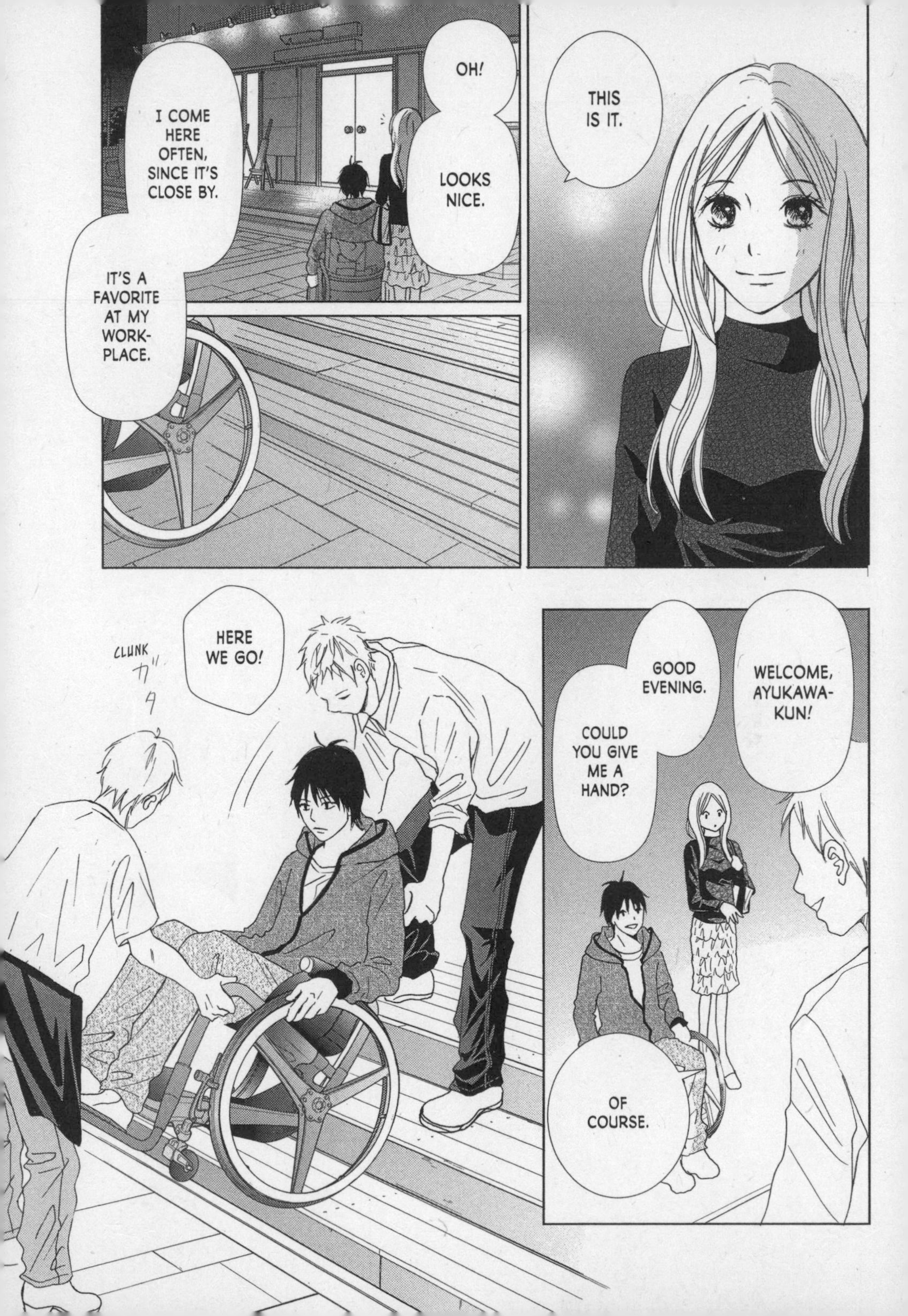
THIS IS IT.
OH!
LOOKS NICE.
I COME HERE OFTEN, SINCE IT'S CLOSE BY.
IT'S A FAVORITE AT MY WORKPLACE.
WELCOME, AYUKAWA-KUN!
GOOD EVENING.
COULD YOU GIVE ME A HAND?
OF COURSE.
HERE WE GO!
CLUNK
ガタ

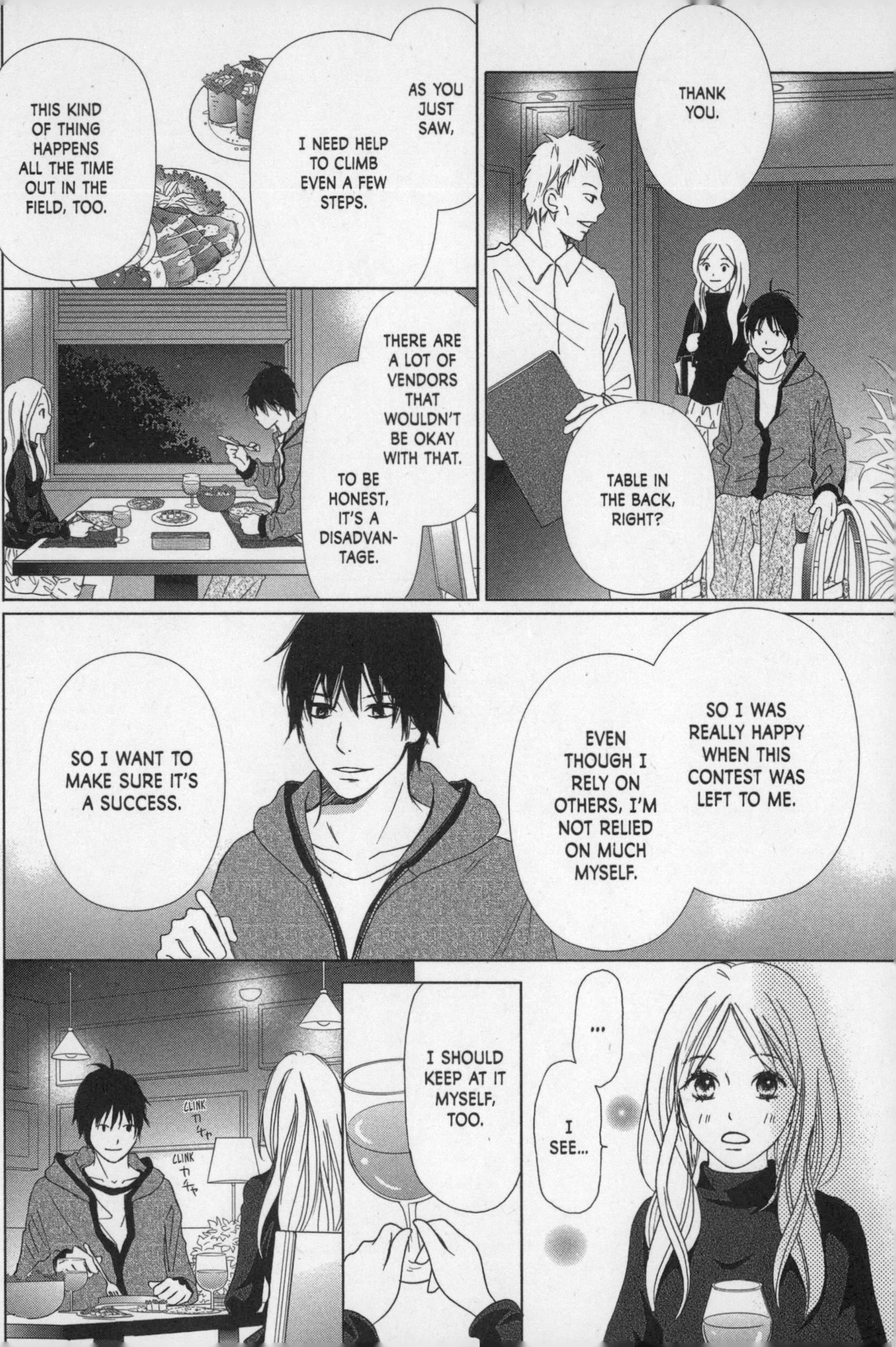
THANK YOU.
TABLE IN THE BACK, RIGHT?
AS YOU JUST SAW, I NEED HELP TO CLIMB EVEN A FEW STEPS.
THIS KIND OF THING HAPPENS ALL THE TIME OUT IN THE FIELD, TOO.
THERE ARE A LOT OF VENDORS THAT WOULDN'T BE OKAY WITH THAT.
TO BE HONEST, IT'S A DISADVANTAGE.
EVEN THOUGH I RELY ON OTHERS, I'M NOT RELIED ON MUCH MYSELF.
SO I WAS REALLY HAPPY WHEN THIS CONTEST WAS LEFT TO ME.
SO I WANT TO MAKE SURE IT'S A SUCCESS.
...
I SEE...
I SHOULD KEEP AT IT MYSELF, TOO.
CLINK カチャ
CLINK カチャ

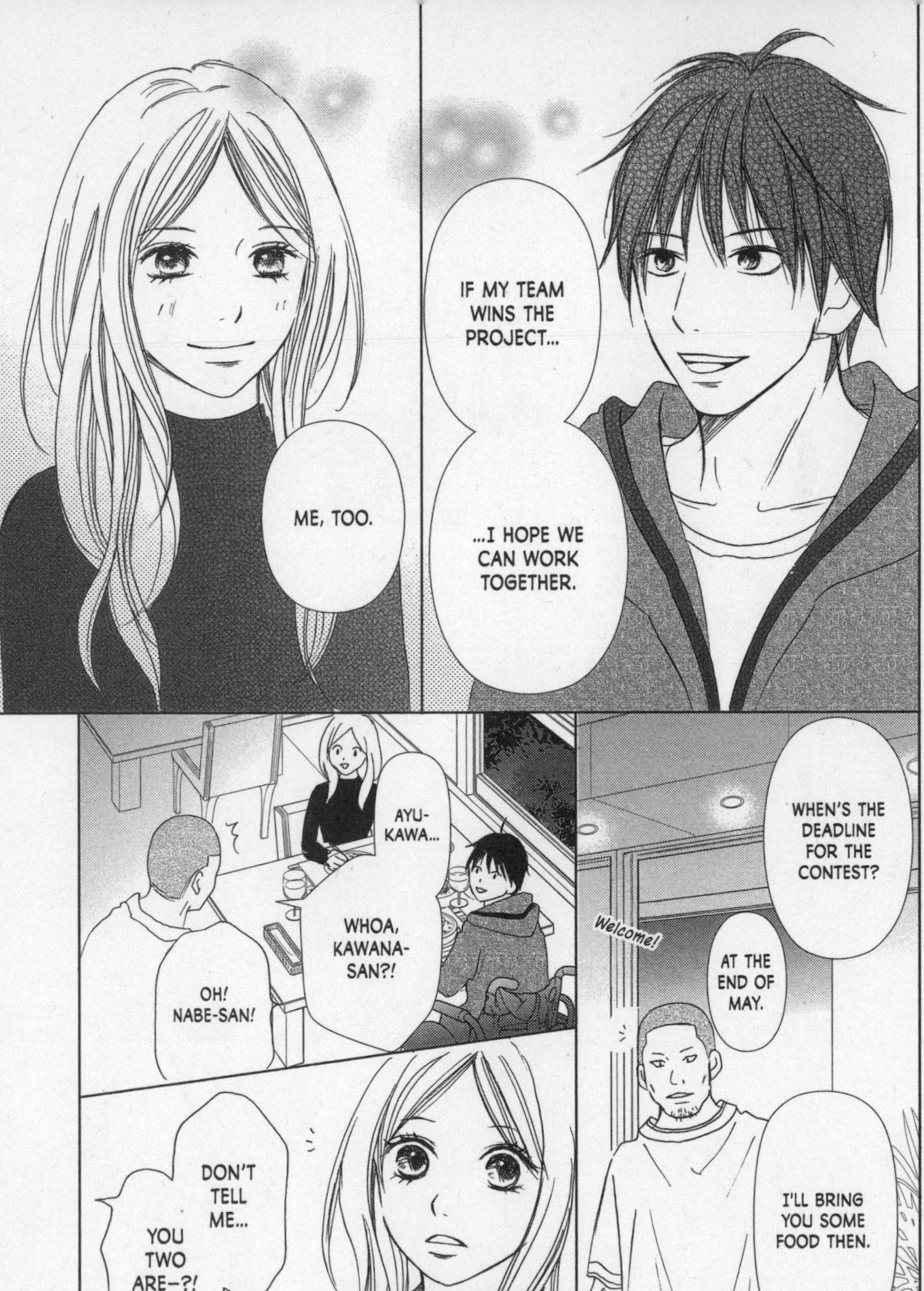
IF MY TEAM WINS THE PROJECT...
...I HOPE WE CAN WORK TOGETHER.
ME, TOO.
WHEN'S THE DEADLINE FOR THE CONTEST?
Welcome!
AT THE END OF MAY.
I'LL BRING YOU SOME FOOD THEN.
AYU-KAWA...
WHOA, KAWANA-SAN?!
OH! NABE-SAN!
DON'T TELL ME...
YOU TWO ARE-?!

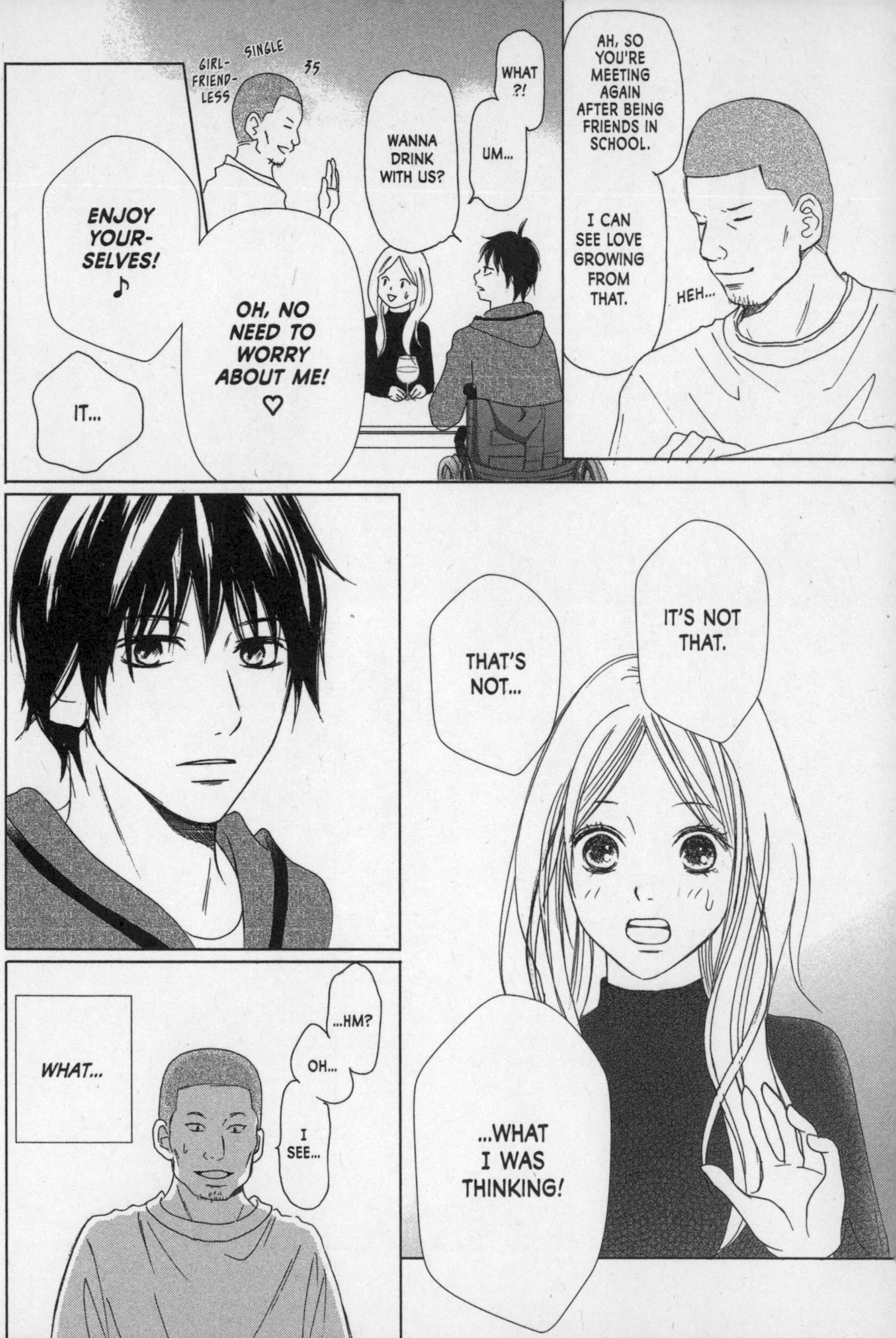
AH, SO YOU'RE MEETING AGAIN AFTER BEING FRIENDS IN SCHOOL.
I CAN SEE LOVE GROWING FROM THAT.
HEH...
WHAT?!
UM...
WANNA DRINK WITH US?
SINGLE
35
GIRL-FRIEND-LESS
ENJOY YOUR-SELVES! ♪
OH, NO NEED TO WORRY ABOUT ME! ♡
IT...
IT'S NOT THAT.
THAT'S NOT...
...WHAT I WAS THINKING!
...HM?
OH...
I SEE...
WHAT...

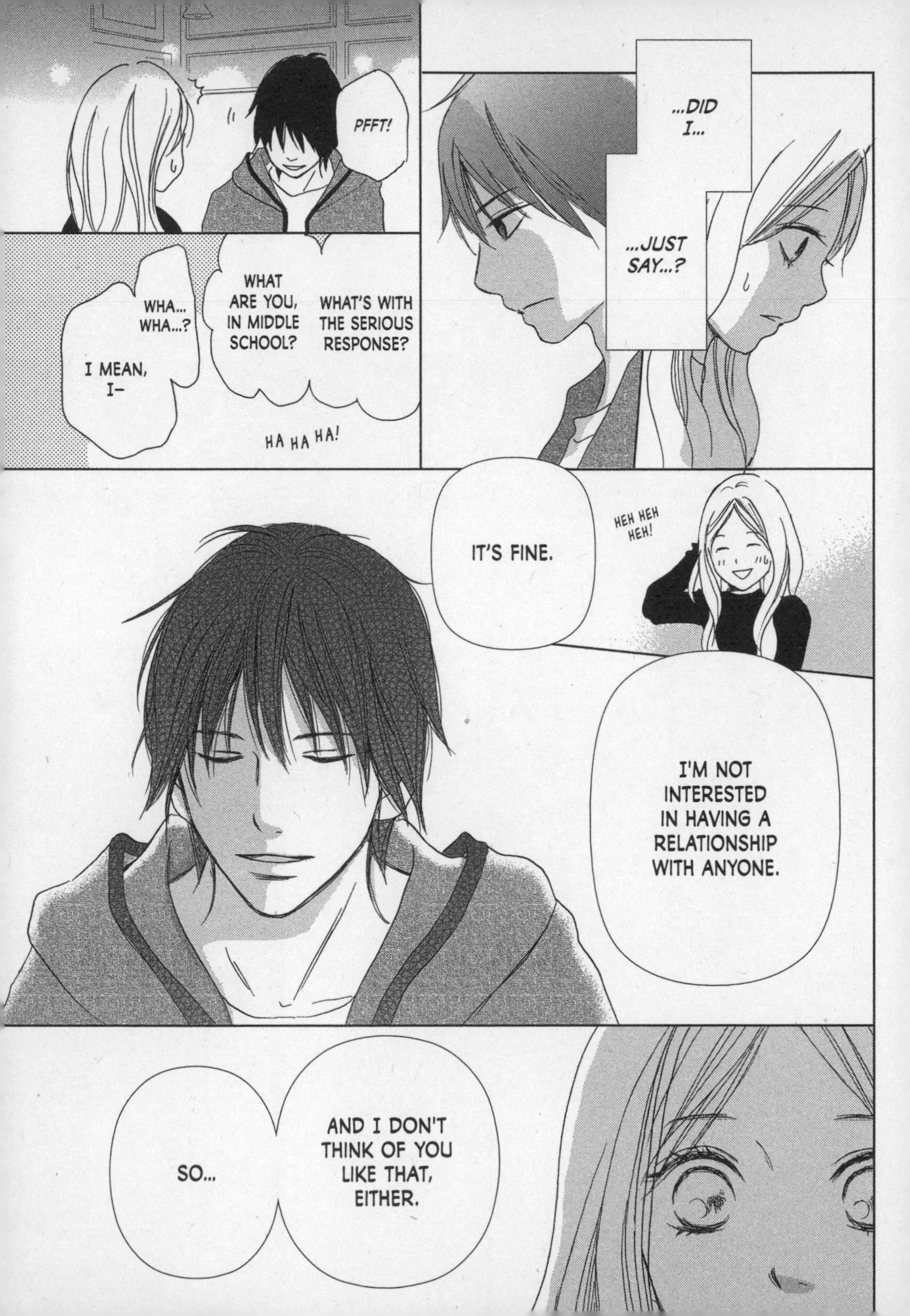
...DID I...
...JUST SAY...?
PFFT!
WHAT'S WITH THE SERIOUS RESPONSE?
WHAT ARE YOU, IN MIDDLE SCHOOL?
WHA... WHA...?
I MEAN, I–
HA HA HA!
HEH HEH HEH!
IT'S FINE.
I'M NOT INTERESTED IN HAVING A RELATIONSHIP WITH ANYONE.
AND I DON'T THINK OF YOU LIKE THAT, EITHER.
SO...

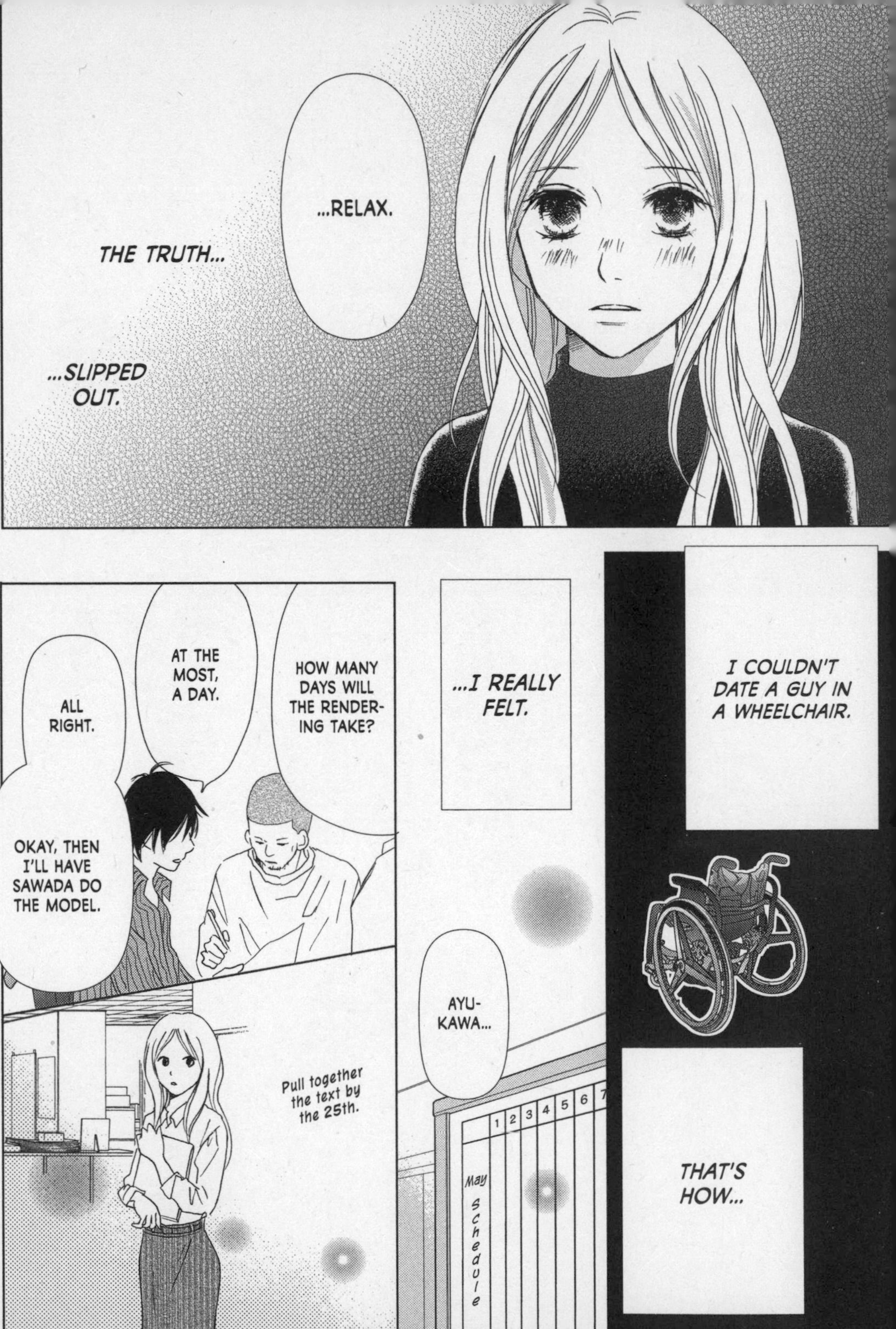
...RELAX.
THE TRUTH...
...SLIPPED OUT.
I COULDN'T DATE A GUY IN A WHEELCHAIR.
THAT'S HOW...
...I REALLY FELT.
HOW MANY DAYS WILL THE RENDER-ING TAKE?
AT THE MOST, A DAY.
ALL RIGHT.
OKAY, THEN I'LL HAVE SAWADA DO THE MODEL.
AYU-KAWA...
Pull together the text by the 25th.
1 2 3 4 5 6 7
May Schedule

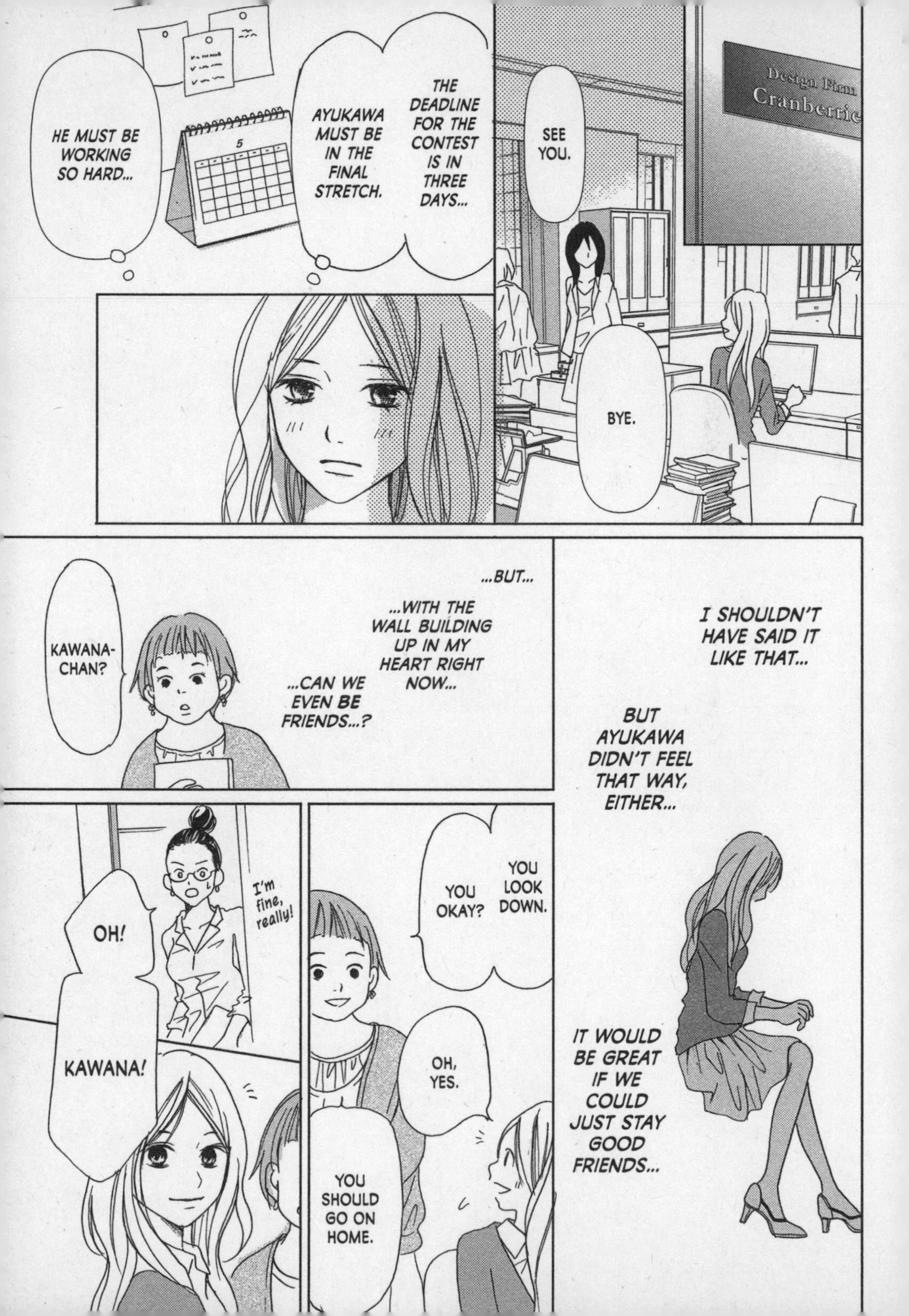
Design Firm
Cranberrie
SEE YOU.
BYE.
THE DEADLINE FOR THE CONTEST IS IN THREE DAYS...
AYUKAWA MUST BE IN THE FINAL STRETCH.
HE MUST BE WORKING SO HARD...
I SHOULDN'T HAVE SAID IT LIKE THAT...
BUT AYUKAWA DIDN'T FEEL THAT WAY, EITHER...
IT WOULD BE GREAT IF WE COULD JUST STAY GOOD FRIENDS...
...BUT...
...WITH THE WALL BUILDING UP IN MY HEART RIGHT NOW...
...CAN WE EVEN BE FRIENDS...?
KAWANA-CHAN?
YOU LOOK DOWN.
YOU OKAY?
OH, YES.
YOU SHOULD GO ON HOME.
I'm fine, really!
OH!
KAWANA!

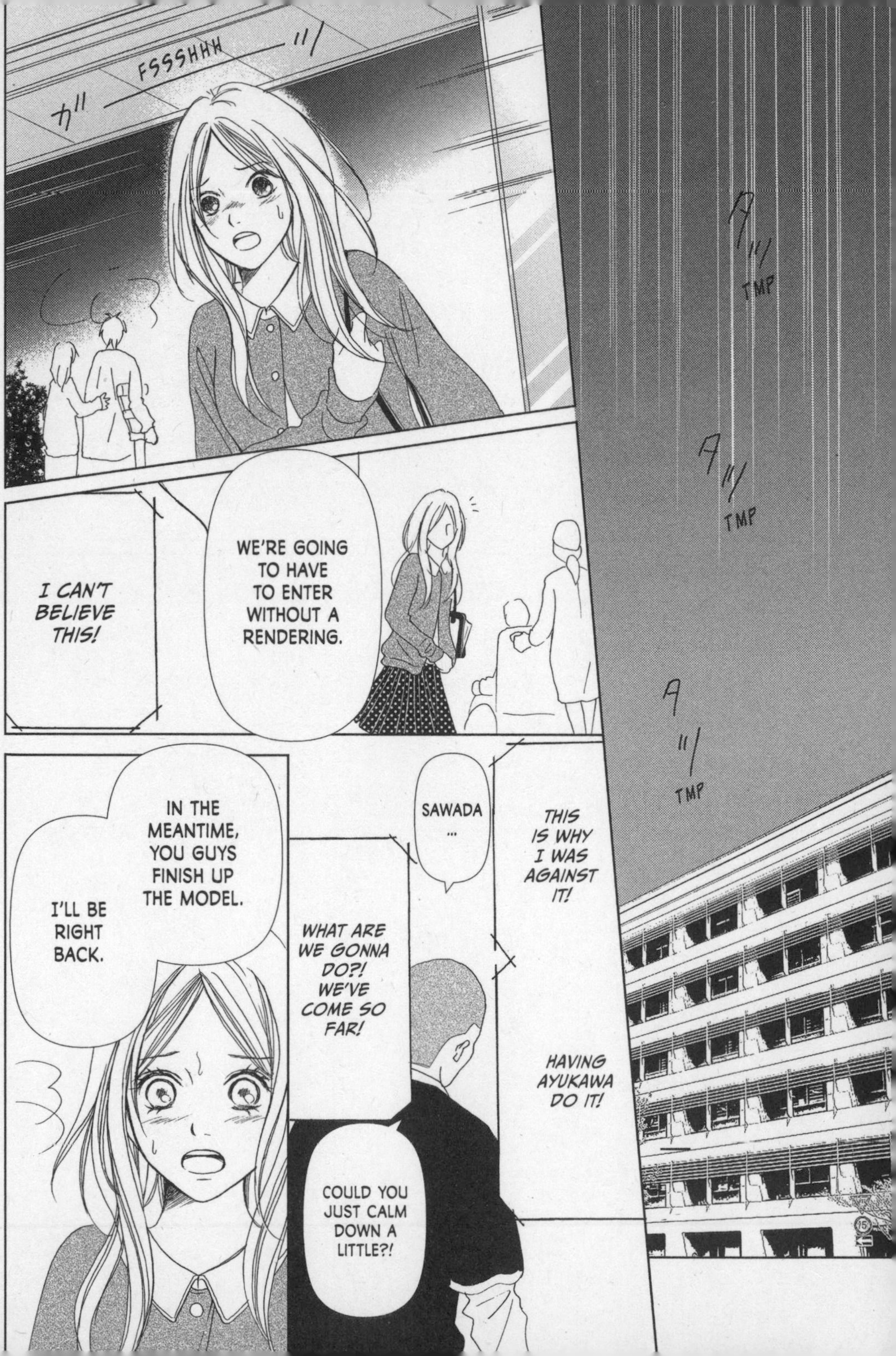
TMP
TMP
TMP
FSSSHHH
WE'RE GOING TO HAVE TO ENTER WITHOUT A RENDERING.
I CAN'T BELIEVE THIS!
SAWADA ...
THIS IS WHY I WAS AGAINST IT!
HAVING AYUKAWA DO IT!
WHAT ARE WE GONNA DO?! WE'VE COME SO FAR!
IN THE MEANTIME, YOU GUYS FINISH UP THE MODEL.
I'LL BE RIGHT BACK.
COULD YOU JUST CALM DOWN A LITTLE?!

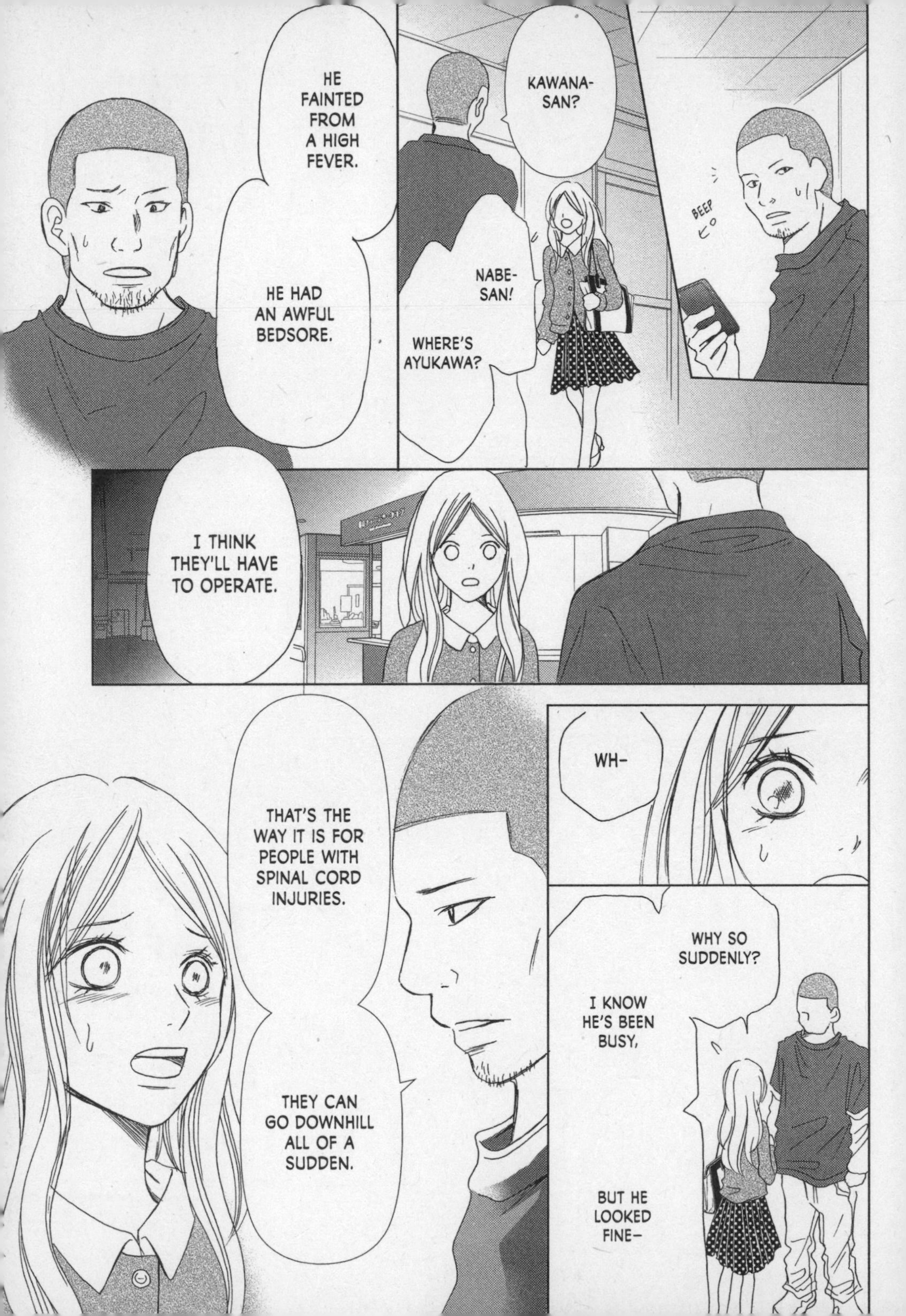
BEEP
ピ
KAWANA-SAN?
NABE-SAN!
WHERE'S AYUKAWA?
HE FAINTED FROM A HIGH FEVER.
HE HAD AN AWFUL BEDSORE.
I THINK THEY'LL HAVE TO OPERATE.
WH–
WHY SO SUDDENLY?
I KNOW HE'S BEEN BUSY,
BUT HE LOOKED FINE–
THAT'S THE WAY IT IS FOR PEOPLE WITH SPINAL CORD INJURIES.
THEY CAN GO DOWNHILL ALL OF A SUDDEN.

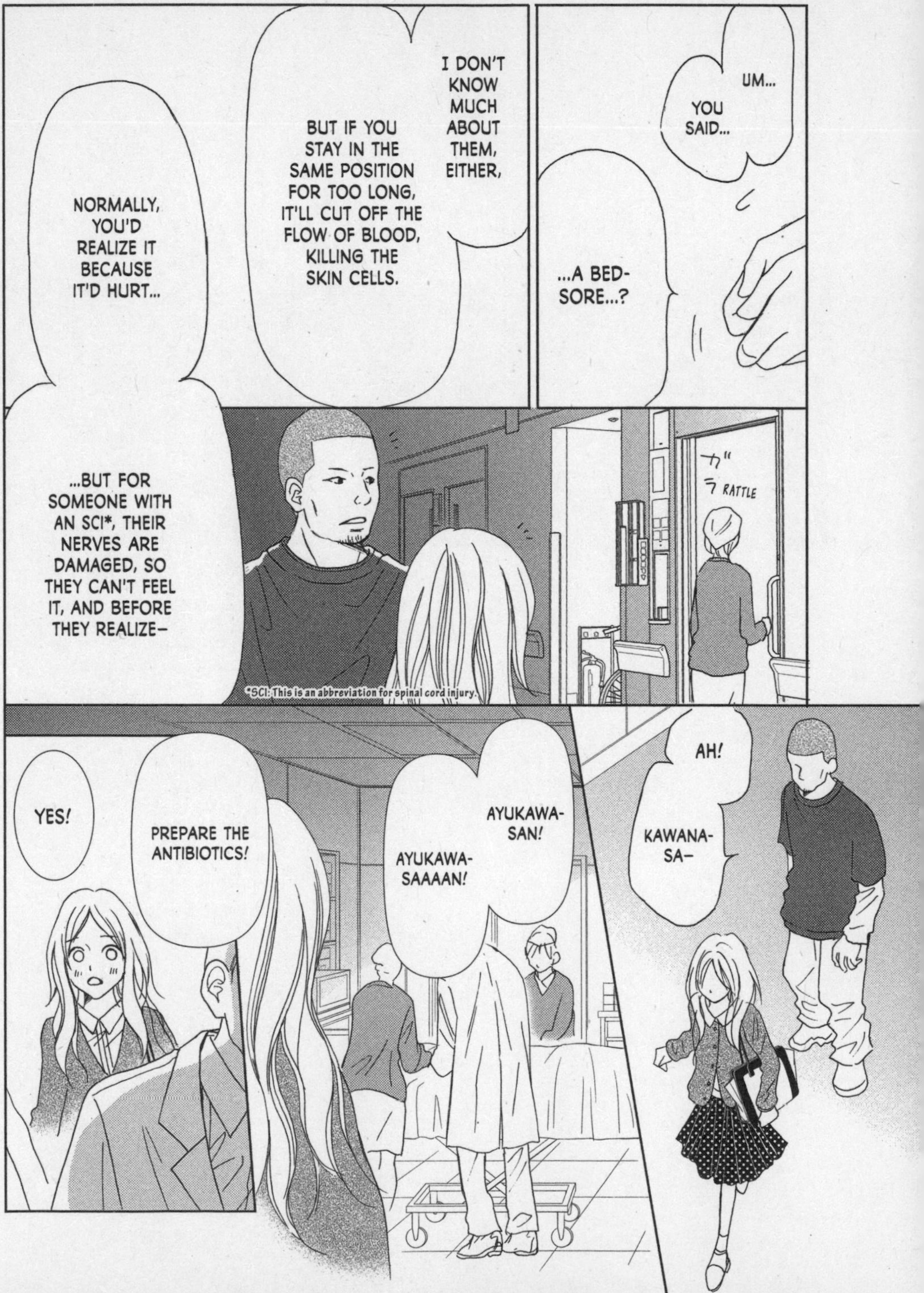
UM...
YOU SAID...
...A BED-SORE...?
I DON'T KNOW MUCH ABOUT THEM, EITHER,
BUT IF YOU STAY IN THE SAME POSITION FOR TOO LONG, IT'LL CUT OFF THE FLOW OF BLOOD, KILLING THE SKIN CELLS.
NORMALLY, YOU'D REALIZE IT BECAUSE IT'D HURT...
...BUT FOR SOMEONE WITH AN SCI*, THEIR NERVES ARE DAMAGED, SO THEY CAN'T FEEL IT, AND BEFORE THEY REALIZE–
ガラ RATTLE
*SCI: This is an abbreviation for spinal cord injury.
AH!
KAWANA-SA–
AYUKAWA-SAN!
AYUKAWA-SAAAAN!
PREPARE THE ANTIBIOTICS!
YES!

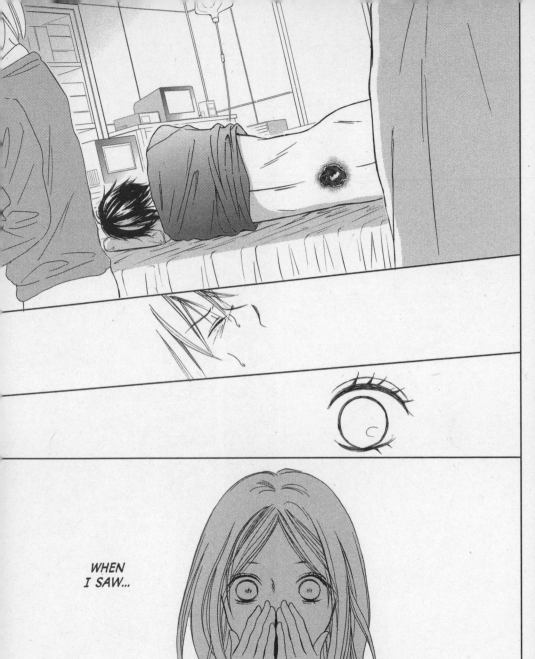

WHEN
I SAW...

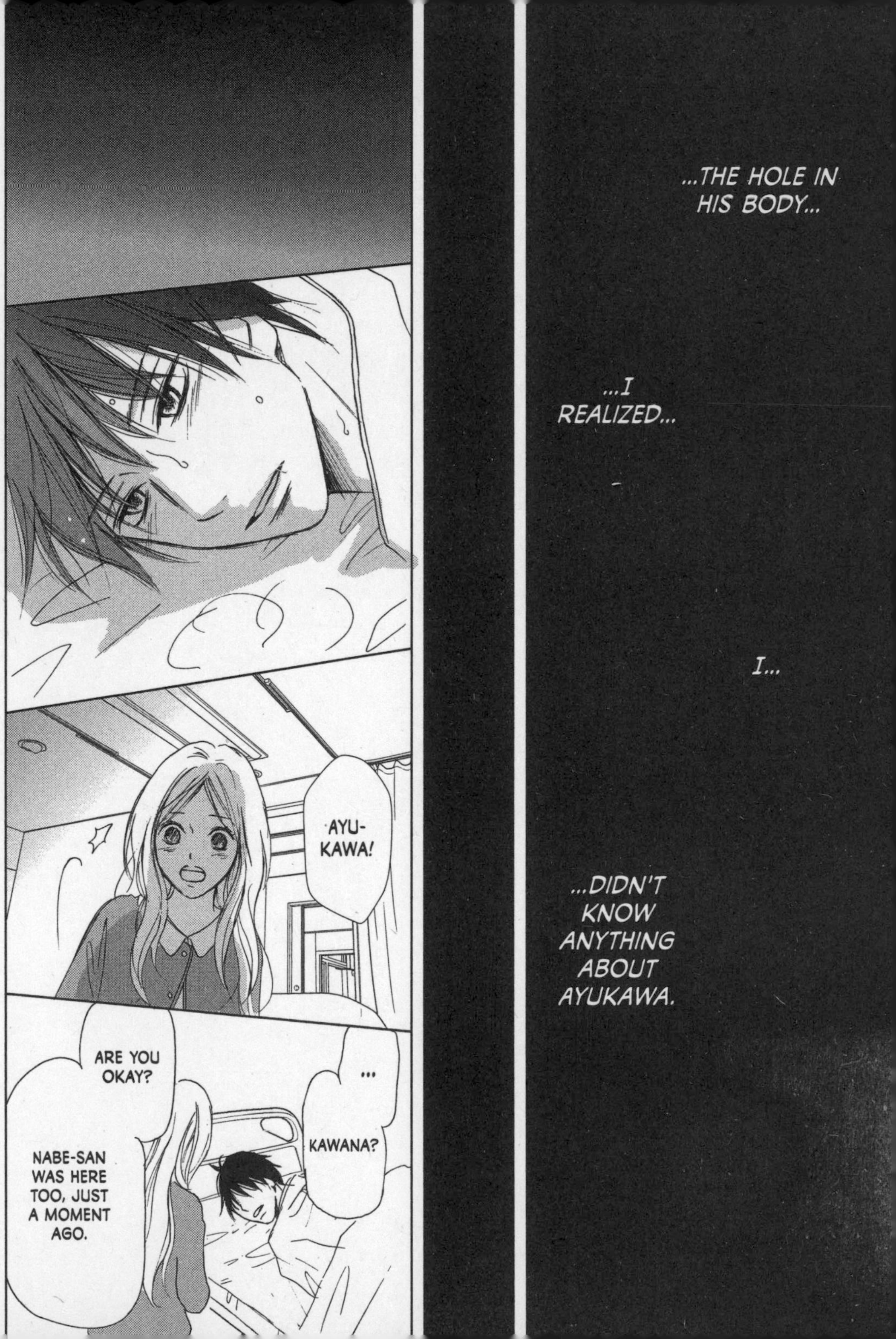
...THE HOLE IN HIS BODY...
...I REALIZED...
I...
...DIDN'T KNOW ANYTHING ABOUT AYUKAWA.
AYU-KAWA!
... KAWANA?
ARE YOU OKAY?
NABE-SAN WAS HERE TOO, JUST A MOMENT AGO.

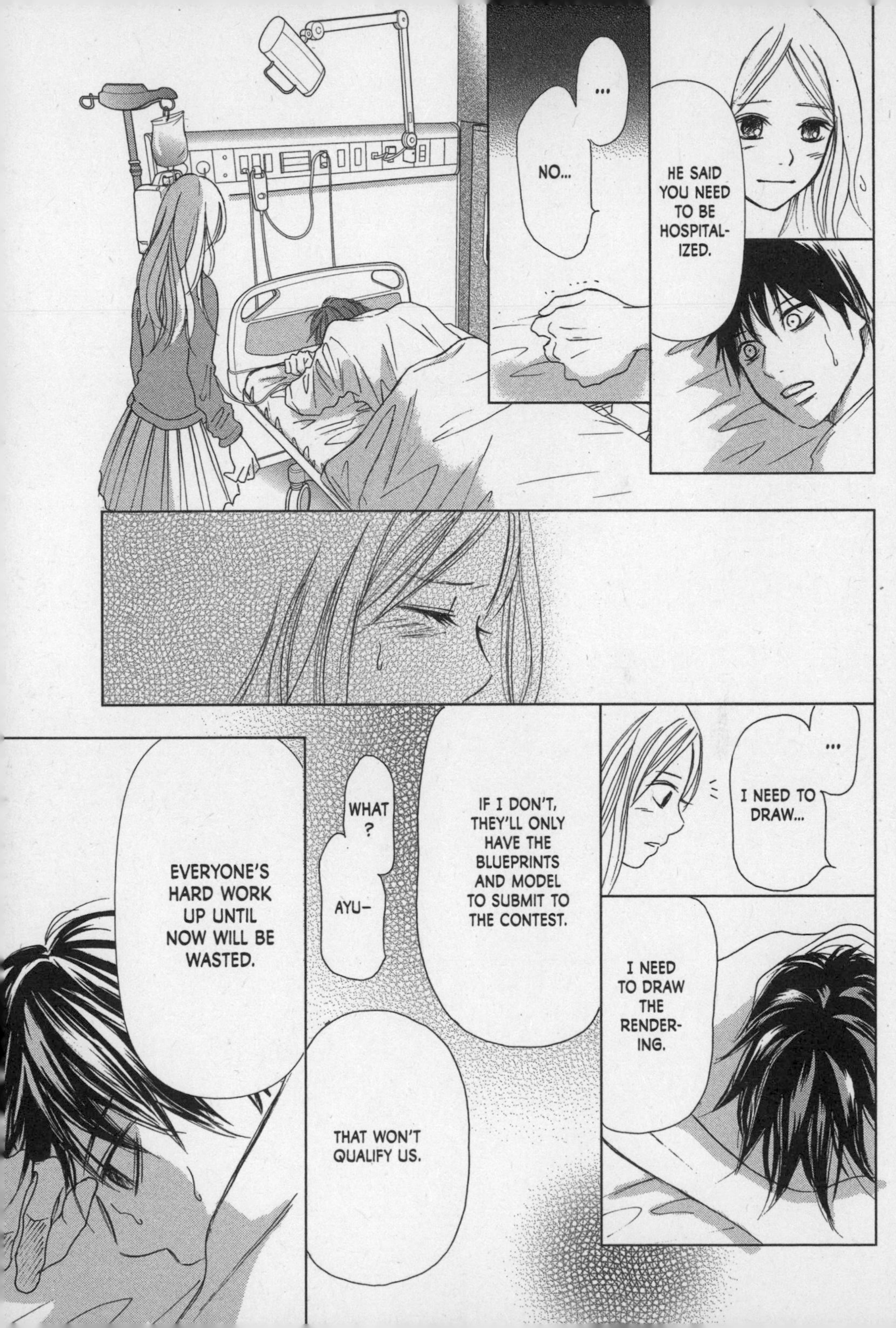
HE SAID YOU NEED TO BE HOSPITAL-IZED.
...
NO...
...
I NEED TO DRAW...
I NEED TO DRAW THE RENDER-ING.
IF I DON'T, THEY'LL ONLY HAVE THE BLUEPRINTS AND MODEL TO SUBMIT TO THE CONTEST.
WHAT?
AYU—
THAT WON'T QUALIFY US.
EVERYONE'S HARD WORK UP UNTIL NOW WILL BE WASTED.

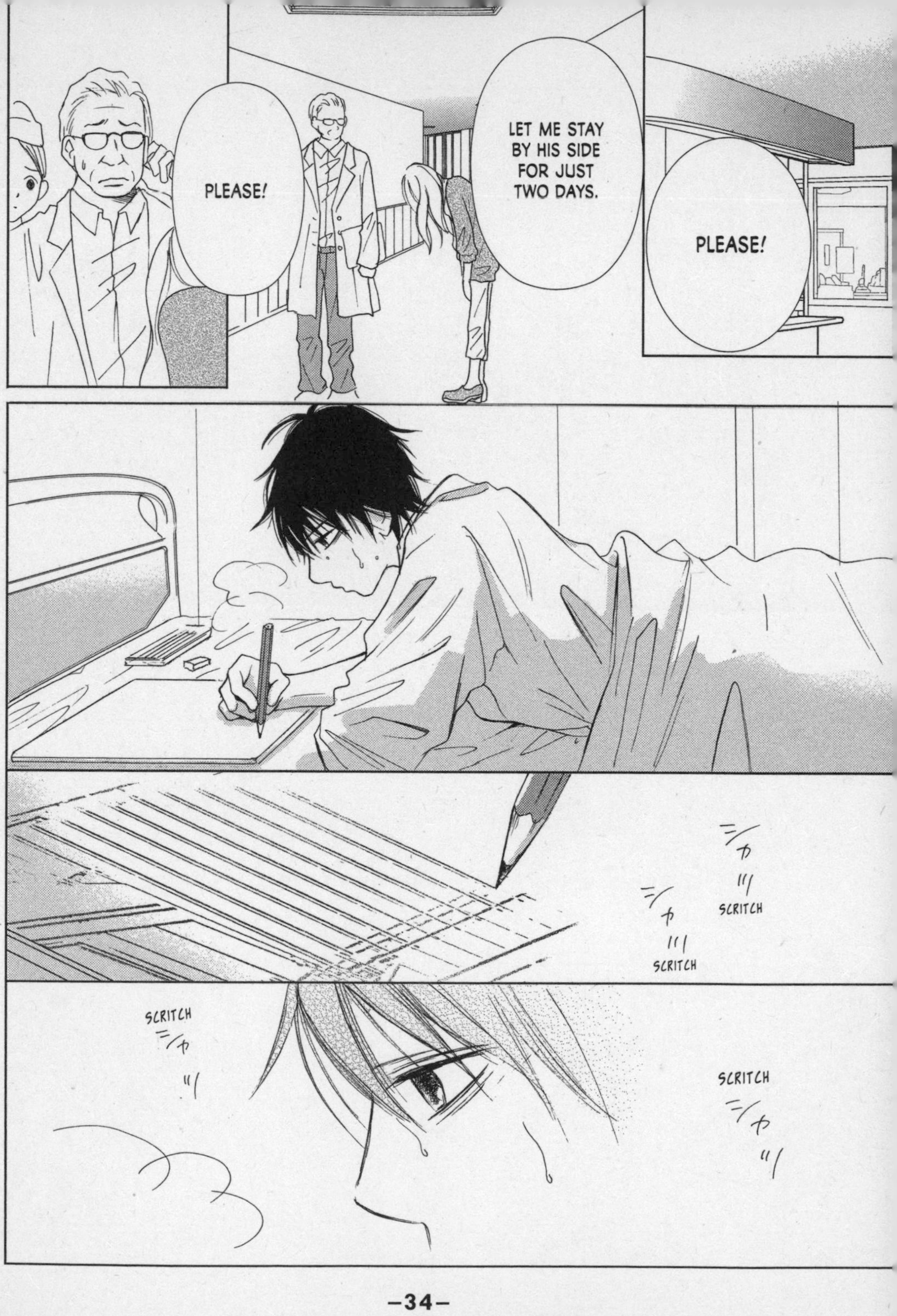
PLEASE!
LET ME STAY BY HIS SIDE FOR JUST TWO DAYS.
PLEASE!
SCRITCH
SCRITCH
SCRITCH
SCRITCH

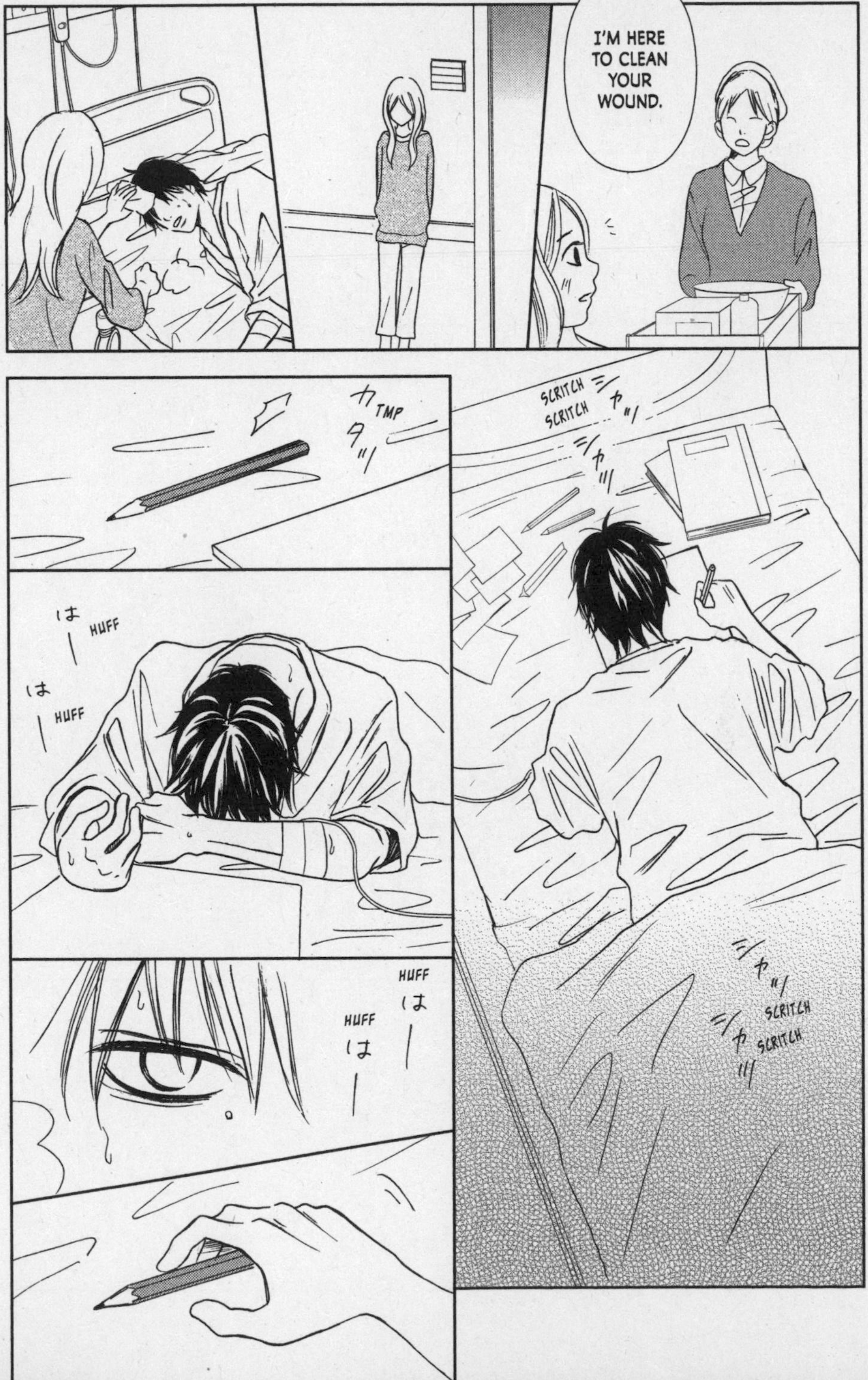
I'M HERE TO CLEAN YOUR WOUND.
SCRITCH SCRITCH
シャッ シャッ
シャッ シャッ
SCRITCH SCRITCH
カタッ
TMP
は HUFF
は HUFF
は HUFF
は HUFF

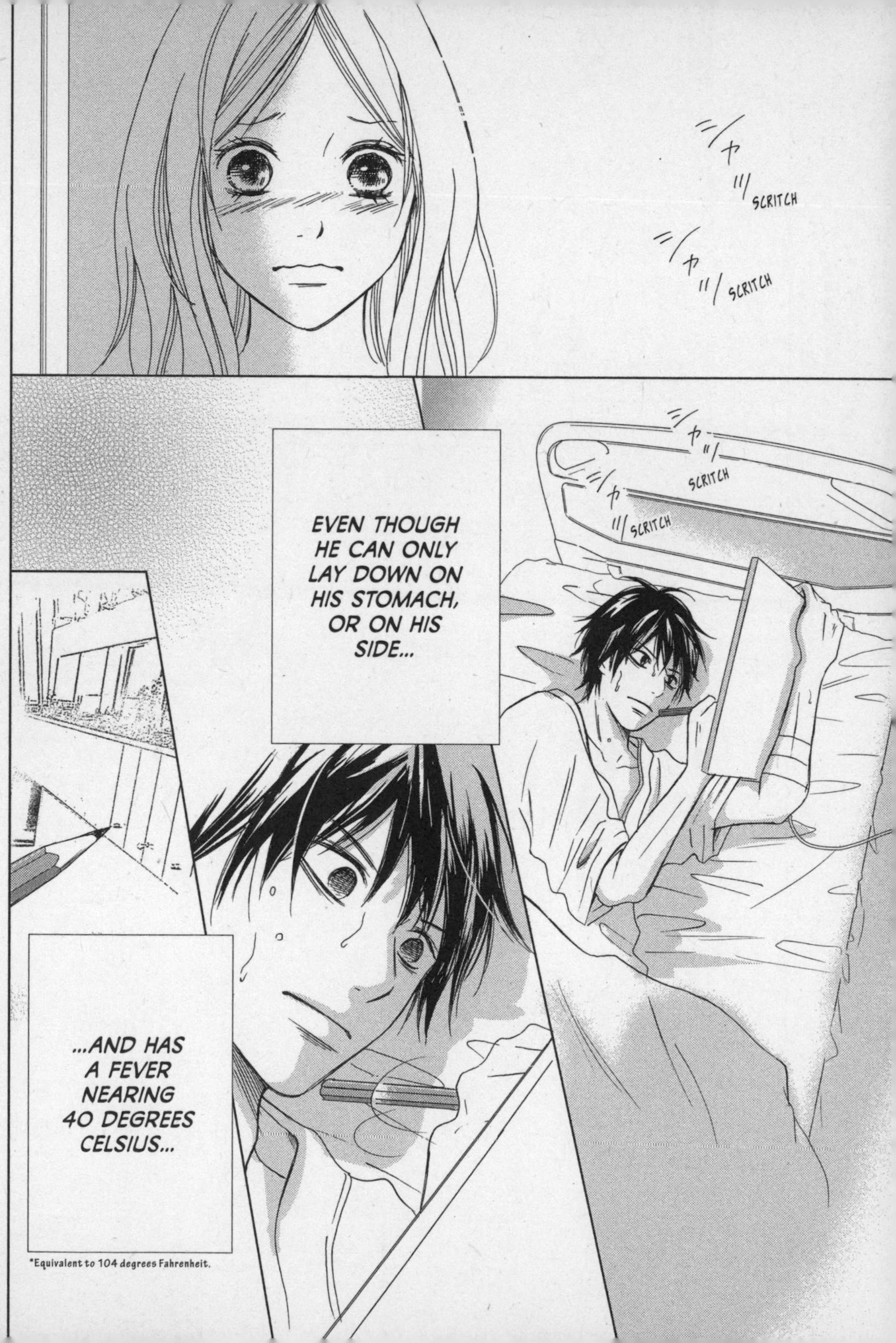
SCRITCH
SCRITCH
SCRITCH
SCRITCH
EVEN THOUGH HE CAN ONLY LAY DOWN ON HIS STOMACH, OR ON HIS SIDE...
...AND HAS A FEVER NEARING 40 DEGREES CELSIUS...

*Equivalent to 104 degrees Fahrenheit.

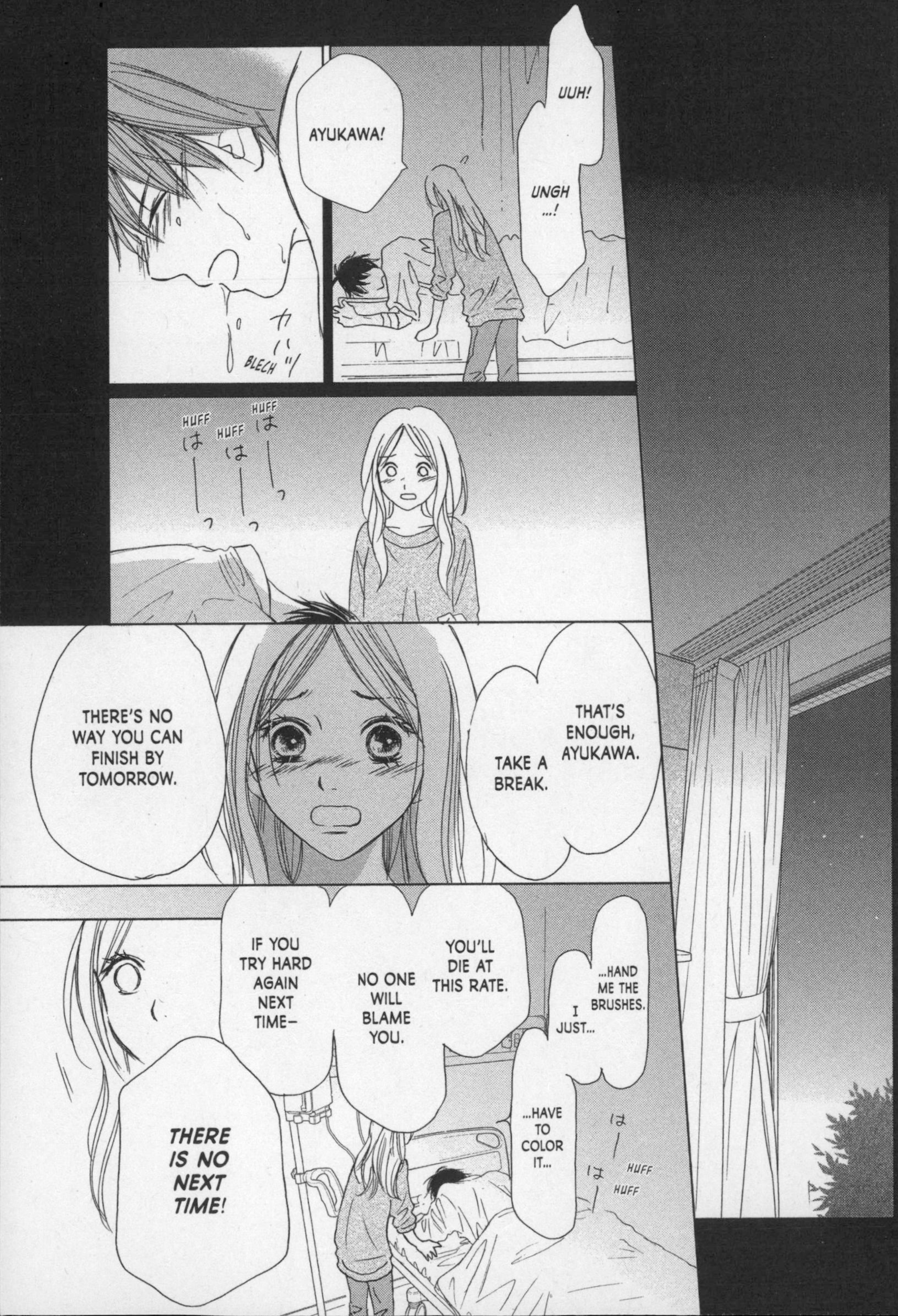

UUH!
UNGH ...!
AYUKAWA!
BLECH
HUFF
HUFF
HUFF
THAT'S ENOUGH, AYUKAWA.
TAKE A BREAK.
THERE'S NO WAY YOU CAN FINISH BY TOMORROW.
...HAND ME THE BRUSHES.
I JUST...
...HAVE TO COLOR IT...
HUFF
HUFF
YOU'LL DIE AT THIS RATE.
NO ONE WILL BLAME YOU.
IF YOU TRY HARD AGAIN NEXT TIME—
THERE IS NO NEXT TIME!

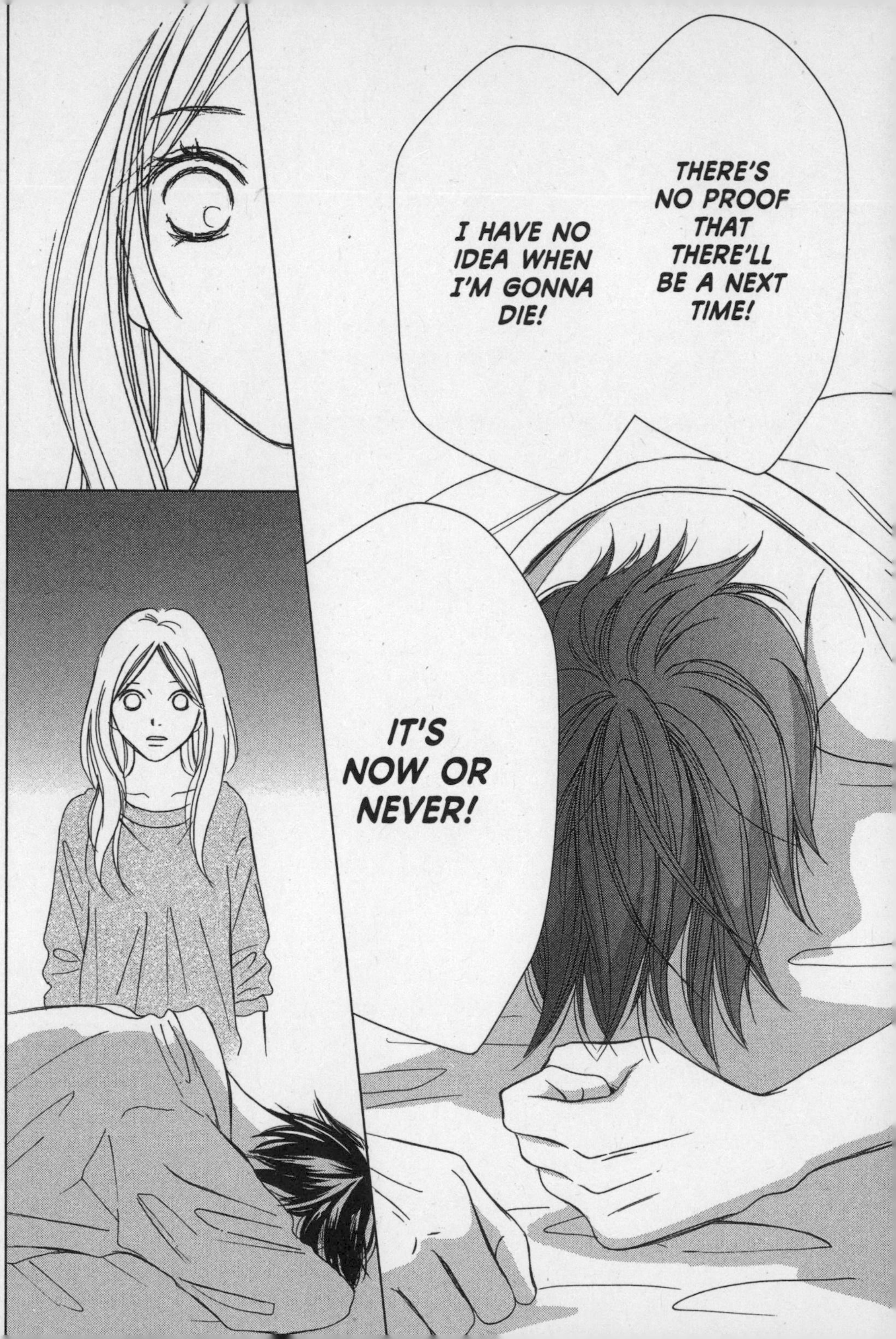
THERE'S NO PROOF THAT THERE'LL BE A NEXT TIME!
I HAVE NO IDEA WHEN I'M GONNA DIE!
IT'S NOW OR NEVER!

I'M GONNA HOLD ONTO IT TIGHT.

HOW...

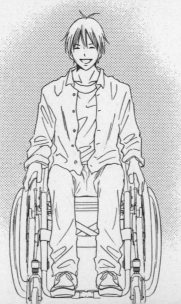

...FRUSTRATING...

...THINGS MUST HAVE BEEN FOR HIM...

...UP UNTIL NOW.

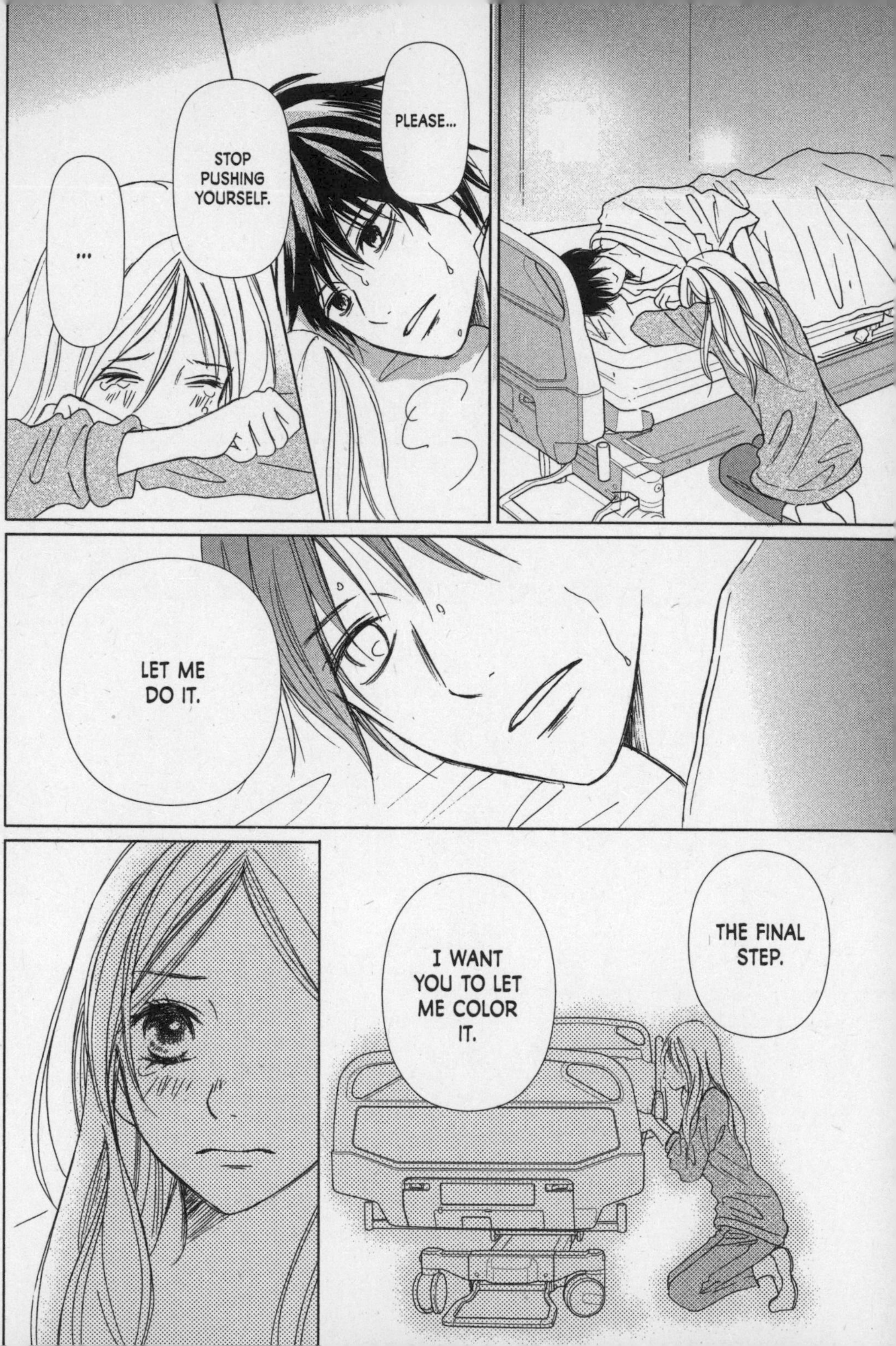
PLEASE...
STOP PUSHING YOURSELF.
...
LET ME DO IT.
THE FINAL STEP.
I WANT YOU TO LET ME COLOR IT.

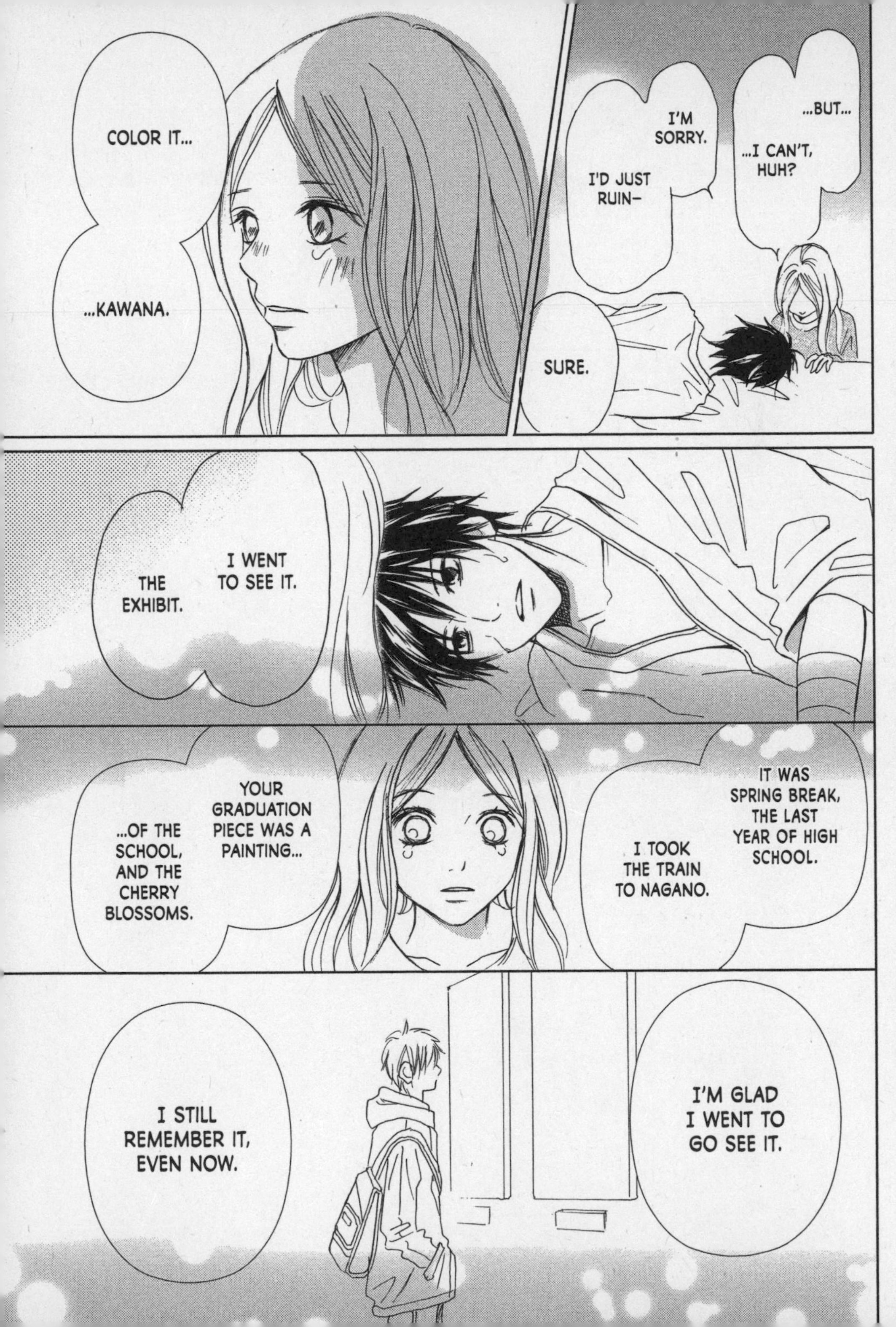
...BUT... ...I CAN'T, HUH?
I'M SORRY. I'D JUST RUIN–
SURE.
COLOR IT...
...KAWANA.
I WENT TO SEE IT.
THE EXHIBIT.
IT WAS SPRING BREAK, THE LAST YEAR OF HIGH SCHOOL.
I TOOK THE TRAIN TO NAGANO.
YOUR GRADUATION PIECE WAS A PAINTING...
...OF THE SCHOOL, AND THE CHERRY BLOSSOMS.
I'M GLAD I WENT TO GO SEE IT.
I STILL REMEMBER IT, EVEN NOW.

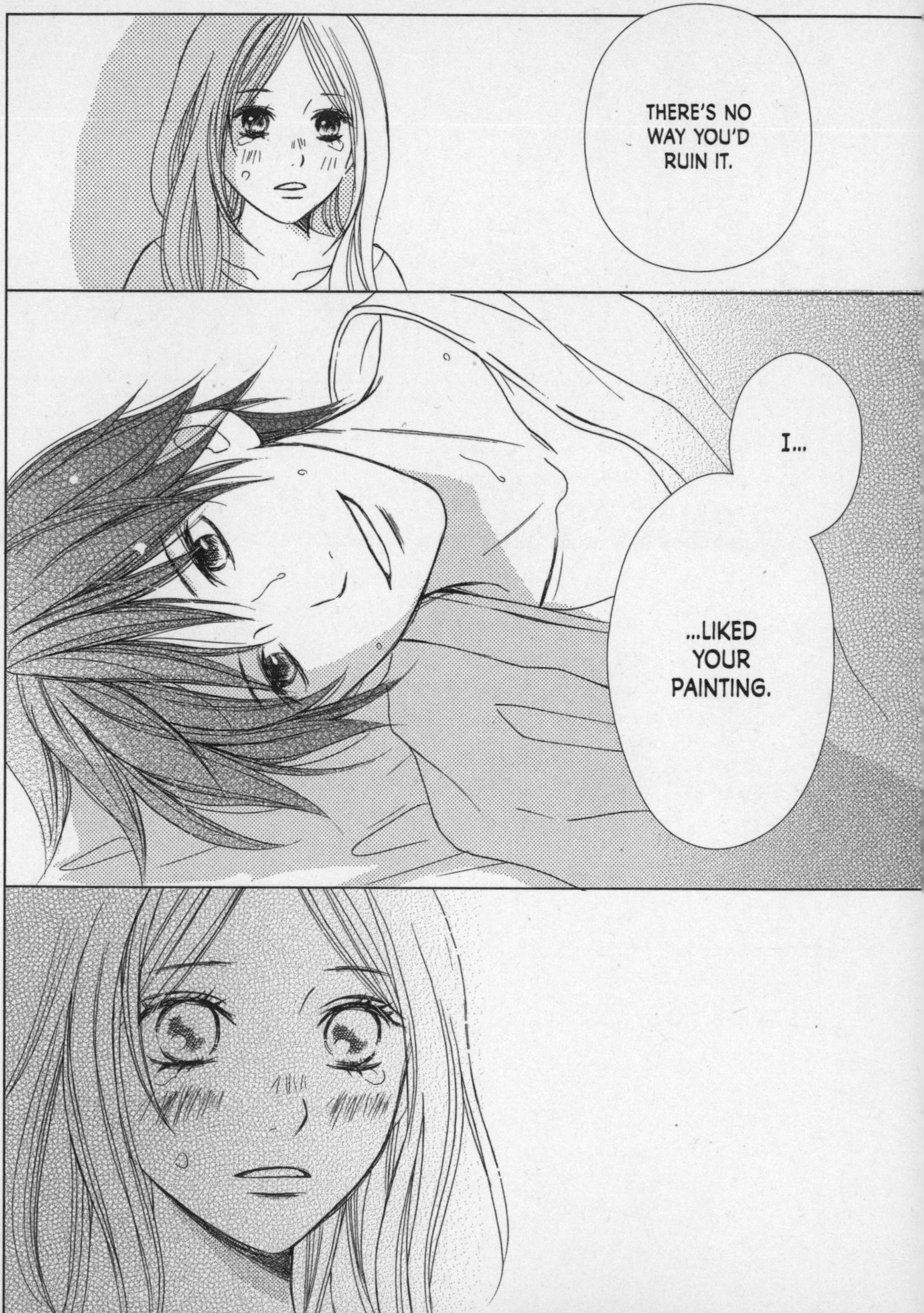
THERE'S NO WAY YOU'D RUIN IT.
I...
...LIKED YOUR PAINTING.

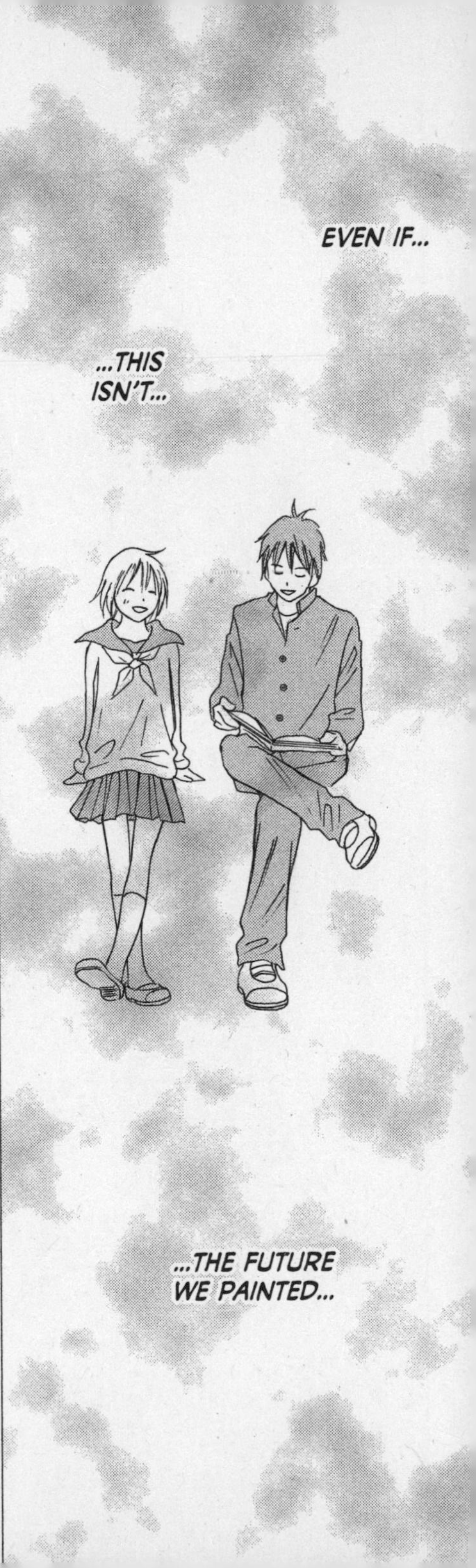
EVEN IF...
...THIS ISN'T...
...THE FUTURE WE PAINTED...

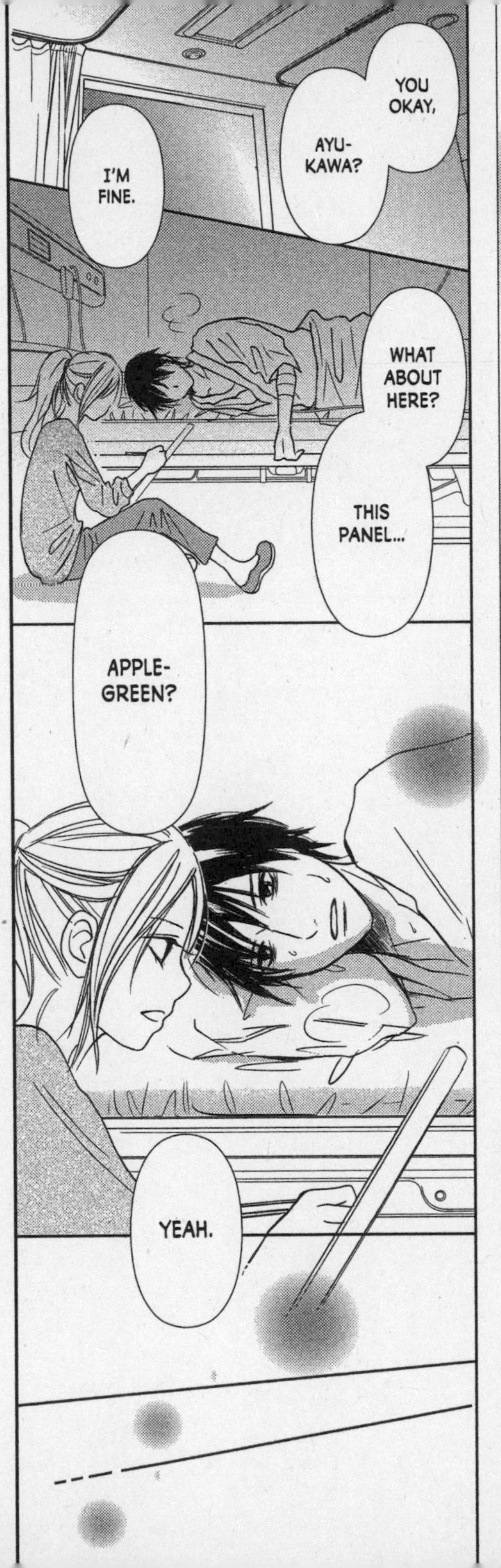
YOU OKAY, AYU-KAWA?
I'M FINE.
WHAT ABOUT HERE?
THIS PANEL...
APPLE-GREEN?
YEAH.

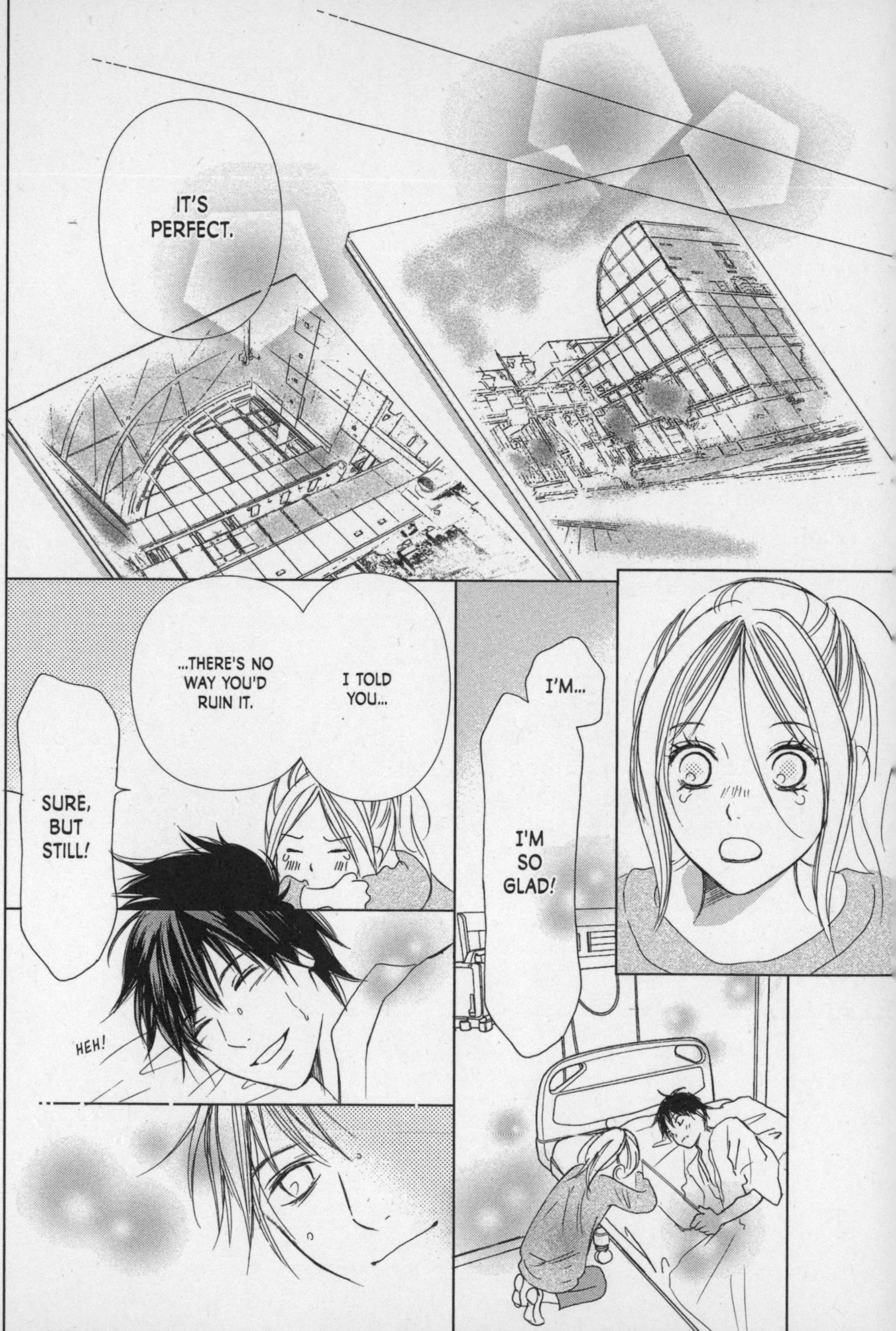
IT'S PERFECT.
I'M... I'M SO GLAD!
I TOLD YOU... ...THERE'S NO WAY YOU'D RUIN IT.
SURE, BUT STILL!
HEH!

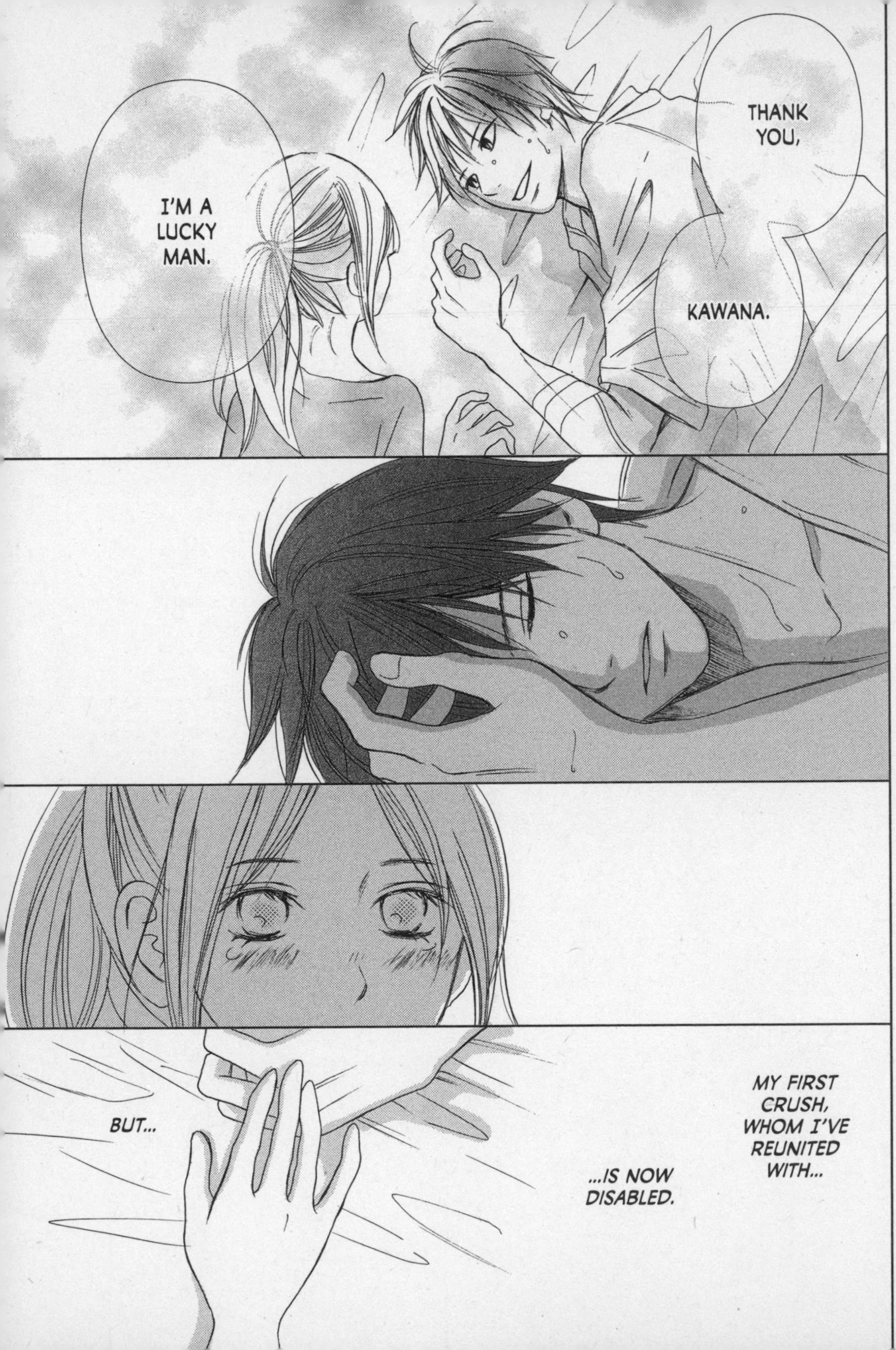
THANK YOU,
KAWANA.
I'M A LUCKY MAN.
MY FIRST CRUSH, WHOM I'VE REUNITED WITH...
...IS NOW DISABLED.
BUT...

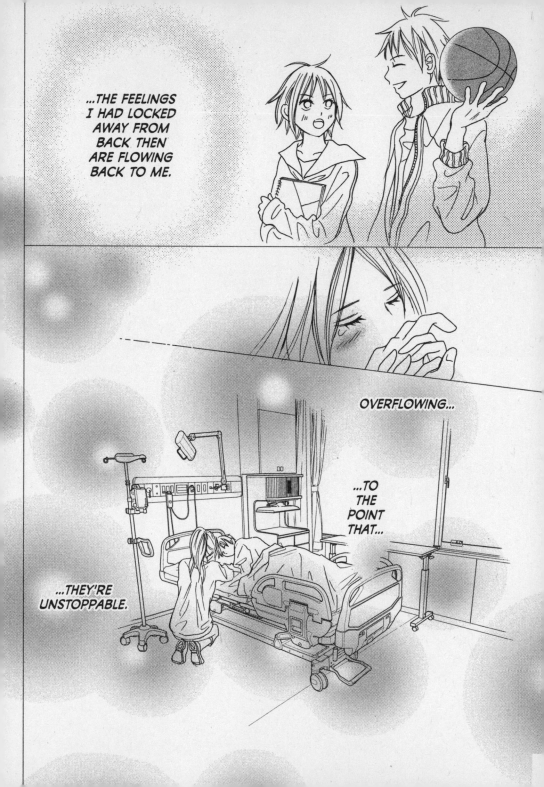

...THE FEELINGS I HAD LOCKED AWAY FROM BACK THEN ARE FLOWING BACK TO ME.

OVERFLOWING...

...TO THE POINT THAT...

...THEY'RE UNSTOPPABLE.

PERFECT WORLD.

PERFECT WORLD

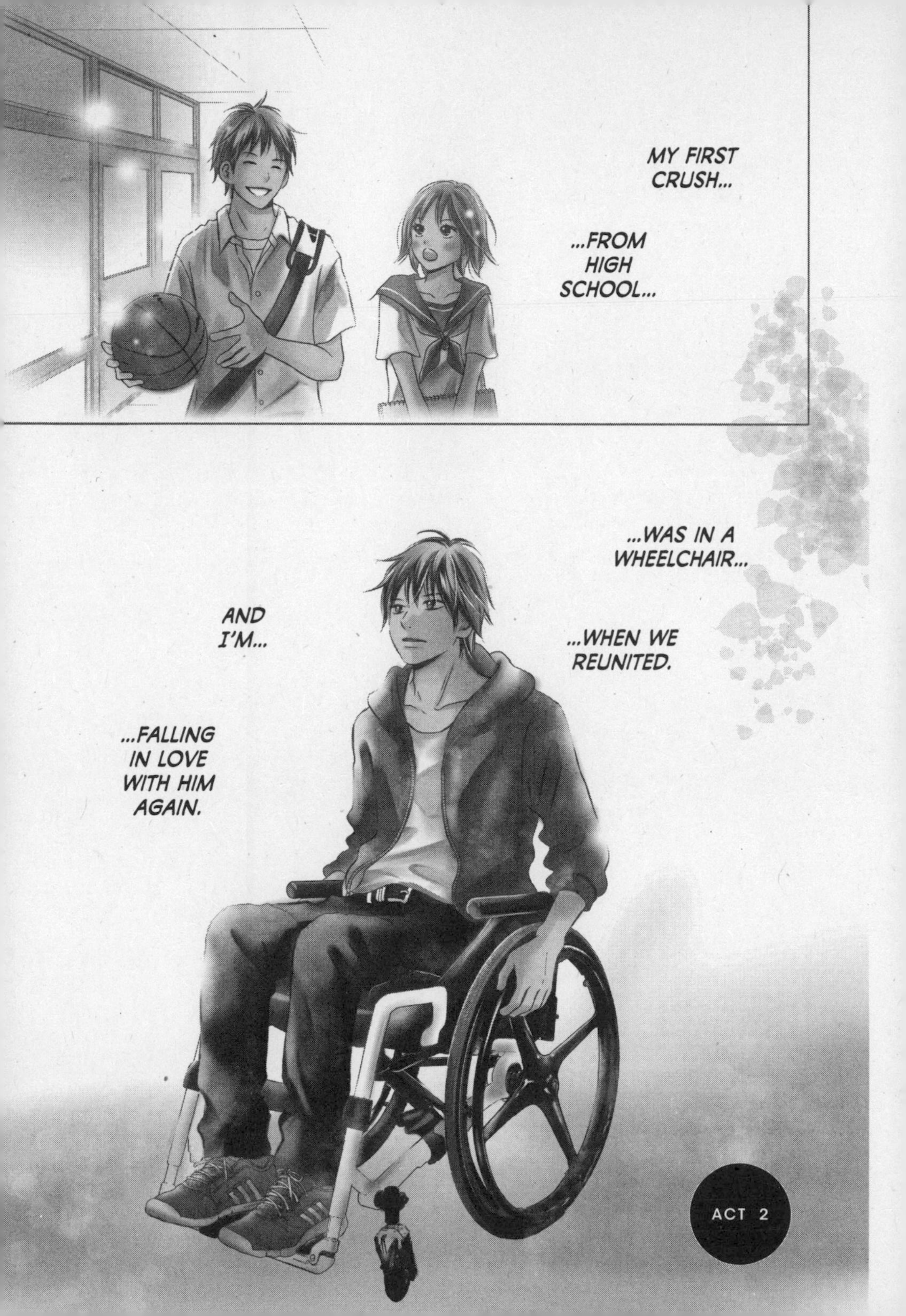
MY FIRST CRUSH...
...FROM HIGH SCHOOL...
...WAS IN A WHEELCHAIR...
...WHEN WE REUNITED.
AND I'M...
...FALLING IN LOVE WITH HIM AGAIN.
ACT 2

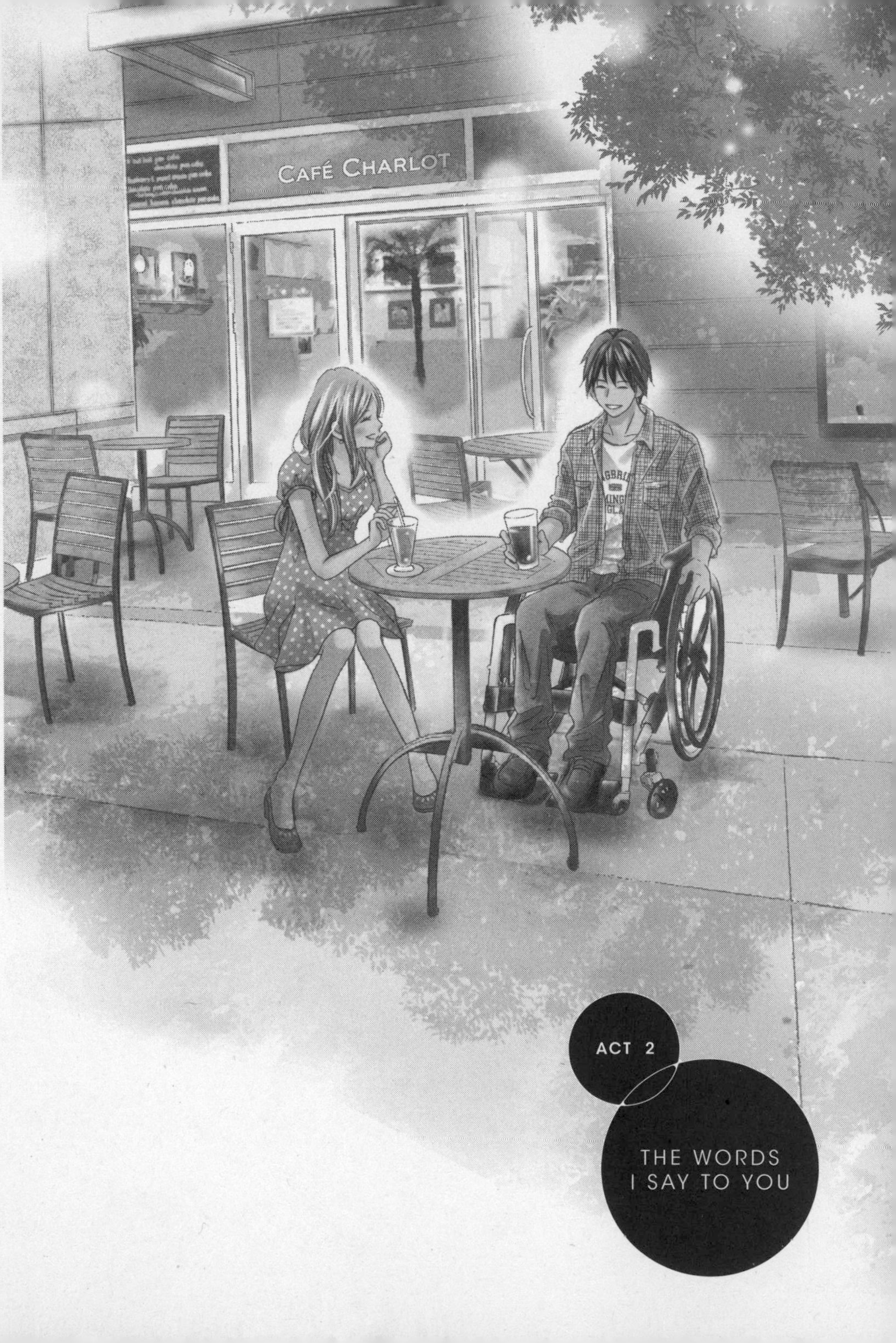
CAFÉ CHARLOT

ACT 2

THE WORDS I SAY TO YOU

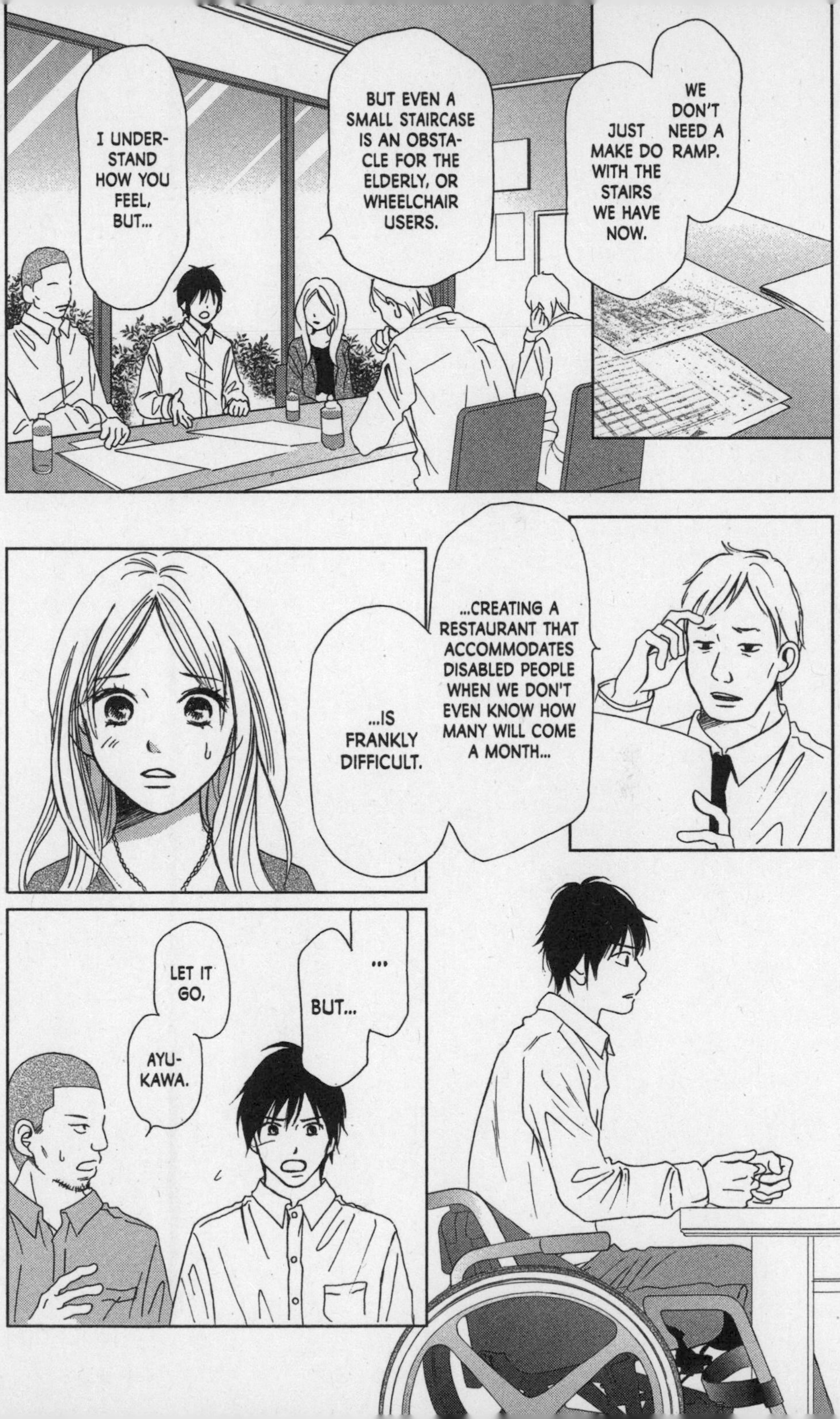
WE DON'T NEED A RAMP.
JUST MAKE DO WITH THE STAIRS WE HAVE NOW.
BUT EVEN A SMALL STAIRCASE IS AN OBSTACLE FOR THE ELDERLY, OR WHEELCHAIR USERS.
I UNDERSTAND HOW YOU FEEL, BUT...
...CREATING A RESTAURANT THAT ACCOMMODATES DISABLED PEOPLE WHEN WE DON'T EVEN KNOW HOW MANY WILL COME A MONTH...
...IS FRANKLY DIFFICULT.
...
BUT...
LET IT GO,
AYUKAWA.

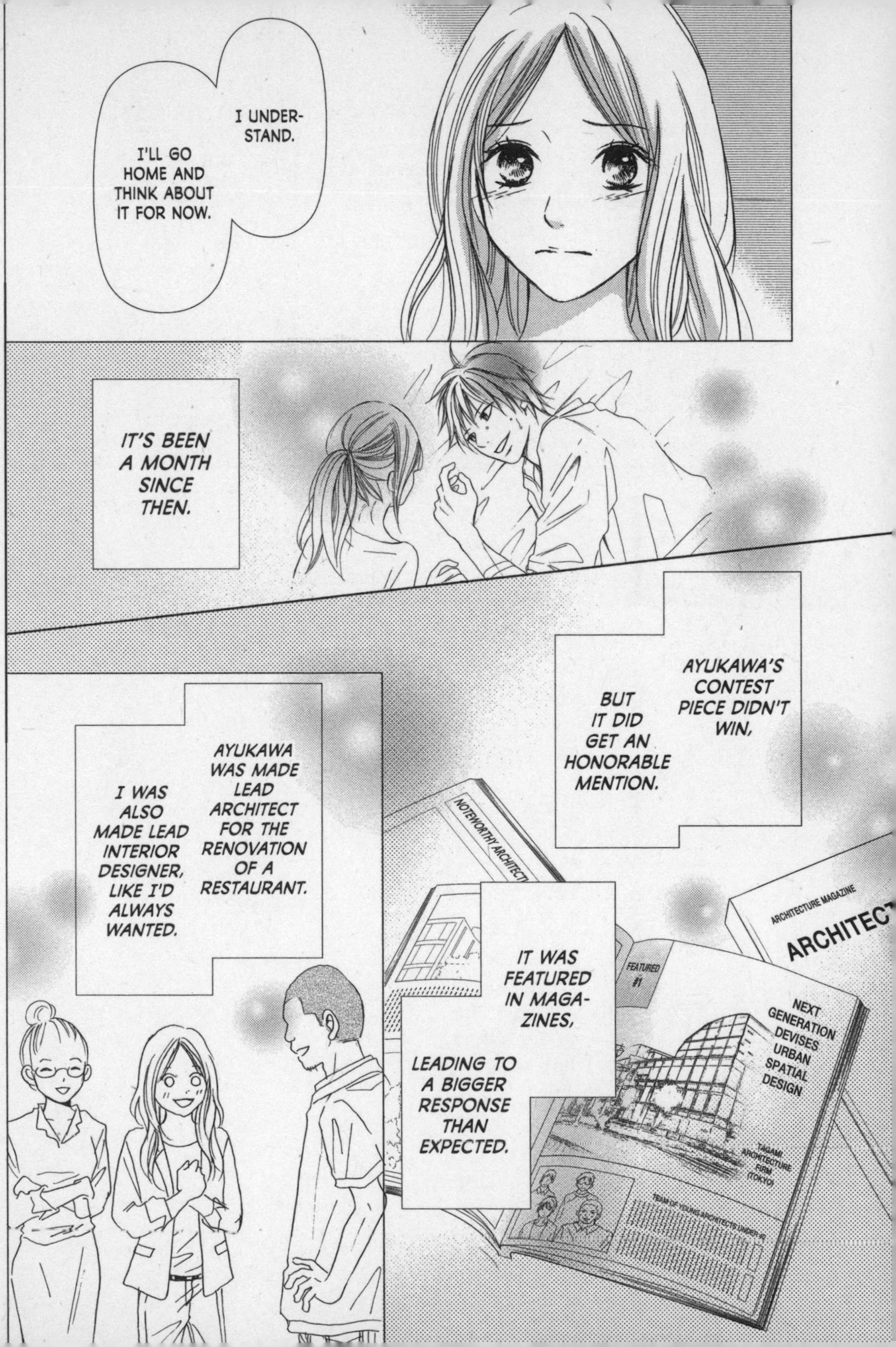

I UNDER-STAND.
I'LL GO HOME AND THINK ABOUT IT FOR NOW.
IT'S BEEN A MONTH SINCE THEN.
AYUKAWA'S CONTEST PIECE DIDN'T WIN,
BUT IT DID GET AN HONORABLE MENTION.
NOTEWORTHY ARCHITECT
ARCHITECTURE MAGAZINE
ARCHITECT
FEATURED #1
NEXT GENERATION DEVISES URBAN SPATIAL DESIGN
TAGAMI ARCHITECTURE FIRM (TOKYO)
IT WAS FEATURED IN MAGA-ZINES,
LEADING TO A BIGGER RESPONSE THAN EXPECTED.
AYUKAWA WAS MADE LEAD ARCHITECT FOR THE RENOVATION OF A RESTAURANT.
I WAS ALSO MADE LEAD INTERIOR DESIGNER, LIKE I'D ALWAYS WANTED.

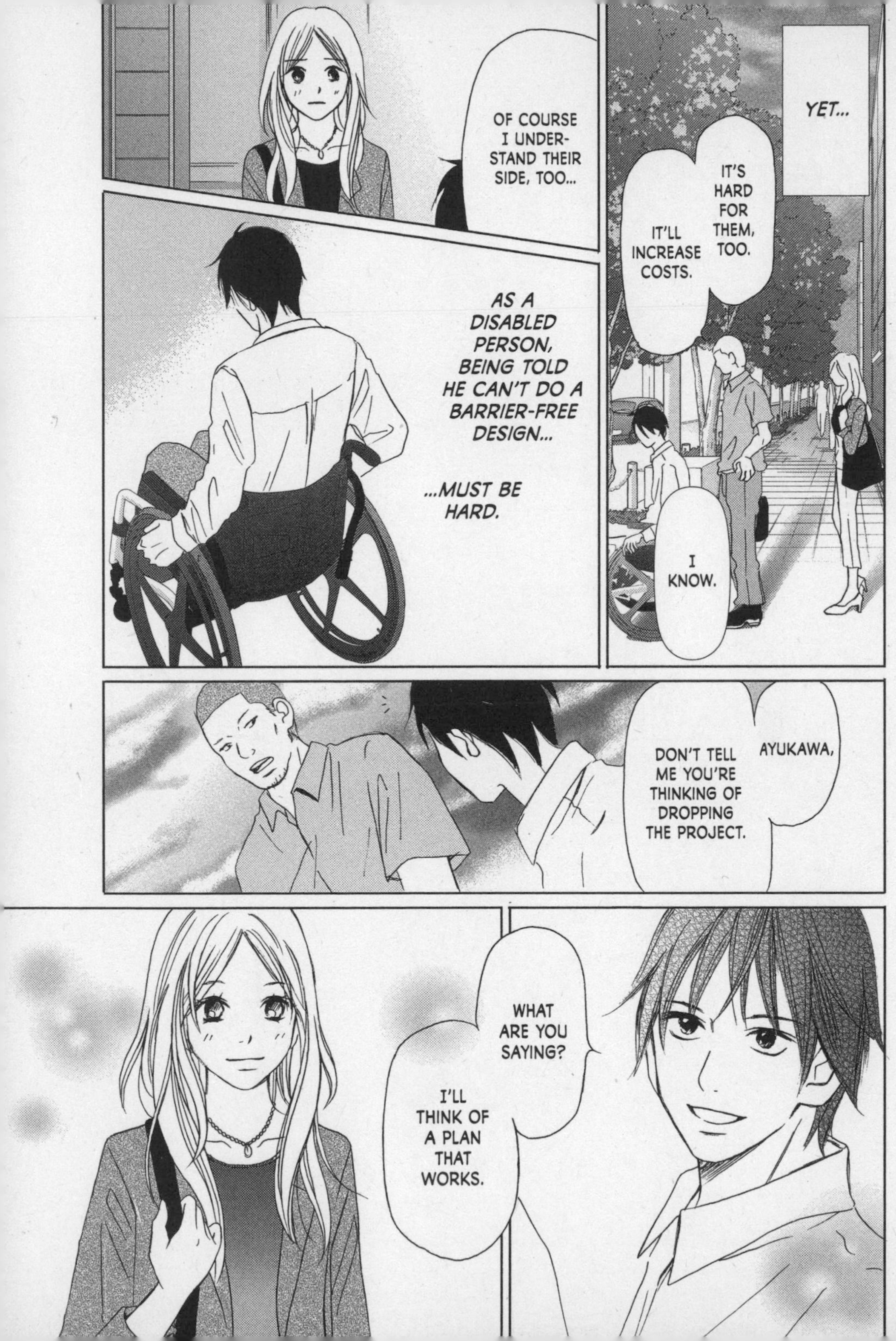
YET...
IT'S HARD FOR THEM, TOO.
IT'LL INCREASE COSTS.
I KNOW.
OF COURSE I UNDER-STAND THEIR SIDE, TOO...
AS A DISABLED PERSON, BEING TOLD HE CAN'T DO A BARRIER-FREE DESIGN...
...MUST BE HARD.
AYUKAWA,
DON'T TELL ME YOU'RE THINKING OF DROPPING THE PROJECT.
WHAT ARE YOU SAYING?
I'LL THINK OF A PLAN THAT WORKS.

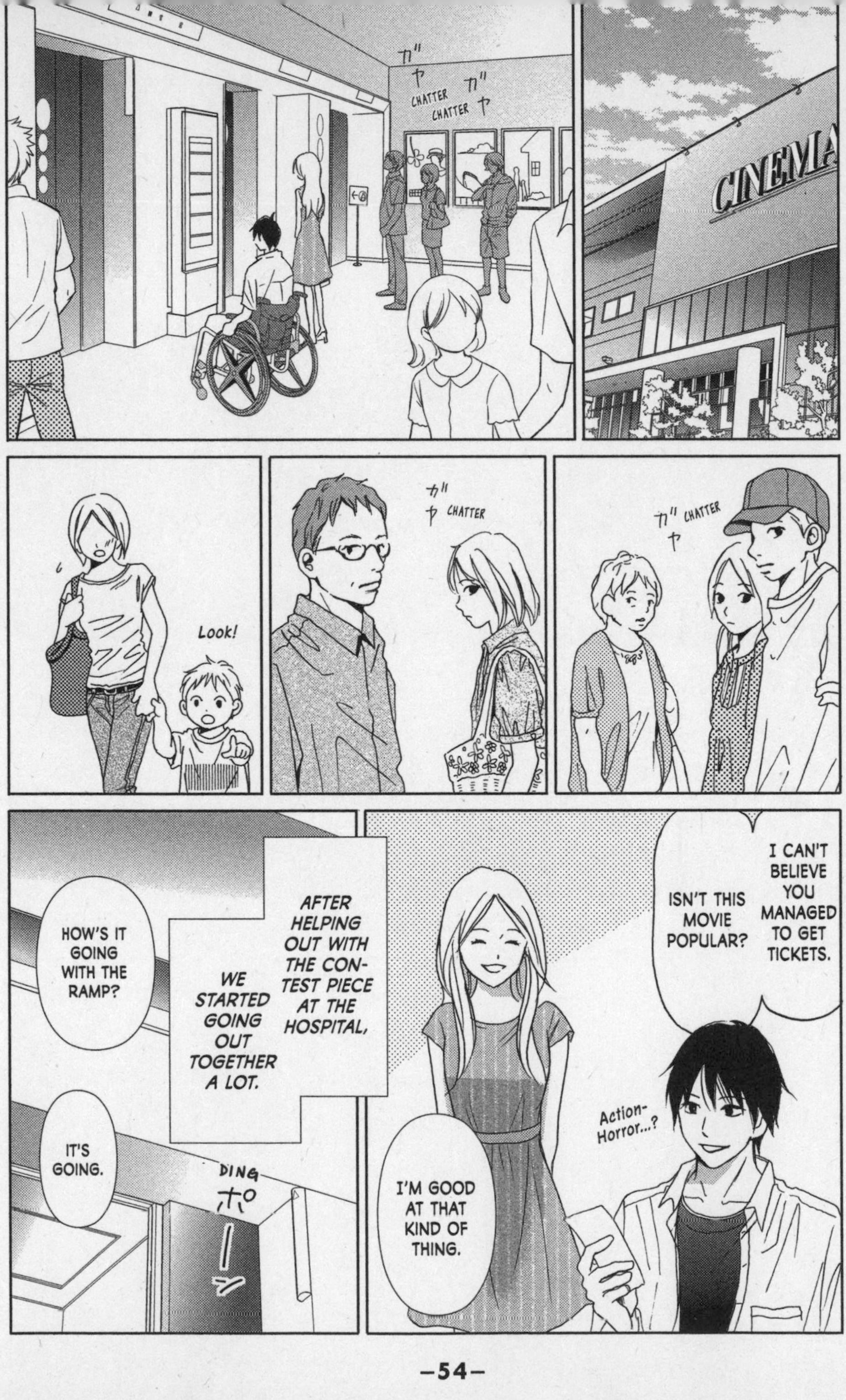
CINEMA
ガヤ
CHATTER
ガヤ
CHATTER
ガヤ
CHATTER
ガヤ
CHATTER
Look!
I CAN'T BELIEVE YOU MANAGED TO GET TICKETS.
ISN'T THIS MOVIE POPULAR?
Action-Horror...?
I'M GOOD AT THAT KIND OF THING.
AFTER HELPING OUT WITH THE CON-TEST PIECE AT THE HOSPITAL,
WE STARTED GOING OUT TOGETHER A LOT.
HOW'S IT GOING WITH THE RAMP?
IT'S GOING.
DING
ポーン

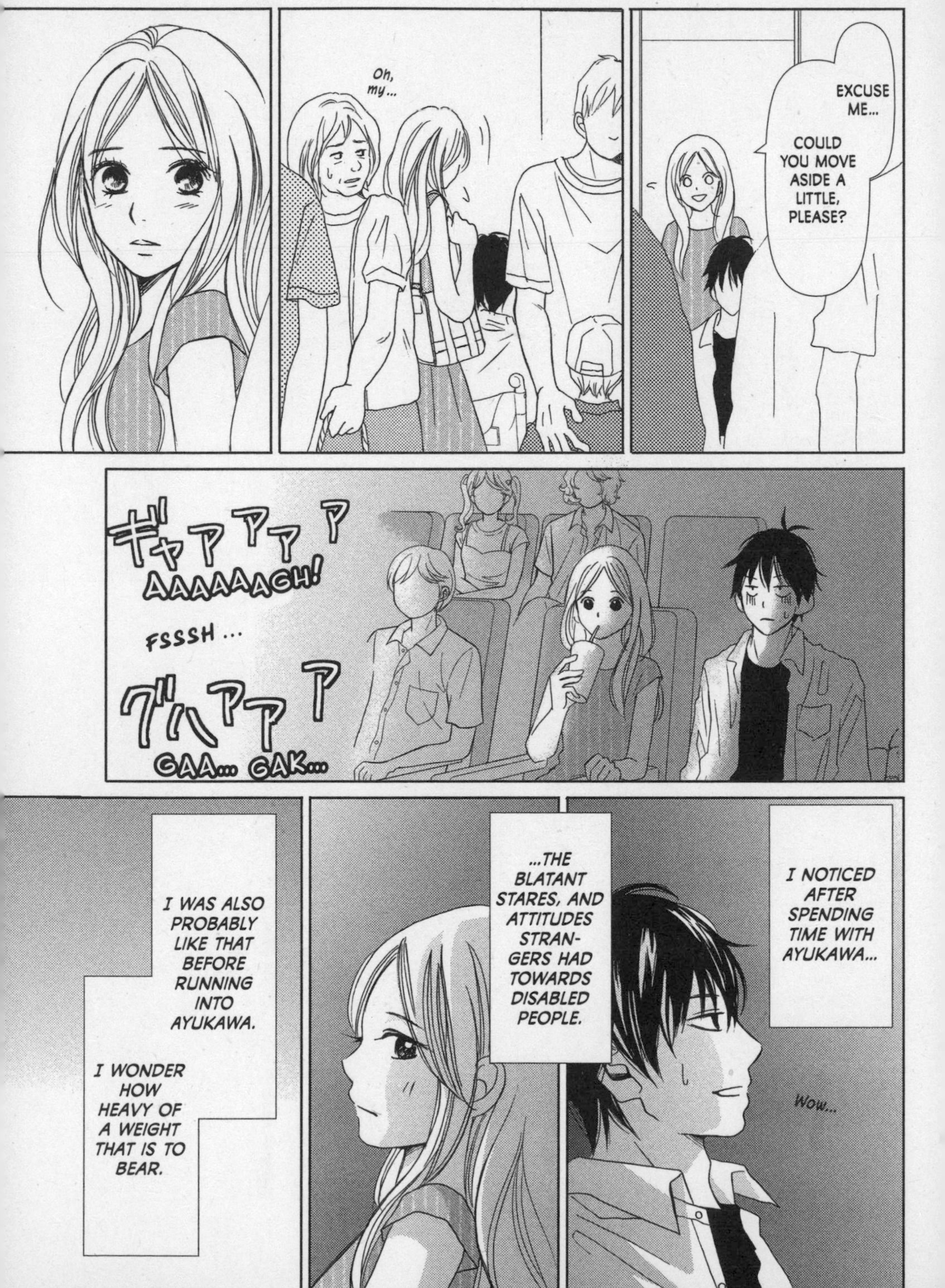
EXCUSE ME... COULD YOU MOVE ASIDE A LITTLE, PLEASE?
Oh, my...
ギャアアアア
AAAAAAGH!
FSSSH...
グハアアア
GAA... GAK...
I NOTICED AFTER SPENDING TIME WITH AYUKAWA...
Wow...
...THE BLATANT STARES, AND ATTITUDES STRAN-GERS HAD TOWARDS DISABLED PEOPLE.
I WAS ALSO PROBABLY LIKE THAT BEFORE RUNNING INTO AYUKAWA.
I WONDER HOW HEAVY OF A WEIGHT THAT IS TO BEAR.

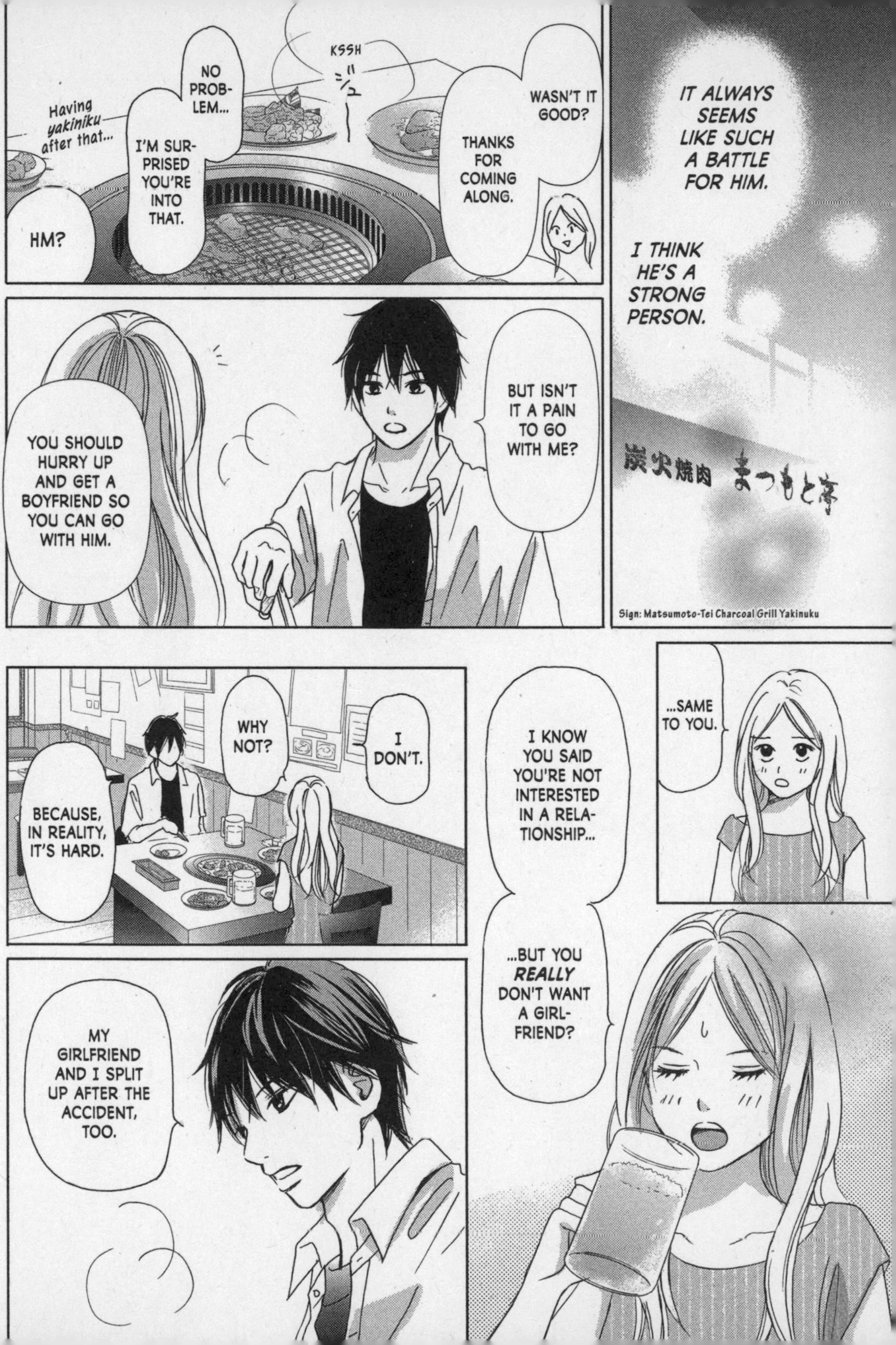
IT ALWAYS SEEMS LIKE SUCH A BATTLE FOR HIM.
I THINK HE'S A STRONG PERSON.
炭火焼肉 まつもと亭
Sign: Matsumoto-Tei Charcoal Grill Yakinuku
WASN'T IT GOOD?
THANKS FOR COMING ALONG.
KSSH
NO PROBLEM...
I'M SURPRISED YOU'RE INTO THAT.
Having yakiniku after that...
HM?
BUT ISN'T IT A PAIN TO GO WITH ME?
YOU SHOULD HURRY UP AND GET A BOYFRIEND SO YOU CAN GO WITH HIM.
...SAME TO YOU.
I DON'T.
WHY NOT?
BECAUSE, IN REALITY, IT'S HARD.
I KNOW YOU SAID YOU'RE NOT INTERESTED IN A RELATIONSHIP...
...BUT YOU REALLY DON'T WANT A GIRLFRIEND?
MY GIRLFRIEND AND I SPLIT UP AFTER THE ACCIDENT, TOO.

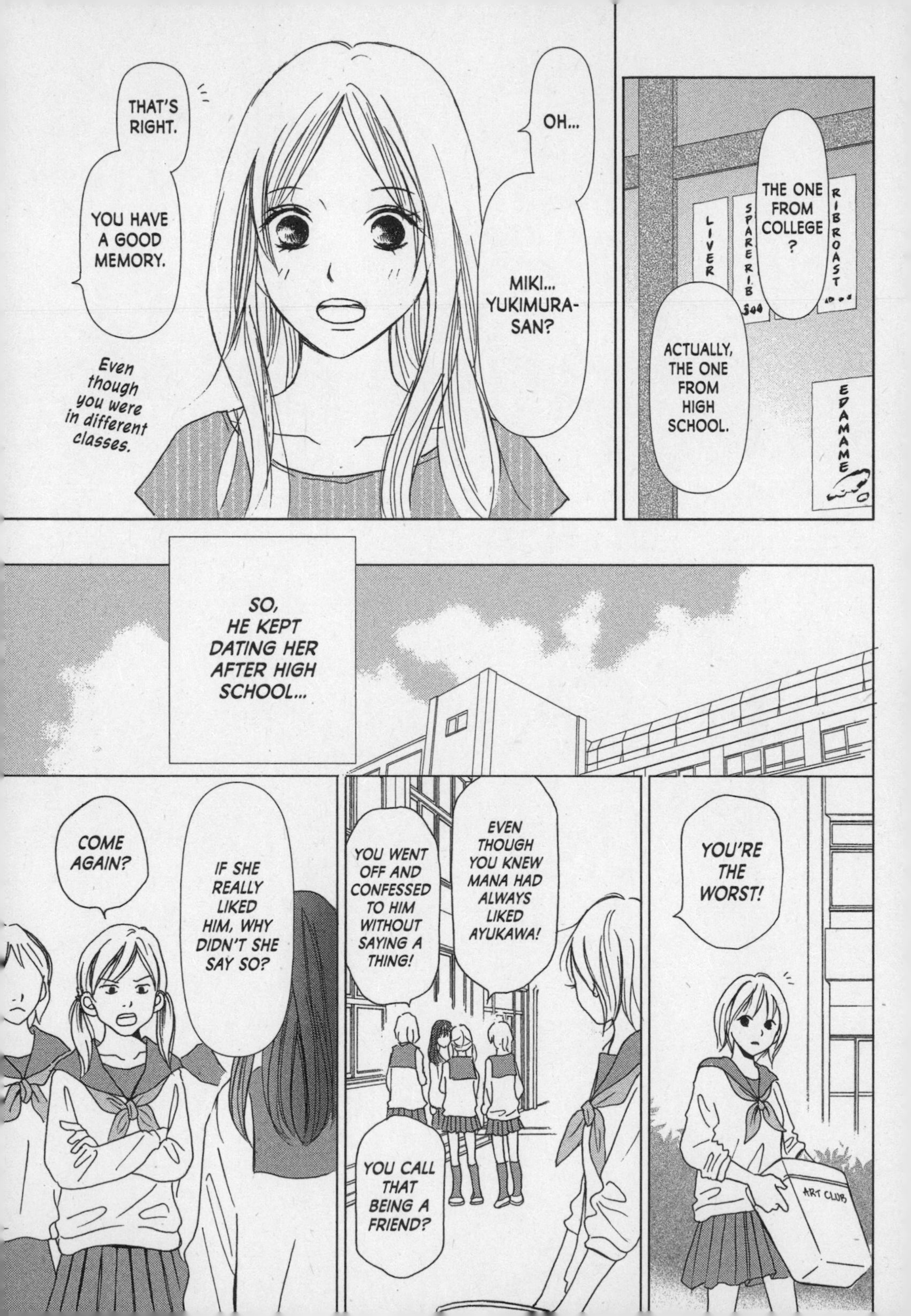
RIBROAST
THE ONE FROM COLLEGE?
SPARE RIB
LIVER
ACTUALLY, THE ONE FROM HIGH SCHOOL.
EDAMAME
OH...
MIKI... YUKIMURA-SAN?
THAT'S RIGHT.
YOU HAVE A GOOD MEMORY.
Even though you were in different classes.
SO, HE KEPT DATING HER AFTER HIGH SCHOOL...
YOU'RE THE WORST!
ART CLUB
EVEN THOUGH YOU KNEW MANA HAD ALWAYS LIKED AYUKAWA!
YOU WENT OFF AND CONFESSED TO HIM WITHOUT SAYING A THING!
YOU CALL THAT BEING A FRIEND?
IF SHE REALLY LIKED HIM, WHY DIDN'T SHE SAY SO?
COME AGAIN?

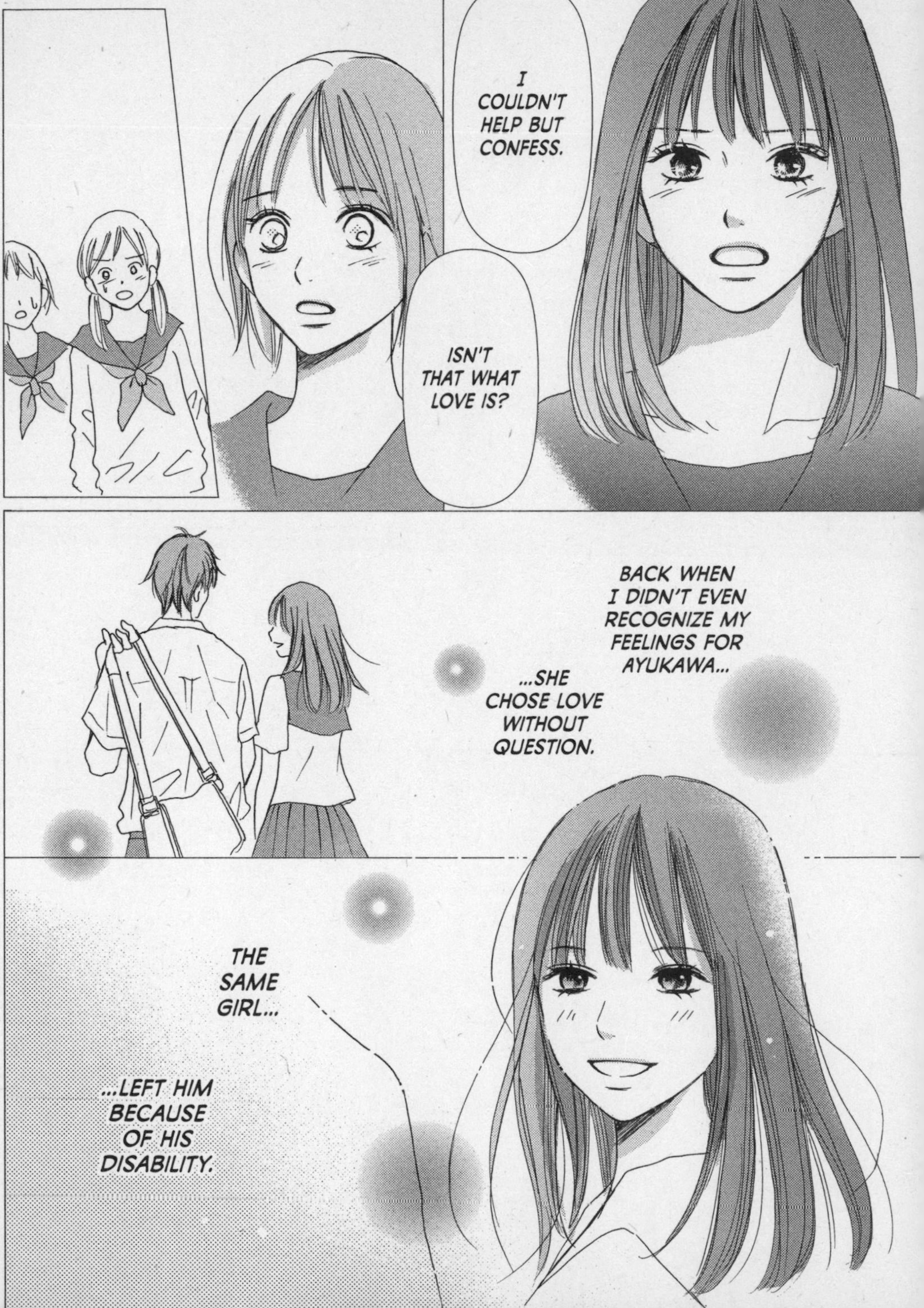
I COULDN'T HELP BUT CONFESS.
ISN'T THAT WHAT LOVE IS?
BACK WHEN I DIDN'T EVEN RECOGNIZE MY FEELINGS FOR AYUKAWA...
...SHE CHOSE LOVE WITHOUT QUESTION.
THE SAME GIRL...
...LEFT HIM BECAUSE OF HIS DISABILITY.

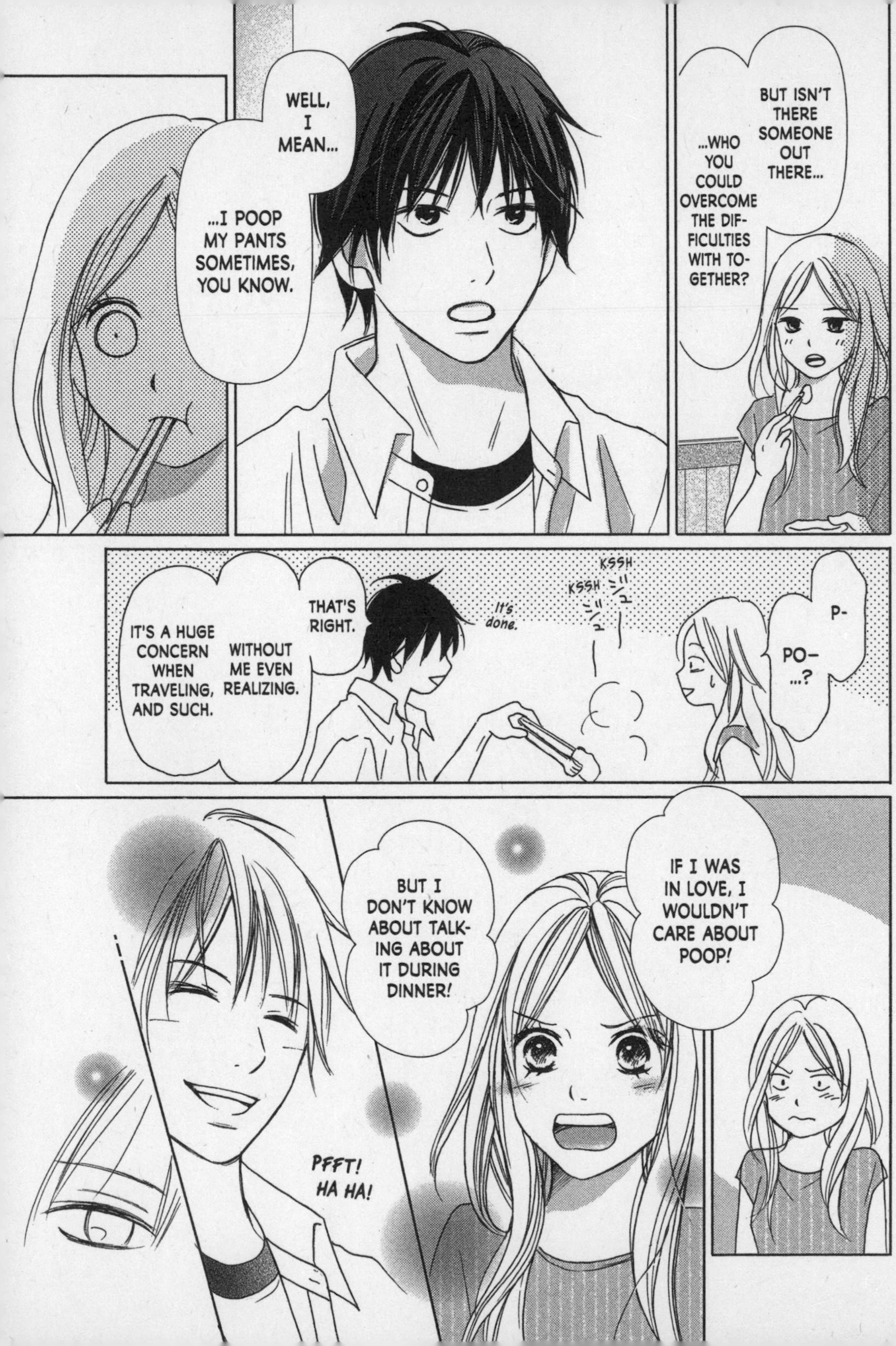
BUT ISN'T THERE SOMEONE OUT THERE...
...WHO YOU COULD OVERCOME THE DIF-FICULTIES WITH TO-GETHER?
WELL, I MEAN...
...I POOP MY PANTS SOMETIMES, YOU KNOW.
P- PO-...?
KSSH KSSH
It's done.
THAT'S RIGHT. WITHOUT ME EVEN REALIZING.
IT'S A HUGE CONCERN WHEN TRAVELING, AND SUCH.
IF I WAS IN LOVE, I WOULDN'T CARE ABOUT POOP!
BUT I DON'T KNOW ABOUT TALK-ING ABOUT IT DURING DINNER!
PFFT! HA HA!

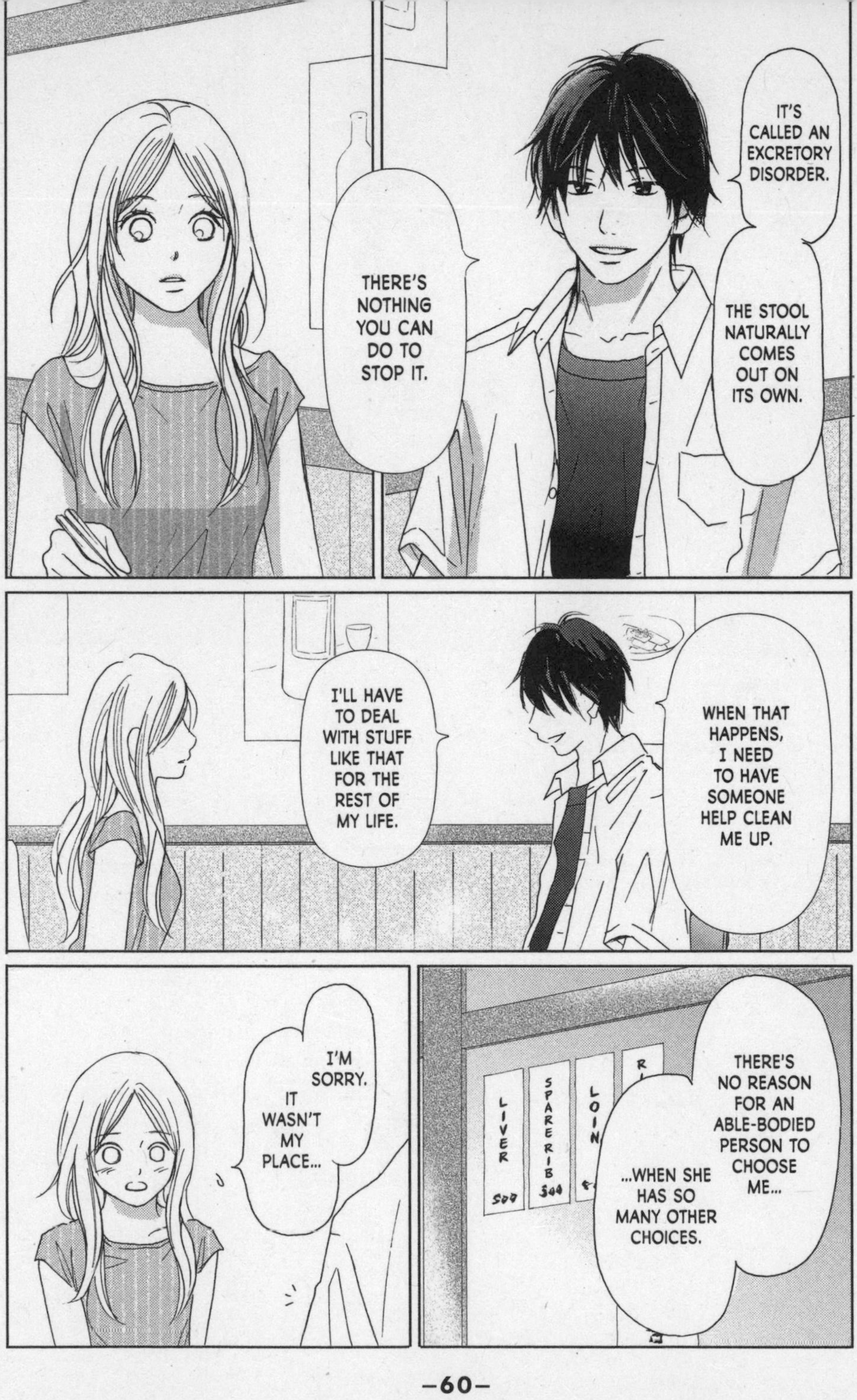
IT'S CALLED AN EXCRETORY DISORDER.
THE STOOL NATURALLY COMES OUT ON ITS OWN.
THERE'S NOTHING YOU CAN DO TO STOP IT.
WHEN THAT HAPPENS, I NEED TO HAVE SOMEONE HELP CLEAN ME UP.
I'LL HAVE TO DEAL WITH STUFF LIKE THAT FOR THE REST OF MY LIFE.
THERE'S NO REASON FOR AN ABLE-BODIED PERSON TO CHOOSE ME...
...WHEN SHE HAS SO MANY OTHER CHOICES.
LIVER
SPARERIB
LOIN
I'M SORRY.
IT WASN'T MY PLACE...

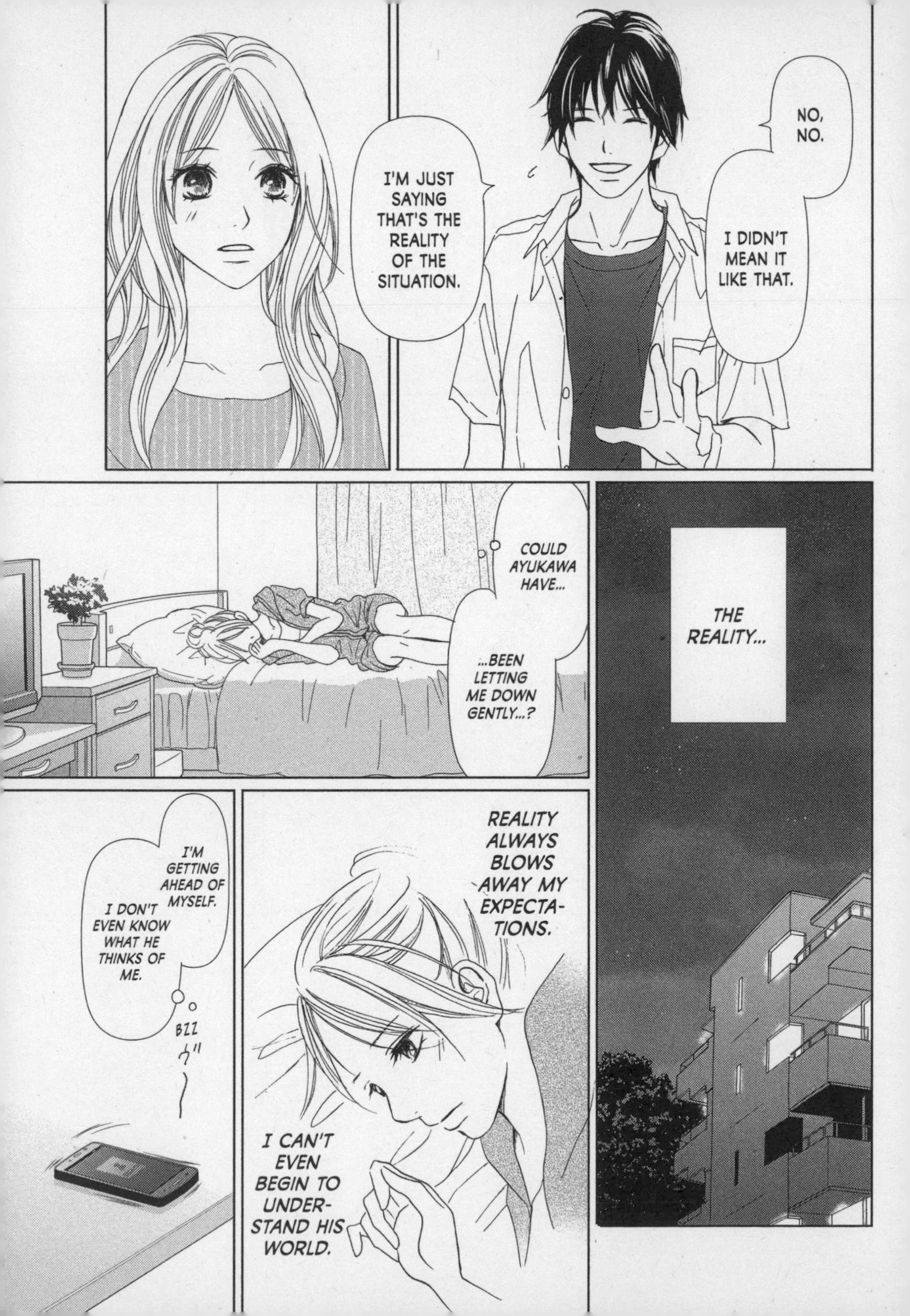
NO, NO.
I DIDN'T MEAN IT LIKE THAT.
I'M JUST SAYING THAT'S THE REALITY OF THE SITUATION.
THE REALITY...
COULD AYUKAWA HAVE...
...BEEN LETTING ME DOWN GENTLY...?
REALITY ALWAYS BLOWS AWAY MY EXPECTA-TIONS.
I CAN'T EVEN BEGIN TO UNDER-STAND HIS WORLD.
I'M GETTING AHEAD OF MYSELF.
I DON'T EVEN KNOW WHAT HE THINKS OF ME.
BZZ

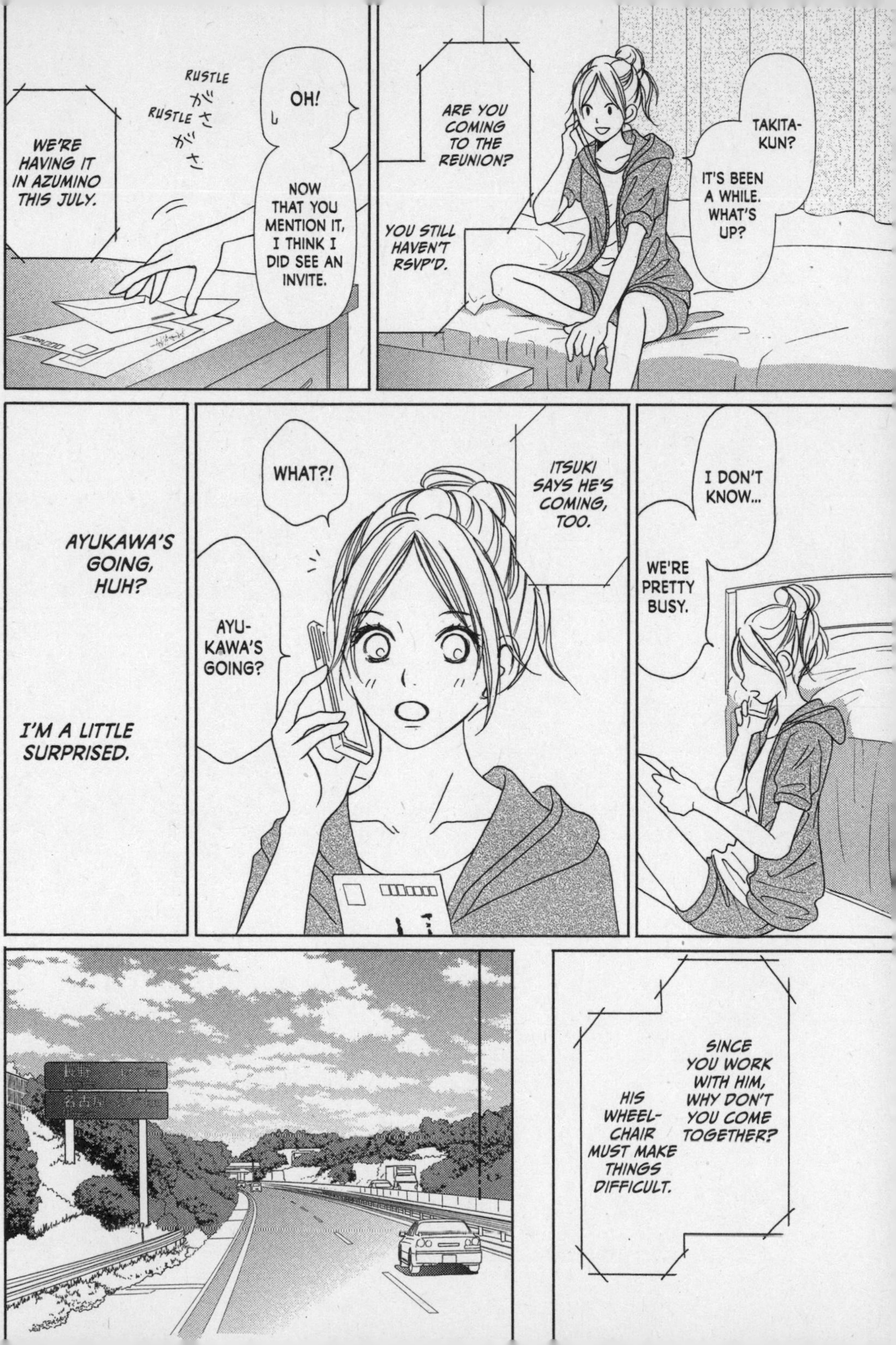
TAKITA-KUN?
IT'S BEEN A WHILE. WHAT'S UP?
ARE YOU COMING TO THE REUNION?
YOU STILL HAVEN'T RSVP'D.
OH!
NOW THAT YOU MENTION IT, I THINK I DID SEE AN INVITE.
RUSTLE がさ
RUSTLE がさ
WE'RE HAVING IT IN AZUMINO THIS JULY.
I DON'T KNOW...
WE'RE PRETTY BUSY.
ITSUKI SAYS HE'S COMING, TOO.
WHAT?!
AYU-KAWA'S GOING?
AYUKAWA'S GOING, HUH?
I'M A LITTLE SURPRISED.
SINCE YOU WORK WITH HIM, WHY DON'T YOU COME TOGETHER?
HIS WHEEL-CHAIR MUST MAKE THINGS DIFFICULT.
長野
名古屋

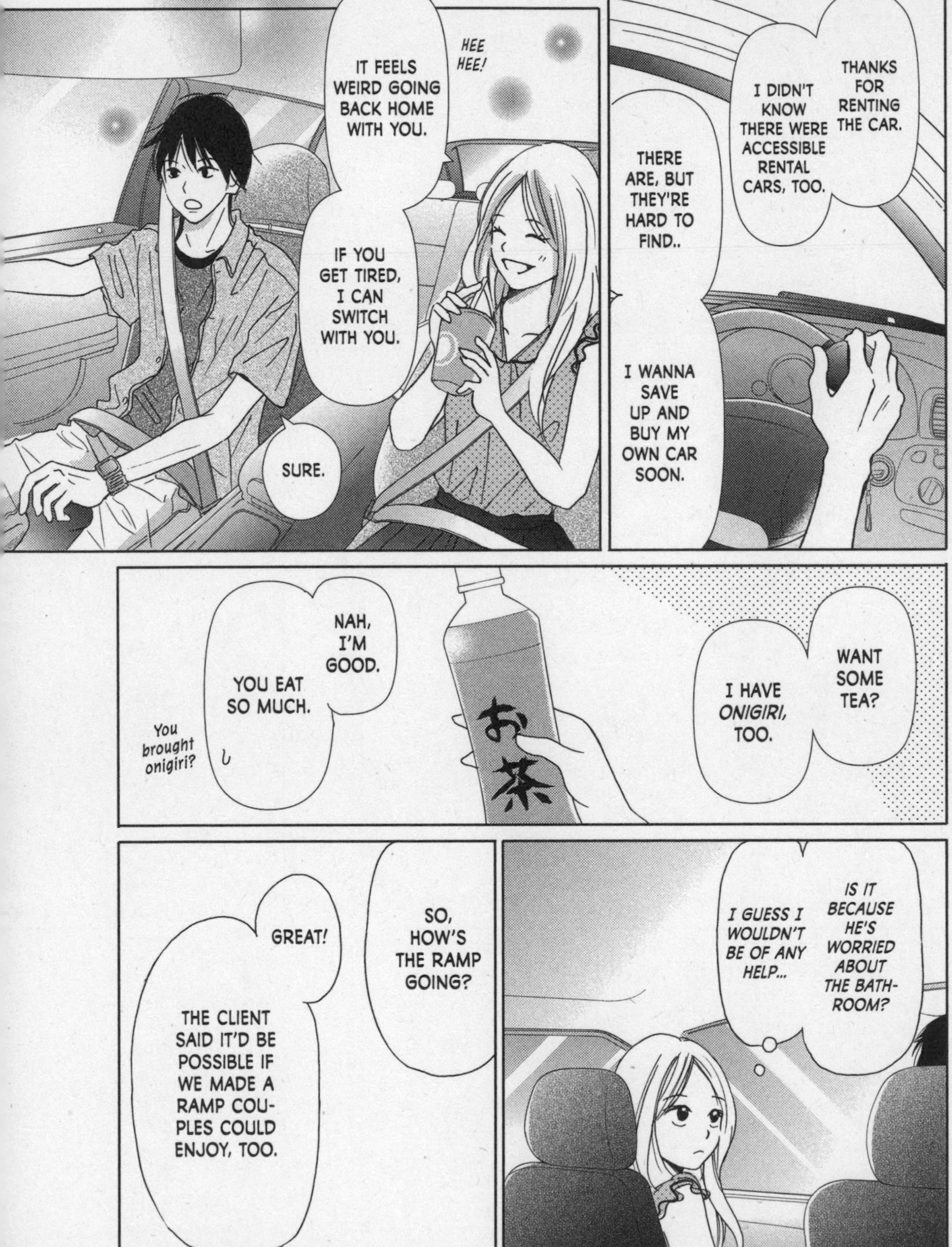

THANKS FOR RENTING THE CAR.
I DIDN'T KNOW THERE WERE ACCESSIBLE RENTAL CARS, TOO.
THERE ARE, BUT THEY'RE HARD TO FIND..
I WANNA SAVE UP AND BUY MY OWN CAR SOON.
HEE HEE!
IT FEELS WEIRD GOING BACK HOME WITH YOU.
IF YOU GET TIRED, I CAN SWITCH WITH YOU.
SURE.
WANT SOME TEA?
I HAVE *ONIGIRI*, TOO.
お茶
NAH, I'M GOOD.
YOU EAT SO MUCH.
You brought onigiri?
IS IT BECAUSE HE'S WORRIED ABOUT THE BATH-ROOM?
I GUESS I WOULDN'T BE OF ANY HELP...
SO, HOW'S THE RAMP GOING?
GREAT!
THE CLIENT SAID IT'D BE POSSIBLE IF WE MADE A RAMP COU-PLES COULD ENJOY, TOO.

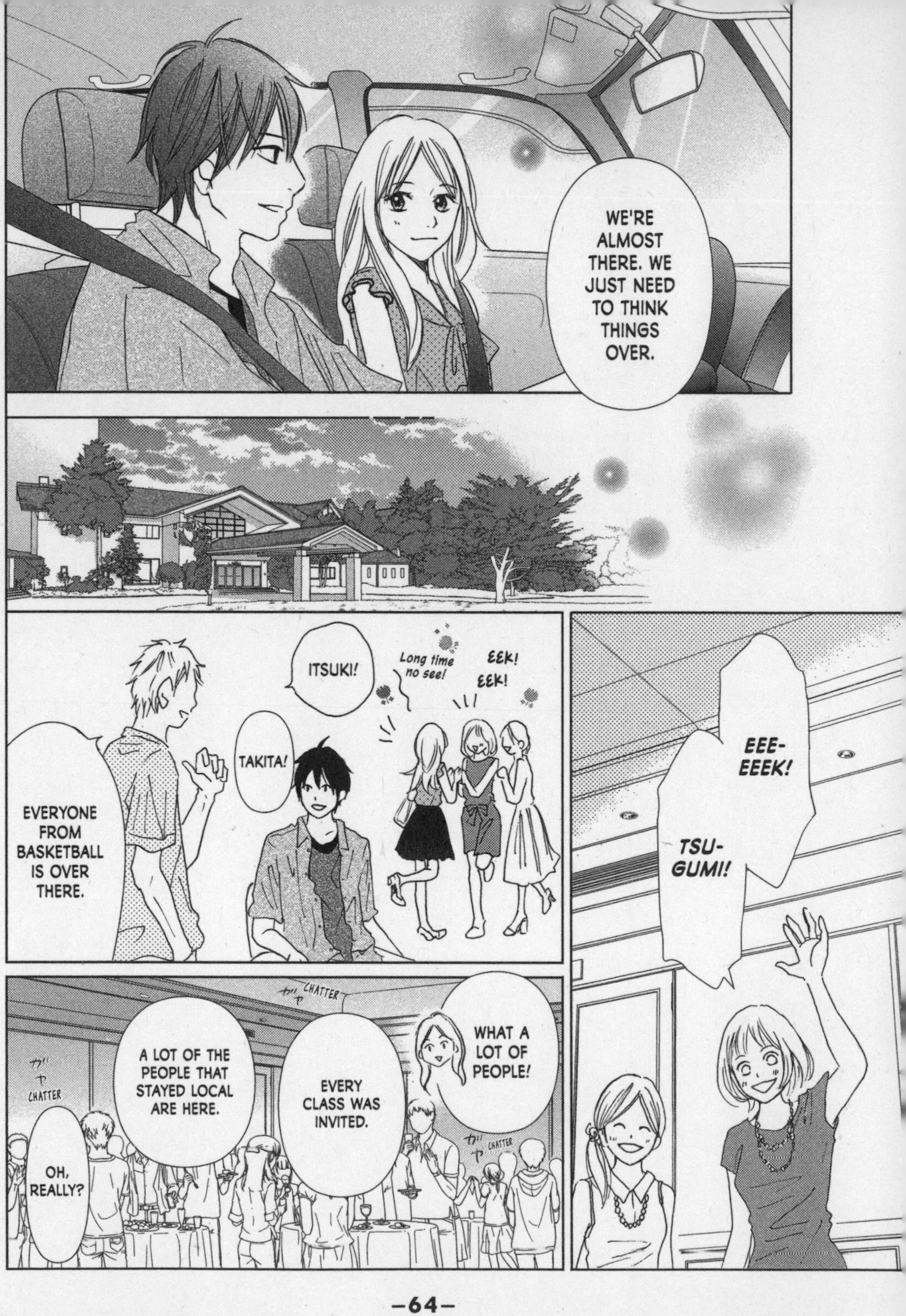
WE'RE ALMOST THERE. WE JUST NEED TO THINK THINGS OVER.
EEE-EEEK!
TSU-GUMI!
EEK!
EEK!
Long time no see!
ITSUKI!
TAKITA!
EVERYONE FROM BASKETBALL IS OVER THERE.
ガヤ CHATTER
WHAT A LOT OF PEOPLE!
ガヤ CHATTER
EVERY CLASS WAS INVITED.
A LOT OF THE PEOPLE THAT STAYED LOCAL ARE HERE.
ガヤ CHATTER
OH, REALLY?

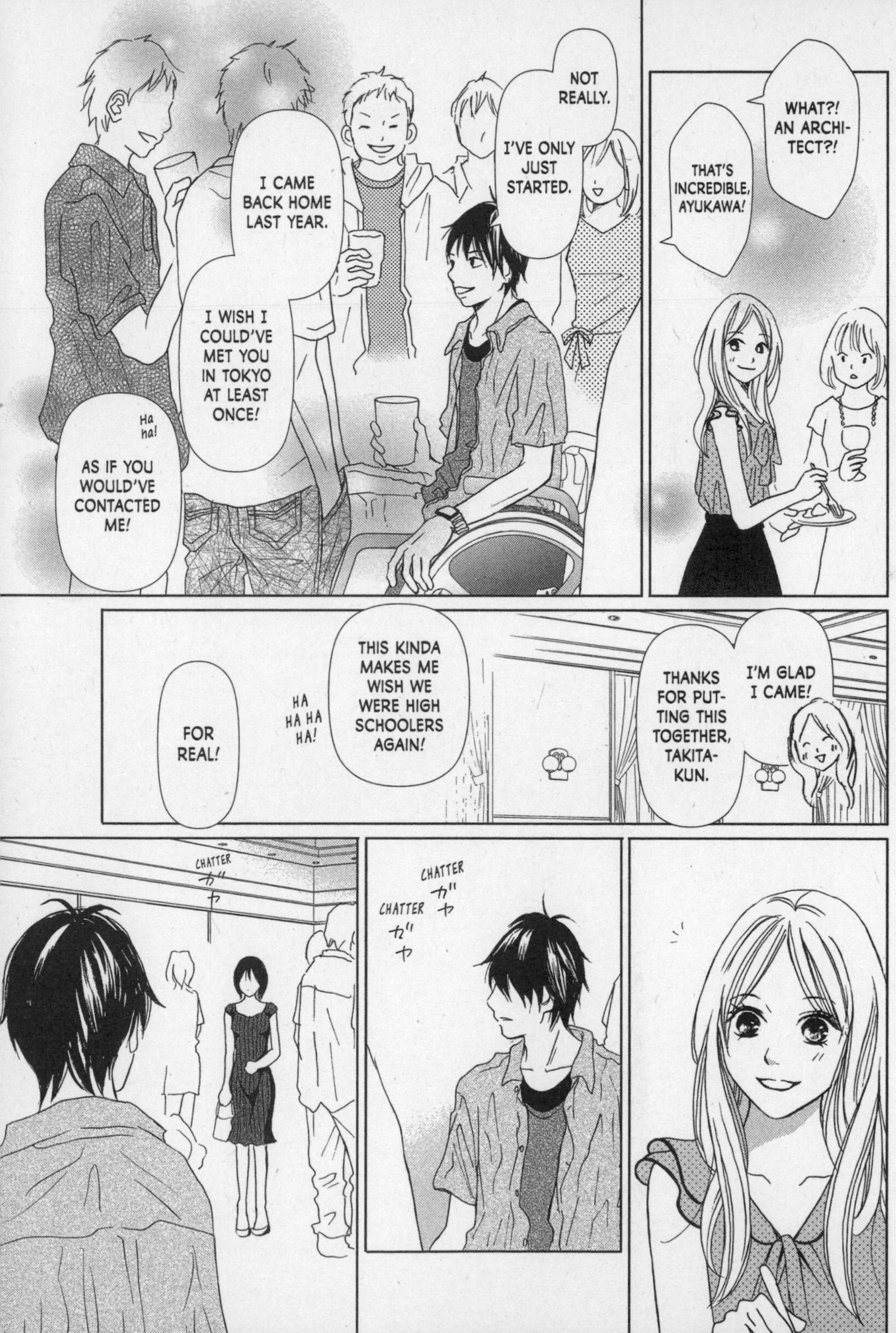
WHAT?! AN ARCHITECT?!
THAT'S INCREDIBLE, AYUKAWA!
NOT REALLY.
I'VE ONLY JUST STARTED.
I CAME BACK HOME LAST YEAR.
I WISH I COULD'VE MET YOU IN TOKYO AT LEAST ONCE!
Ha ha!
AS IF YOU WOULD'VE CONTACTED ME!
I'M GLAD I CAME!
THANKS FOR PUTTING THIS TOGETHER, TAKITA-KUN.
THIS KINDA MAKES ME WISH WE WERE HIGH SCHOOLERS AGAIN!
HA HA HA HA!
FOR REAL!
CHATTER ガヤ
CHATTER ガヤ
CHATTER ガヤ

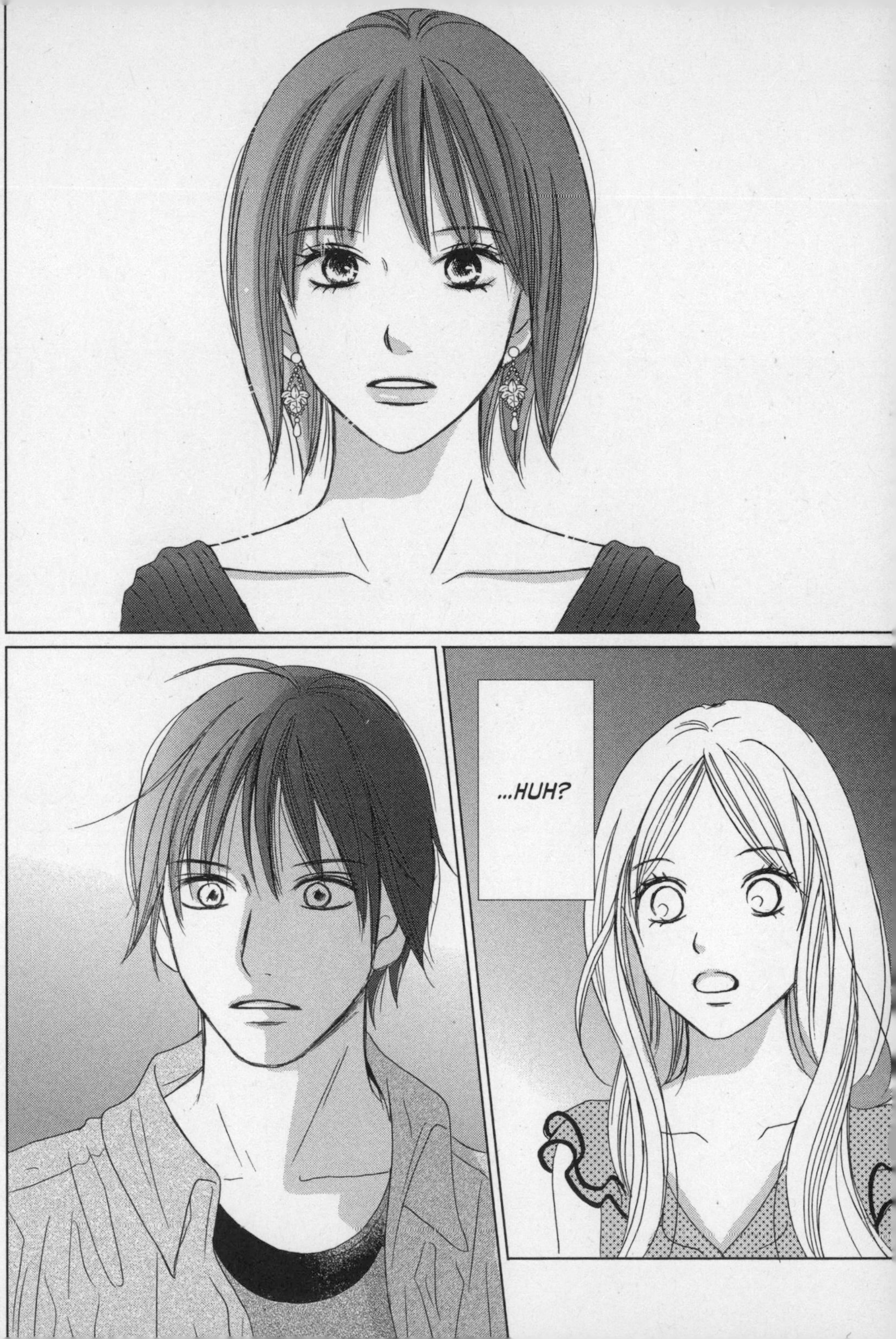
...HUH?

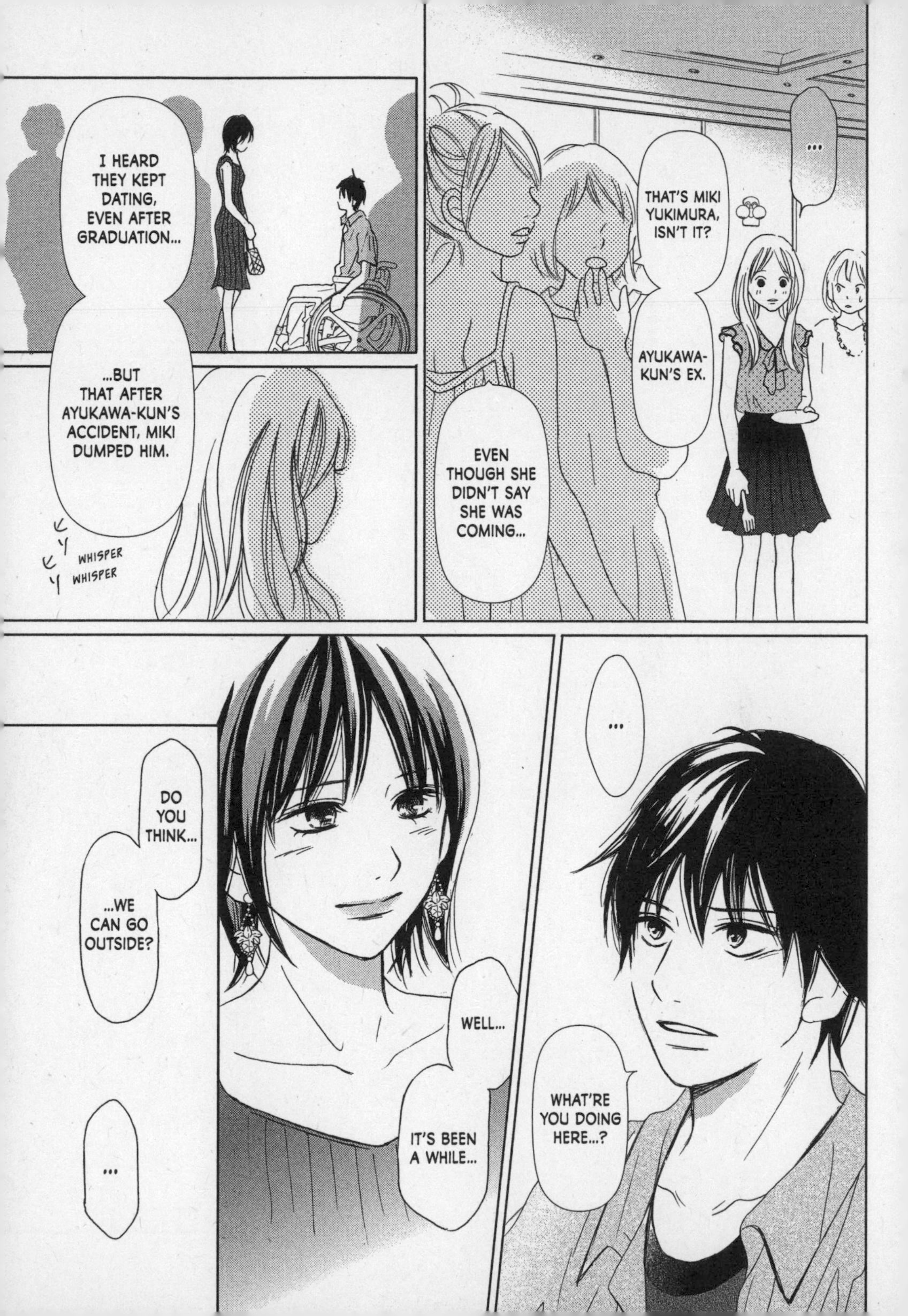
...
THAT'S MIKI YUKIMURA, ISN'T IT?
AYUKAWA-KUN'S EX.
EVEN THOUGH SHE DIDN'T SAY SHE WAS COMING...
I HEARD THEY KEPT DATING, EVEN AFTER GRADUATION...
...BUT THAT AFTER AYUKAWA-KUN'S ACCIDENT, MIKI DUMPED HIM.
WHISPER WHISPER
...
WHAT'RE YOU DOING HERE...?
WELL...
IT'S BEEN A WHILE...
DO YOU THINK...
...WE CAN GO OUTSIDE?
...

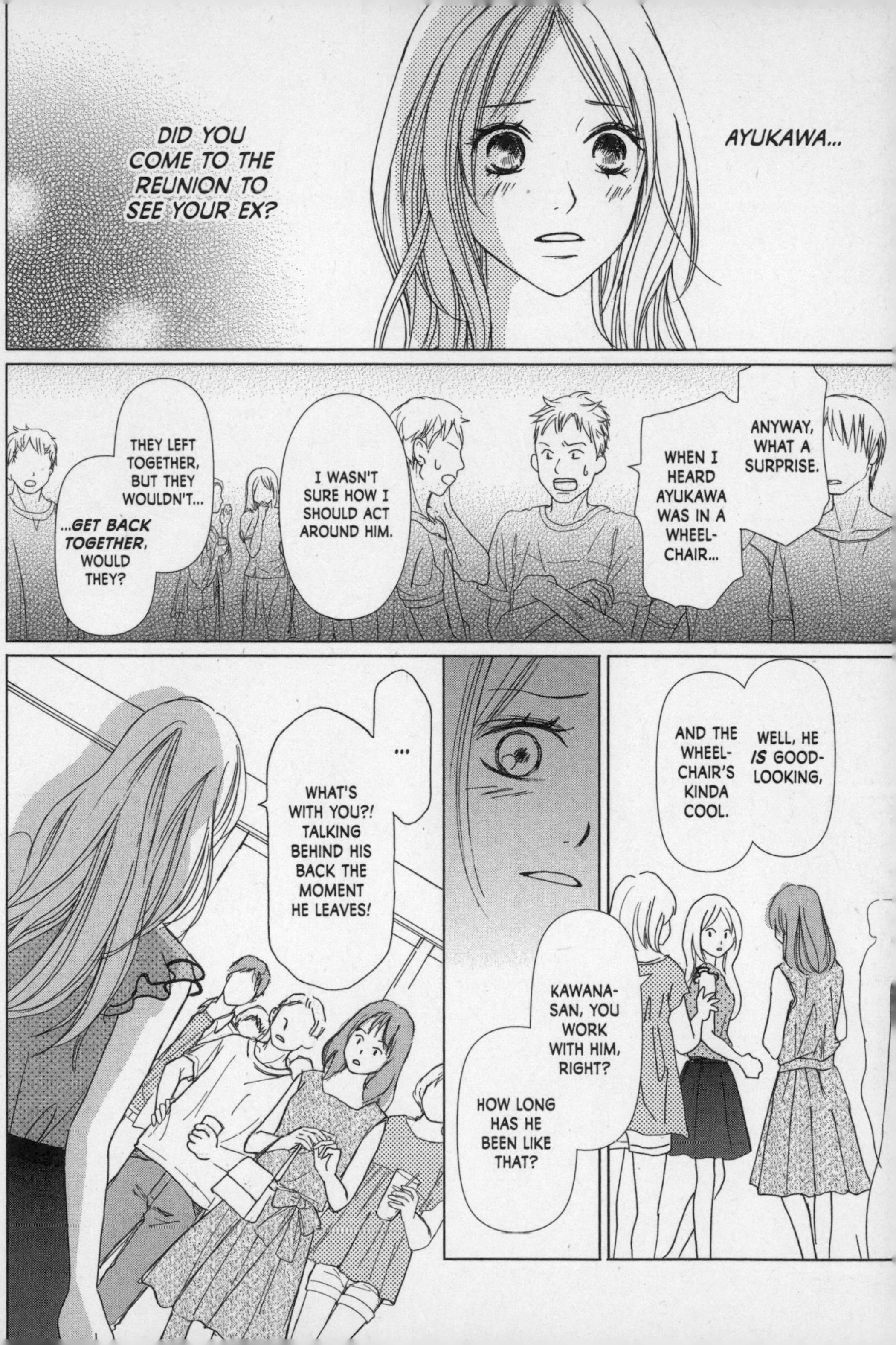
AYUKAWA...
DID YOU COME TO THE REUNION TO SEE YOUR EX?
ANYWAY, WHAT A SURPRISE.
WHEN I HEARD AYUKAWA WAS IN A WHEEL-CHAIR...
I WASN'T SURE HOW I SHOULD ACT AROUND HIM.
THEY LEFT TOGETHER, BUT THEY WOULDN'T...
...*GET BACK TOGETHER*, WOULD THEY?
WELL, HE *IS* GOOD-LOOKING,
AND THE WHEEL-CHAIR'S KINDA COOL.
KAWANA-SAN, YOU WORK WITH HIM, RIGHT?
HOW LONG HAS HE BEEN LIKE THAT?
...
WHAT'S WITH YOU?! TALKING BEHIND HIS BACK THE MOMENT HE LEAVES!

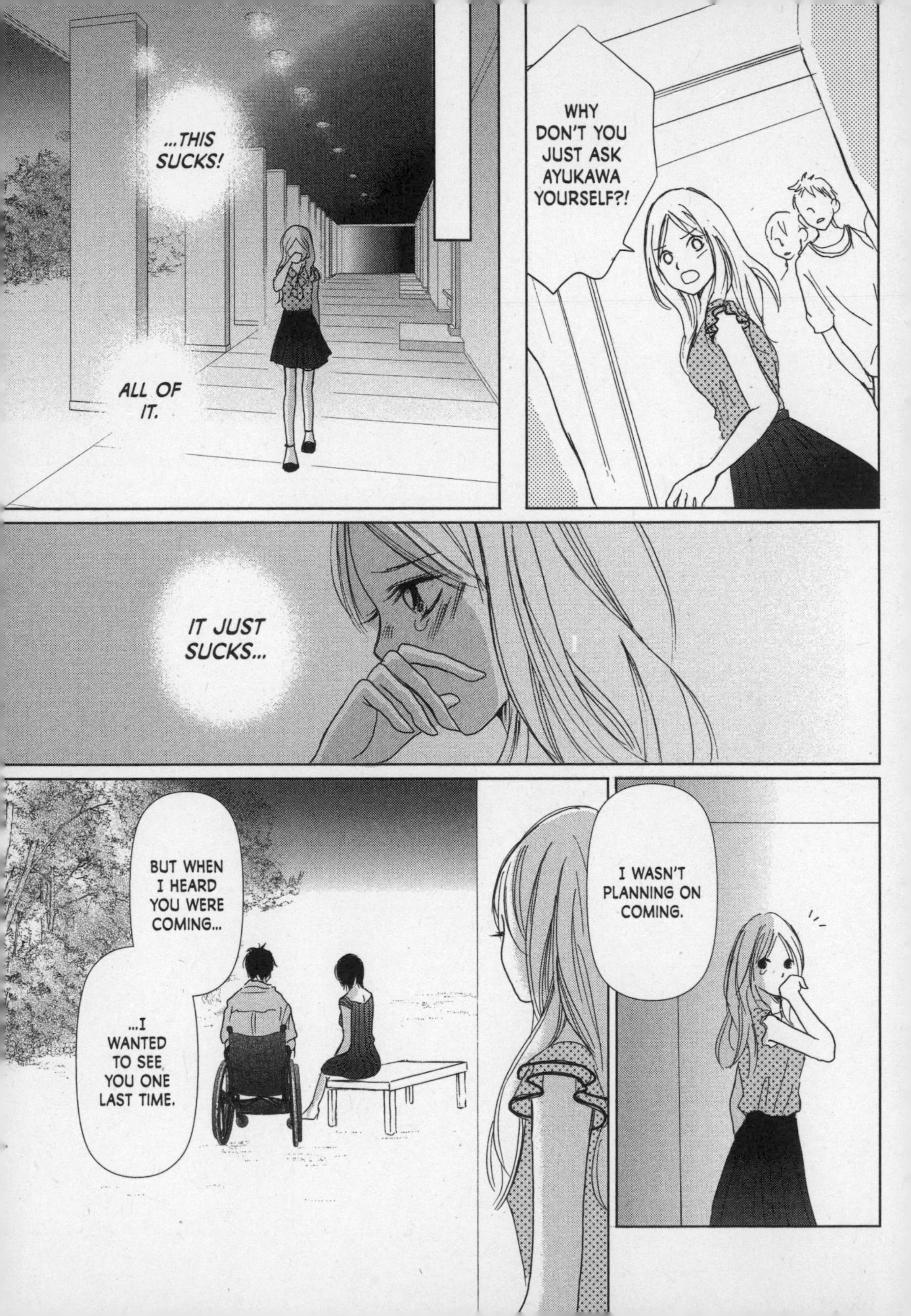
WHY DON'T YOU JUST ASK AYUKAWA YOURSELF?!
...THIS SUCKS!
ALL OF IT.
IT JUST SUCKS...
I WASN'T PLANNING ON COMING.
BUT WHEN I HEARD YOU WERE COMING...
...I WANTED TO SEE YOU ONE LAST TIME.

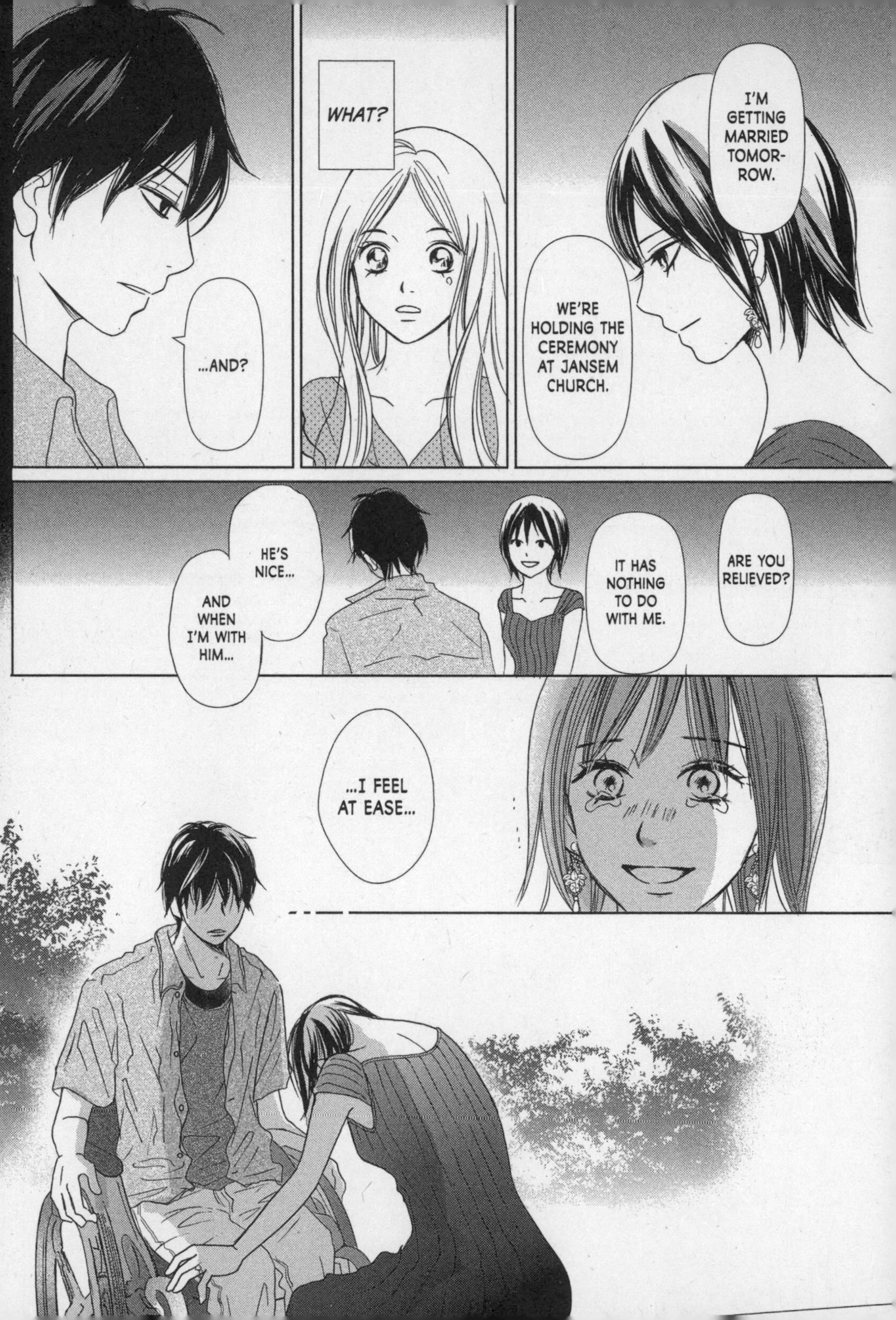

I'M GETTING MARRIED TOMOR-ROW.
WE'RE HOLDING THE CEREMONY AT JANSEM CHURCH.
WHAT?
...AND?
ARE YOU RELIEVED?
IT HAS NOTHING TO DO WITH ME.
HE'S NICE...
AND WHEN I'M WITH HIM...
...I FEEL AT EASE...

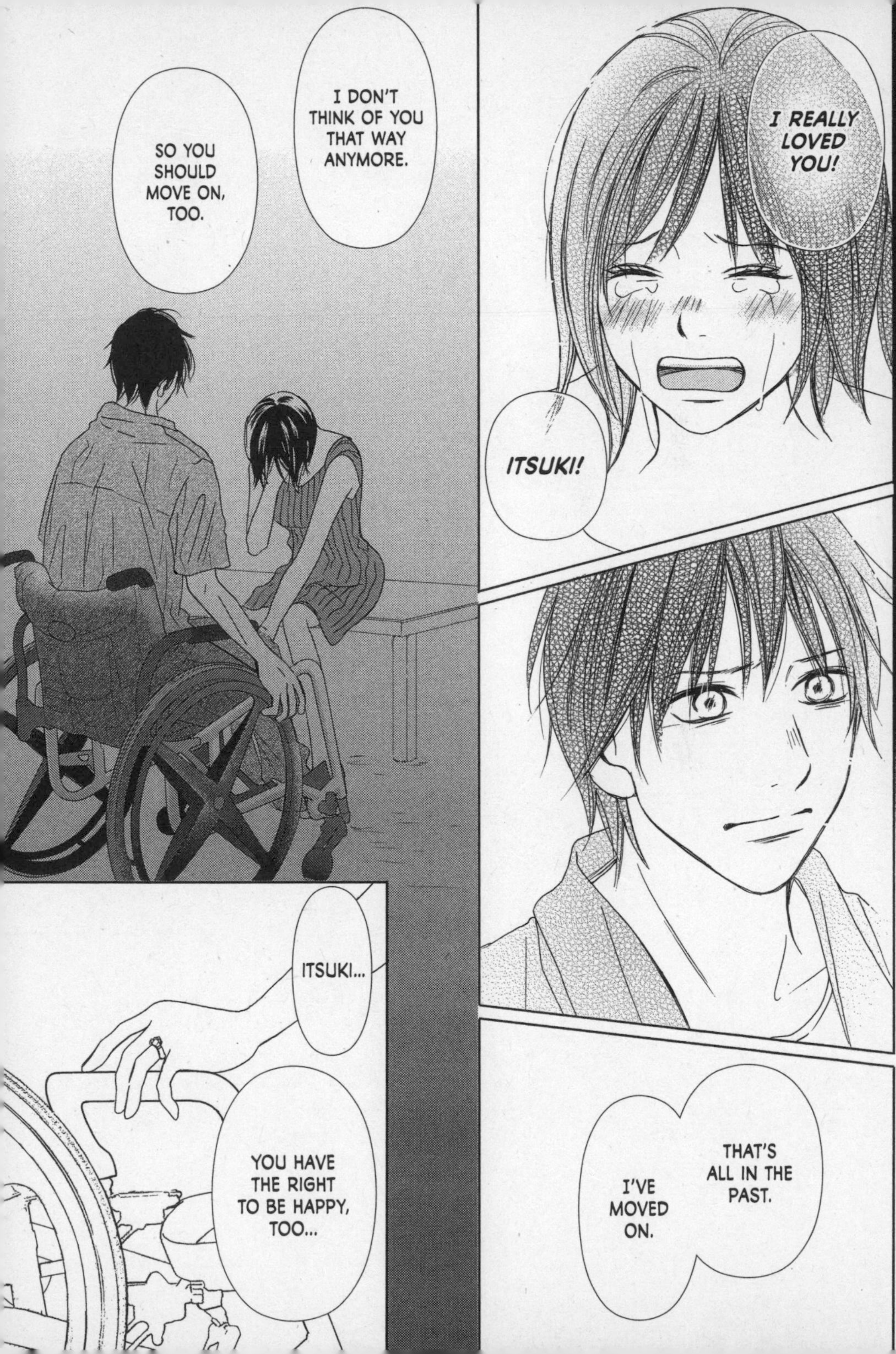
I REALLY LOVED YOU!
ITSUKI!
THAT'S ALL IN THE PAST.
I'VE MOVED ON.
I DON'T THINK OF YOU THAT WAY ANYMORE.
SO YOU SHOULD MOVE ON, TOO.
ITSUKI...
YOU HAVE THE RIGHT TO BE HAPPY, TOO...

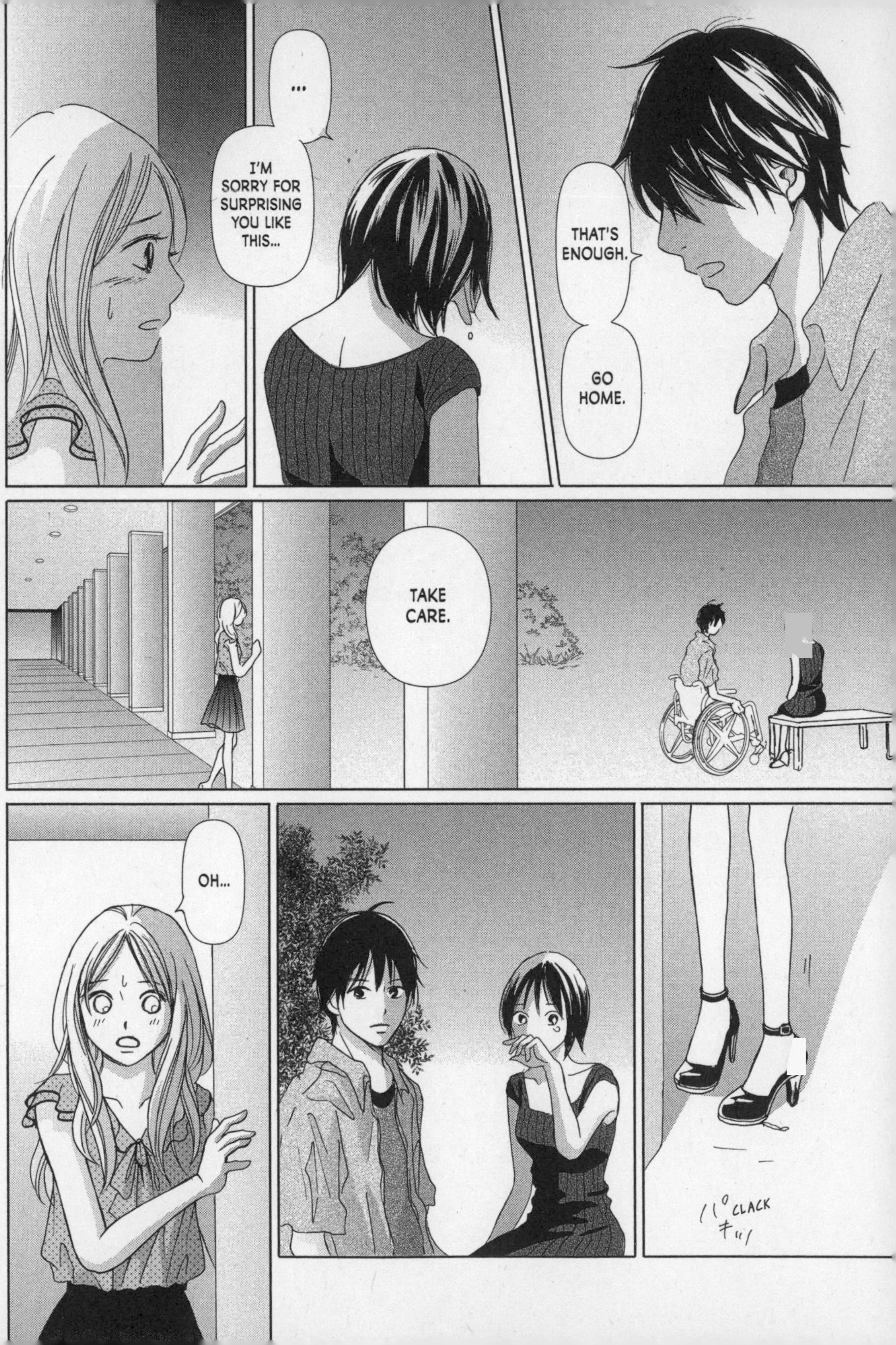
THAT'S ENOUGH.
GO HOME.
...
I'M SORRY FOR SURPRISING YOU LIKE THIS...
TAKE CARE.
CLACK
OH...

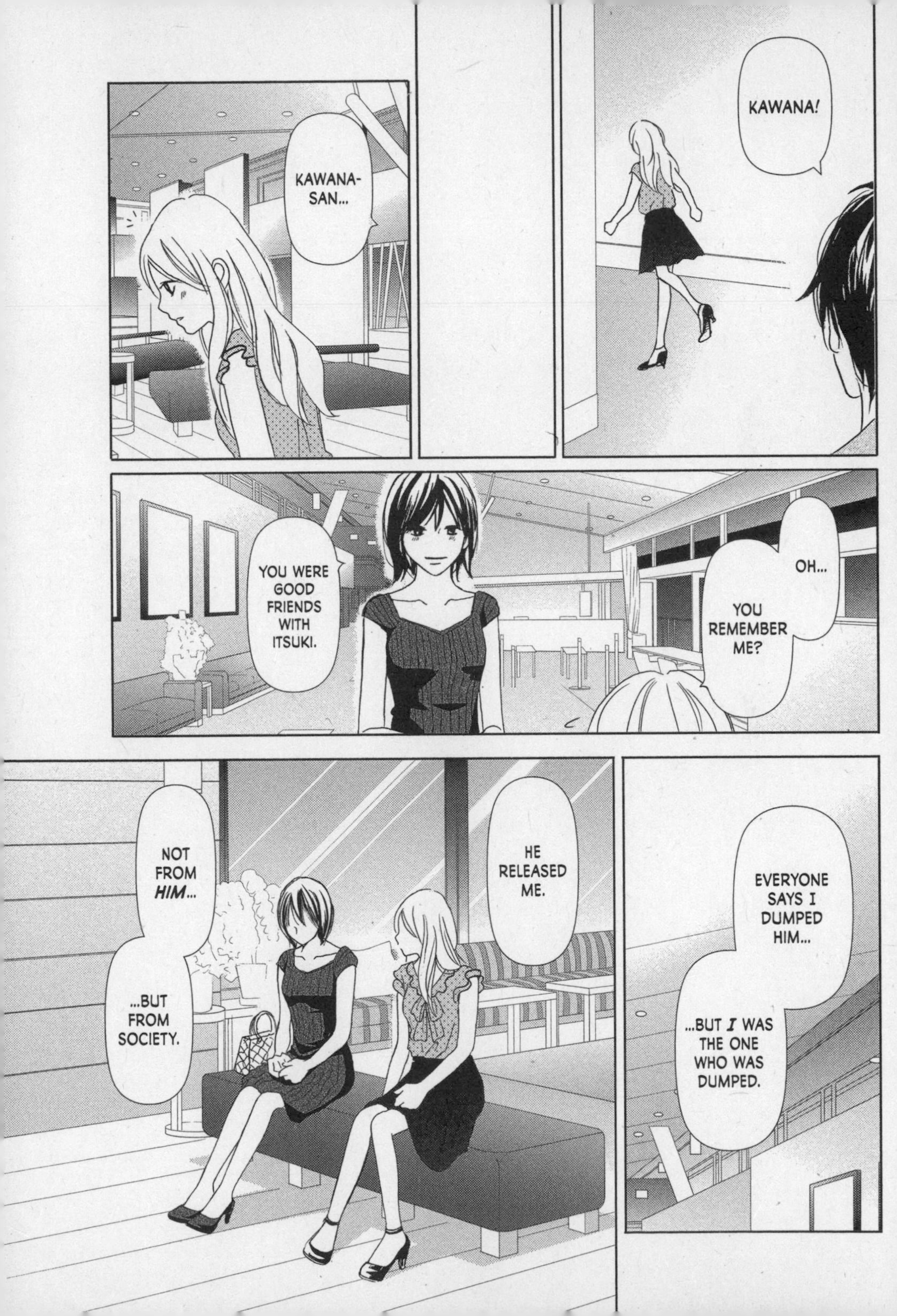
KAWANA!
KAWANA-SAN...
OH...
YOU REMEMBER ME?
YOU WERE GOOD FRIENDS WITH ITSUKI.
EVERYONE SAYS I DUMPED HIM...
...BUT *I* WAS THE ONE WHO WAS DUMPED.
HE RELEASED ME.
NOT FROM ***HIM***...
...BUT FROM SOCIETY.

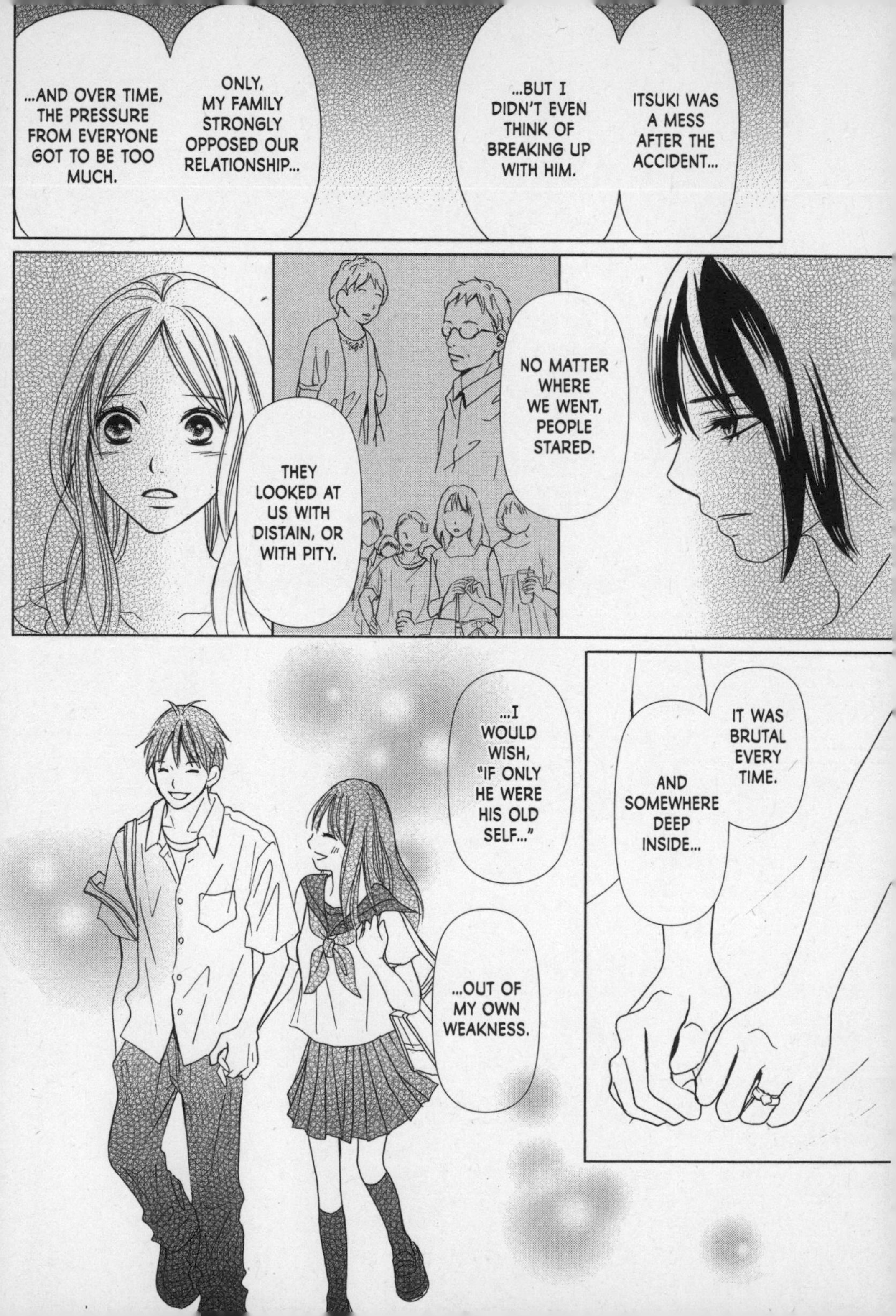
ITSUKI WAS A MESS AFTER THE ACCIDENT...
...BUT I DIDN'T EVEN THINK OF BREAKING UP WITH HIM.
ONLY, MY FAMILY STRONGLY OPPOSED OUR RELATIONSHIP...
...AND OVER TIME, THE PRESSURE FROM EVERYONE GOT TO BE TOO MUCH.
NO MATTER WHERE WE WENT, PEOPLE STARED.
THEY LOOKED AT US WITH DISTAIN, OR WITH PITY.
IT WAS BRUTAL EVERY TIME.
AND SOMEWHERE DEEP INSIDE...
...I WOULD WISH, "IF ONLY HE WERE HIS OLD SELF..."
...OUT OF MY OWN WEAKNESS.

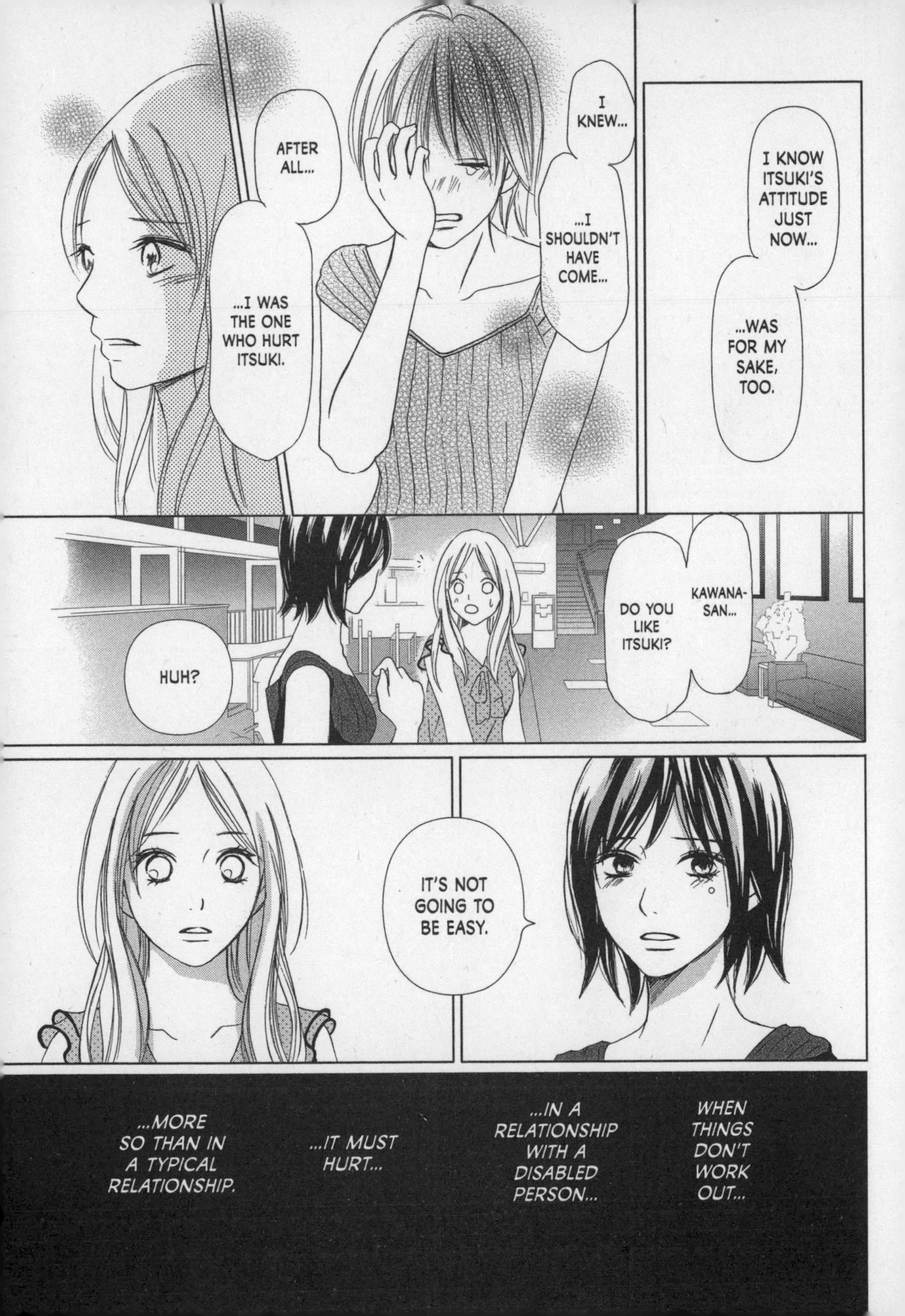
I KNOW ITSUKI'S ATTITUDE JUST NOW...
...WAS FOR MY SAKE, TOO.
I KNEW...
...I SHOULDN'T HAVE COME...
AFTER ALL...
...I WAS THE ONE WHO HURT ITSUKI.
KAWANA-SAN...
DO YOU LIKE ITSUKI?
HUH?
IT'S NOT GOING TO BE EASY.
WHEN THINGS DON'T WORK OUT...
...IN A RELATIONSHIP WITH A DISABLED PERSON...
...IT MUST HURT...
...MORE SO THAN IN A TYPICAL RELATIONSHIP.

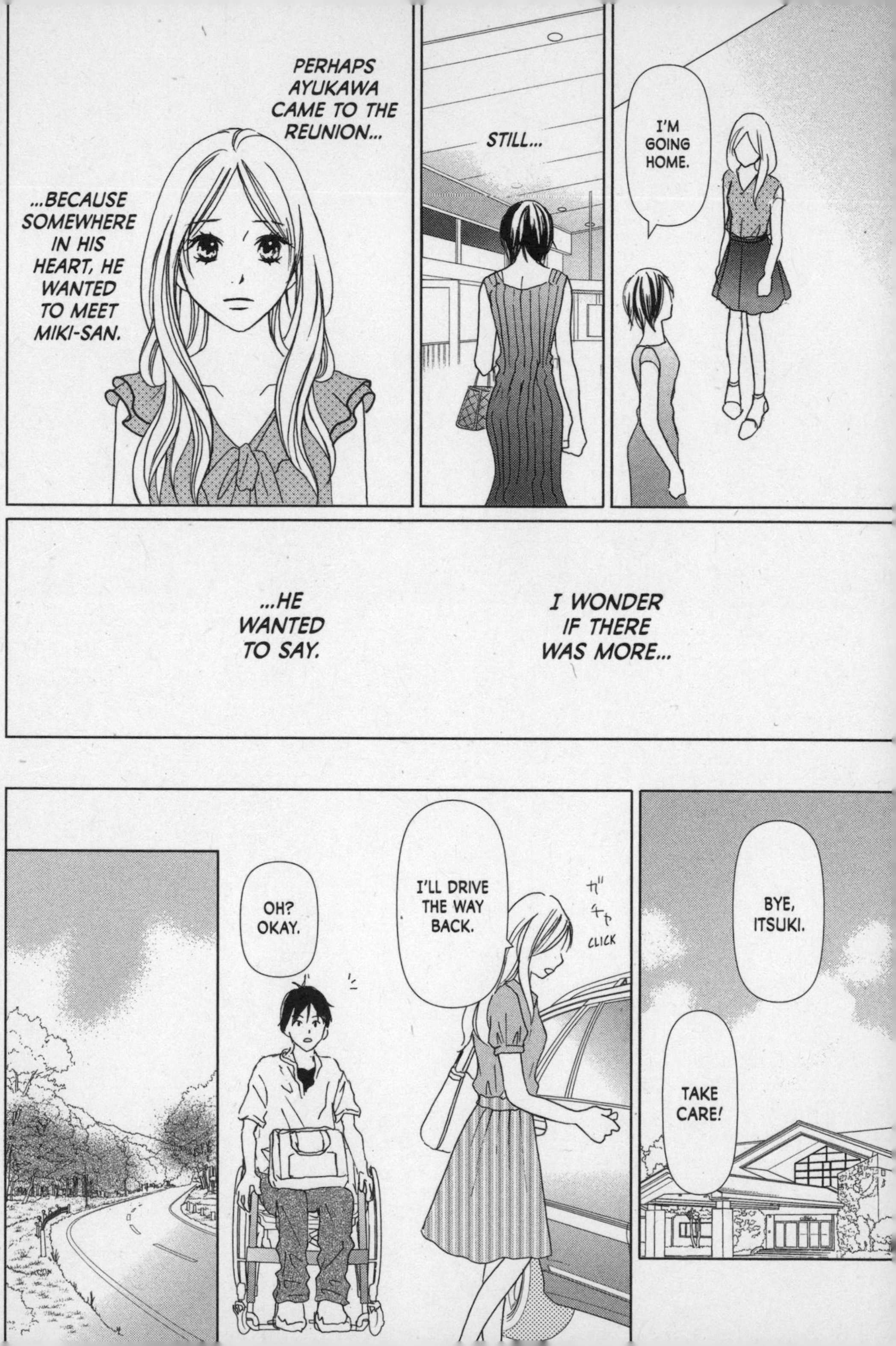
I'M GOING HOME.
STILL...
PERHAPS AYUKAWA CAME TO THE REUNION...
...BECAUSE SOMEWHERE IN HIS HEART, HE WANTED TO MEET MIKI-SAN.
I WONDER IF THERE WAS MORE...
...HE WANTED TO SAY.
BYE, ITSUKI.
TAKE CARE!
I'LL DRIVE THE WAY BACK.
ガチャ
CLICK
OH? OKAY.

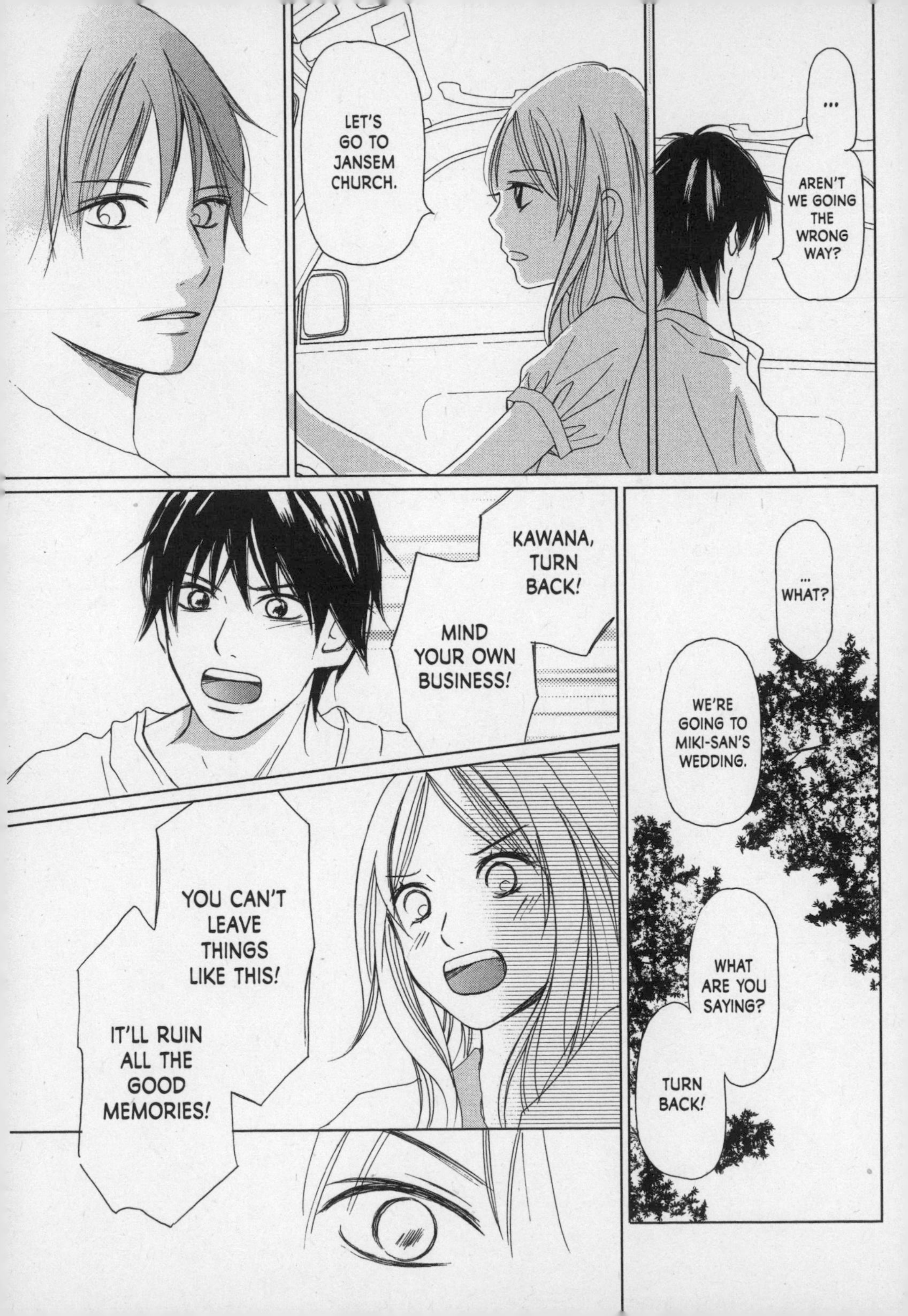
...
AREN'T WE GOING THE WRONG WAY?
LET'S GO TO JANSEM CHURCH.
... WHAT?
WE'RE GOING TO MIKI-SAN'S WEDDING.
WHAT ARE YOU SAYING?
TURN BACK!
KAWANA, TURN BACK!
MIND YOUR OWN BUSINESS!
YOU CAN'T LEAVE THINGS LIKE THIS!
IT'LL RUIN ALL THE GOOD MEMORIES!

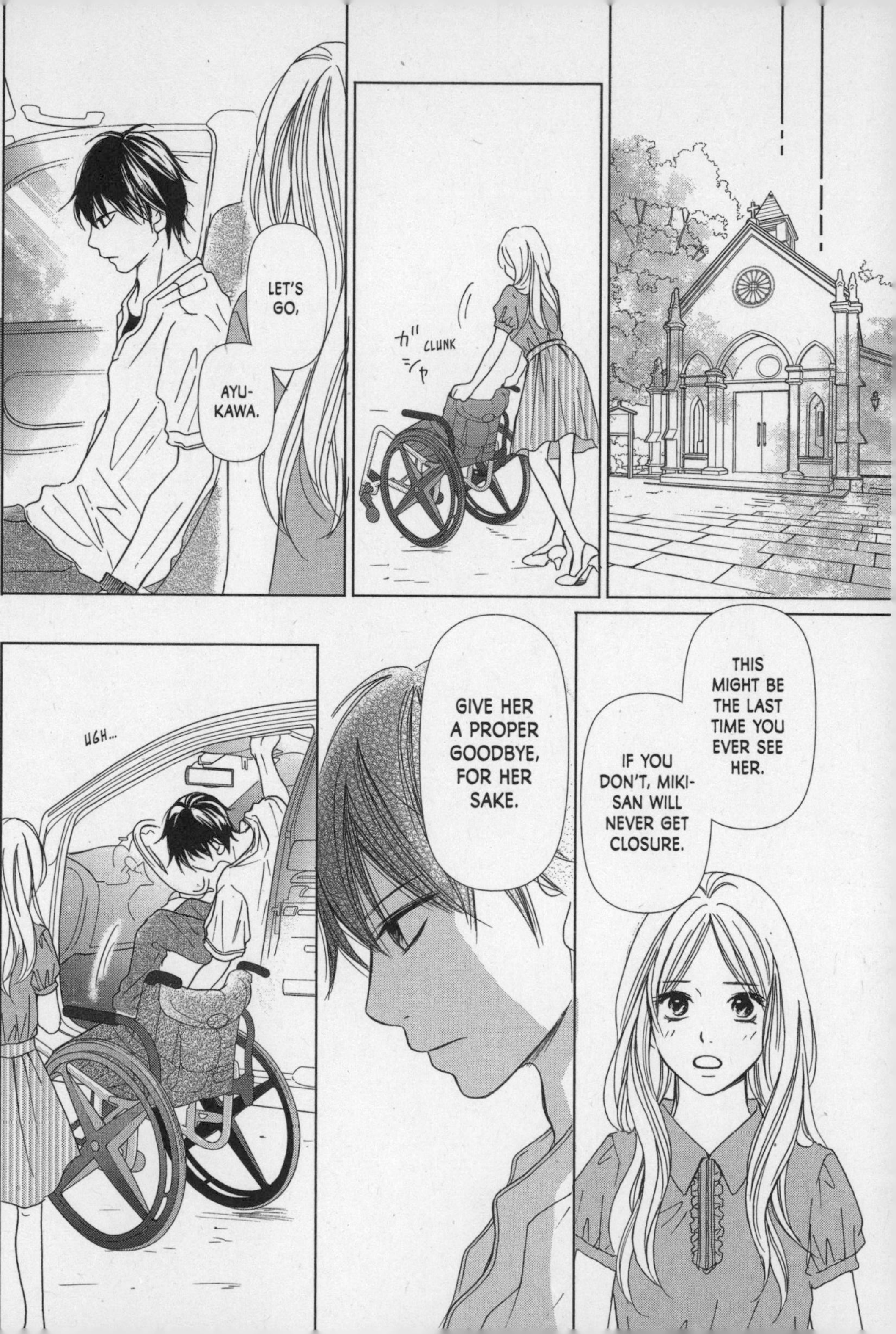
ガシャ
CLUNK
LET'S GO,
AYU-KAWA.
THIS MIGHT BE THE LAST TIME YOU EVER SEE HER.
IF YOU DON'T, MIKI-SAN WILL NEVER GET CLOSURE.
GIVE HER A PROPER GOODBYE, FOR HER SAKE.
UGH...

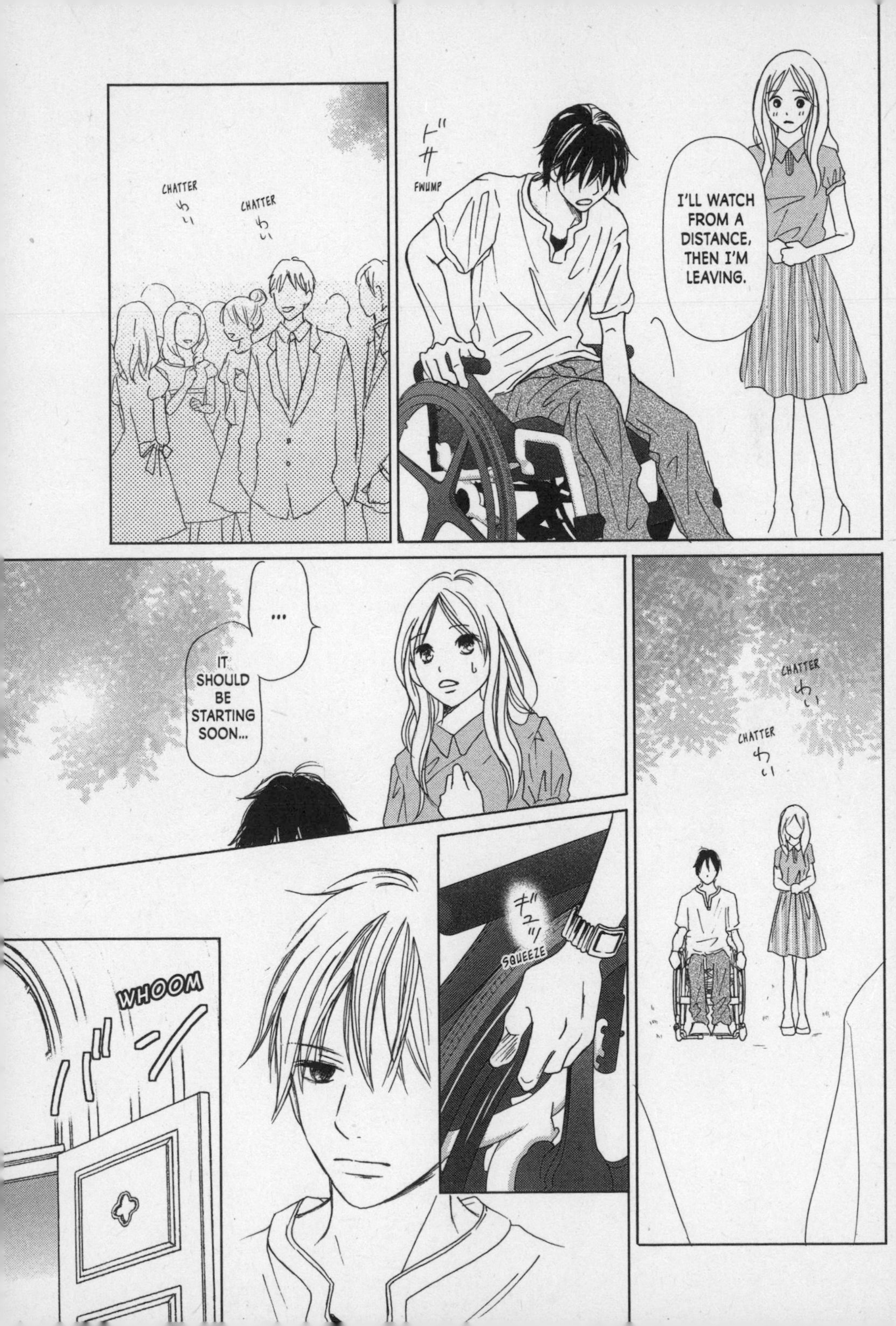
ドサ
FWUMP
I'LL WATCH FROM A DISTANCE, THEN I'M LEAVING.
CHATTER
わい
CHATTER
わい
CHATTER
わい
CHATTER
わい
...
IT SHOULD BE STARTING SOON...
ギュッ
SQUEEZE
WHOOM

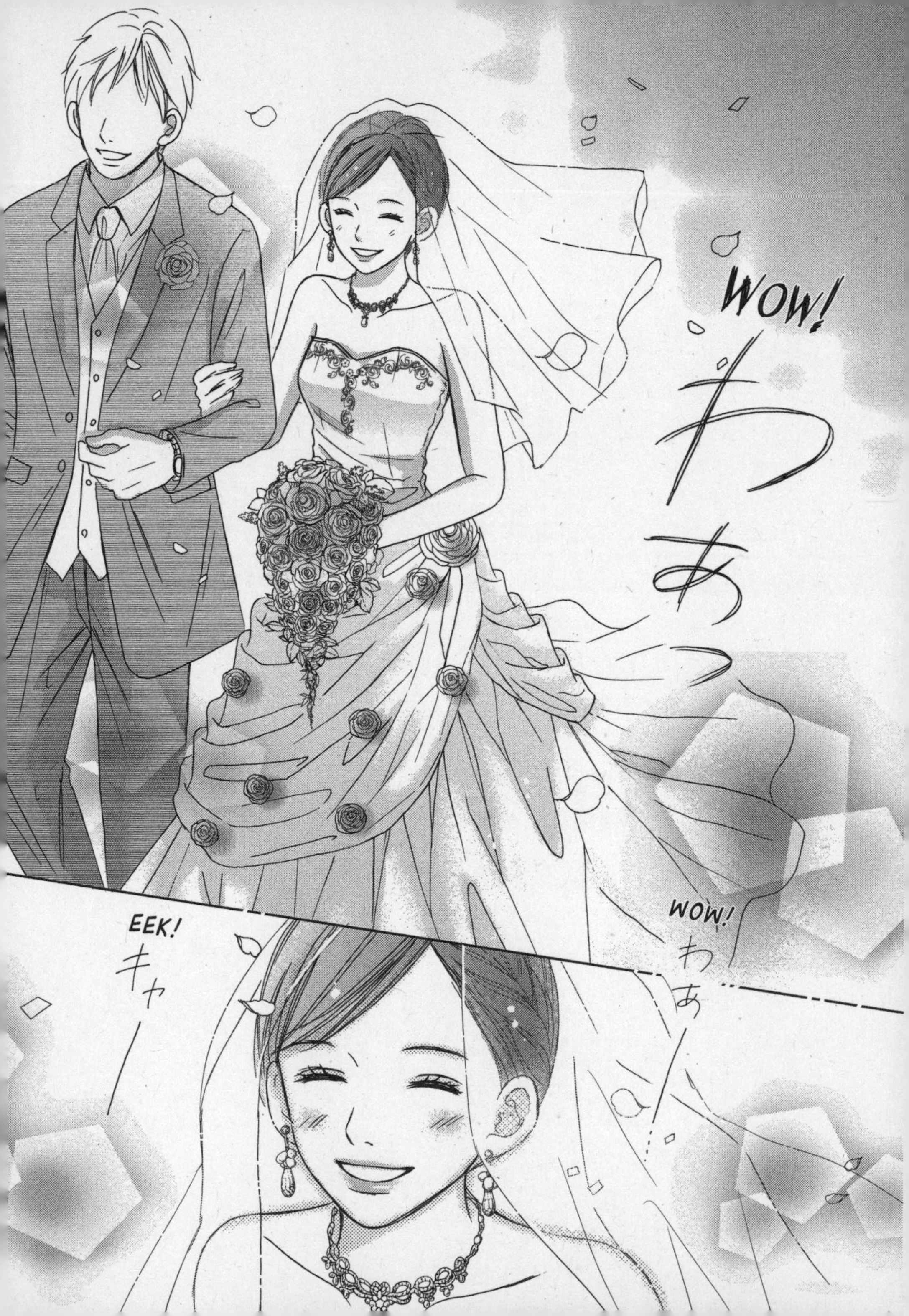
WOW!
わあっ
WOW!
わあー
EEK!
キャー

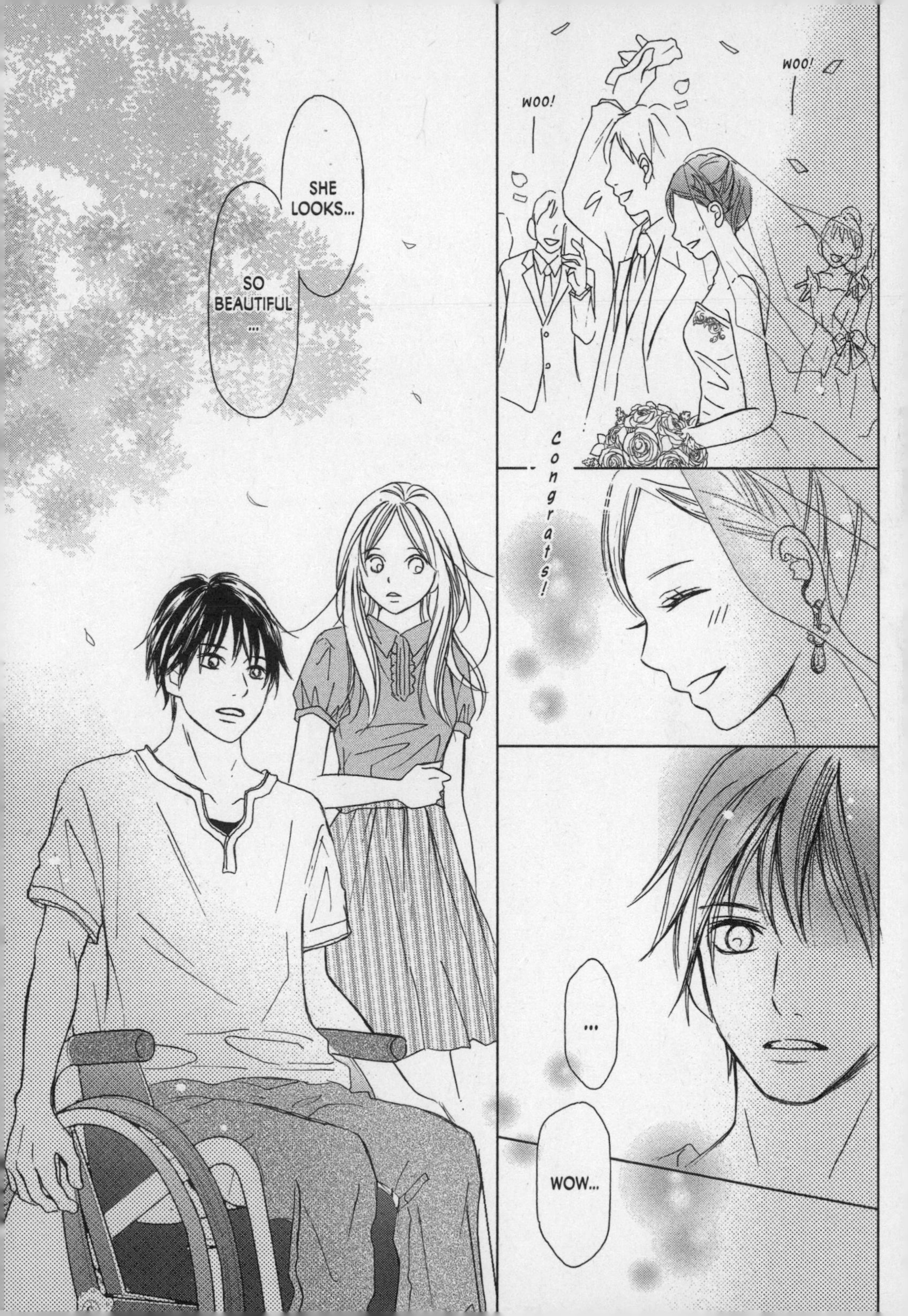
WOO!
WOO!
Congrats!
...
WOW...
SHE LOOKS...
SO BEAUTIFUL ...

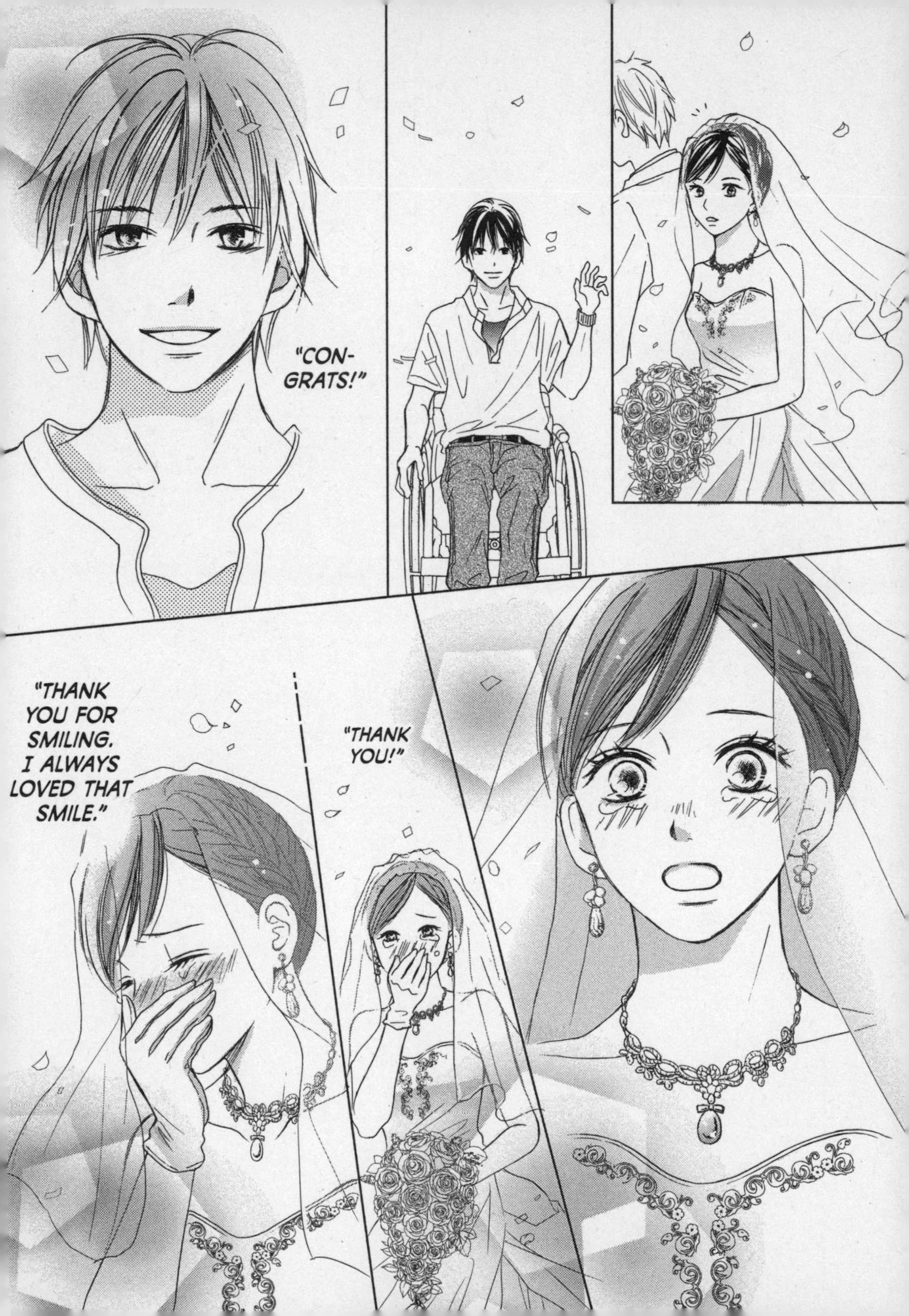
"CON-GRATS!"
"THANK YOU!"
"THANK YOU FOR SMILING. I ALWAYS LOVED THAT SMILE."

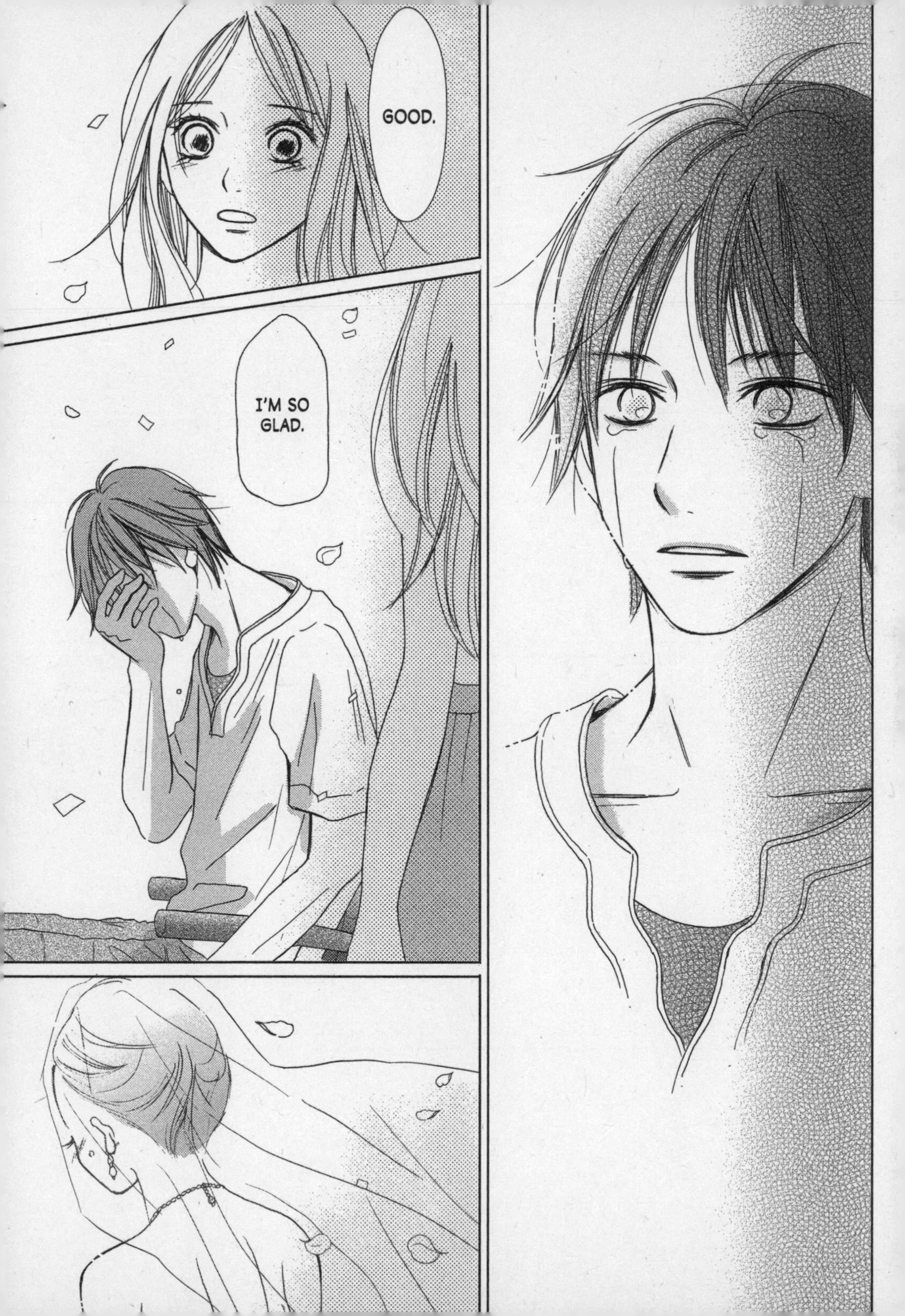
GOOD.
I'M SO GLAD.

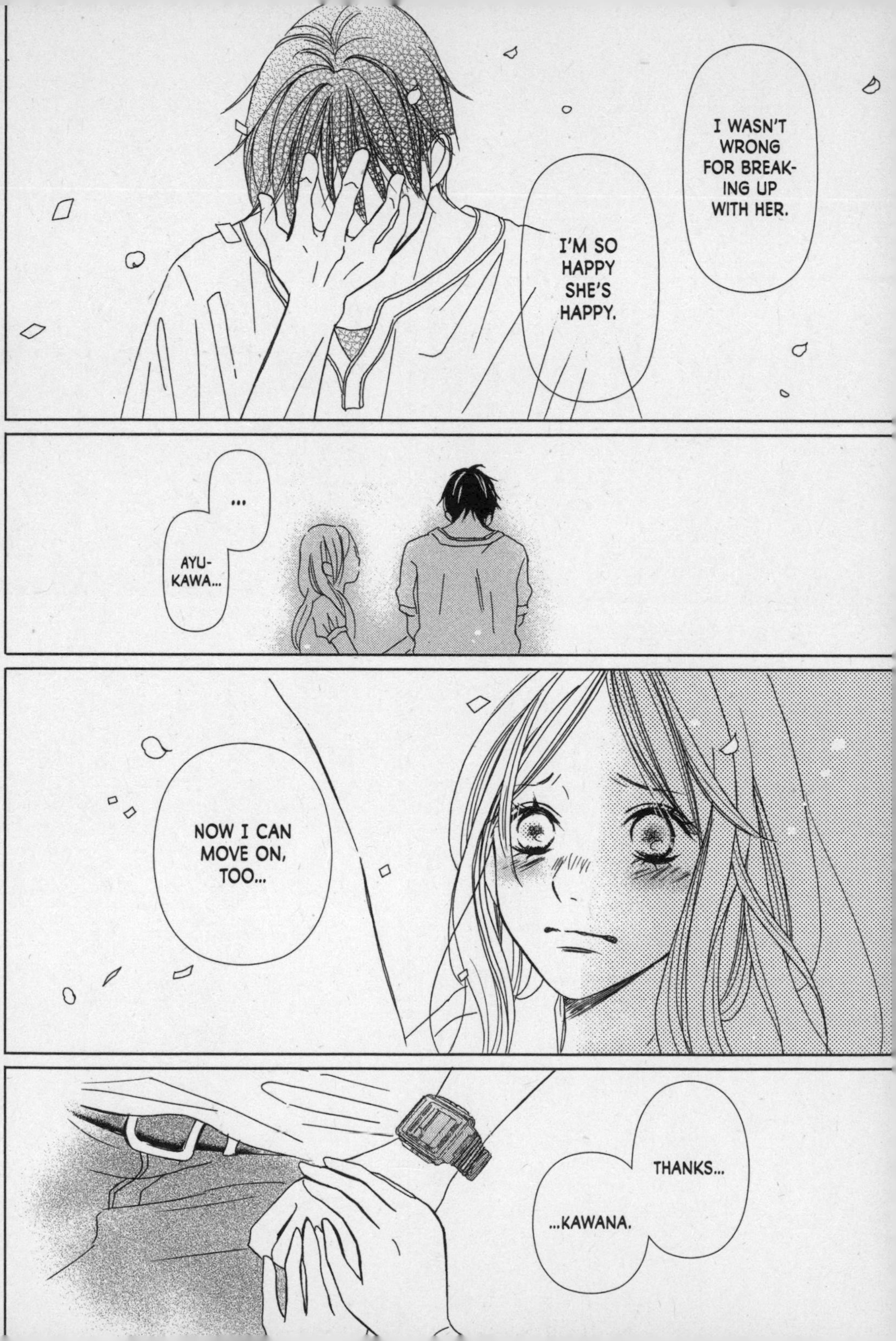
I WASN'T WRONG FOR BREAK-ING UP WITH HER.
I'M SO HAPPY SHE'S HAPPY.
...
AYU-KAWA...
NOW I CAN MOVE ON, TOO...
THANKS...
...KAWANA.

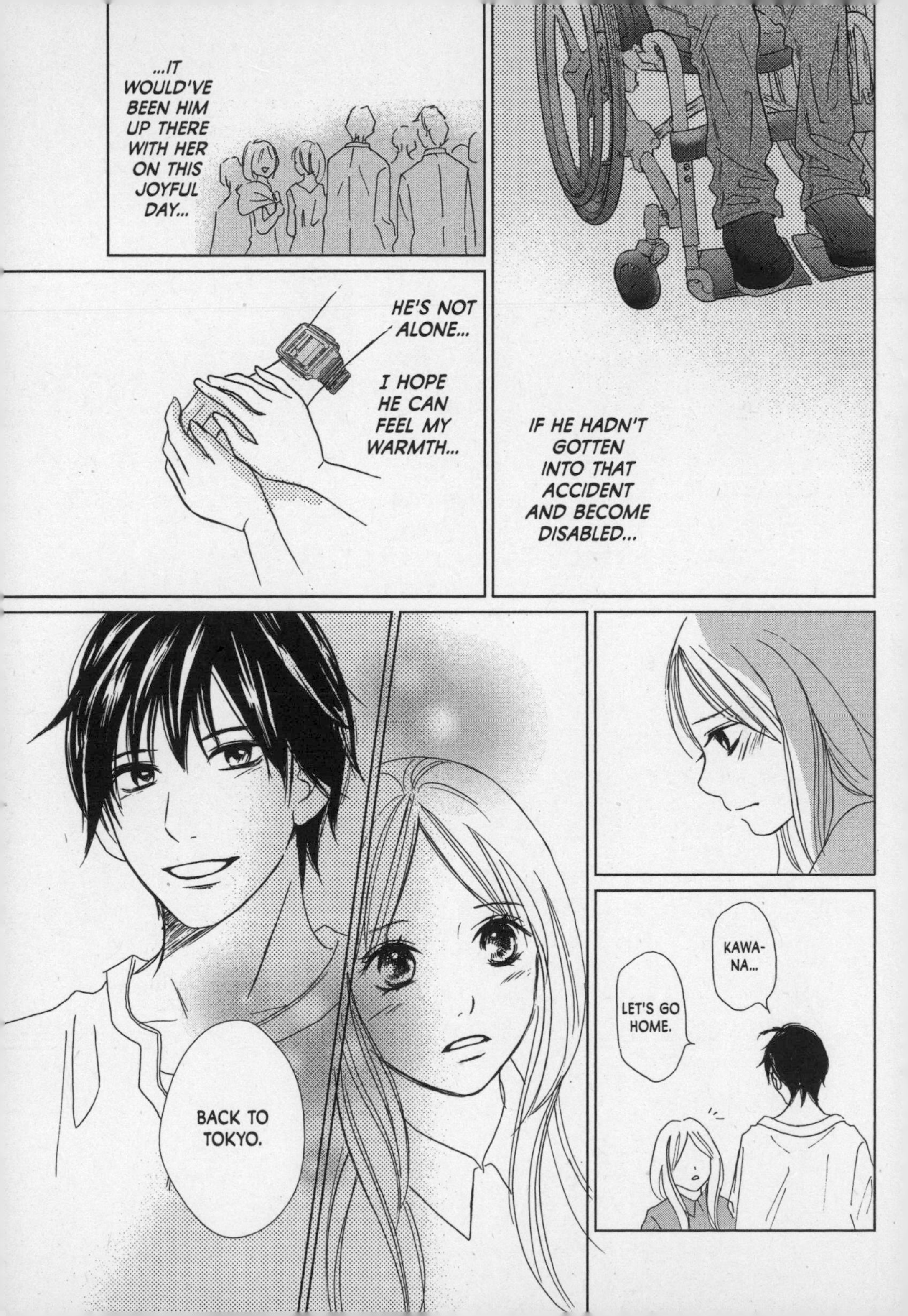
IF HE HADN'T GOTTEN INTO THAT ACCIDENT AND BECOME DISABLED...
...IT WOULD'VE BEEN HIM UP THERE WITH HER ON THIS JOYFUL DAY...
HE'S NOT ALONE...
I HOPE HE CAN FEEL MY WARMTH...
KAWANA...
LET'S GO HOME.
BACK TO TOKYO.

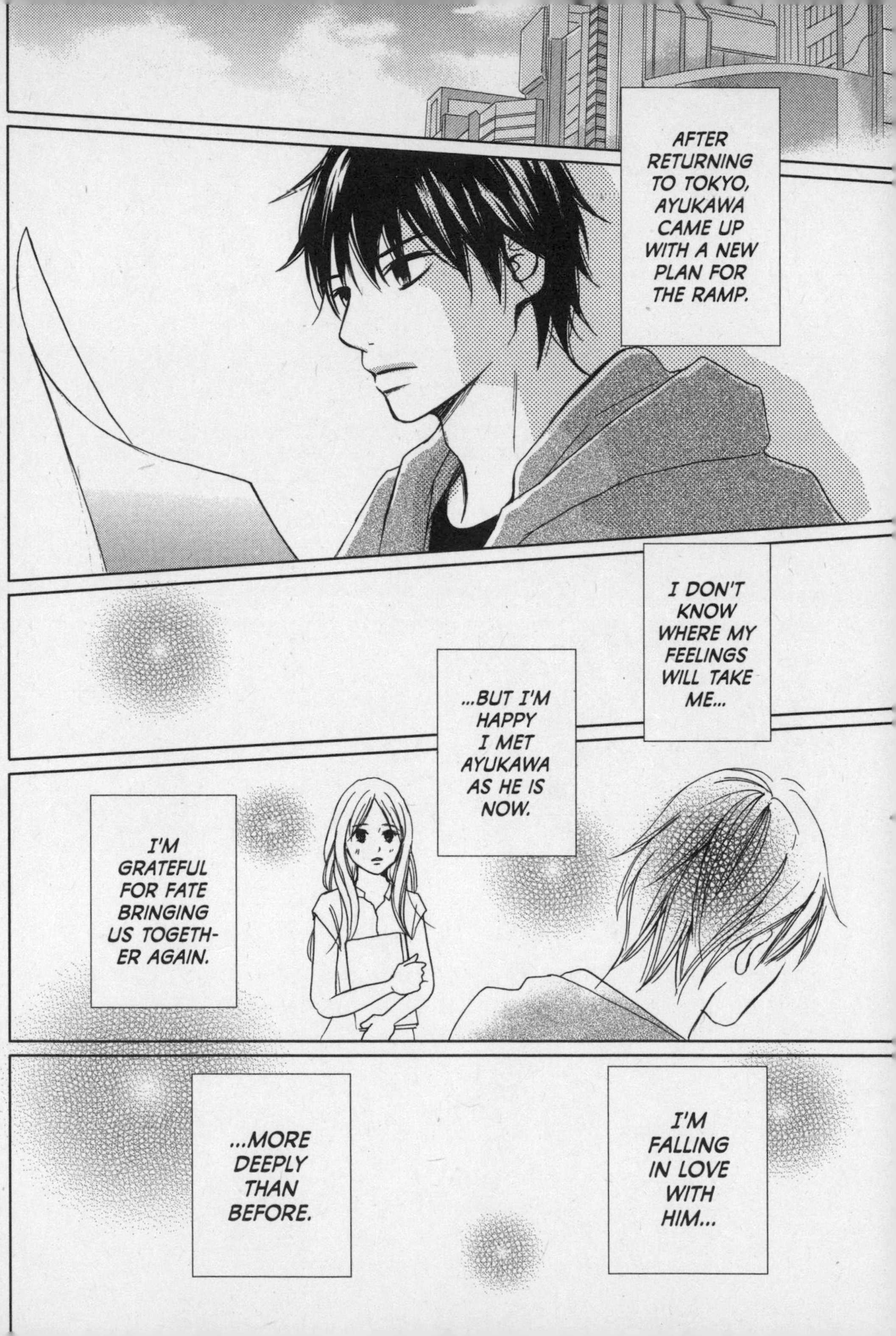
AFTER RETURNING TO TOKYO, AYUKAWA CAME UP WITH A NEW PLAN FOR THE RAMP.
I DON'T KNOW WHERE MY FEELINGS WILL TAKE ME...
...BUT I'M HAPPY I MET AYUKAWA AS HE IS NOW.
I'M GRATEFUL FOR FATE BRINGING US TOGETH-ER AGAIN.
I'M FALLING IN LOVE WITH HIM...
...MORE DEEPLY THAN BEFORE.

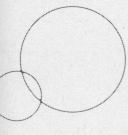
PERFECT WORLD

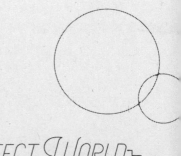

PERFECT WORLD

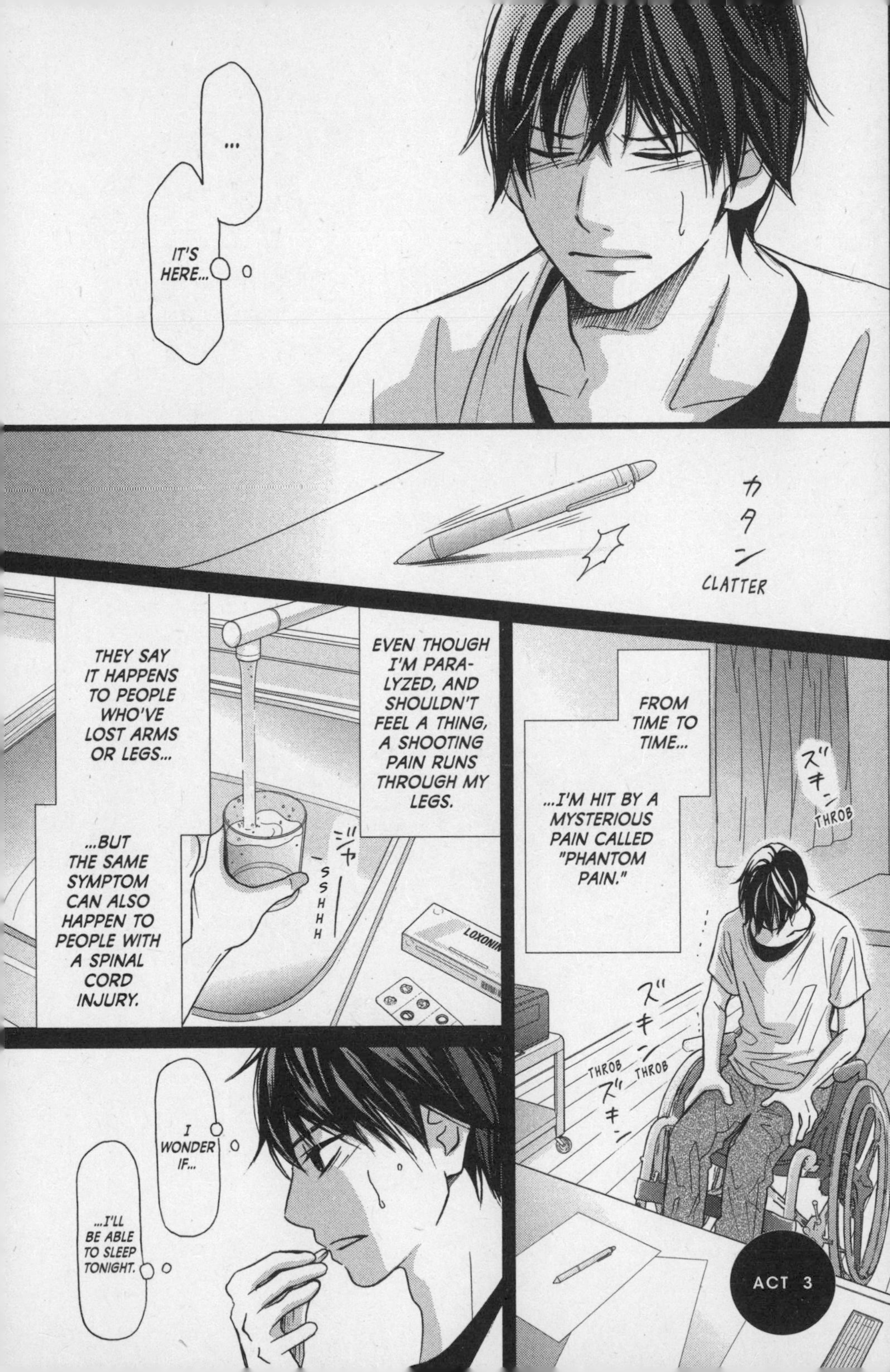
...
IT'S HERE...
カタン
CLATTER
FROM TIME TO TIME...
...I'M HIT BY A MYSTERIOUS PAIN CALLED "PHANTOM PAIN."
ズキン
THROB
ズキン
THROB
ズキン
THROB
ACT 3
EVEN THOUGH I'M PARA-LYZED, AND SHOULDN'T FEEL A THING, A SHOOTING PAIN RUNS THROUGH MY LEGS.
THEY SAY IT HAPPENS TO PEOPLE WHO'VE LOST ARMS OR LEGS...
...BUT THE SAME SYMPTOM CAN ALSO HAPPEN TO PEOPLE WITH A SPINAL CORD INJURY.
ジャー
SSHHH
LOXONIN
I WONDER IF...
...I'LL BE ABLE TO SLEEP TONIGHT.

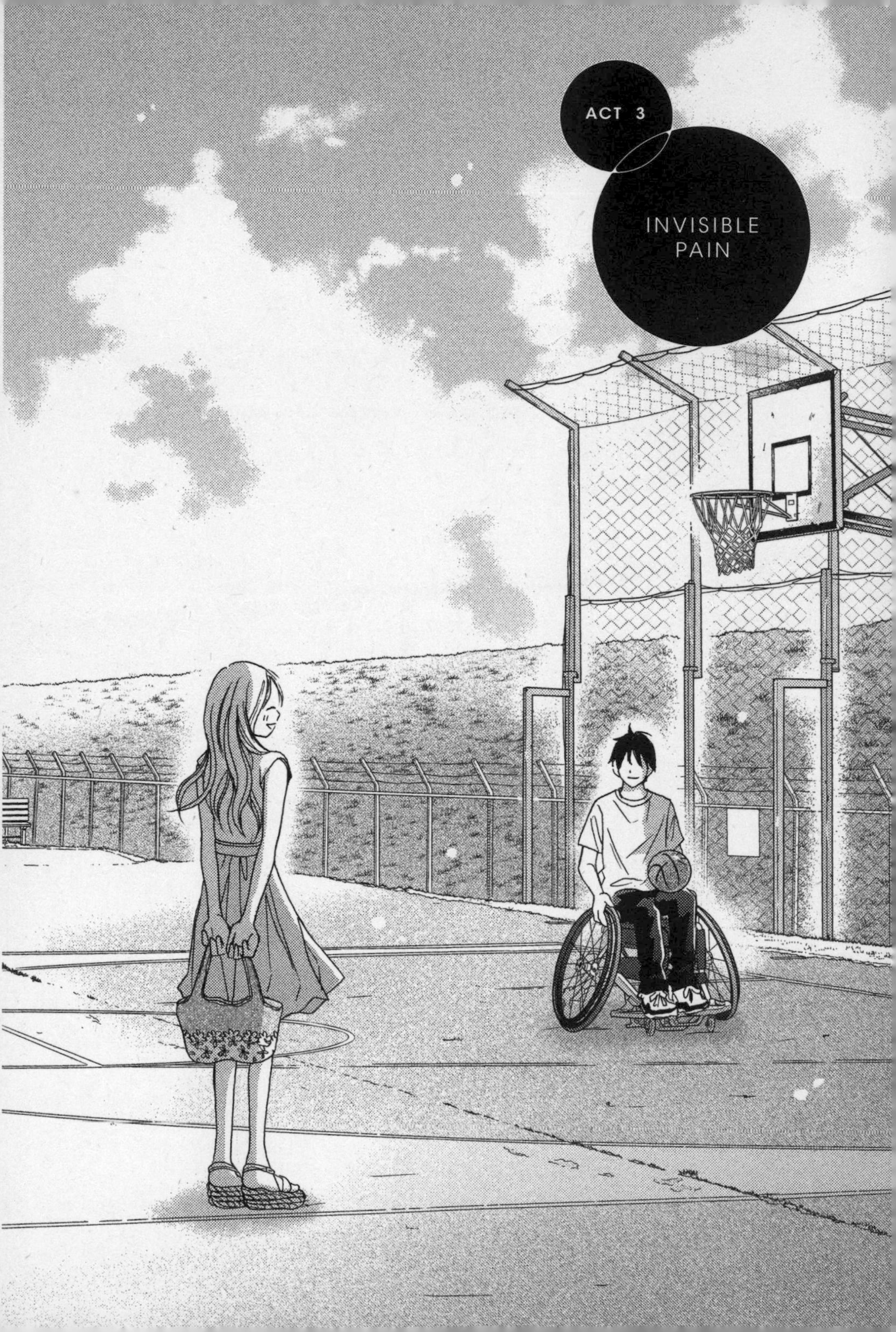
ACT 3
INVISIBLE PAIN

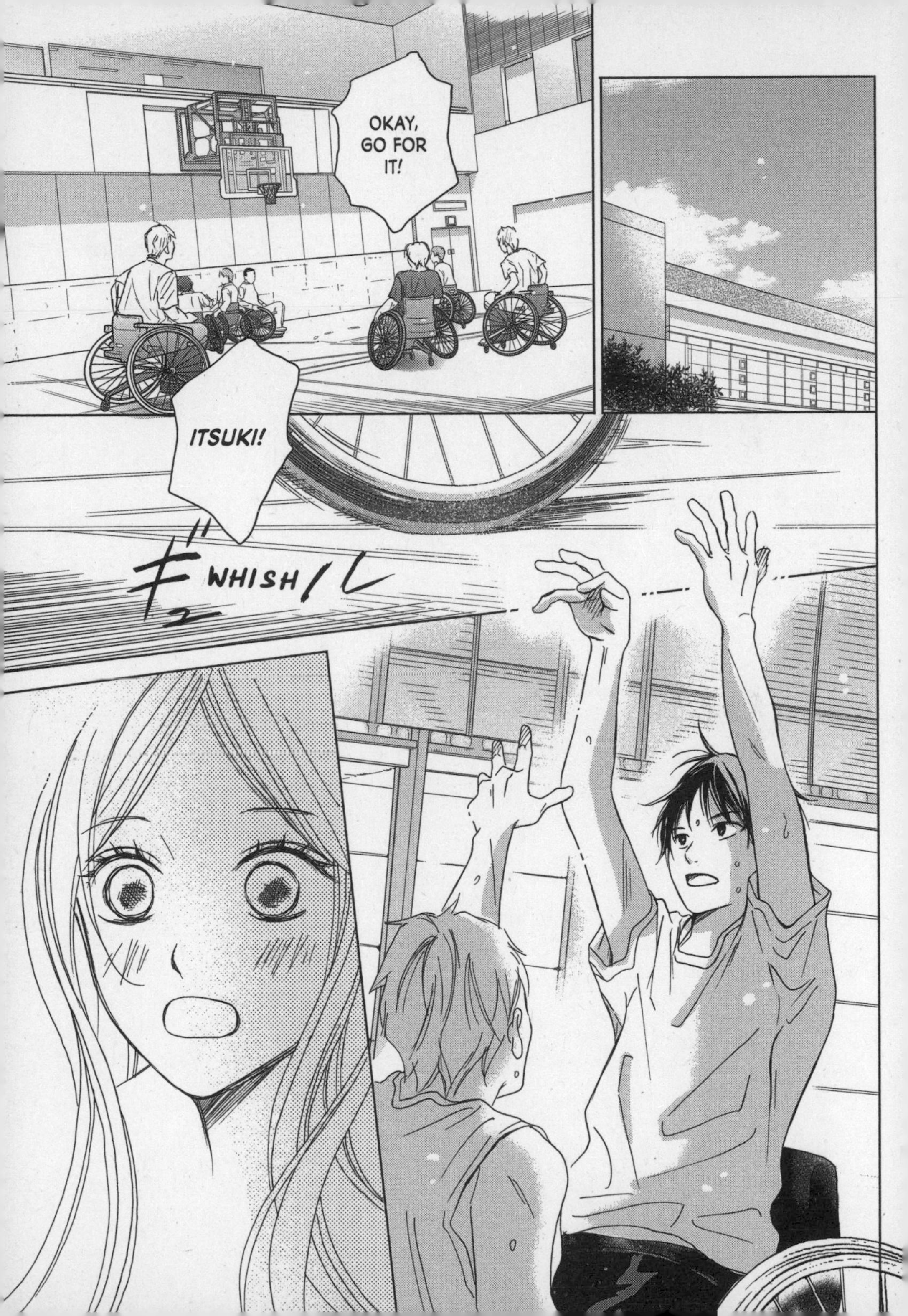
OKAY, GO FOR IT!
ITSUKI!
WHISH

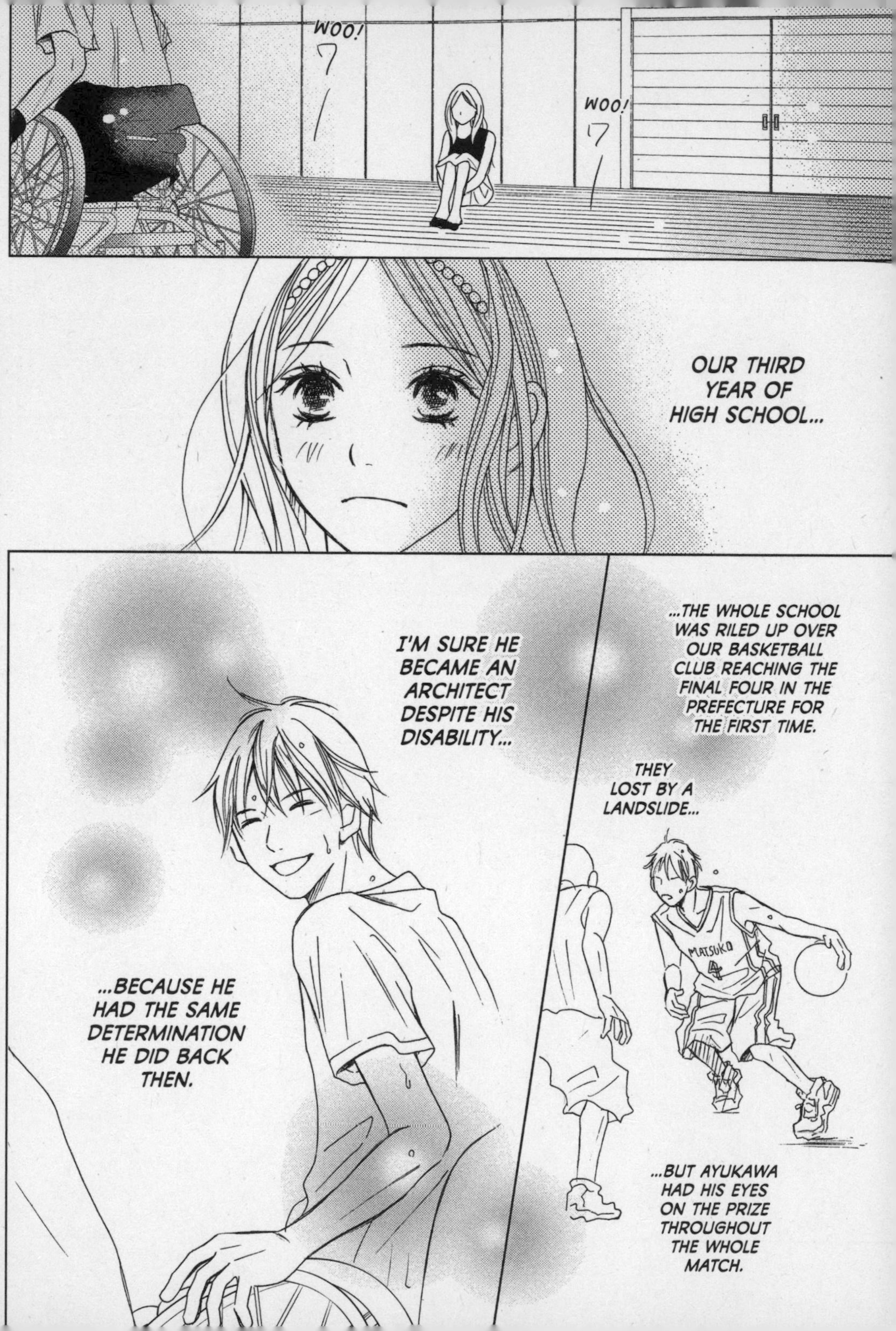
WOO!
WOO!
OUR THIRD YEAR OF HIGH SCHOOL...
...THE WHOLE SCHOOL WAS RILED UP OVER OUR BASKETBALL CLUB REACHING THE FINAL FOUR IN THE PREFECTURE FOR THE FIRST TIME.
THEY LOST BY A LANDSLIDE...
MATSUKO
4
...BUT AYUKAWA HAD HIS EYES ON THE PRIZE THROUGHOUT THE WHOLE MATCH.
I'M SURE HE BECAME AN ARCHITECT DESPITE HIS DISABILITY...
...BECAUSE HE HAD THE SAME DETERMINATION HE DID BACK THEN.

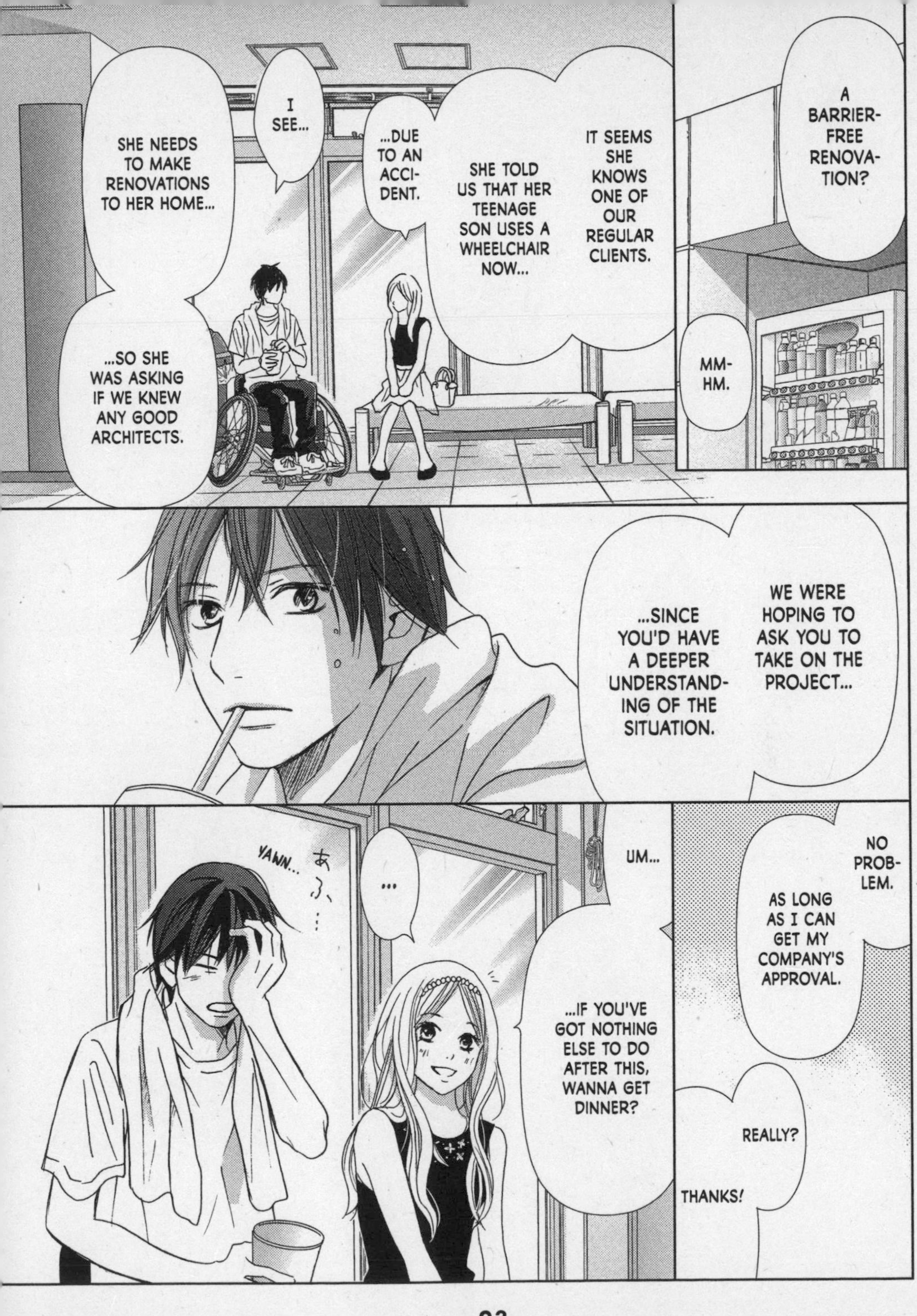
A BARRIER-FREE RENOVATION?
MM-HM.
IT SEEMS SHE KNOWS ONE OF OUR REGULAR CLIENTS.
SHE TOLD US THAT HER TEENAGE SON USES A WHEELCHAIR NOW...
...DUE TO AN ACCIDENT.
I SEE...
SHE NEEDS TO MAKE RENOVATIONS TO HER HOME...
...SO SHE WAS ASKING IF WE KNEW ANY GOOD ARCHITECTS.
WE WERE HOPING TO ASK YOU TO TAKE ON THE PROJECT...
...SINCE YOU'D HAVE A DEEPER UNDERSTANDING OF THE SITUATION.
NO PROBLEM.
AS LONG AS I CAN GET MY COMPANY'S APPROVAL.
REALLY?
THANKS!
UM...
...IF YOU'VE GOT NOTHING ELSE TO DO AFTER THIS, WANNA GET DINNER?
...
YAWN...
あふ...

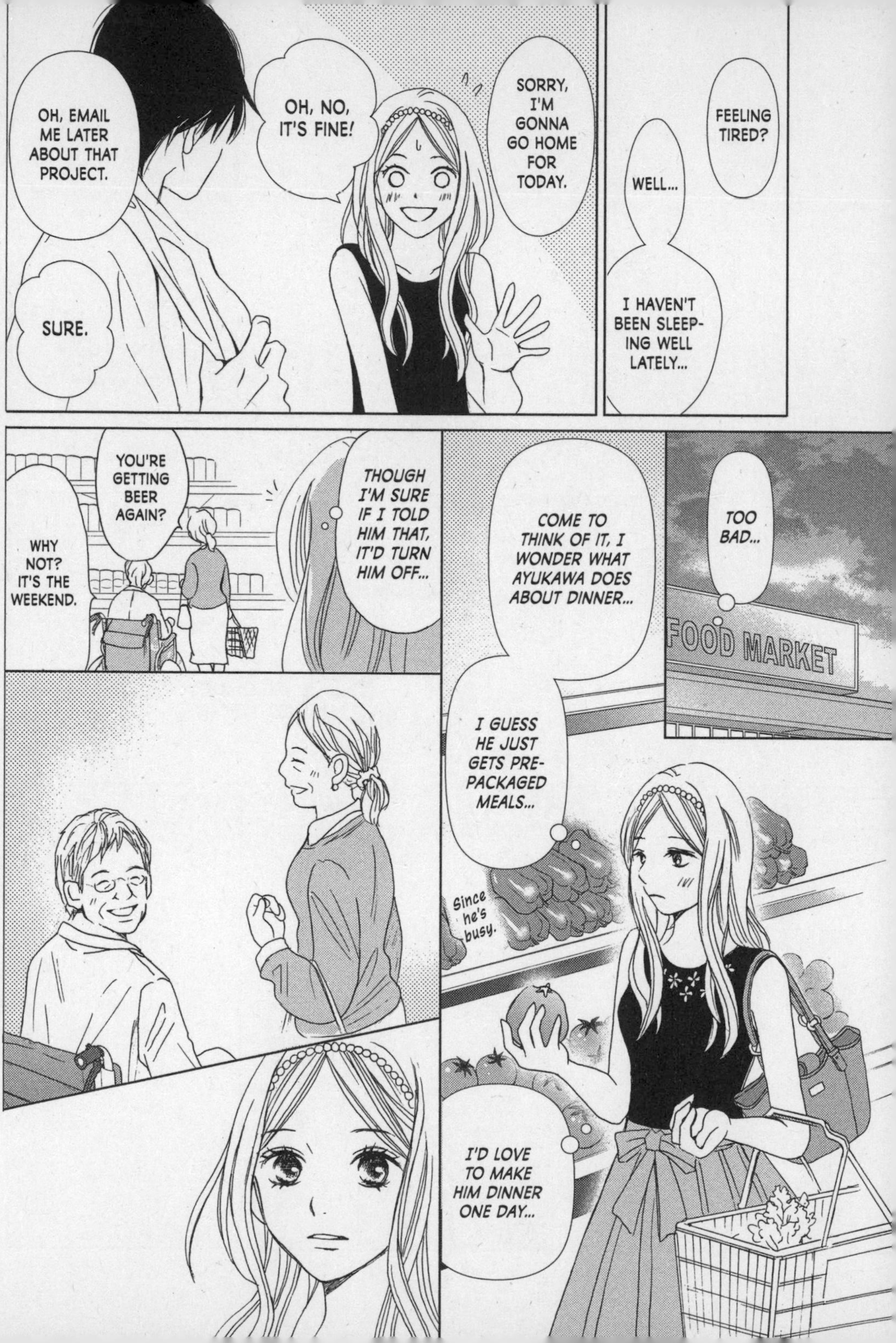

FEELING TIRED?
WELL...
I HAVEN'T BEEN SLEEPING WELL LATELY...
SORRY, I'M GONNA GO HOME FOR TODAY.
OH, NO, IT'S FINE!
OH, EMAIL ME LATER ABOUT THAT PROJECT.
SURE.
FOOD MARKET
TOO BAD...
COME TO THINK OF IT, I WONDER WHAT AYUKAWA DOES ABOUT DINNER...
I GUESS HE JUST GETS PRE-PACKAGED MEALS...
Since he's busy.
I'D LOVE TO MAKE HIM DINNER ONE DAY...
THOUGH I'M SURE IF I TOLD HIM THAT, IT'D TURN HIM OFF...
YOU'RE GETTING BEER AGAIN?
WHY NOT? IT'S THE WEEKEND.

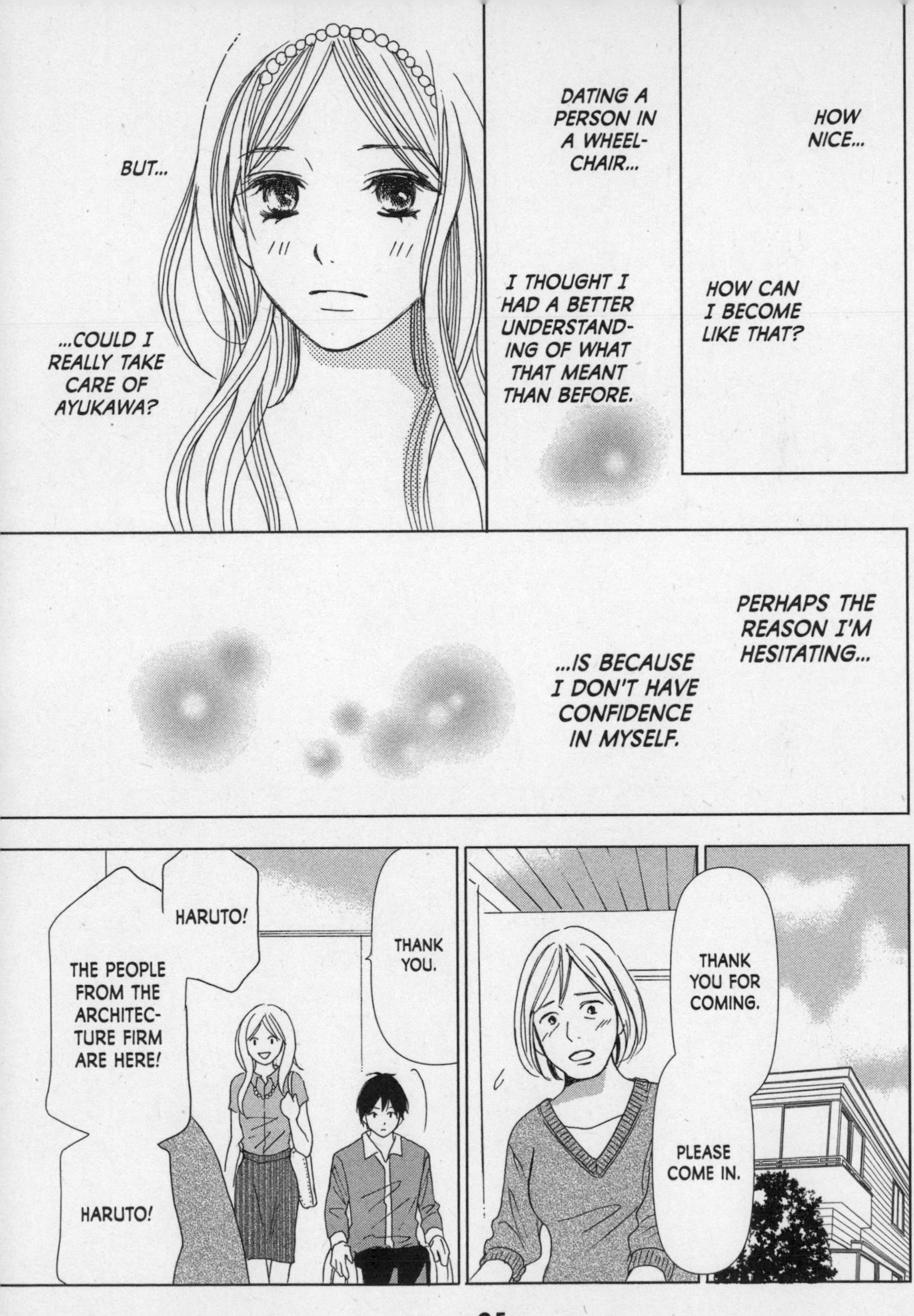

HOW NICE...
HOW CAN I BECOME LIKE THAT?
DATING A PERSON IN A WHEEL-CHAIR...
I THOUGHT I HAD A BETTER UNDERSTAND-ING OF WHAT THAT MEANT THAN BEFORE.
BUT...
...COULD I REALLY TAKE CARE OF AYUKAWA?
PERHAPS THE REASON I'M HESITATING...
...IS BECAUSE I DON'T HAVE CONFIDENCE IN MYSELF.
THANK YOU FOR COMING.
PLEASE COME IN.
THANK YOU.
HARUTO!
THE PEOPLE FROM THE ARCHITEC-TURE FIRM ARE HERE!
HARUTO!

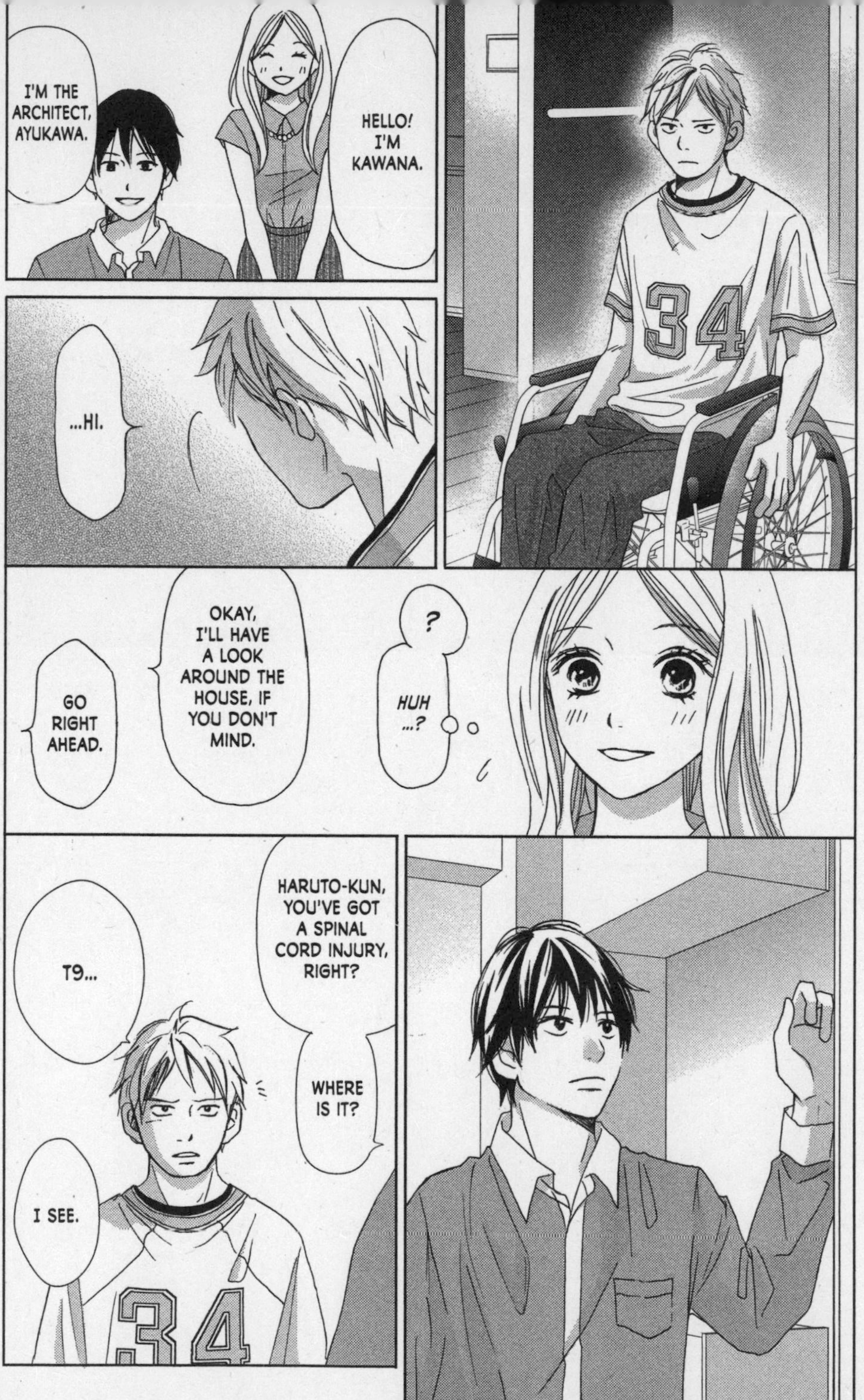
HELLO! I'M KAWANA.
I'M THE ARCHITECT, AYUKAWA.
...HI.
?
HUH ...?
OKAY, I'LL HAVE A LOOK AROUND THE HOUSE, IF YOU DON'T MIND.
GO RIGHT AHEAD.
HARUTO-KUN, YOU'VE GOT A SPINAL CORD INJURY, RIGHT?
WHERE IS IT?
T9...
I SEE.

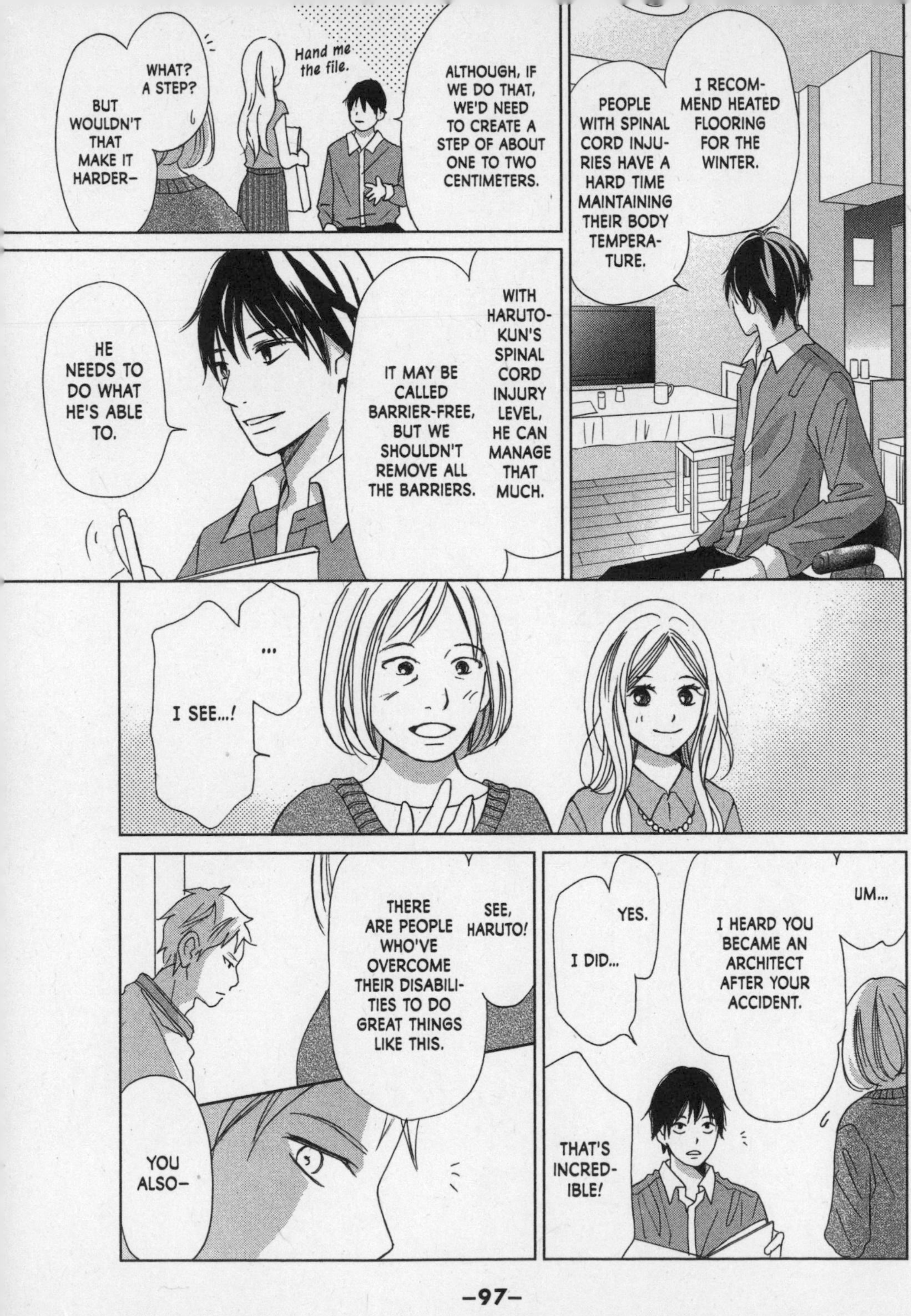
I RECOMMEND HEATED FLOORING FOR THE WINTER.
PEOPLE WITH SPINAL CORD INJURIES HAVE A HARD TIME MAINTAINING THEIR BODY TEMPERATURE.
ALTHOUGH, IF WE DO THAT, WE'D NEED TO CREATE A STEP OF ABOUT ONE TO TWO CENTIMETERS.
Hand me the file.
WHAT? A STEP?
BUT WOULDN'T THAT MAKE IT HARDER—
WITH HARUTO-KUN'S SPINAL CORD INJURY LEVEL, HE CAN MANAGE THAT MUCH.
IT MAY BE CALLED BARRIER-FREE, BUT WE SHOULDN'T REMOVE ALL THE BARRIERS.
HE NEEDS TO DO WHAT HE'S ABLE TO.
...
I SEE...!
UM...
I HEARD YOU BECAME AN ARCHITECT AFTER YOUR ACCIDENT.
YES.
I DID...
THAT'S INCREDIBLE!
SEE, HARUTO!
THERE ARE PEOPLE WHO'VE OVERCOME THEIR DISABILITIES TO DO GREAT THINGS LIKE THIS.
YOU ALSO—

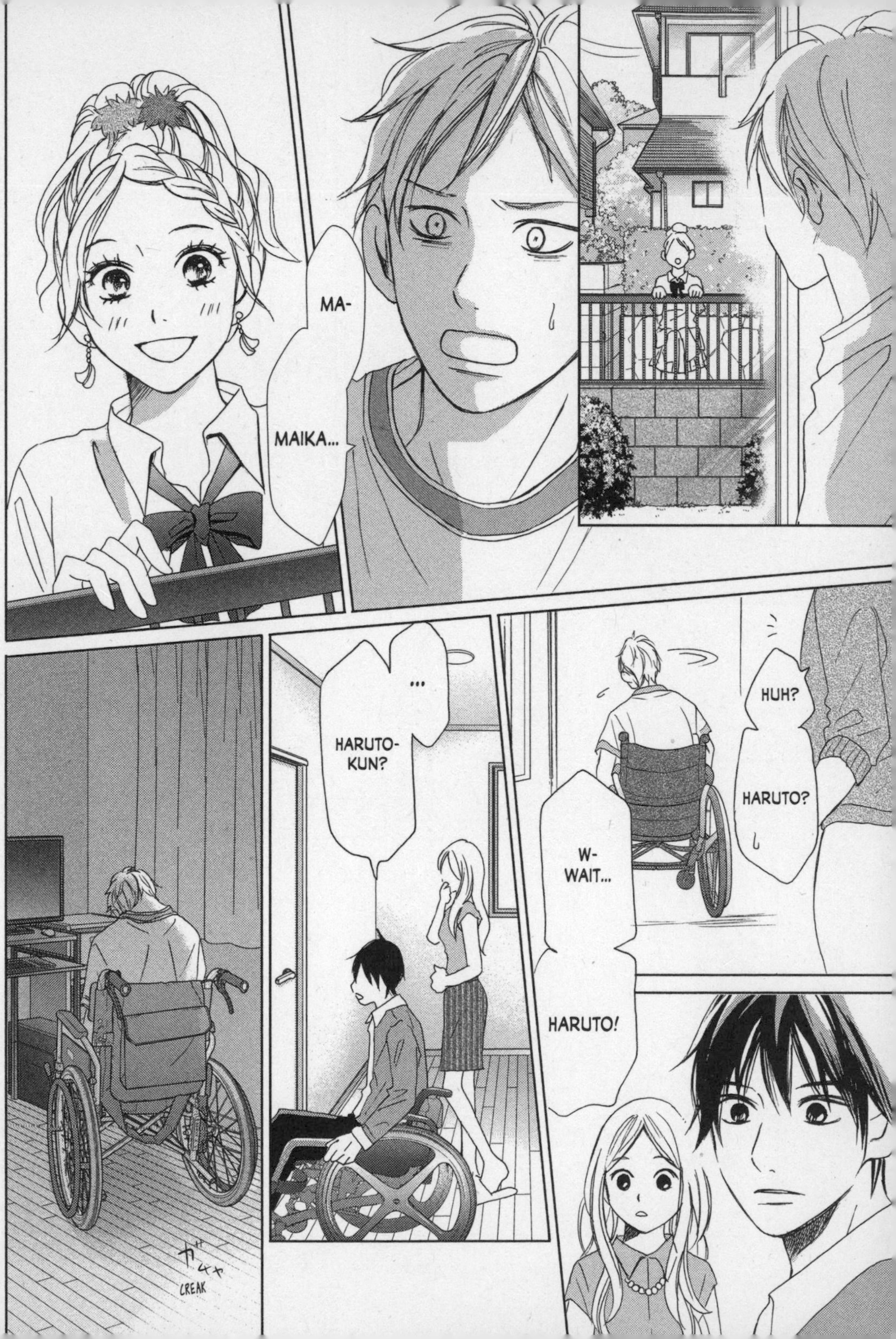
MA-
MAIKA...
HUH?
HARUTO?
W- WAIT...
HARUTO!
...
HARUTO-KUN?
ガチャ
CREAK

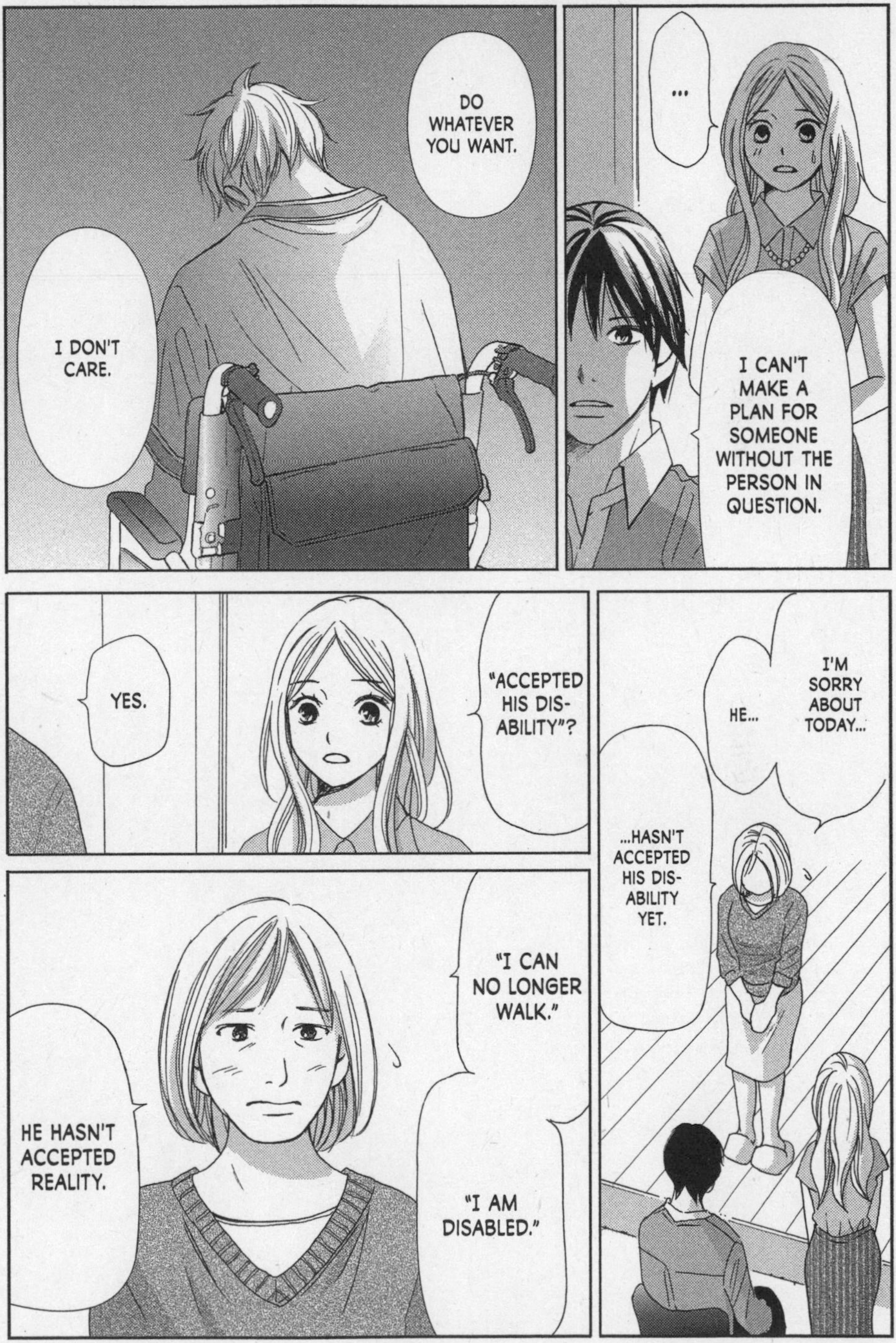
...
I CAN'T MAKE A PLAN FOR SOMEONE WITHOUT THE PERSON IN QUESTION.
DO WHATEVER YOU WANT.
I DON'T CARE.
I'M SORRY ABOUT TODAY...
HE...
...HASN'T ACCEPTED HIS DIS-ABILITY YET.
"ACCEPTED HIS DIS-ABILITY"?
YES.
"I CAN NO LONGER WALK."
"I AM DISABLED."
HE HASN'T ACCEPTED REALITY.

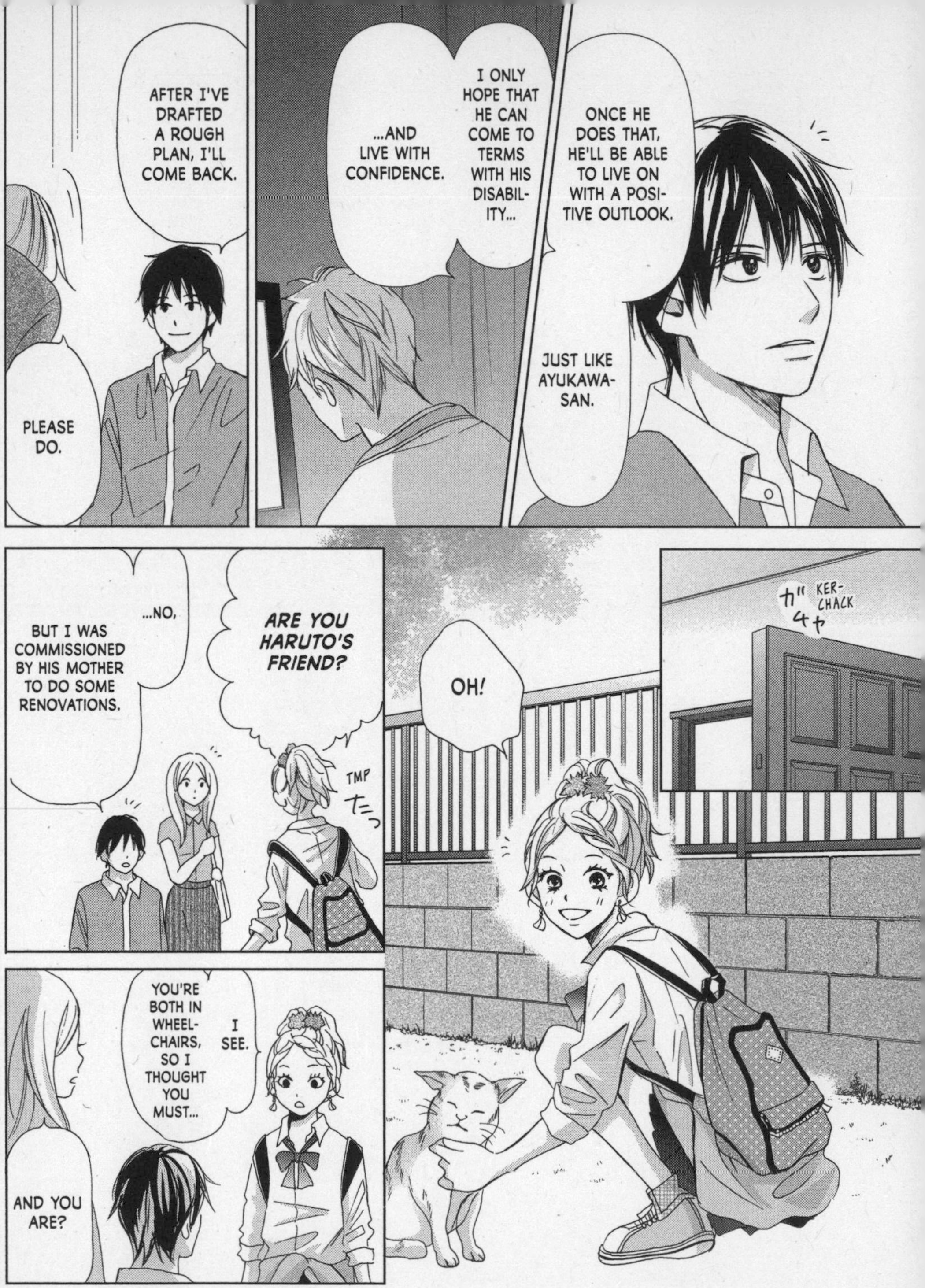
ONCE HE DOES THAT, HE'LL BE ABLE TO LIVE ON WITH A POSITIVE OUTLOOK.
JUST LIKE AYUKAWA-SAN.
I ONLY HOPE THAT HE CAN COME TO TERMS WITH HIS DISABILITY...
...AND LIVE WITH CONFIDENCE.
AFTER I'VE DRAFTED A ROUGH PLAN, I'LL COME BACK.
PLEASE DO.
KER-CHACK
OH!
ARE YOU HARUTO'S FRIEND?
TMP
...NO,
BUT I WAS COMMISSIONED BY HIS MOTHER TO DO SOME RENOVATIONS.
YOU'RE BOTH IN WHEELCHAIRS, SO I THOUGHT YOU MUST...
I SEE.
AND YOU ARE?

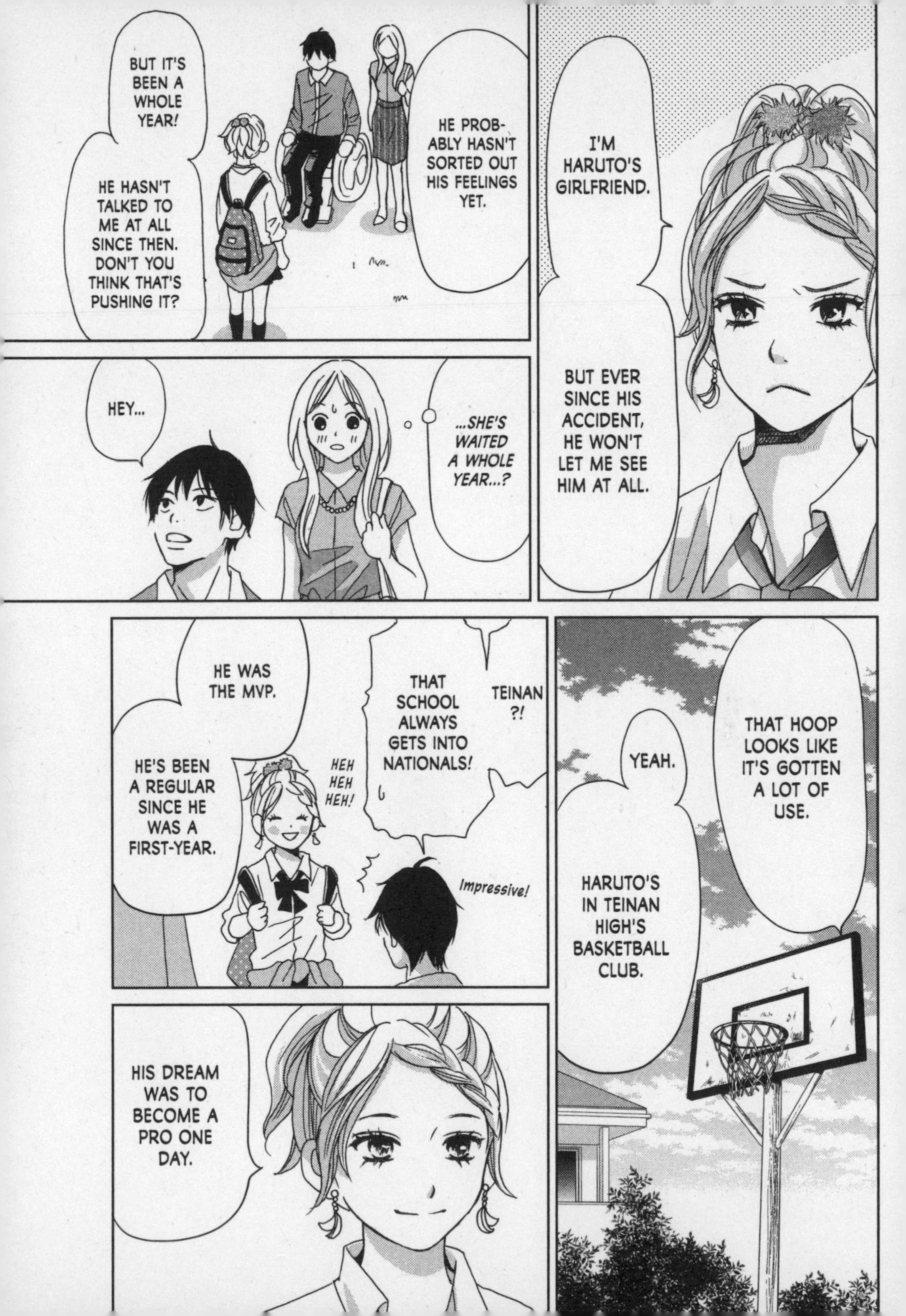
I'M HARUTO'S GIRLFRIEND.
BUT EVER SINCE HIS ACCIDENT, HE WON'T LET ME SEE HIM AT ALL.
HE PROB-ABLY HASN'T SORTED OUT HIS FEELINGS YET.
BUT IT'S BEEN A WHOLE YEAR!
HE HASN'T TALKED TO ME AT ALL SINCE THEN. DON'T YOU THINK THAT'S PUSHING IT?
...SHE'S WAITED A WHOLE YEAR...?
HEY...
THAT HOOP LOOKS LIKE IT'S GOTTEN A LOT OF USE.
YEAH.
HARUTO'S IN TEINAN HIGH'S BASKETBALL CLUB.
TEINAN ?!
THAT SCHOOL ALWAYS GETS INTO NATIONALS!
HE WAS THE MVP.
HEH HEH HEH!
HE'S BEEN A REGULAR SINCE HE WAS A FIRST-YEAR.
Impressive!
HIS DREAM WAS TO BECOME A PRO ONE DAY.

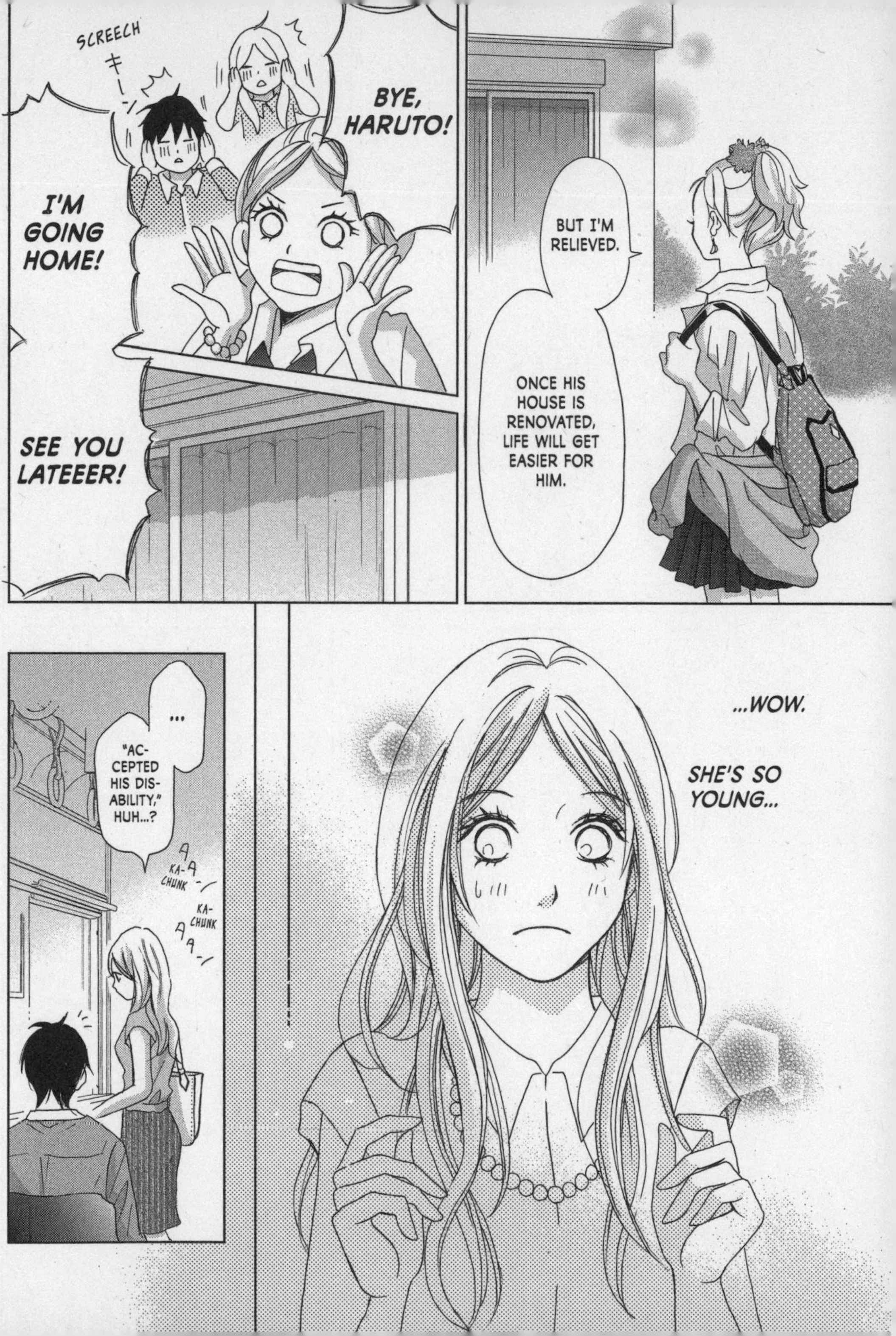
BUT I'M RELIEVED.
ONCE HIS HOUSE IS RENOVATED, LIFE WILL GET EASIER FOR HIM.
BYE, HARUTO!
SCREECH
キーン
I'M GOING HOME!
SEE YOU LATEEER!
...WOW.
SHE'S SO YOUNG...
...
"AC-CEPTED HIS DIS-ABILITY," HUH...?
KA-CHUNK
KA-CHUNK

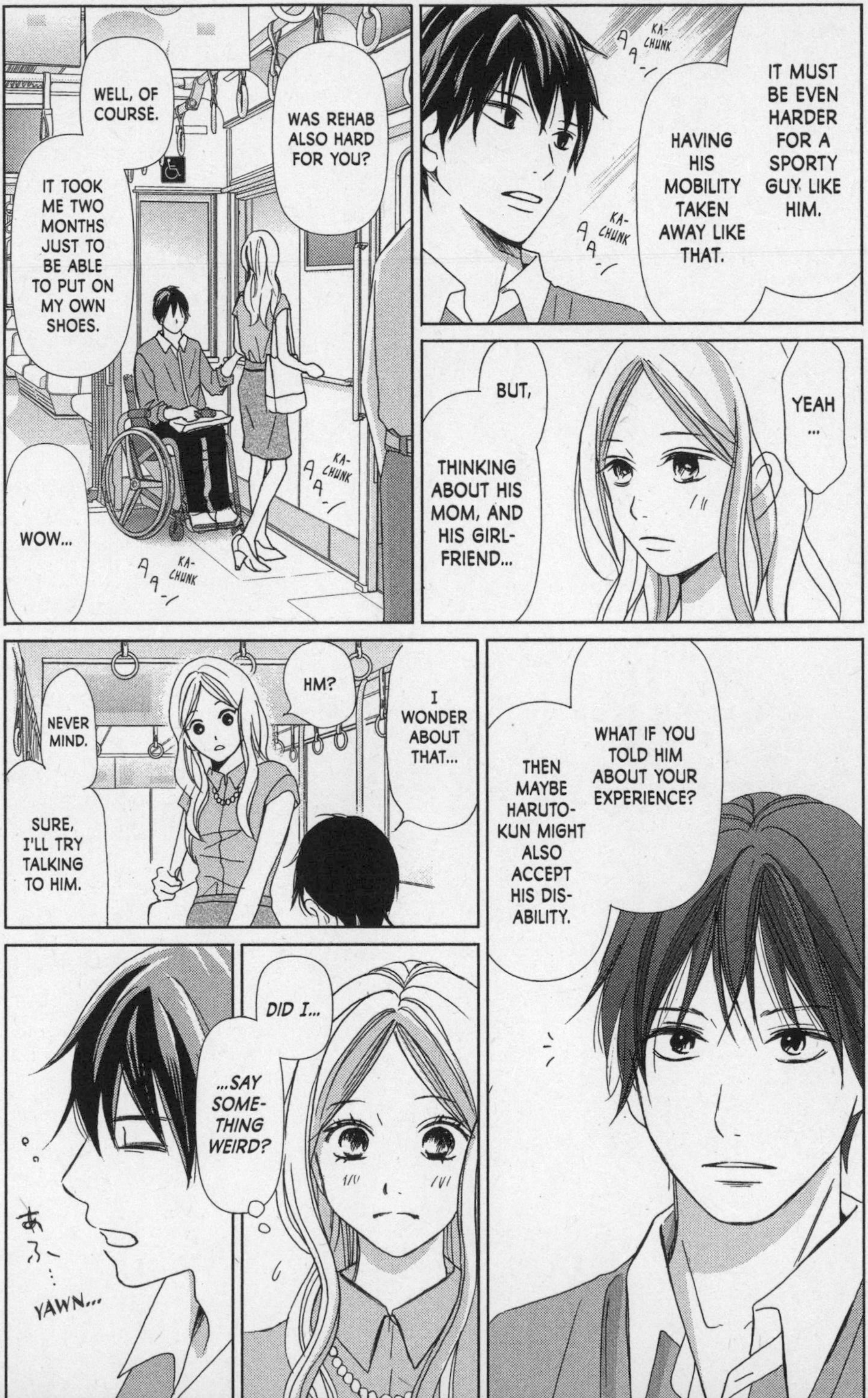
KA-CHUNK
IT MUST BE EVEN HARDER FOR A SPORTY GUY LIKE HIM.
HAVING HIS MOBILITY TAKEN AWAY LIKE THAT.
KA-CHUNK
YEAH ...
BUT,
THINKING ABOUT HIS MOM, AND HIS GIRL-FRIEND...
WAS REHAB ALSO HARD FOR YOU?
WELL, OF COURSE.
IT TOOK ME TWO MONTHS JUST TO BE ABLE TO PUT ON MY OWN SHOES.
KA-CHUNK
KA-CHUNK
WOW...
WHAT IF YOU TOLD HIM ABOUT YOUR EXPERIENCE?
THEN MAYBE HARUTO-KUN MIGHT ALSO ACCEPT HIS DIS-ABILITY.
HM?
I WONDER ABOUT THAT...
NEVER MIND.
SURE, I'LL TRY TALKING TO HIM.
DID I...
...SAY SOME-THING WEIRD?
あふ～
YAWN...

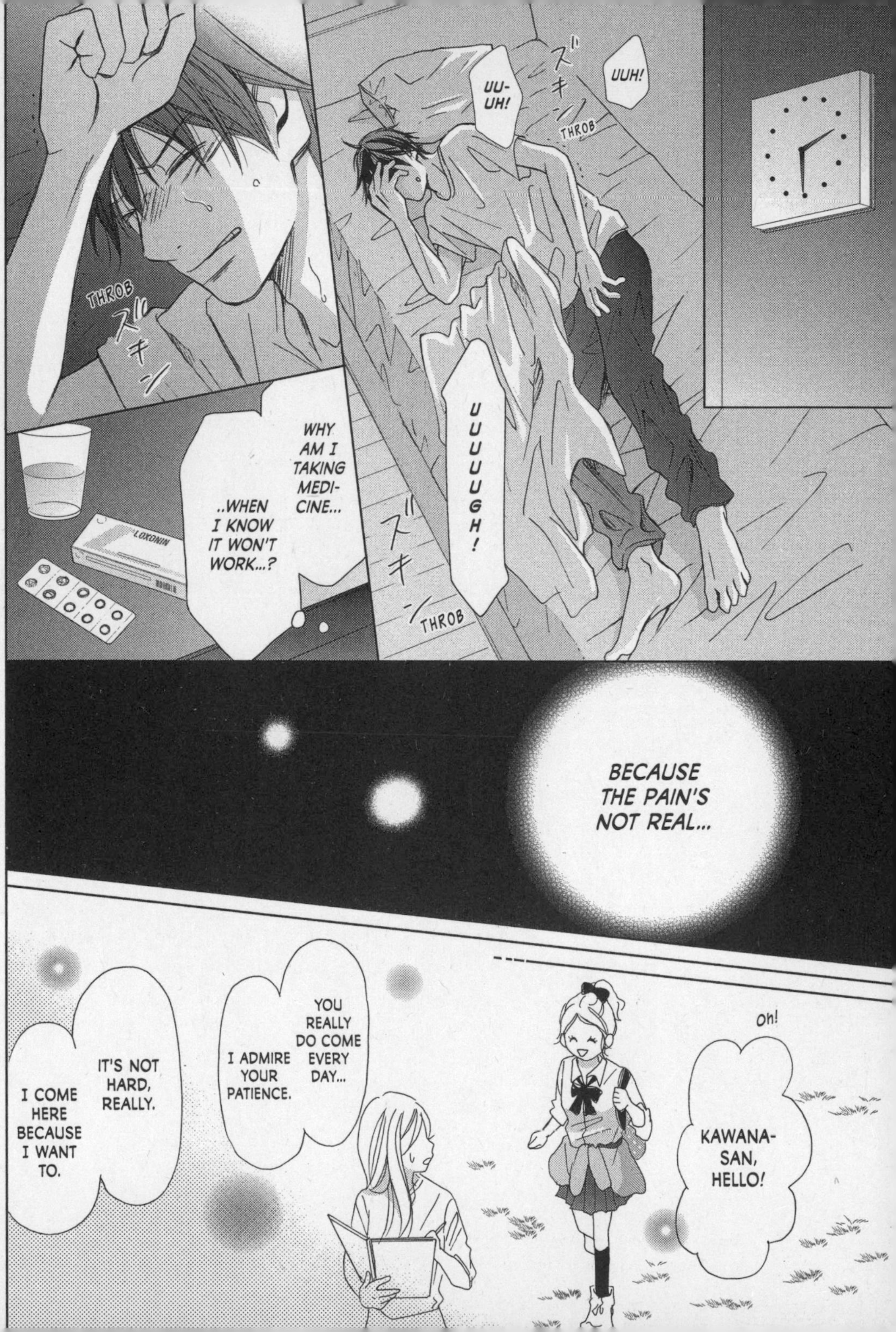
UUH!
UU-UH!
ズキン
THROB
UUUUUUGH!
ズキン
THROB
THROB
ズキン
WHY AM I TAKING MEDICINE...
..WHEN I KNOW IT WON'T WORK...?
LOXONIN
BECAUSE THE PAIN'S NOT REAL...
Oh!
KAWANA-SAN, HELLO!
YOU REALLY DO COME EVERY DAY...
I ADMIRE YOUR PATIENCE.
IT'S NOT HARD, REALLY.
I COME HERE BECAUSE I WANT TO.

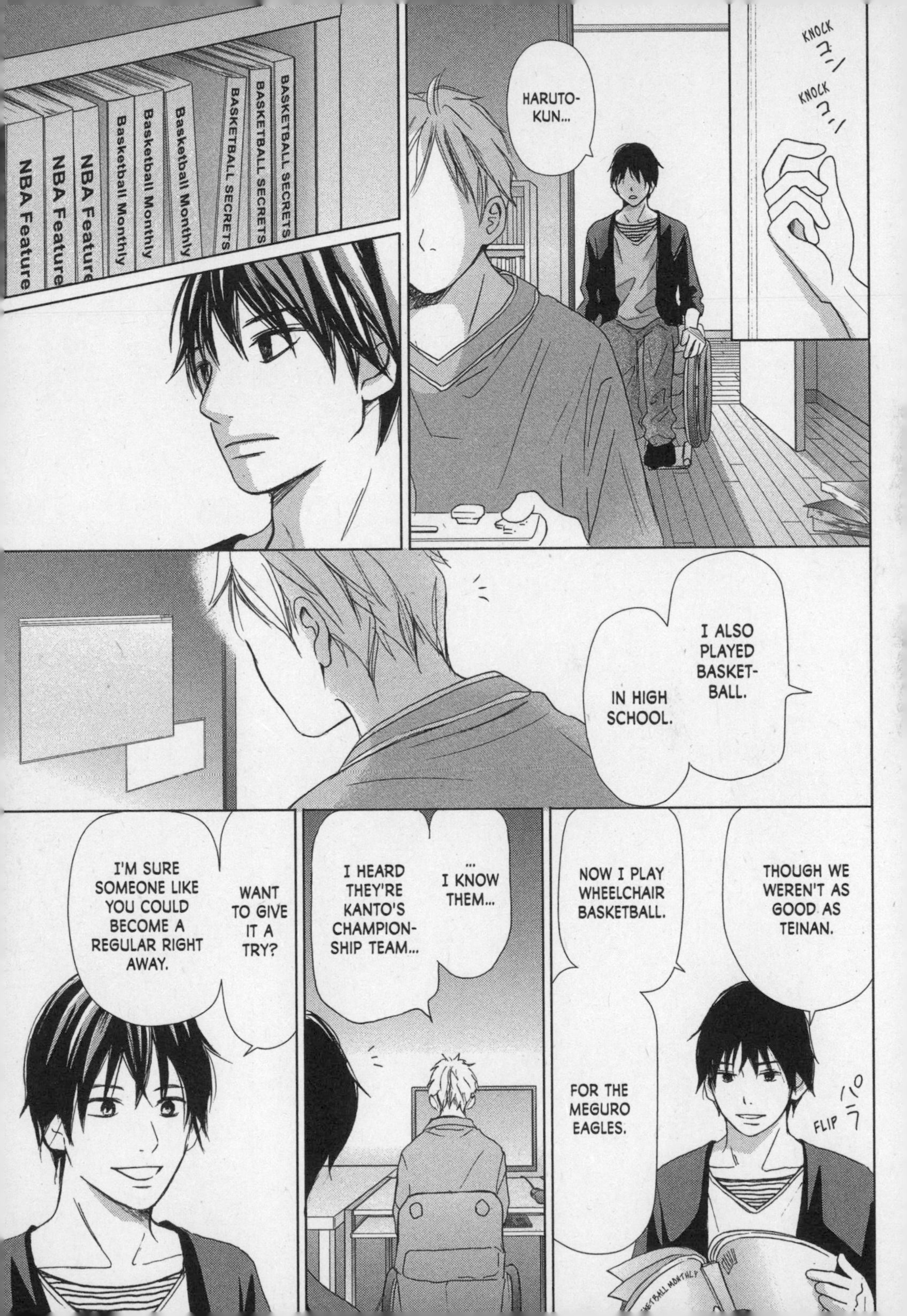
KNOCK
KNOCK
HARUTO-KUN...
BASKETBALL SECRETS
BASKETBALL SECRETS
BASKETBALL SECRETS
Basketball Monthly
Basketball Monthly
Basketball Monthly
NBA Feature
NBA Feature
NBA Feature
I ALSO PLAYED BASKET-BALL.
IN HIGH SCHOOL.
THOUGH WE WEREN'T AS GOOD AS TEINAN.
NOW I PLAY WHEELCHAIR BASKETBALL.
FLIP
FOR THE MEGURO EAGLES.
... I KNOW THEM...
I HEARD THEY'RE KANTO'S CHAMPION-SHIP TEAM...
WANT TO GIVE IT A TRY?
I'M SURE SOMEONE LIKE YOU COULD BECOME A REGULAR RIGHT AWAY.

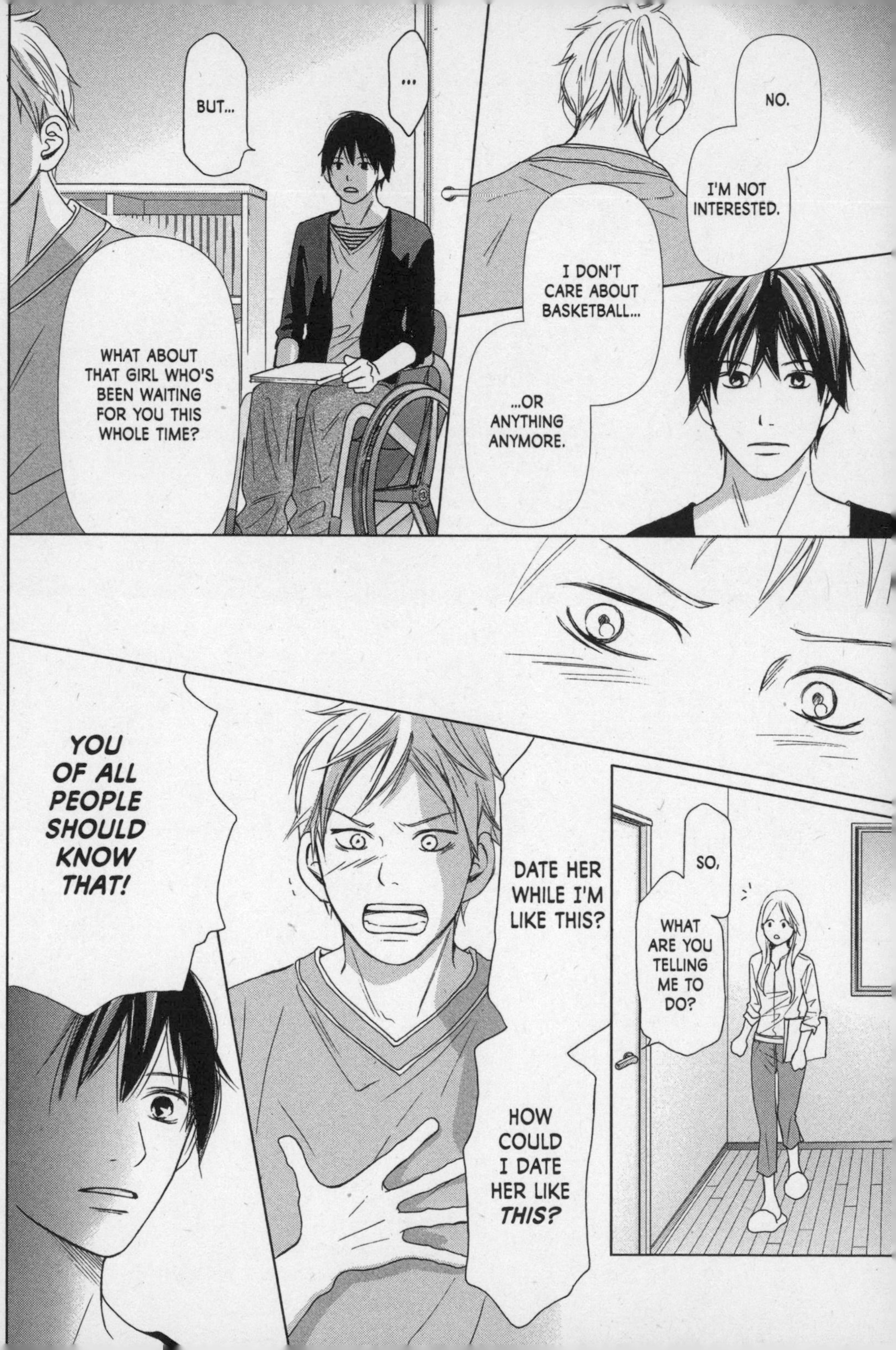
NO.
I'M NOT INTERESTED.
I DON'T CARE ABOUT BASKETBALL...
...OR ANYTHING ANYMORE.
...
BUT...
WHAT ABOUT THAT GIRL WHO'S BEEN WAITING FOR YOU THIS WHOLE TIME?
SO,
WHAT ARE YOU TELLING ME TO DO?
DATE HER WHILE I'M LIKE THIS?
HOW COULD I DATE HER LIKE *THIS?*
YOU OF ALL PEOPLE SHOULD KNOW THAT!

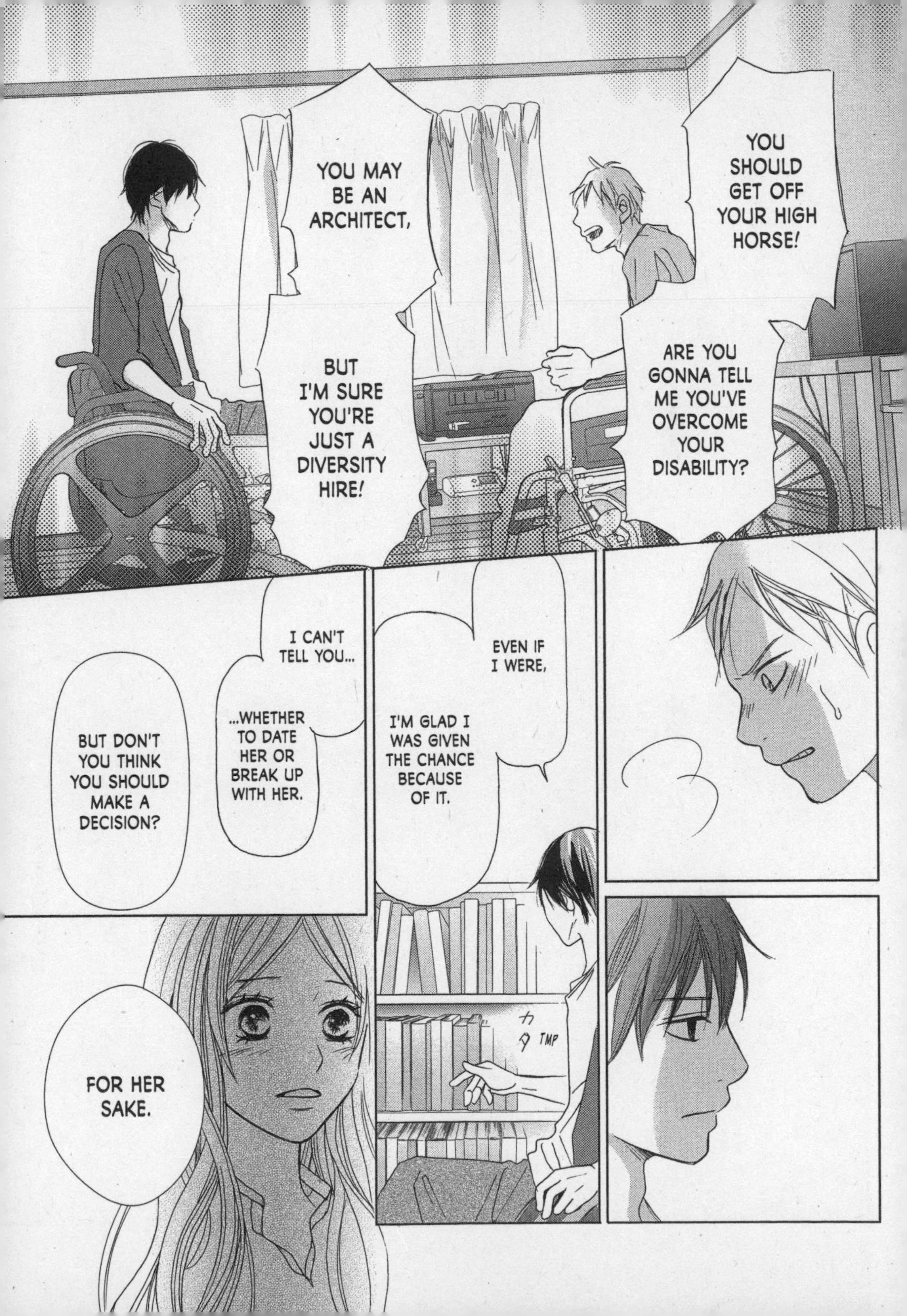
YOU SHOULD GET OFF YOUR HIGH HORSE!
YOU MAY BE AN ARCHITECT,
BUT I'M SURE YOU'RE JUST A DIVERSITY HIRE!
ARE YOU GONNA TELL ME YOU'VE OVERCOME YOUR DISABILITY?
EVEN IF I WERE,
I'M GLAD I WAS GIVEN THE CHANCE BECAUSE OF IT.
I CAN'T TELL YOU...
...WHETHER TO DATE HER OR BREAK UP WITH HER.
BUT DON'T YOU THINK YOU SHOULD MAKE A DECISION?
カタ TMP
FOR HER SAKE.

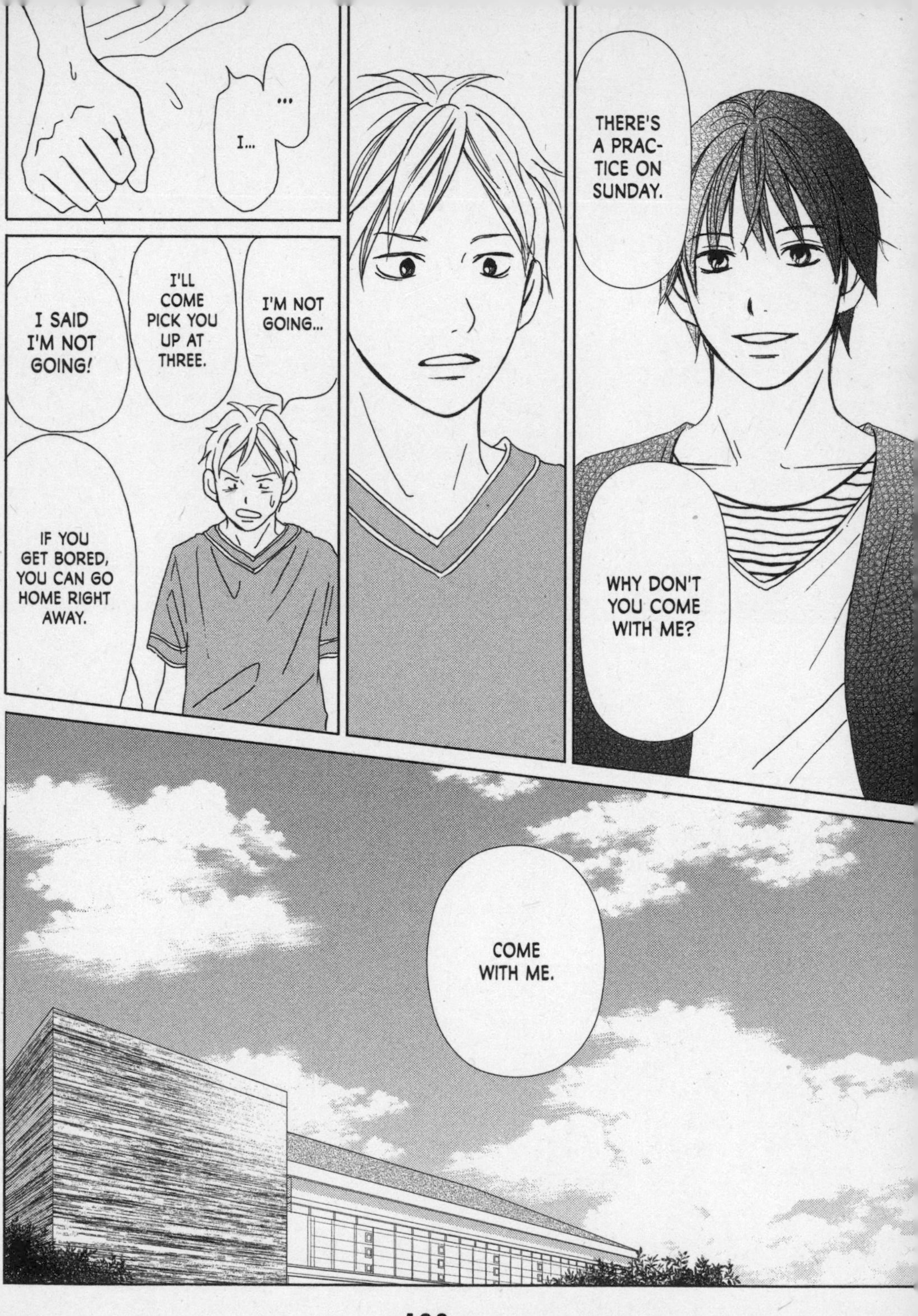
THERE'S A PRACTICE ON SUNDAY.
WHY DON'T YOU COME WITH ME?
... I...
I'M NOT GOING...
I'LL COME PICK YOU UP AT THREE.
I SAID I'M NOT GOING!
IF YOU GET BORED, YOU CAN GO HOME RIGHT AWAY.
COME WITH ME.

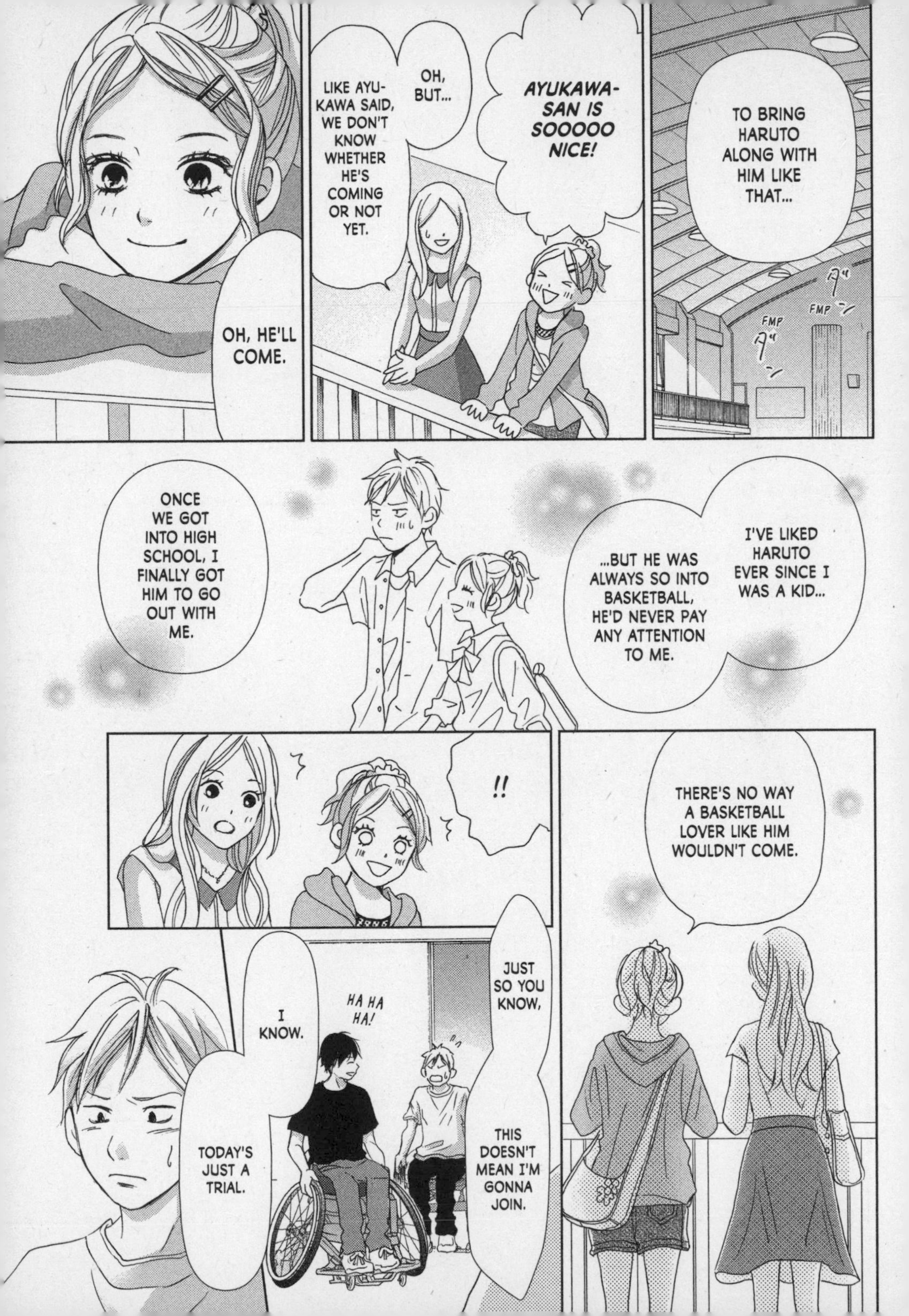
TO BRING HARUTO ALONG WITH HIM LIKE THAT...
FMP
FMP
AYUKAWA-SAN IS SOOOOO NICE!
OH, BUT...
LIKE AYUKAWA SAID, WE DON'T KNOW WHETHER HE'S COMING OR NOT YET.
OH, HE'LL COME.
I'VE LIKED HARUTO EVER SINCE I WAS A KID...
...BUT HE WAS ALWAYS SO INTO BASKETBALL, HE'D NEVER PAY ANY ATTENTION TO ME.
ONCE WE GOT INTO HIGH SCHOOL, I FINALLY GOT HIM TO GO OUT WITH ME.
THERE'S NO WAY A BASKETBALL LOVER LIKE HIM WOULDN'T COME.
!!
JUST SO YOU KNOW,
THIS DOESN'T MEAN I'M GONNA JOIN.
HA HA HA!
I KNOW.
TODAY'S JUST A TRIAL.

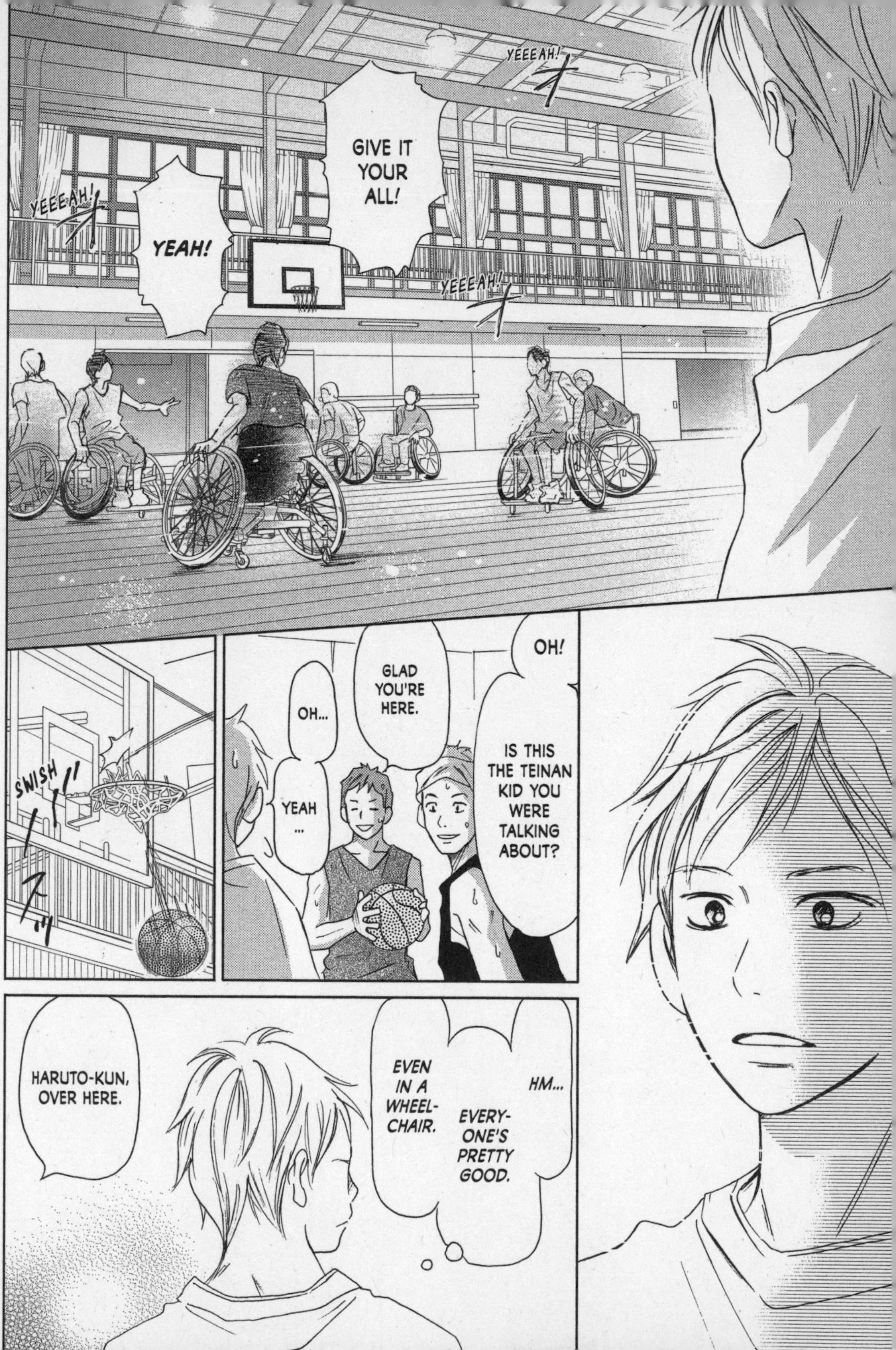
YEEEAH!
GIVE IT YOUR ALL!
YEEEAH!
YEAH!
YEEEAH!
OH!
IS THIS THE TEINAN KID YOU WERE TALKING ABOUT?
GLAD YOU'RE HERE.
OH...
YEAH ...
SWISH
HM...
EVEN IN A WHEEL-CHAIR.
EVERY-ONE'S PRETTY GOOD.
HARUTO-KUN, OVER HERE.

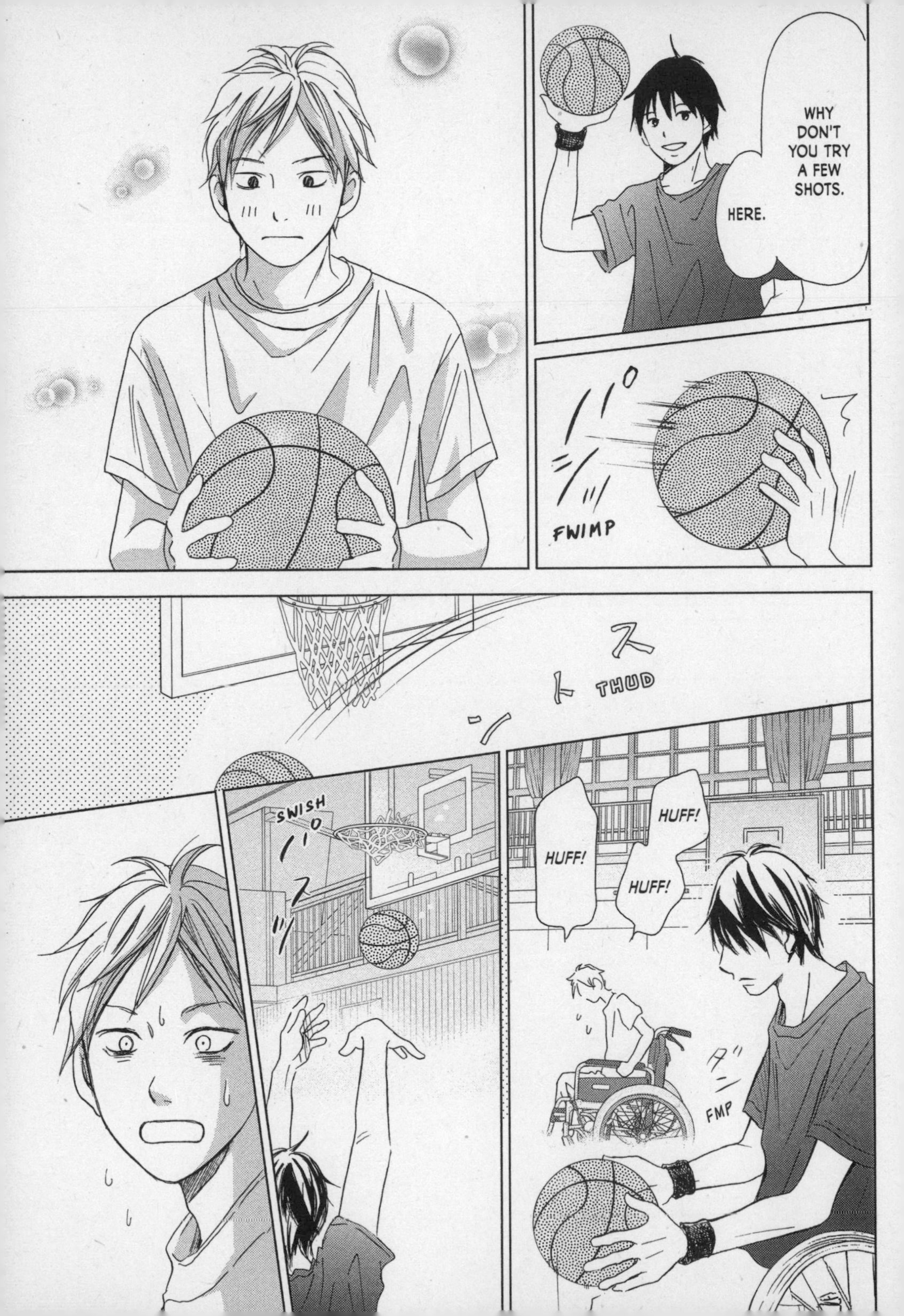

WHY DON'T YOU TRY A FEW SHOTS.
HERE.
FWIMP
THUD
HUFF!
HUFF!
HUFF!
FMP
SWISH

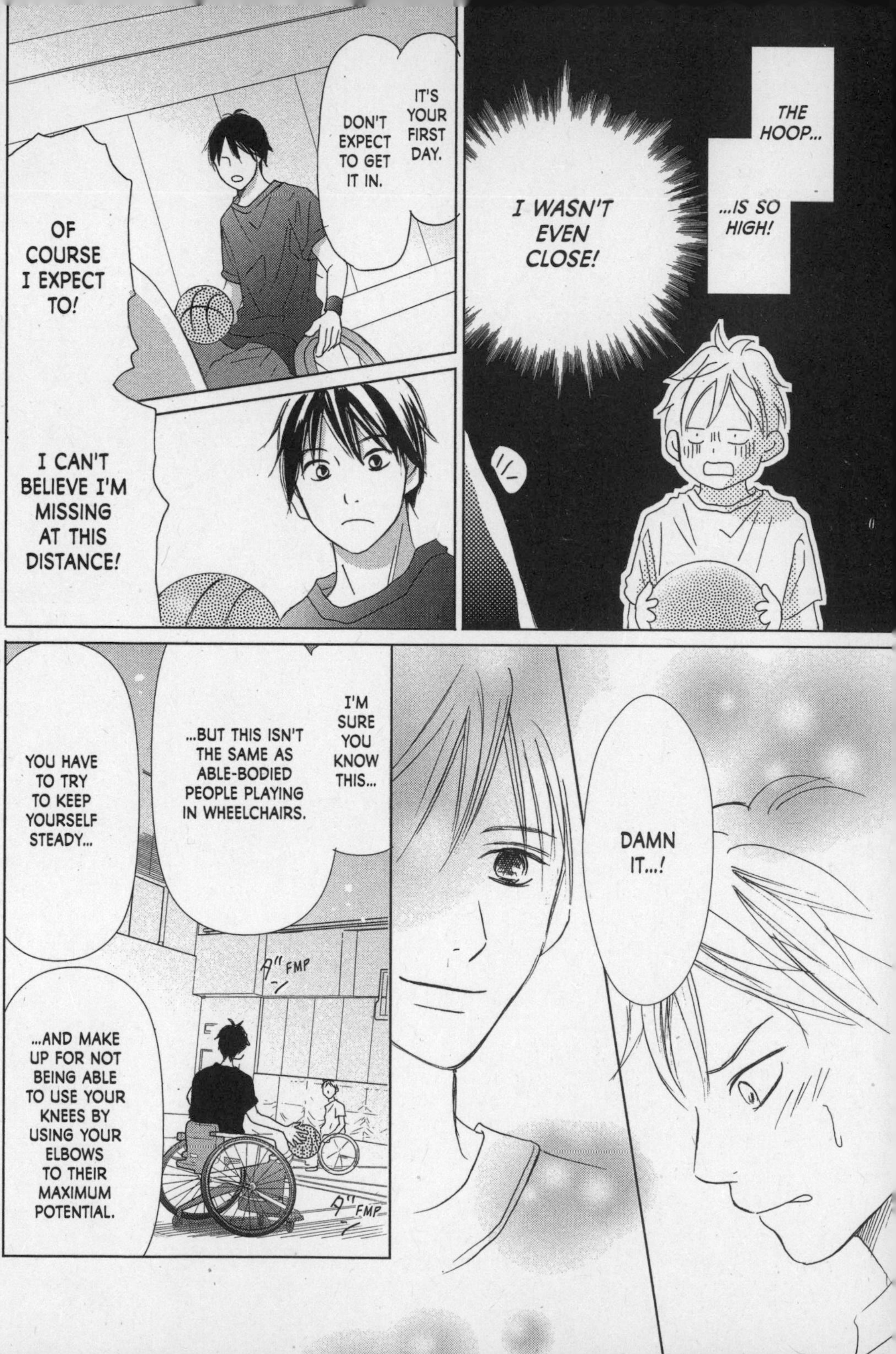
THE HOOP...
...IS SO HIGH!
I WASN'T EVEN CLOSE!
IT'S YOUR FIRST DAY.
DON'T EXPECT TO GET IT IN.
OF COURSE I EXPECT TO!
I CAN'T BELIEVE I'M MISSING AT THIS DISTANCE!
DAMN IT...!
I'M SURE YOU KNOW THIS...
...BUT THIS ISN'T THE SAME AS ABLE-BODIED PEOPLE PLAYING IN WHEELCHAIRS.
YOU HAVE TO TRY TO KEEP YOURSELF STEADY...
FMP
...AND MAKE UP FOR NOT BEING ABLE TO USE YOUR KNEES BY USING YOUR ELBOWS TO THEIR MAXIMUM POTENTIAL.
FMP

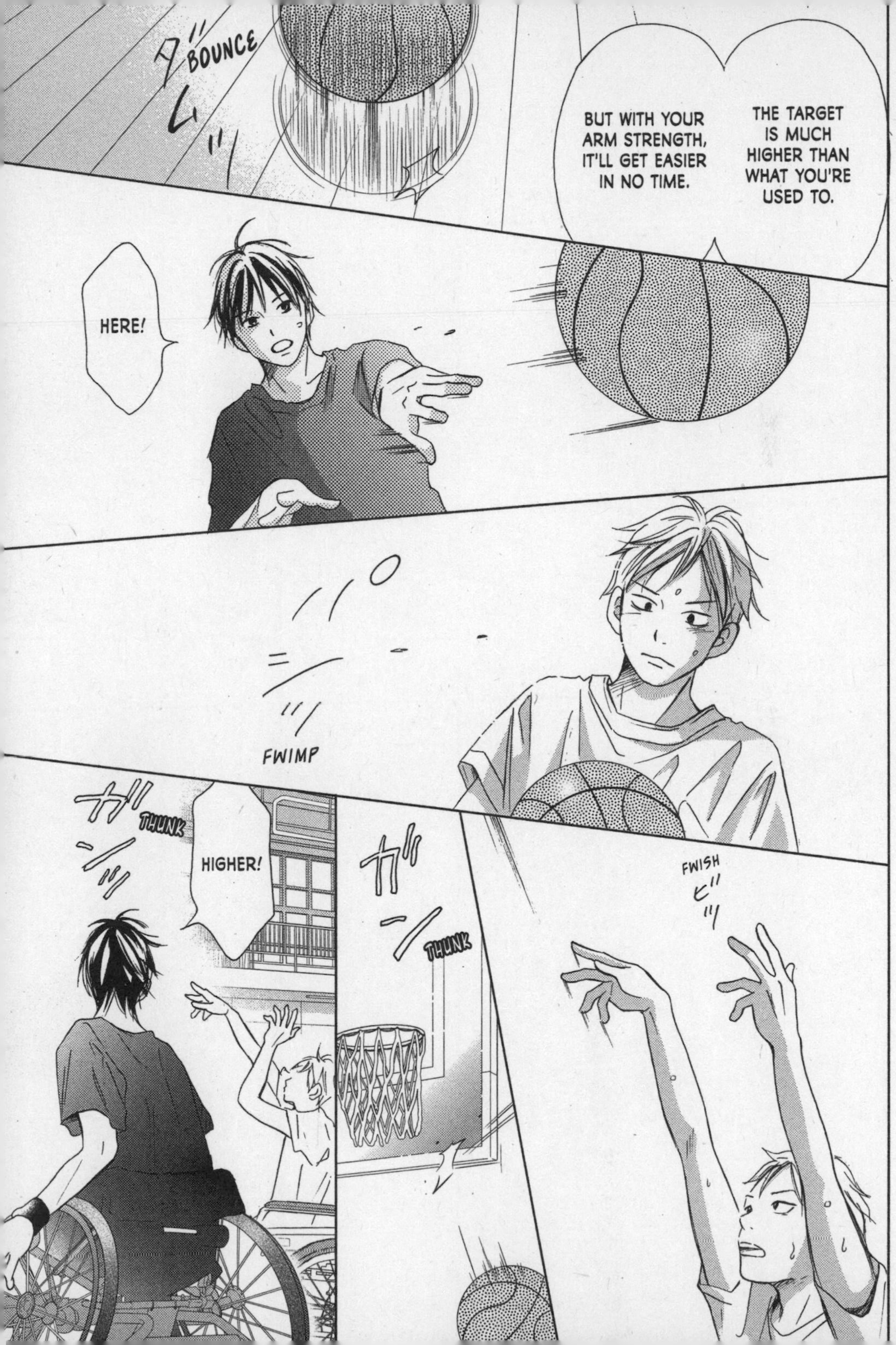
THE TARGET IS MUCH HIGHER THAN WHAT YOU'RE USED TO.
BUT WITH YOUR ARM STRENGTH, IT'LL GET EASIER IN NO TIME.
BOUNCE
HERE!
FWIMP
FWISH
THUNK
HIGHER!
THUNK

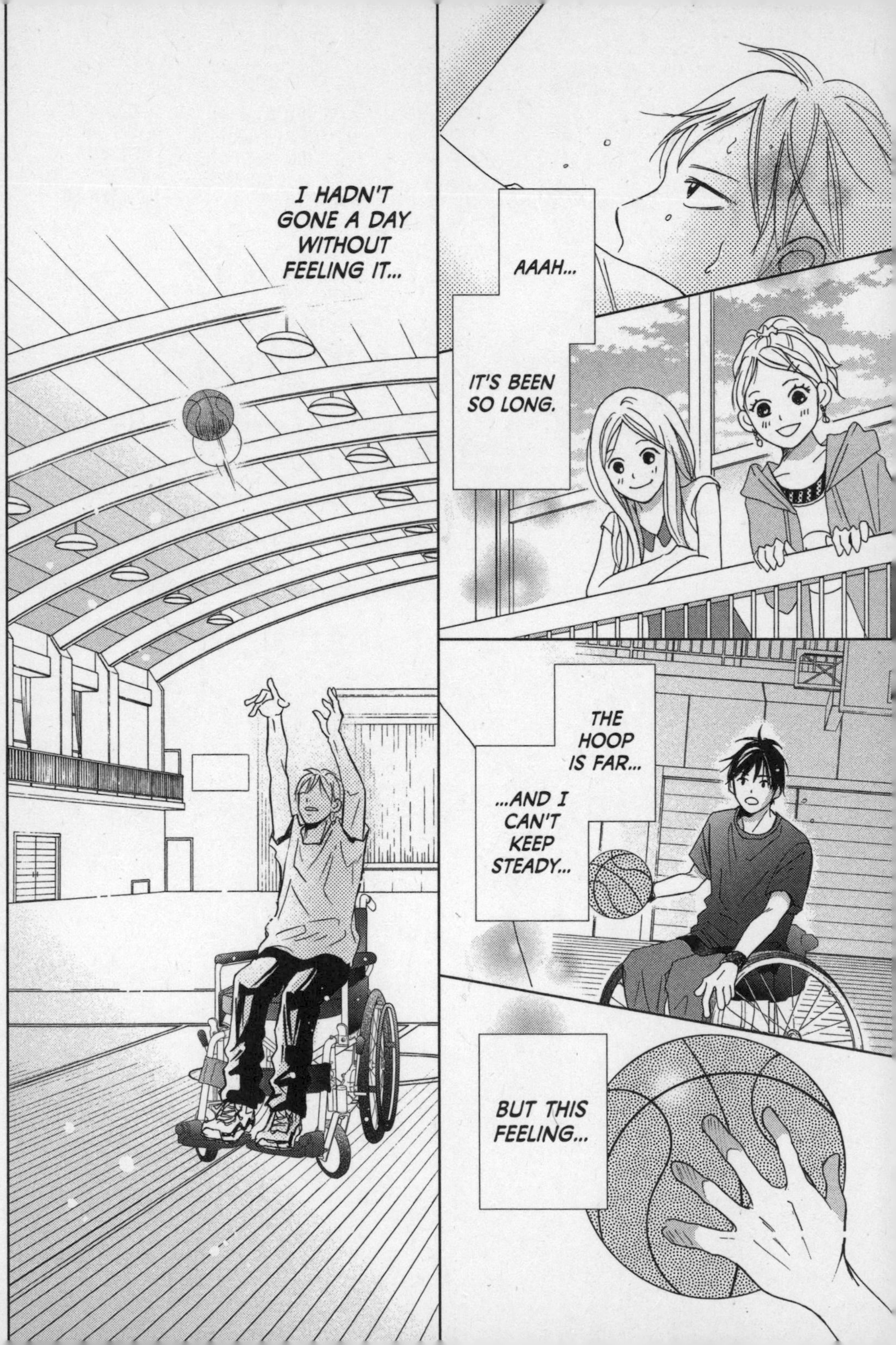
AAAH...
IT'S BEEN SO LONG.
THE HOOP IS FAR...
...AND I CAN'T KEEP STEADY...
BUT THIS FEELING...
I HADN'T GONE A DAY WITHOUT FEELING IT...

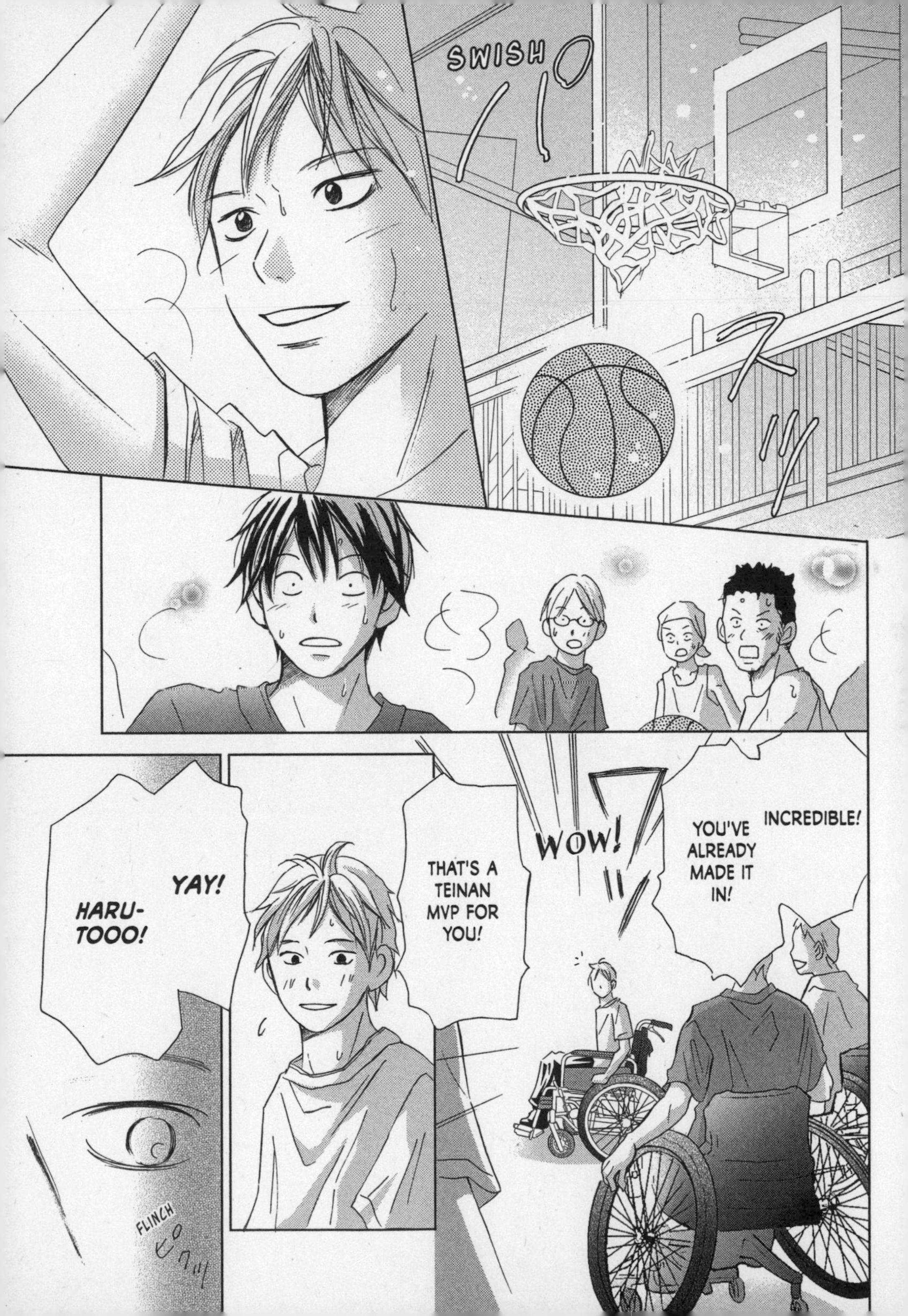
SWISH
INCREDIBLE!
YOU'VE ALREADY MADE IT IN!
WOW!
THAT'S A TEINAN MVP FOR YOU!
YAY!
HARU-TOOO!
FLINCH

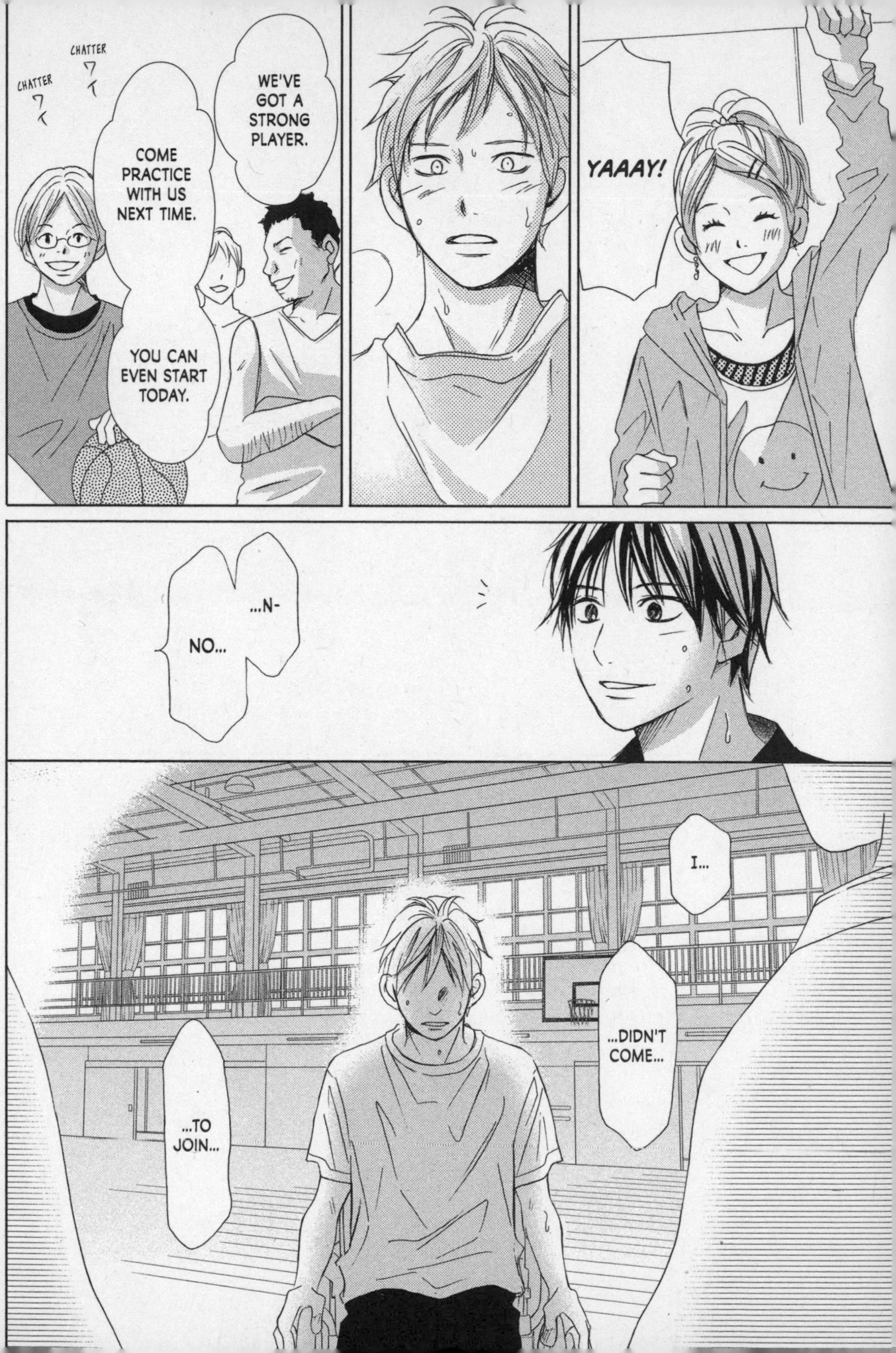
YAAAY!
WE'VE GOT A STRONG PLAYER.
COME PRACTICE WITH US NEXT TIME.
YOU CAN EVEN START TODAY.
CHATTER ワイ
CHATTER ワイ
...N- NO...
I...
...DIDN'T COME...
...TO JOIN...

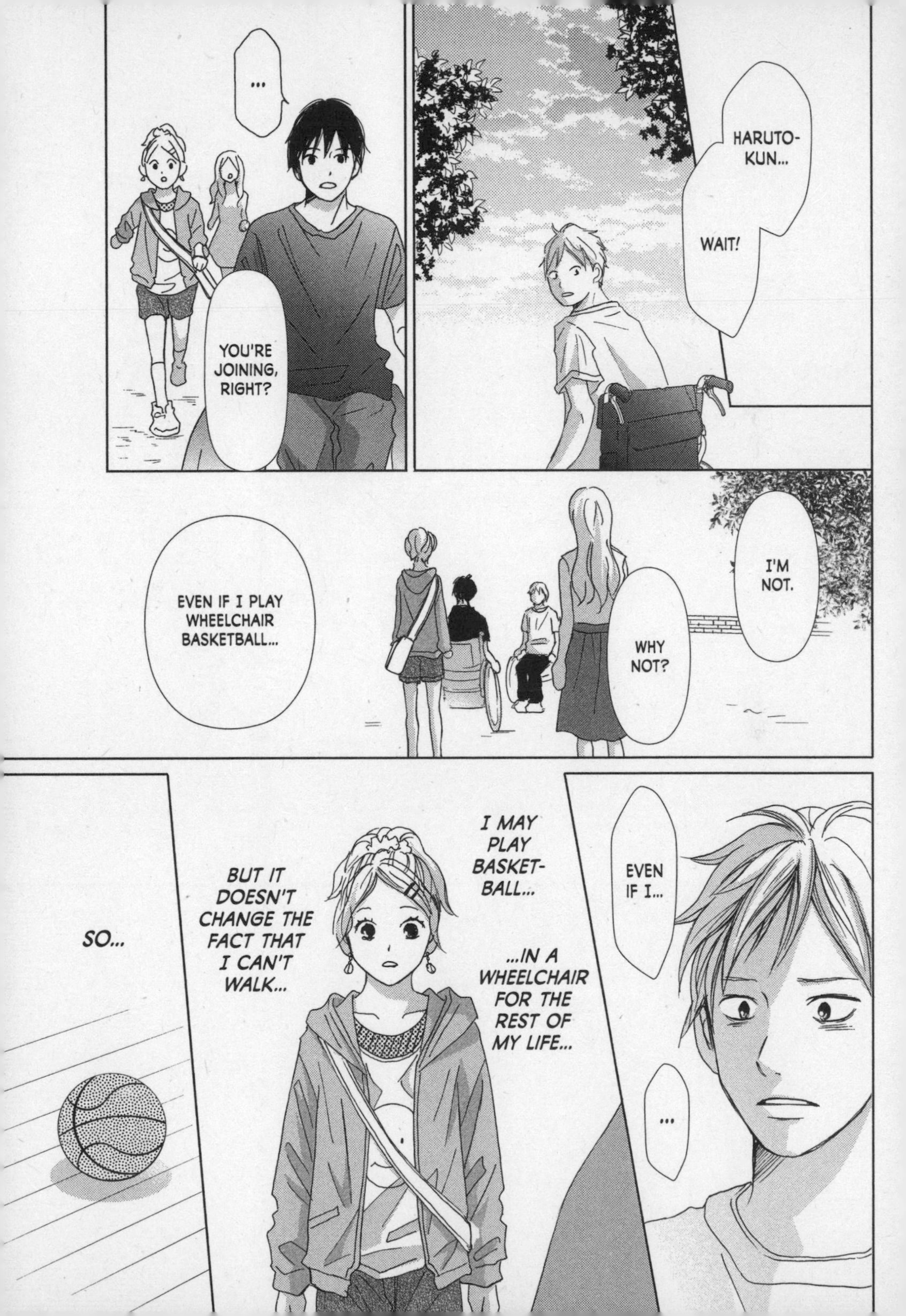
HARUTO-KUN...
WAIT!
...
YOU'RE JOINING, RIGHT?
I'M NOT.
WHY NOT?
EVEN IF I PLAY WHEELCHAIR BASKETBALL...
EVEN IF I...
I MAY PLAY BASKET-BALL...
...
...IN A WHEELCHAIR FOR THE REST OF MY LIFE...
BUT IT DOESN'T CHANGE THE FACT THAT I CAN'T WALK...
SO...

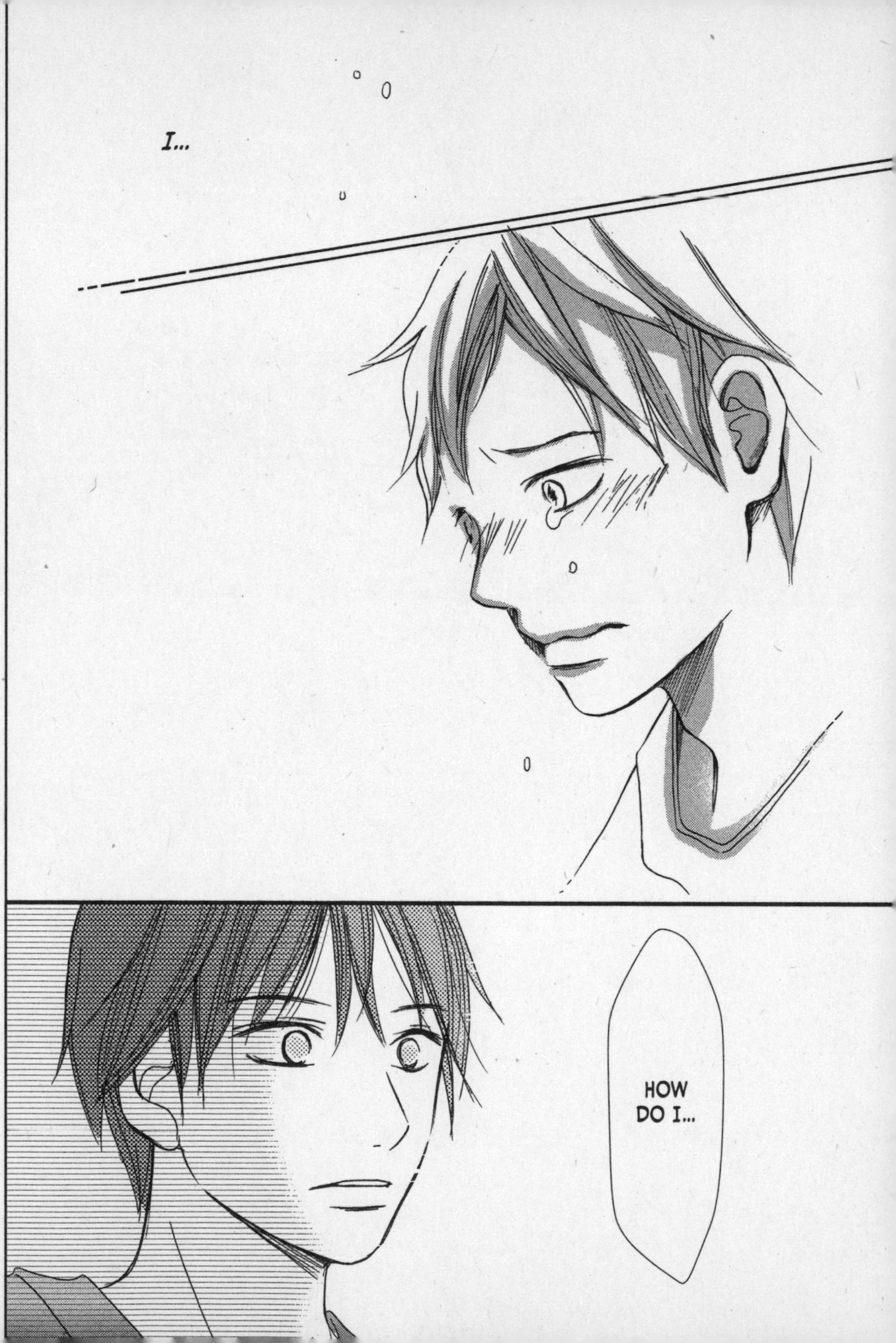

I...
HOW DO I...

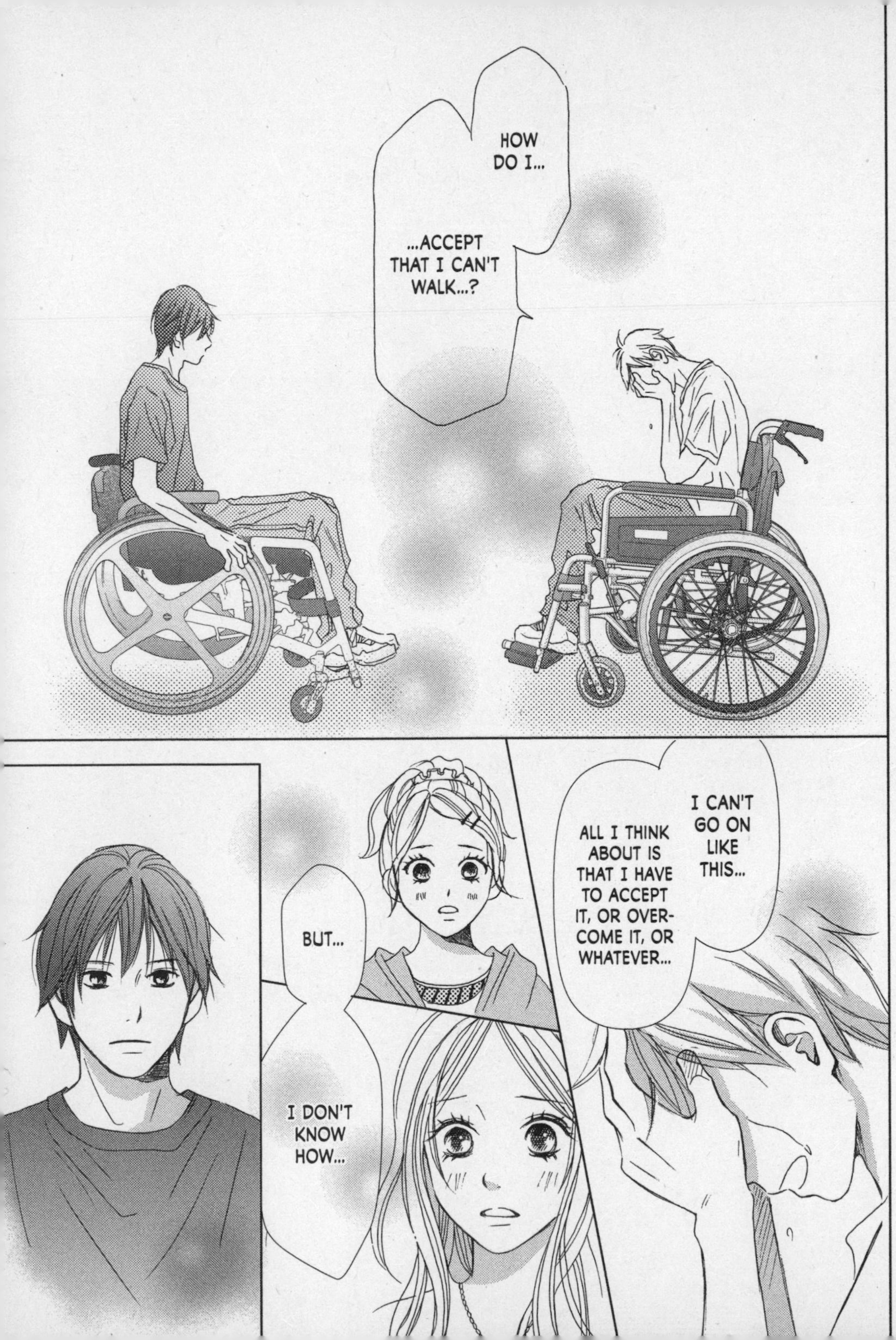
HOW DO I...
...ACCEPT THAT I CAN'T WALK...?
I CAN'T GO ON LIKE THIS...
ALL I THINK ABOUT IS THAT I HAVE TO ACCEPT IT, OR OVER-COME IT, OR WHATEVER...
BUT...
I DON'T KNOW HOW...

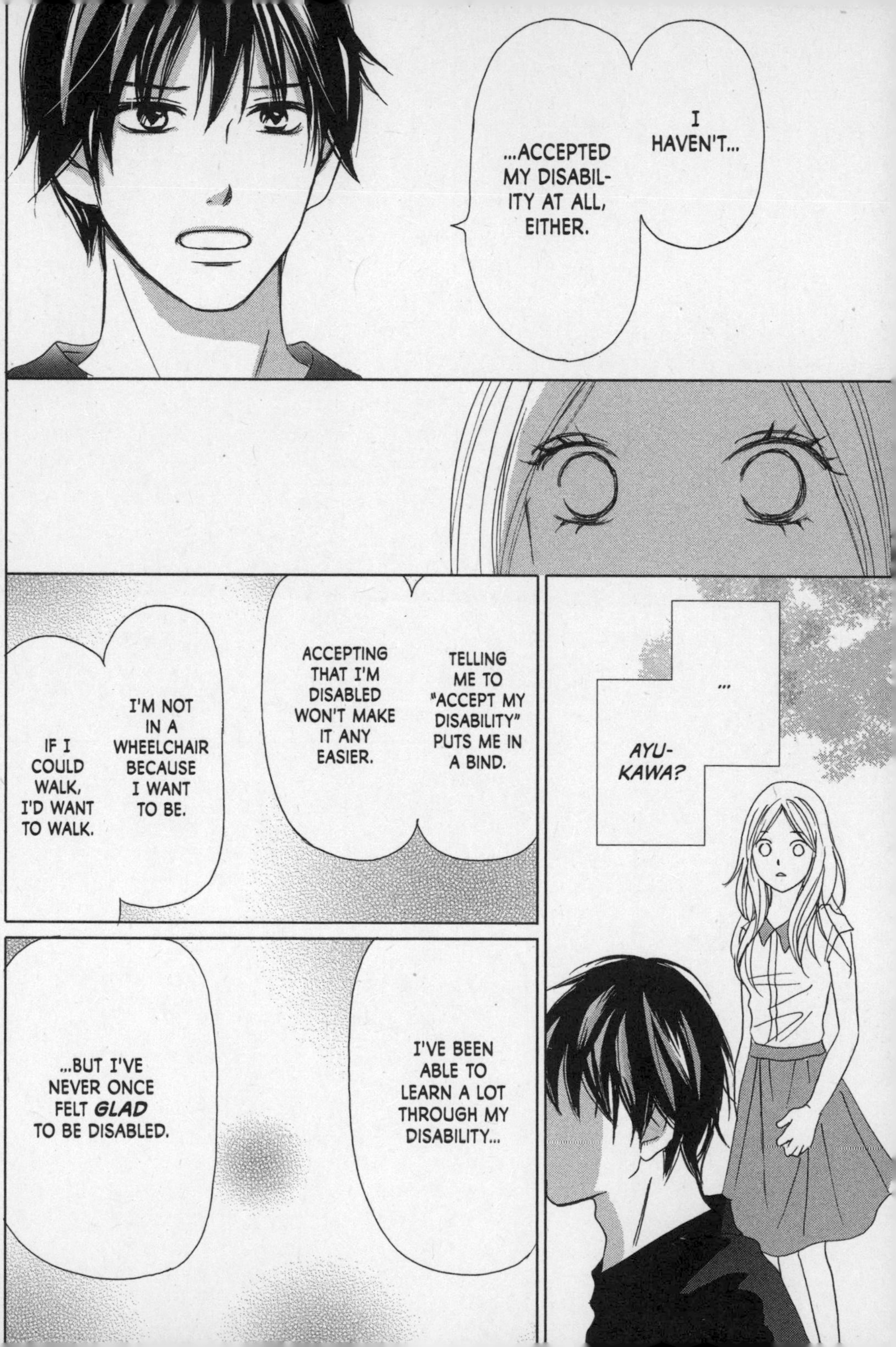

I HAVEN'T...
...ACCEPTED MY DISABIL-ITY AT ALL, EITHER.
...
AYU-KAWA?
TELLING ME TO "ACCEPT MY DISABILITY" PUTS ME IN A BIND.
ACCEPTING THAT I'M DISABLED WON'T MAKE IT ANY EASIER.
I'M NOT IN A WHEELCHAIR BECAUSE I WANT TO BE.
IF I COULD WALK, I'D WANT TO WALK.
I'VE BEEN ABLE TO LEARN A LOT THROUGH MY DISABILITY...
...BUT I'VE NEVER ONCE FELT *GLAD* TO BE DISABLED.

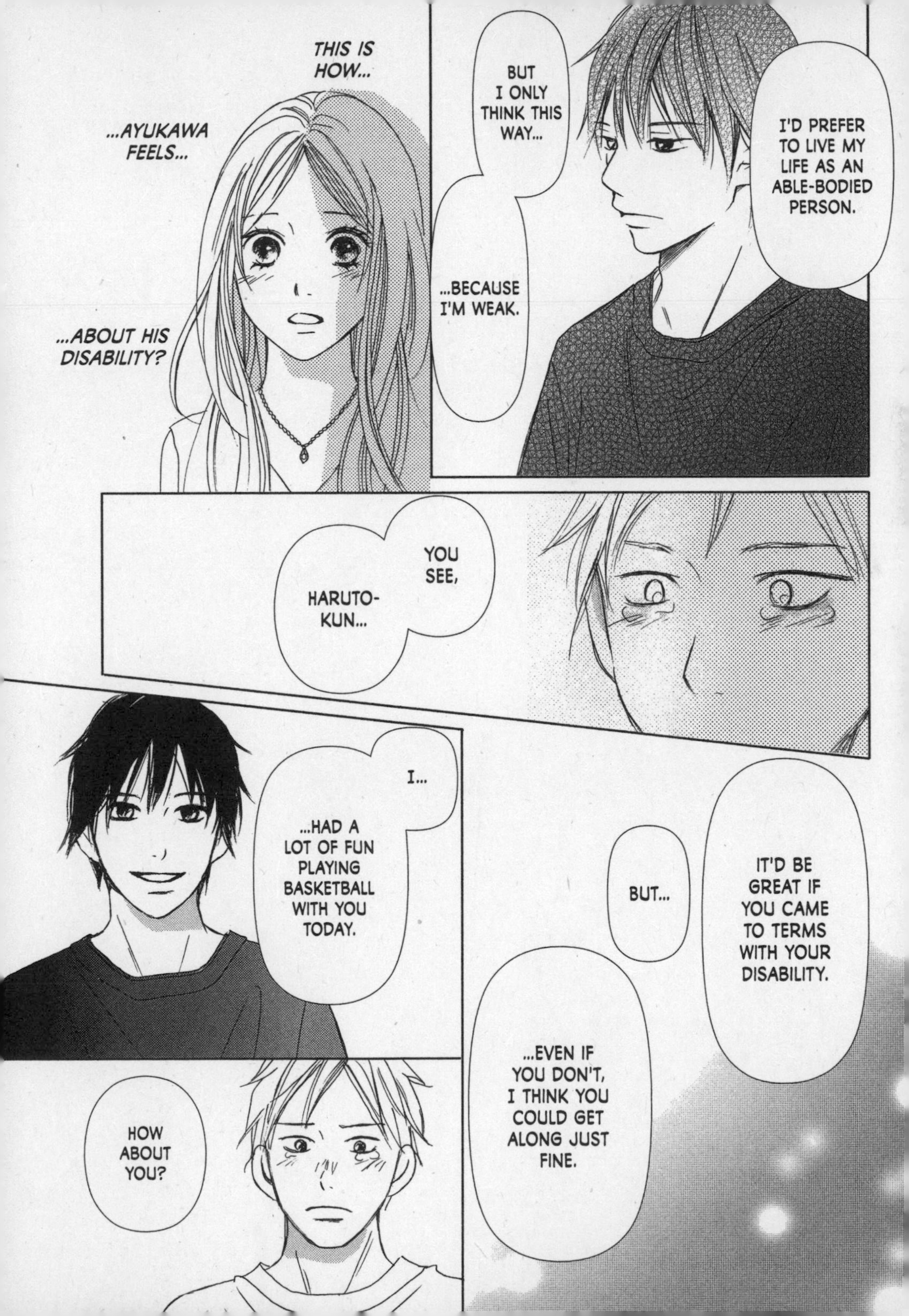
I'D PREFER TO LIVE MY LIFE AS AN ABLE-BODIED PERSON.
BUT I ONLY THINK THIS WAY...
...BECAUSE I'M WEAK.
THIS IS HOW...
...AYUKAWA FEELS...
...ABOUT HIS DISABILITY?
YOU SEE, HARUTO-KUN...
IT'D BE GREAT IF YOU CAME TO TERMS WITH YOUR DISABILITY.
BUT...
...EVEN IF YOU DON'T, I THINK YOU COULD GET ALONG JUST FINE.
I...
...HAD A LOT OF FUN PLAYING BASKETBALL WITH YOU TODAY.
HOW ABOUT YOU?

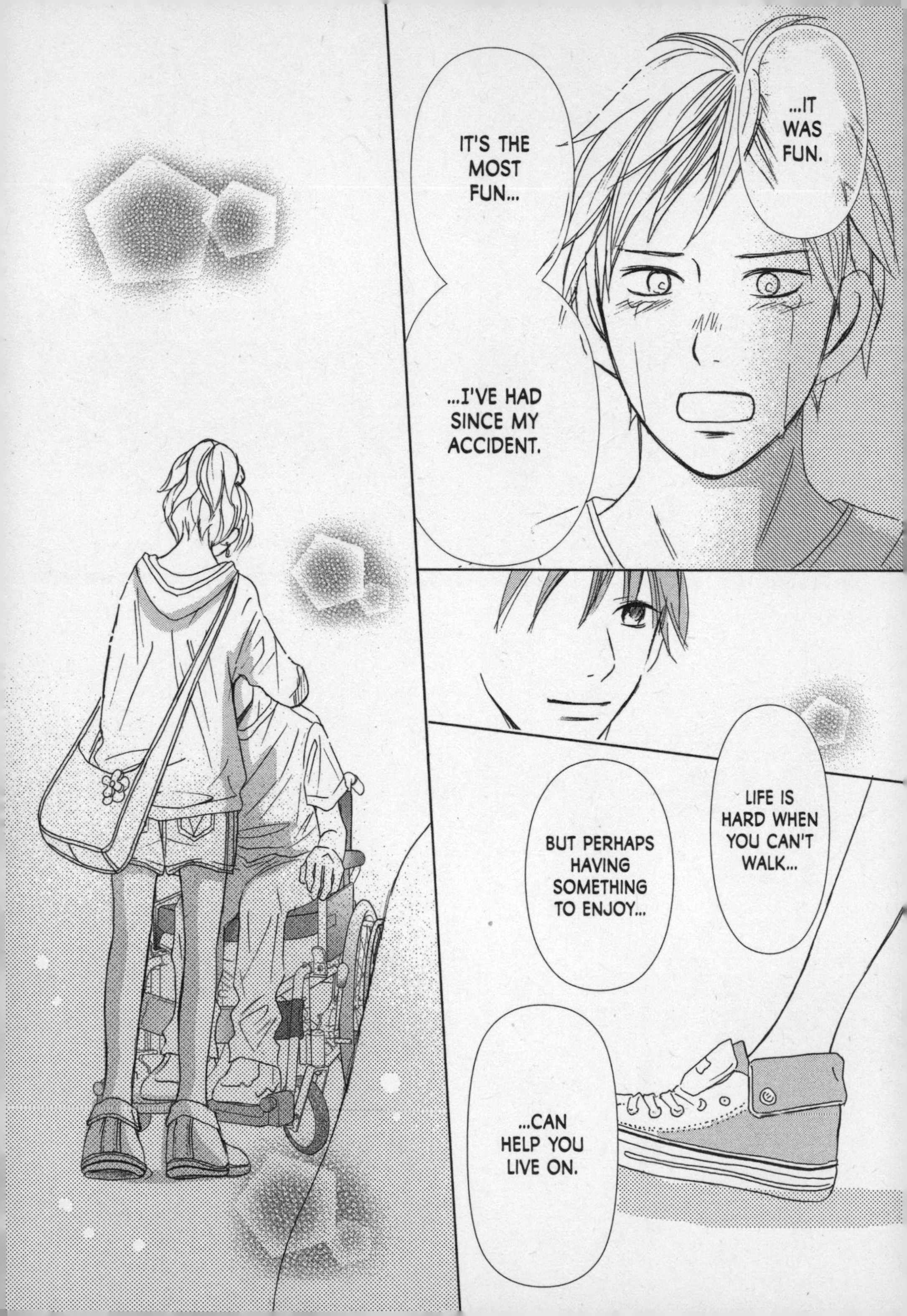
...IT WAS FUN.
IT'S THE MOST FUN...
...I'VE HAD SINCE MY ACCIDENT.
LIFE IS HARD WHEN YOU CAN'T WALK...
BUT PERHAPS HAVING SOMETHING TO ENJOY...
...CAN HELP YOU LIVE ON.

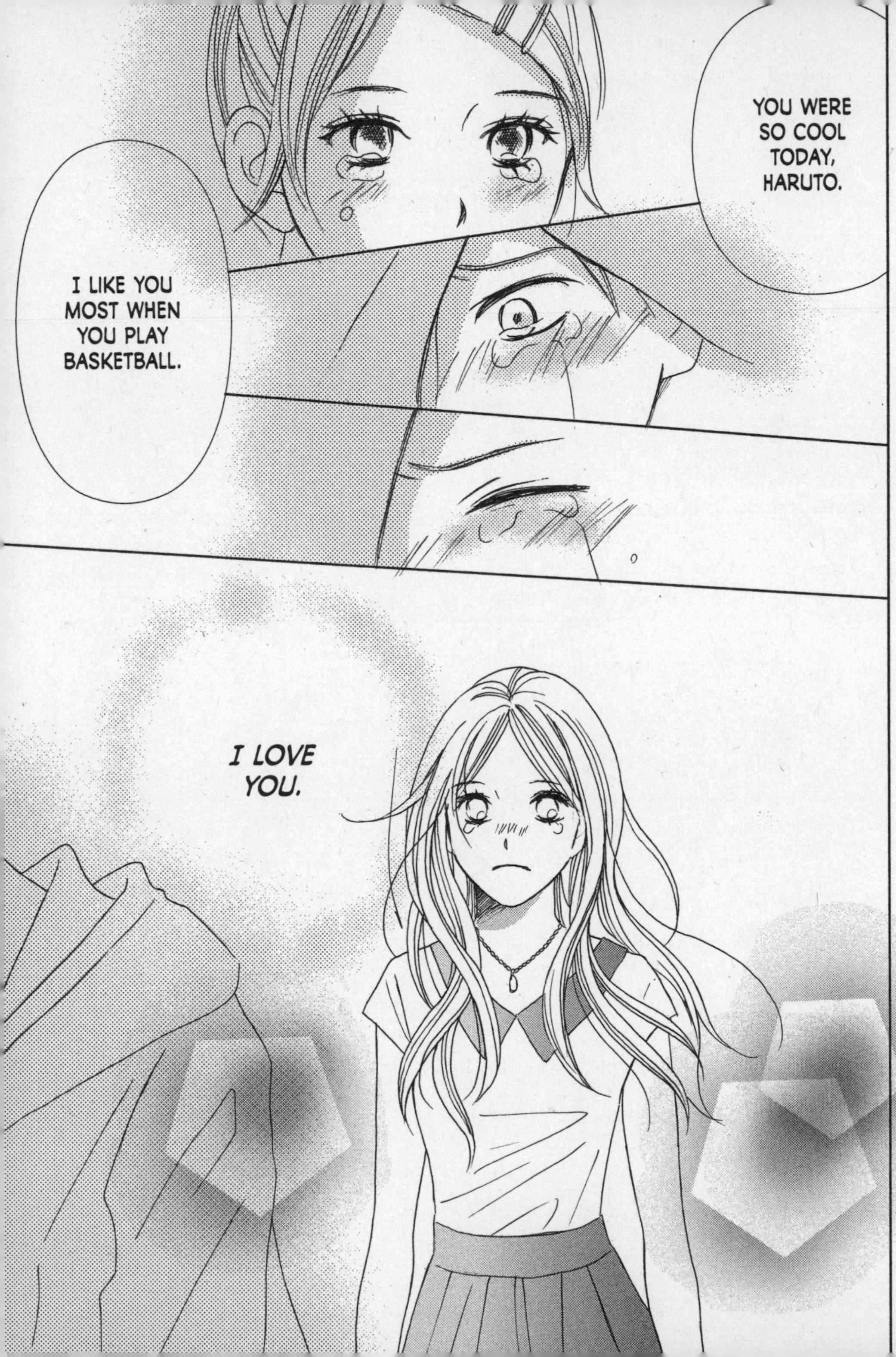
YOU WERE SO COOL TODAY, HARUTO.
I LIKE YOU MOST WHEN YOU PLAY BASKETBALL.
I LOVE YOU.

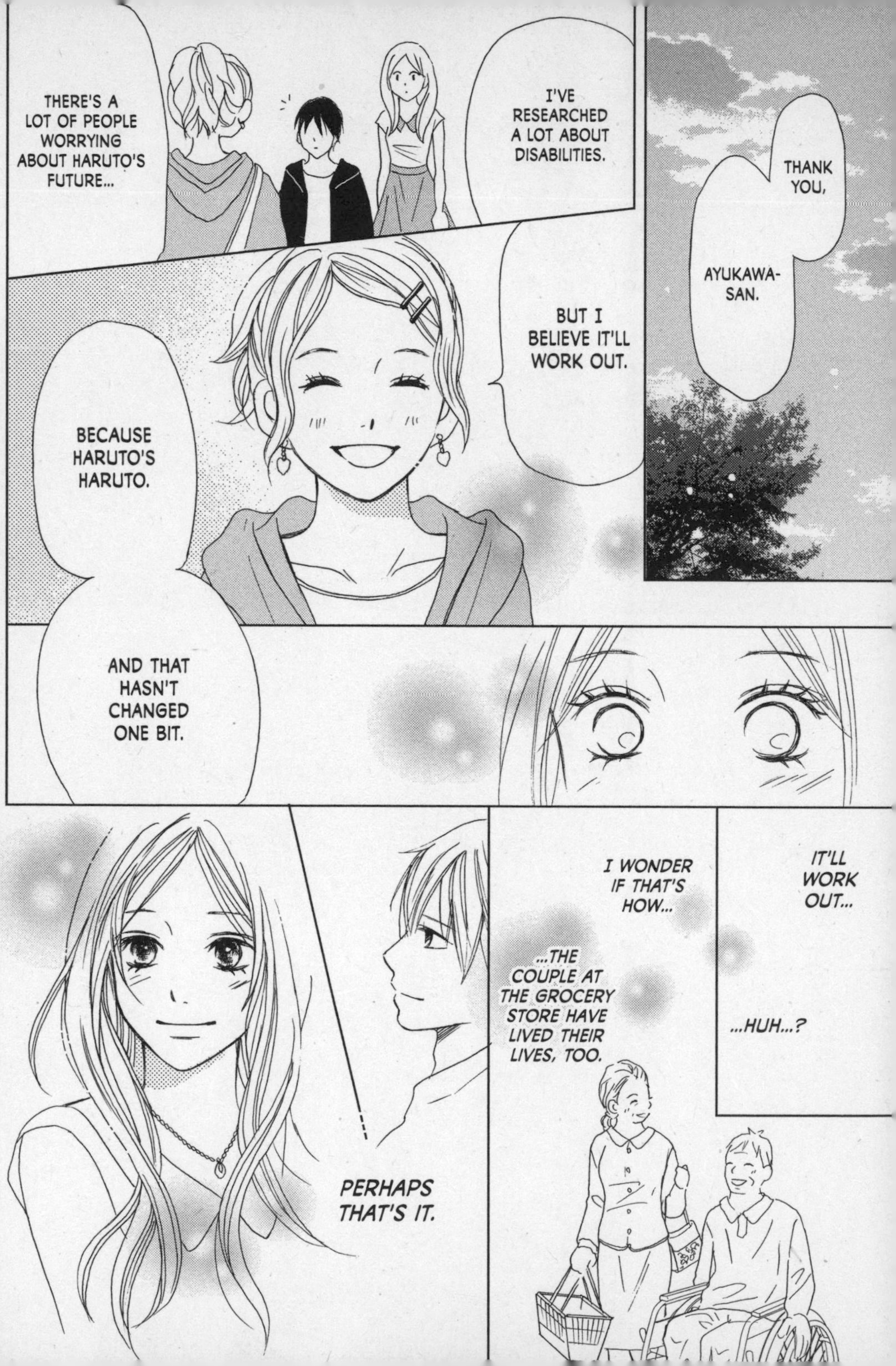
THANK YOU,
AYUKAWA-SAN.
I'VE RESEARCHED A LOT ABOUT DISABILITIES.
THERE'S A LOT OF PEOPLE WORRYING ABOUT HARUTO'S FUTURE...
BUT I BELIEVE IT'LL WORK OUT.
BECAUSE HARUTO'S HARUTO.
AND THAT HASN'T CHANGED ONE BIT.
IT'LL WORK OUT...
...HUH...?
I WONDER IF THAT'S HOW...
...THE COUPLE AT THE GROCERY STORE HAVE LIVED THEIR LIVES, TOO.
PERHAPS THAT'S IT.

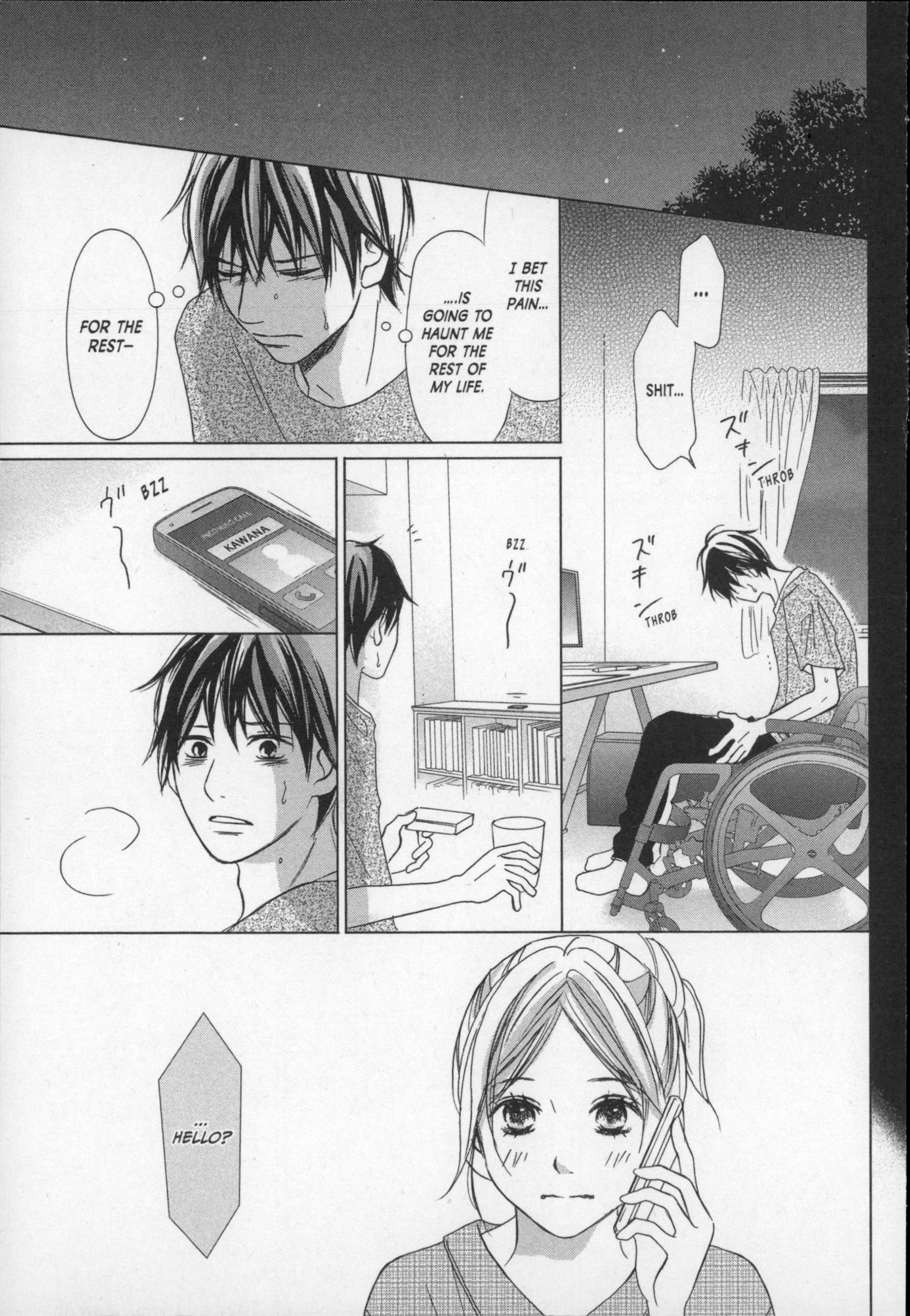
...
SHIT...
ズキン THROB
ズキン THROB
I BET THIS PAIN...
....IS GOING TO HAUNT ME FOR THE REST OF MY LIFE.
FOR THE REST–
ヴ BZZ
ヴ BZZ
KAWANA
...HELLO?

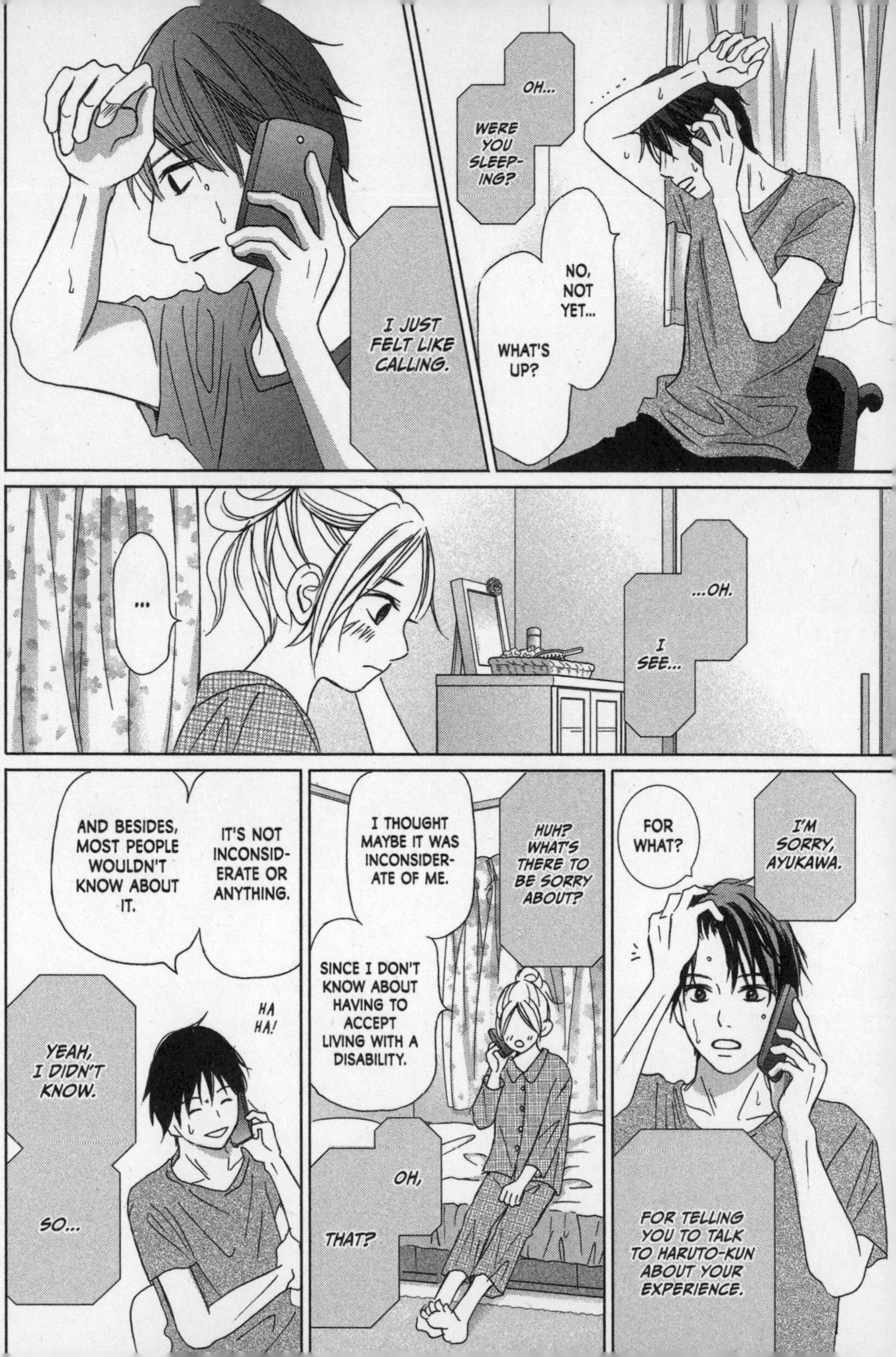
OH...
WERE YOU SLEEPING?
NO, NOT YET...
WHAT'S UP?
I JUST FELT LIKE CALLING.
...OH.
I SEE...
...
I'M SORRY, AYUKAWA.
FOR WHAT?
FOR TELLING YOU TO TALK TO HARUTO-KUN ABOUT YOUR EXPERIENCE.
HUH? WHAT'S THERE TO BE SORRY ABOUT?
I THOUGHT MAYBE IT WAS INCONSIDERATE OF ME.
SINCE I DON'T KNOW ABOUT HAVING TO ACCEPT LIVING WITH A DISABILITY.
OH,
THAT?
IT'S NOT INCONSIDERATE OR ANYTHING.
AND BESIDES, MOST PEOPLE WOULDN'T KNOW ABOUT IT.
HA HA!
YEAH, I DIDN'T KNOW.
SO...

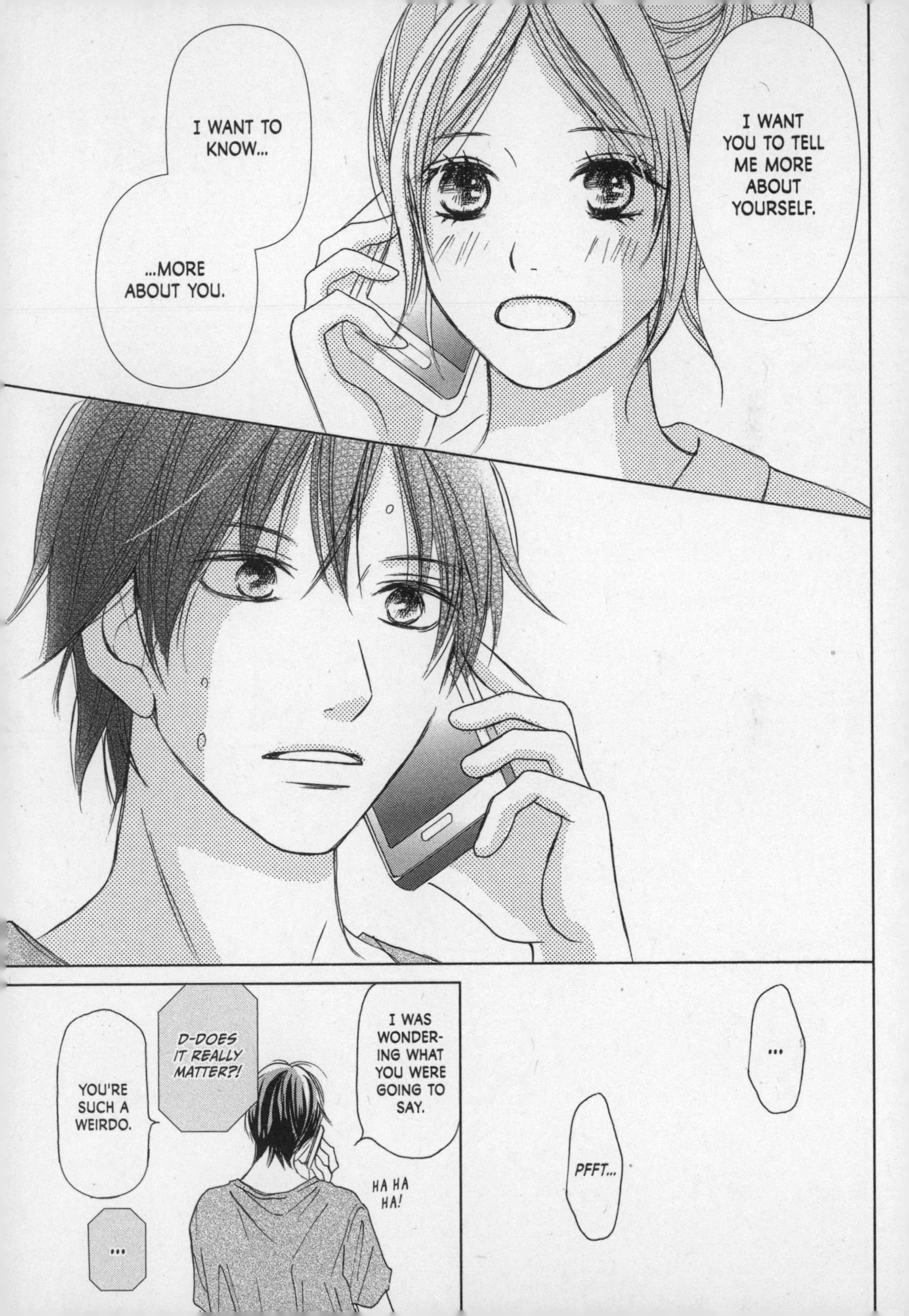
I WANT YOU TO TELL ME MORE ABOUT YOURSELF.
I WANT TO KNOW...
...MORE ABOUT YOU.
...
PFFT...
I WAS WONDERING WHAT YOU WERE GOING TO SAY.
HA HA HA!
D-DOES IT REALLY MATTER?!
YOU'RE SUCH A WEIRDO.
...

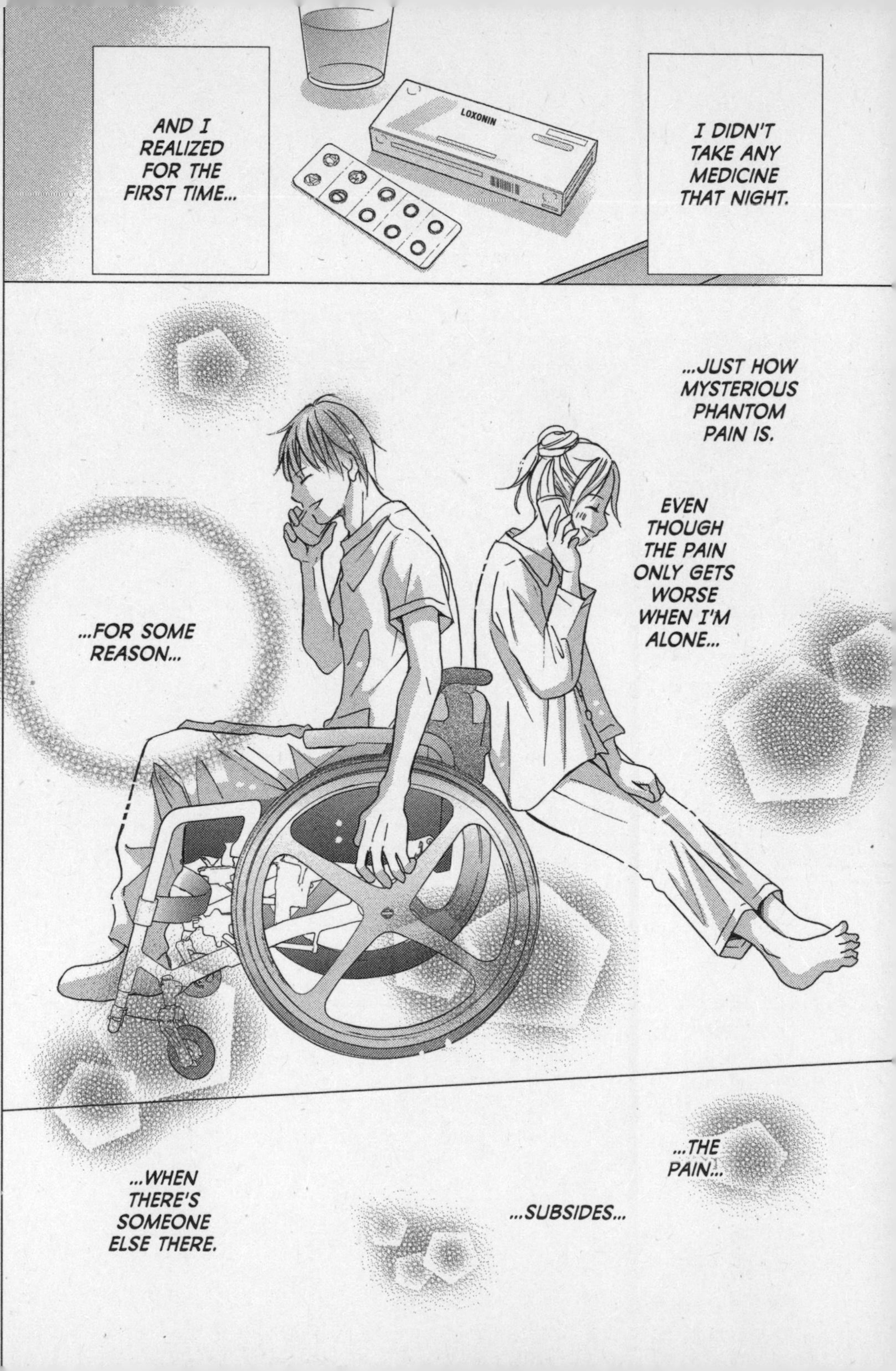
I DIDN'T TAKE ANY MEDICINE THAT NIGHT.
LOXONIN
AND I REALIZED FOR THE FIRST TIME...
...JUST HOW MYSTERIOUS PHANTOM PAIN IS.
EVEN THOUGH THE PAIN ONLY GETS WORSE WHEN I'M ALONE...
...FOR SOME REASON...
...THE PAIN...
...SUBSIDES...
...WHEN THERE'S SOMEONE ELSE THERE.

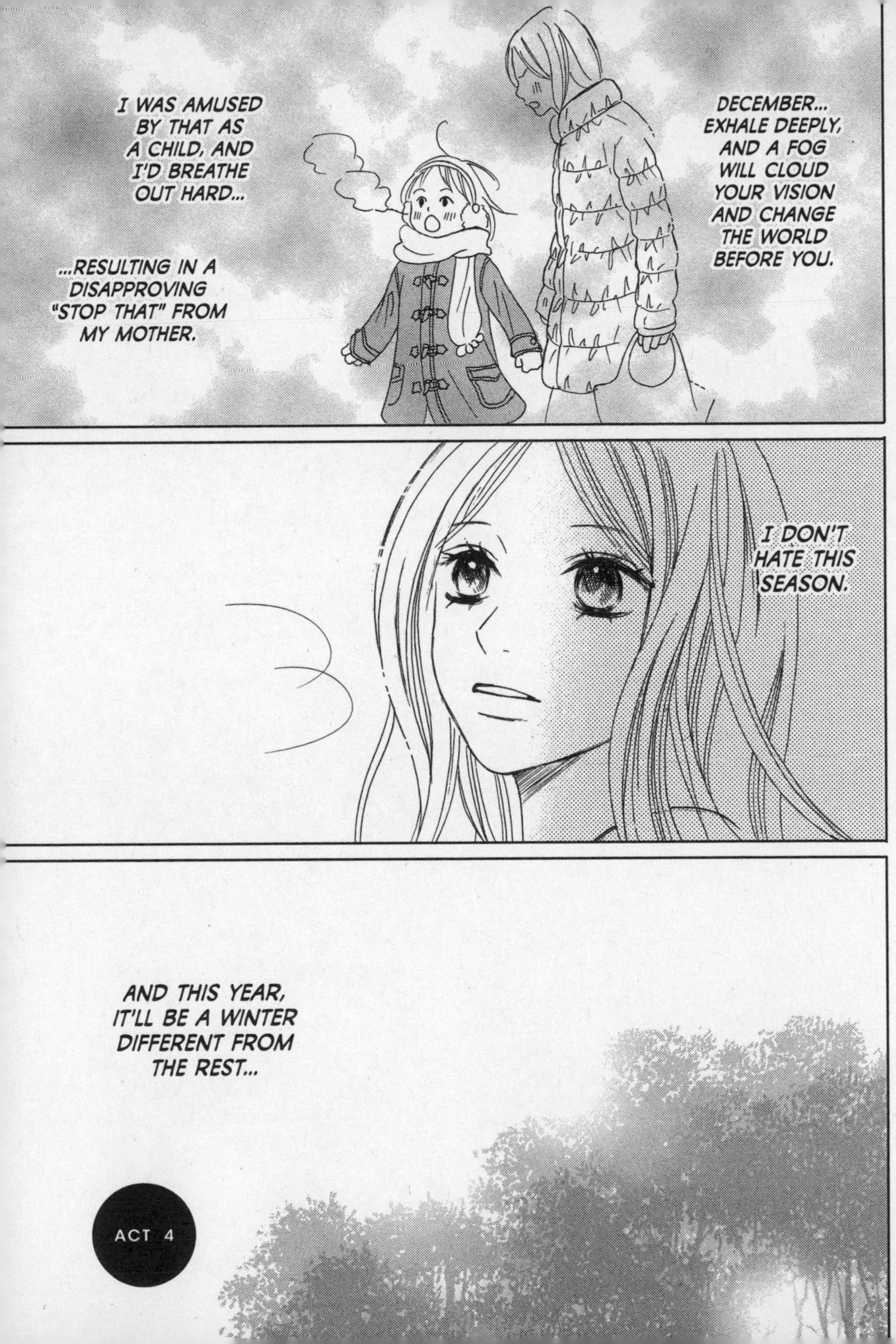
DECEMBER... EXHALE DEEPLY, AND A FOG WILL CLOUD YOUR VISION AND CHANGE THE WORLD BEFORE YOU.
I WAS AMUSED BY THAT AS A CHILD, AND I'D BREATHE OUT HARD...
...RESULTING IN A DISAPPROVING "STOP THAT" FROM MY MOTHER.
I DON'T HATE THIS SEASON.
AND THIS YEAR, IT'LL BE A WINTER DIFFERENT FROM THE REST...
ACT 4

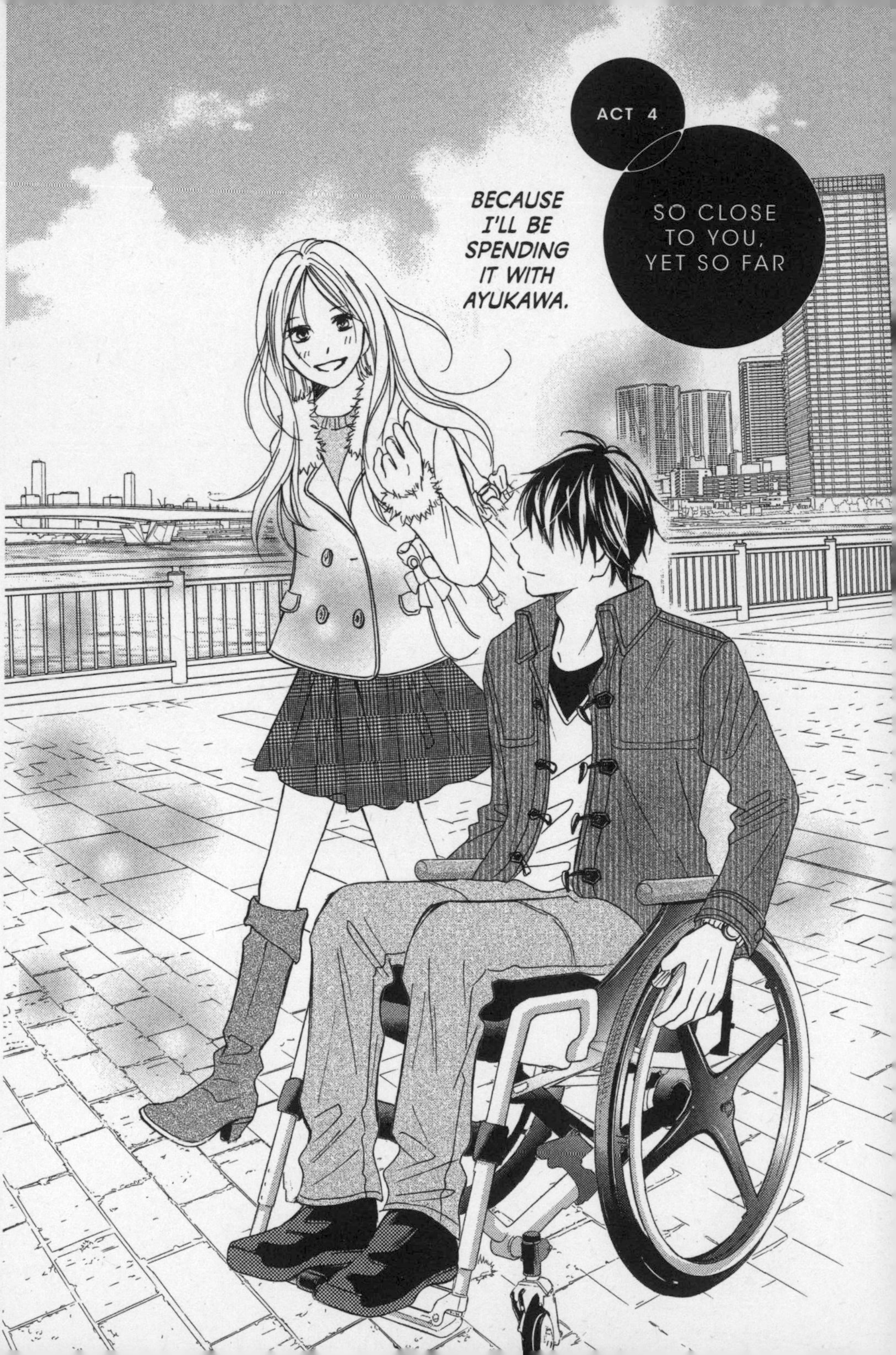
ACT 4
SO CLOSE TO YOU, YET SO FAR
BECAUSE I'LL BE SPENDING IT WITH AYUKAWA.

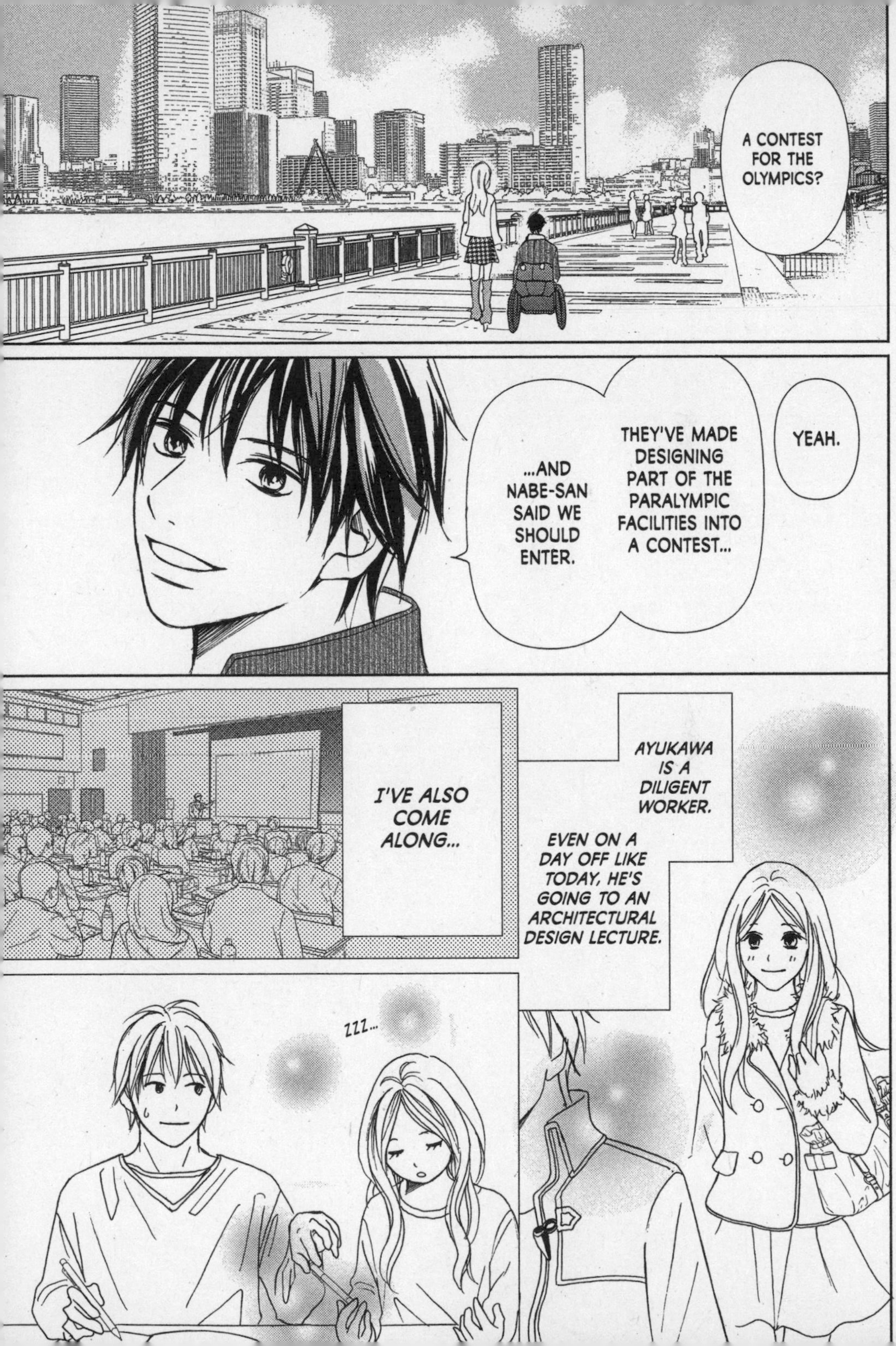
A CONTEST FOR THE OLYMPICS?
YEAH.
THEY'VE MADE DESIGNING PART OF THE PARALYMPIC FACILITIES INTO A CONTEST...
...AND NABE-SAN SAID WE SHOULD ENTER.
AYUKAWA IS A DILIGENT WORKER.
EVEN ON A DAY OFF LIKE TODAY, HE'S GOING TO AN ARCHITECTURAL DESIGN LECTURE.
I'VE ALSO COME ALONG...
ZZZ...

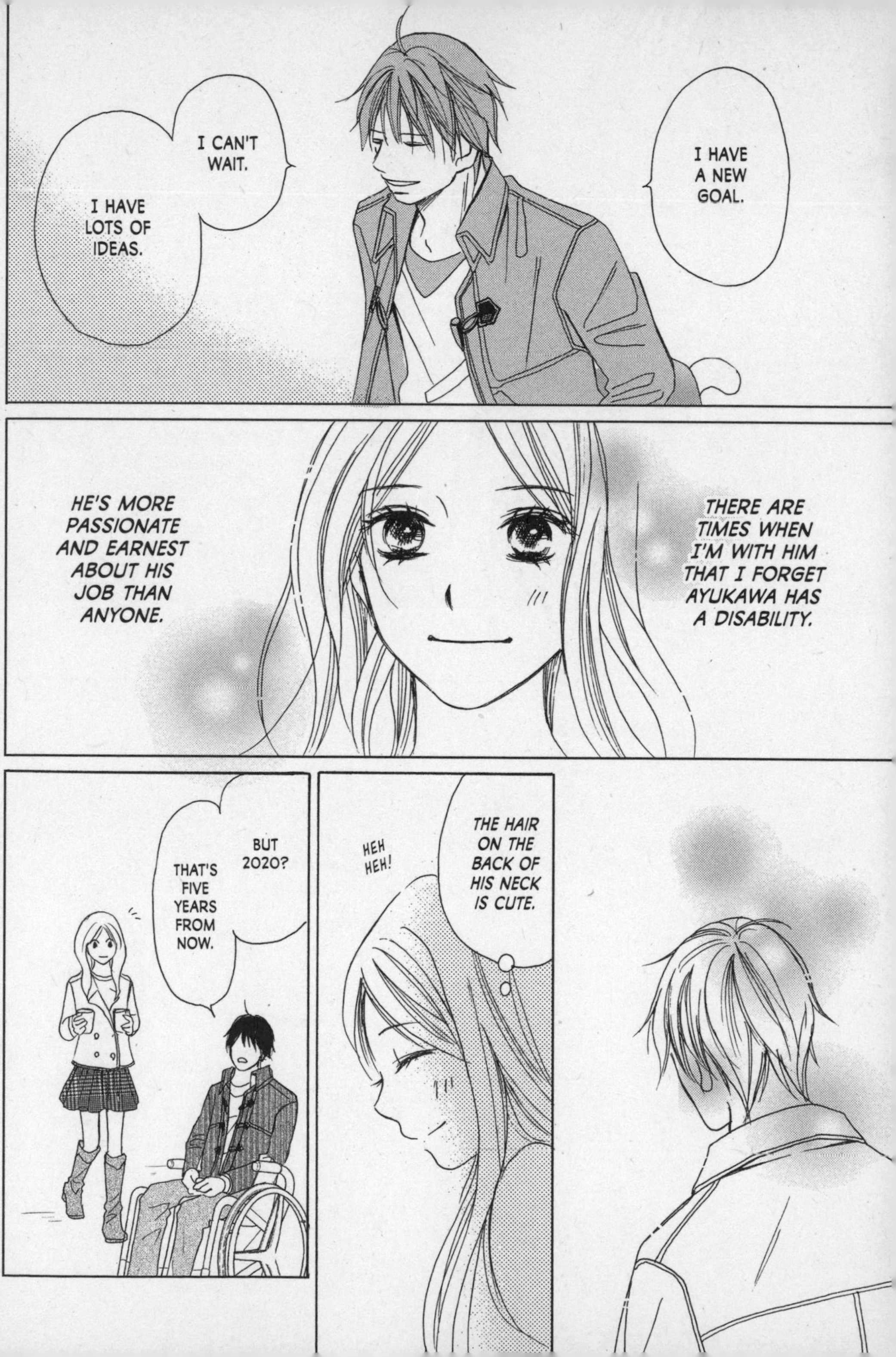
I HAVE A NEW GOAL.
I CAN'T WAIT.
I HAVE LOTS OF IDEAS.
THERE ARE TIMES WHEN I'M WITH HIM THAT I FORGET AYUKAWA HAS A DISABILITY.
HE'S MORE PASSIONATE AND EARNEST ABOUT HIS JOB THAN ANYONE.
THE HAIR ON THE BACK OF HIS NECK IS CUTE.
HEH HEH!
BUT 2020?
THAT'S FIVE YEARS FROM NOW.

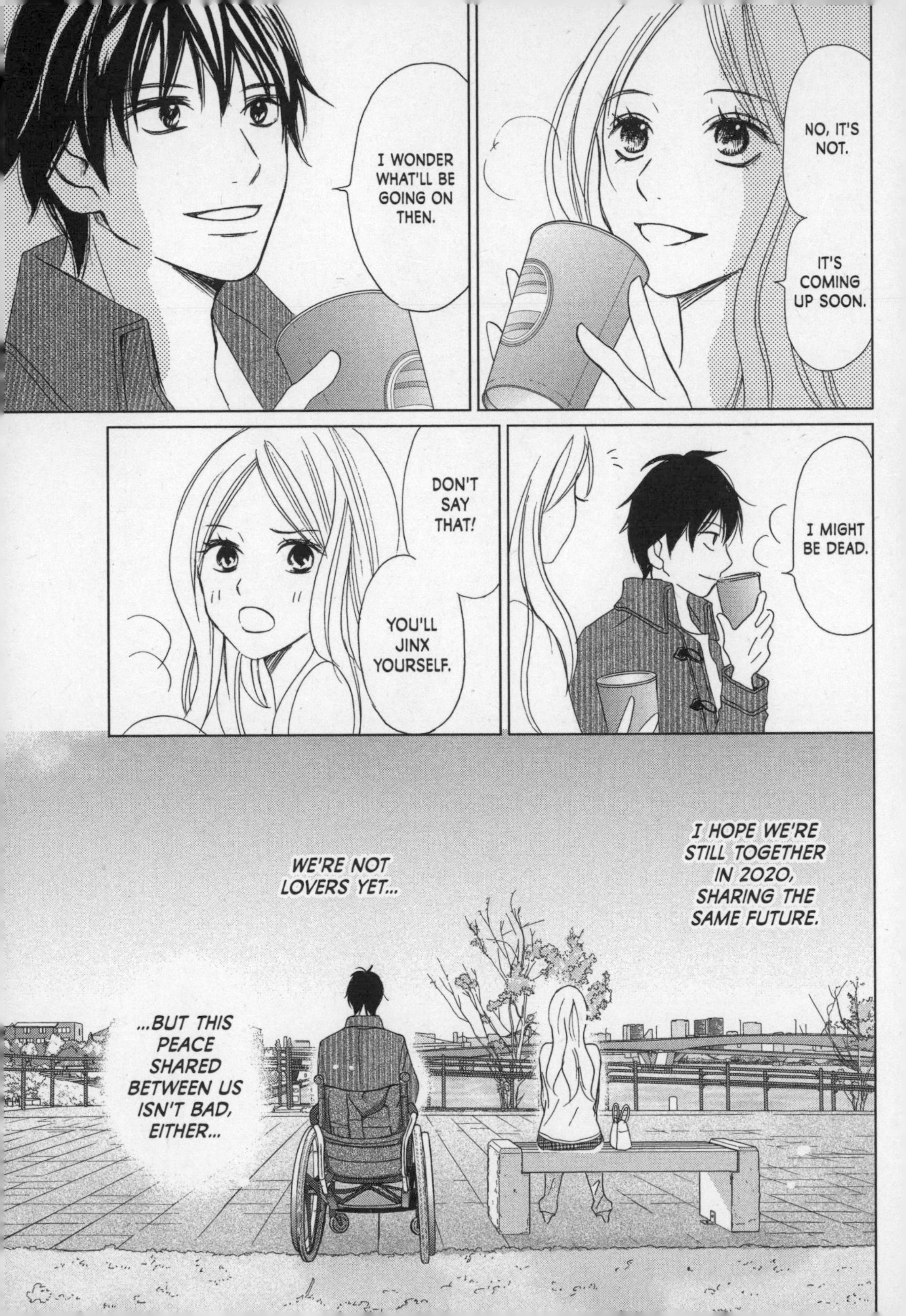
NO, IT'S NOT.
IT'S COMING UP SOON.
I WONDER WHAT'LL BE GOING ON THEN.
I MIGHT BE DEAD.
DON'T SAY THAT!
YOU'LL JINX YOURSELF.
I HOPE WE'RE STILL TOGETHER IN 2020, SHARING THE SAME FUTURE.
WE'RE NOT LOVERS YET...
...BUT THIS PEACE SHARED BETWEEN US ISN'T BAD, EITHER...

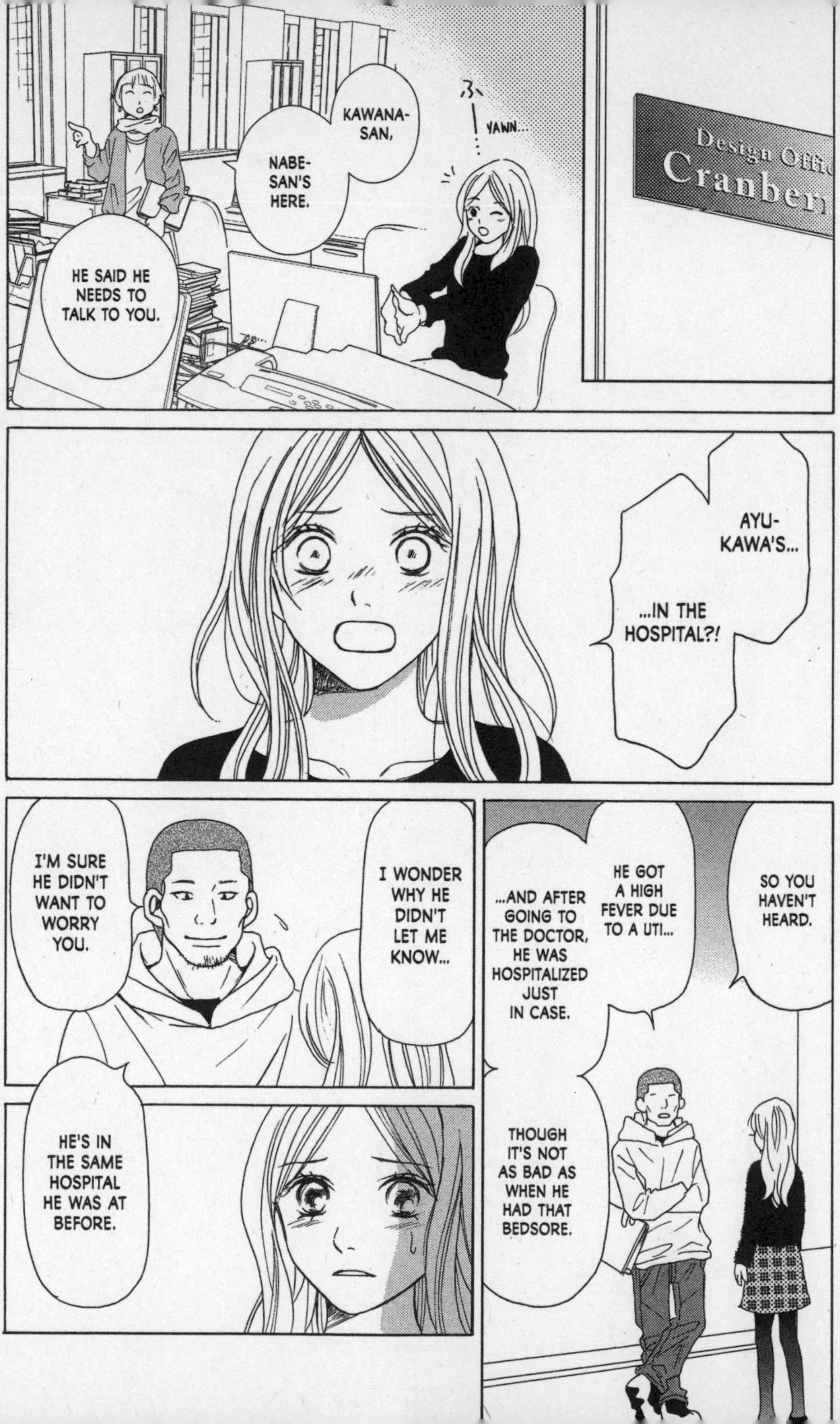
Design Offic
Cranber
ふ
YAWN...
KAWANA-SAN, NABE-SAN'S HERE.
HE SAID HE NEEDS TO TALK TO YOU.
AYU-KAWA'S...
...IN THE HOSPITAL?!
SO YOU HAVEN'T HEARD.
HE GOT A HIGH FEVER DUE TO A UTI...
...AND AFTER GOING TO THE DOCTOR, HE WAS HOSPITALIZED JUST IN CASE.
THOUGH IT'S NOT AS BAD AS WHEN HE HAD THAT BEDSORE.
I WONDER WHY HE DIDN'T LET ME KNOW...
I'M SURE HE DIDN'T WANT TO WORRY YOU.
HE'S IN THE SAME HOSPITAL HE WAS AT BEFORE.

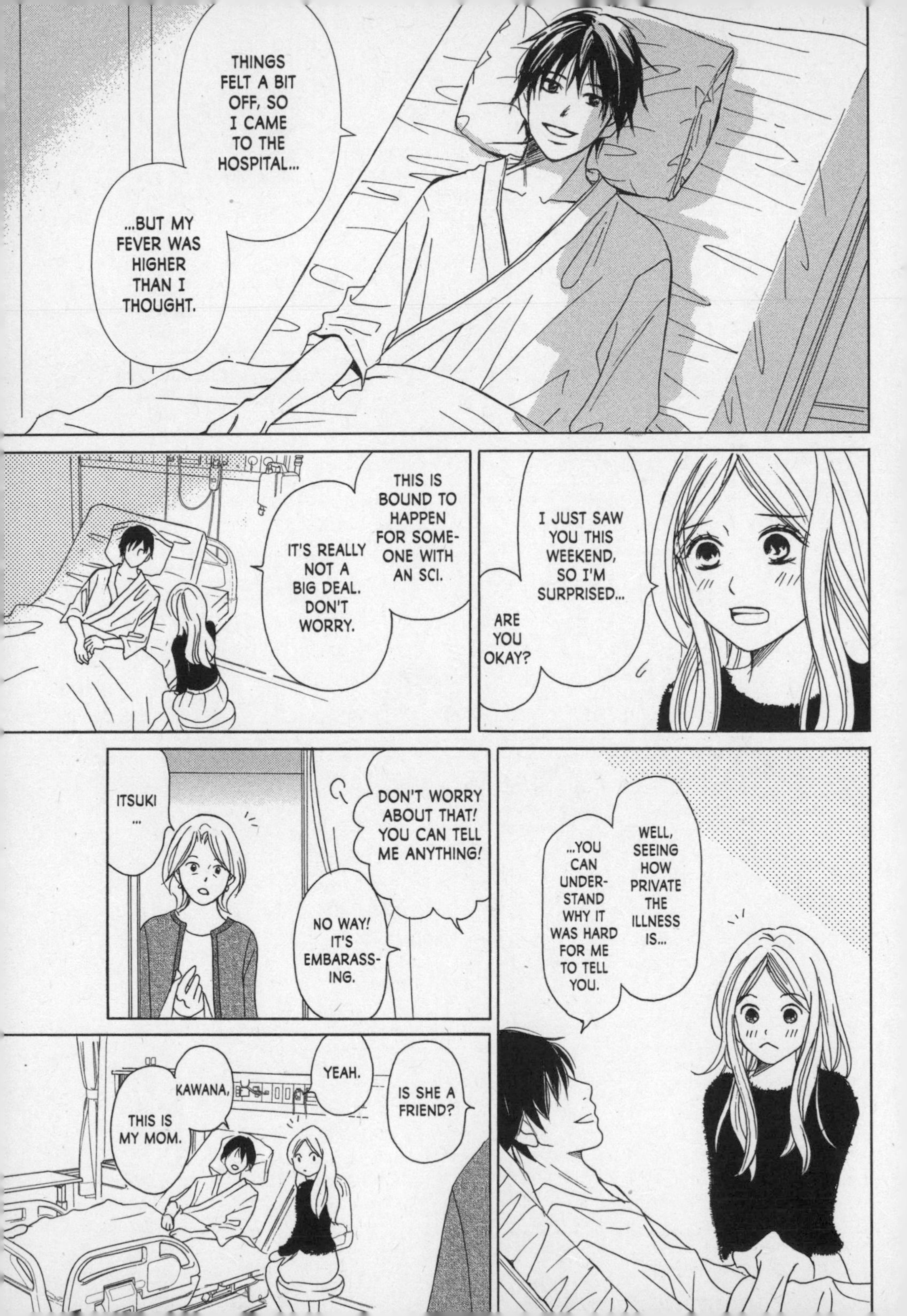
THINGS FELT A BIT OFF, SO I CAME TO THE HOSPITAL...
...BUT MY FEVER WAS HIGHER THAN I THOUGHT.
I JUST SAW YOU THIS WEEKEND, SO I'M SURPRISED...
ARE YOU OKAY?
THIS IS BOUND TO HAPPEN FOR SOME-ONE WITH AN SCI.
IT'S REALLY NOT A BIG DEAL. DON'T WORRY.
WELL, SEEING HOW PRIVATE THE ILLNESS IS...
...YOU CAN UNDER-STAND WHY IT WAS HARD FOR ME TO TELL YOU.
DON'T WORRY ABOUT THAT! YOU CAN TELL ME ANYTHING!
NO WAY! IT'S EMBARASS-ING.
ITSUKI ...
IS SHE A FRIEND?
YEAH.
KAWANA, THIS IS MY MOM.

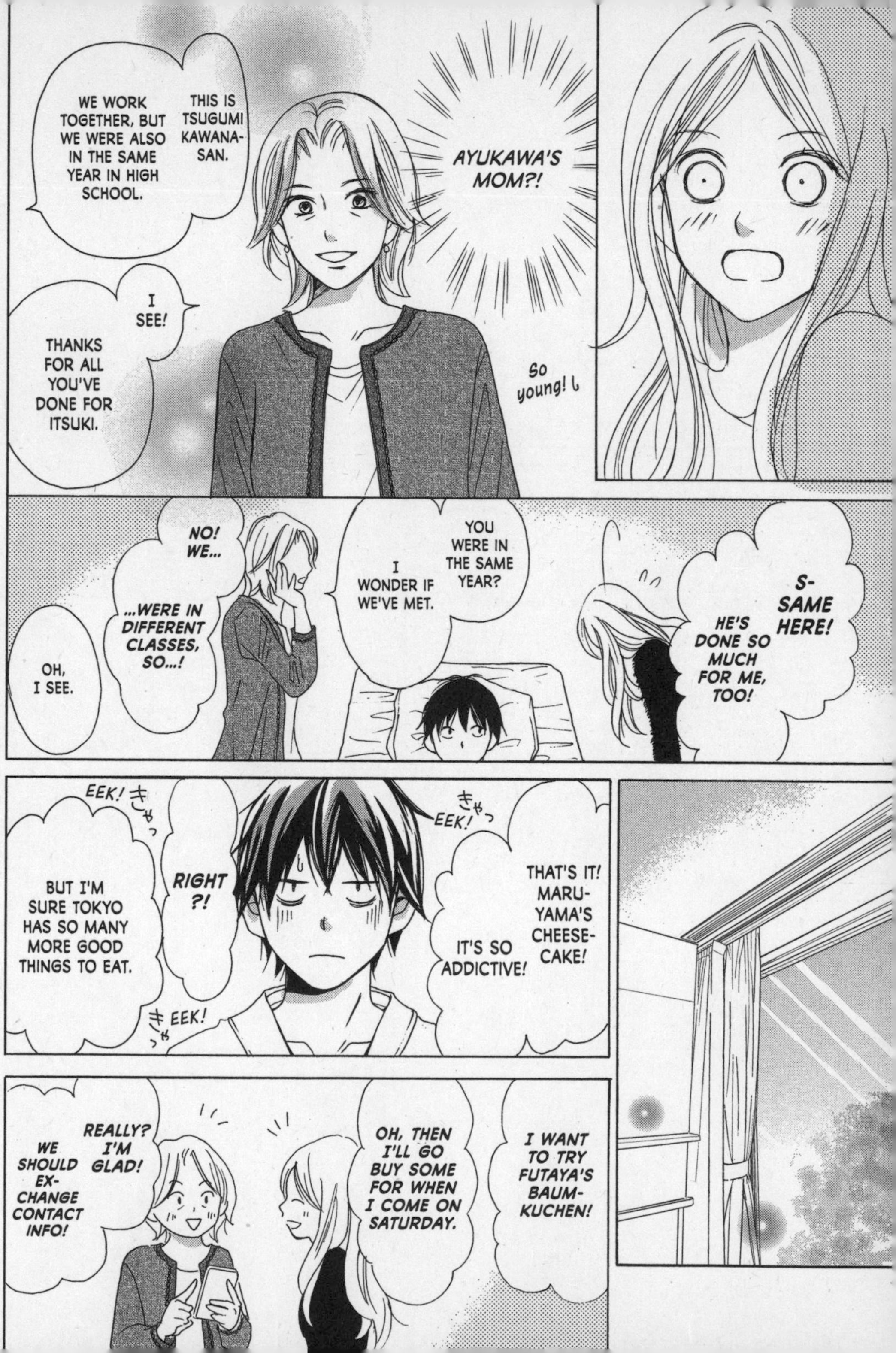
AYUKAWA'S MOM?!
THIS IS TSUGUMI KAWANA-SAN.
WE WORK TOGETHER, BUT WE WERE ALSO IN THE SAME YEAR IN HIGH SCHOOL.
So young!
I SEE!
THANKS FOR ALL YOU'VE DONE FOR ITSUKI.
S-SAME HERE!
HE'S DONE SO MUCH FOR ME, TOO!
YOU WERE IN THE SAME YEAR?
I WONDER IF WE'VE MET.
NO! WE...
...WERE IN DIFFERENT CLASSES, SO...!
OH, I SEE.
きゃっ EEK!
THAT'S IT! MARUYAMA'S CHEESE-CAKE!
IT'S SO ADDICTIVE!
RIGHT?!
EEK! きゃっ
BUT I'M SURE TOKYO HAS SO MANY MORE GOOD THINGS TO EAT.
きゃっ EEK!
I WANT TO TRY FUTAYA'S BAUM-KUCHEN!
OH, THEN I'LL GO BUY SOME FOR WHEN I COME ON SATURDAY.
REALLY? I'M GLAD!
WE SHOULD EX-CHANGE CONTACT INFO!

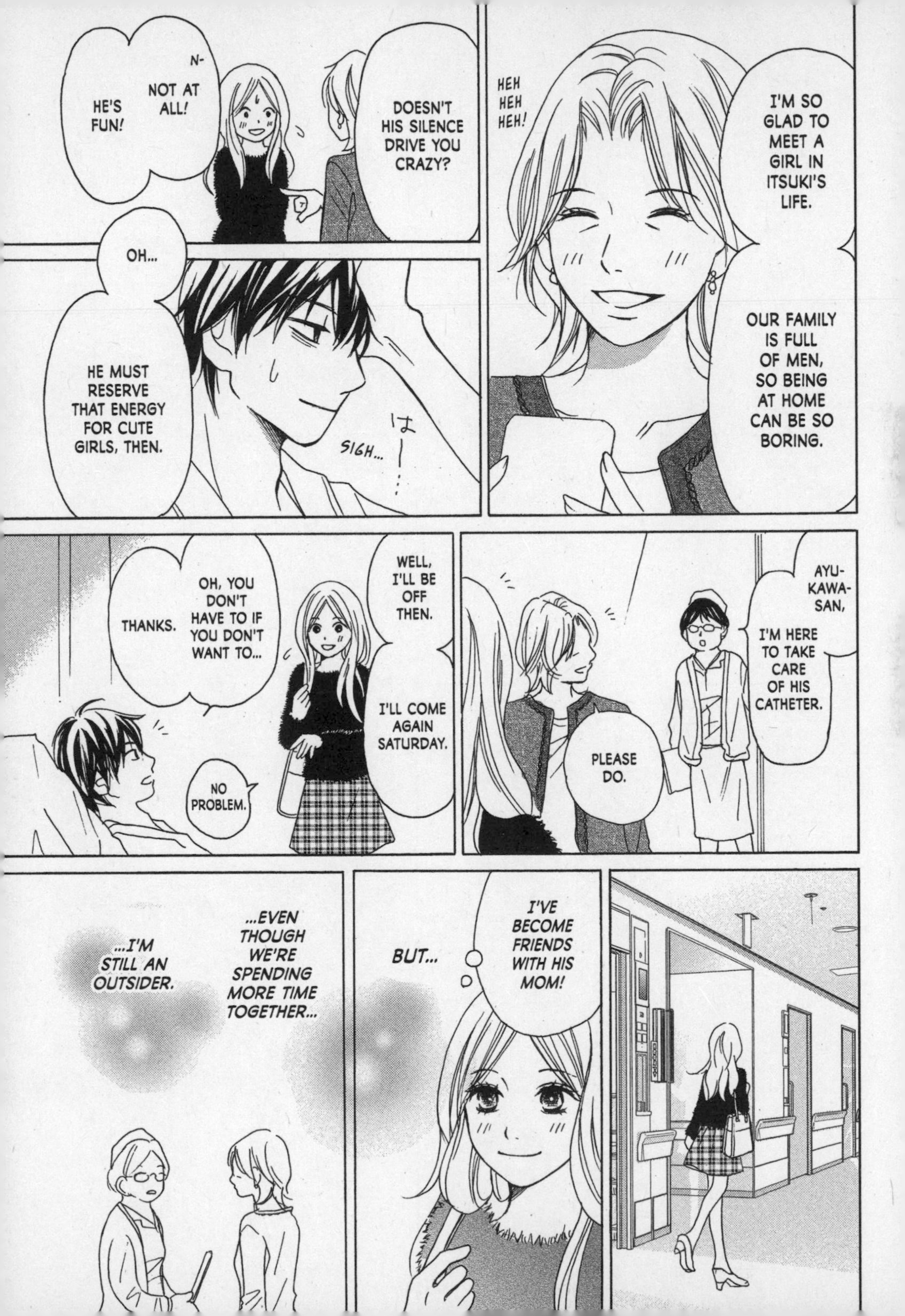
HEH HEH HEH!
I'M SO GLAD TO MEET A GIRL IN ITSUKI'S LIFE.
OUR FAMILY IS FULL OF MEN, SO BEING AT HOME CAN BE SO BORING.
DOESN'T HIS SILENCE DRIVE YOU CRAZY?
N- NOT AT ALL!
HE'S FUN!
OH...
HE MUST RESERVE THAT ENERGY FOR CUTE GIRLS, THEN.
は—…
SIGH...
AYU-KAWA-SAN,
I'M HERE TO TAKE CARE OF HIS CATHETER.
PLEASE DO.
WELL, I'LL BE OFF THEN.
I'LL COME AGAIN SATURDAY.
OH, YOU DON'T HAVE TO IF YOU DON'T WANT TO...
THANKS.
NO PROBLEM.
I'VE BECOME FRIENDS WITH HIS MOM!
BUT...
...EVEN THOUGH WE'RE SPENDING MORE TIME TOGETHER...
...I'M STILL AN OUTSIDER.

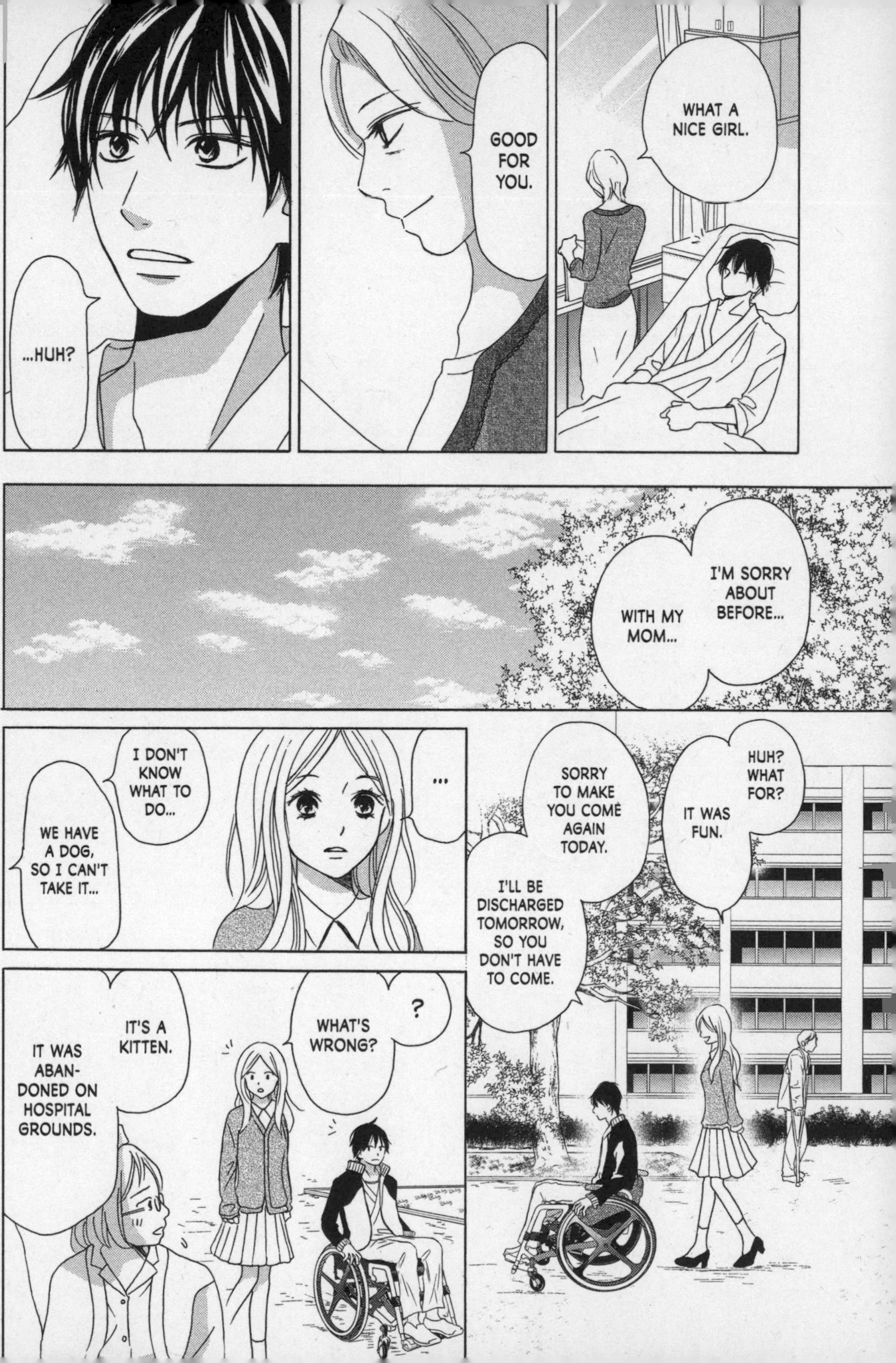
WHAT A NICE GIRL.
GOOD FOR YOU.
...HUH?
I'M SORRY ABOUT BEFORE...
WITH MY MOM...
SORRY TO MAKE YOU COME AGAIN TODAY.
HUH? WHAT FOR?
IT WAS FUN.
I'LL BE DISCHARGED TOMORROW, SO YOU DON'T HAVE TO COME.
...
I DON'T KNOW WHAT TO DO...
WE HAVE A DOG, SO I CAN'T TAKE IT...
?
WHAT'S WRONG?
IT'S A KITTEN.
IT WAS ABANDONED ON HOSPITAL GROUNDS.

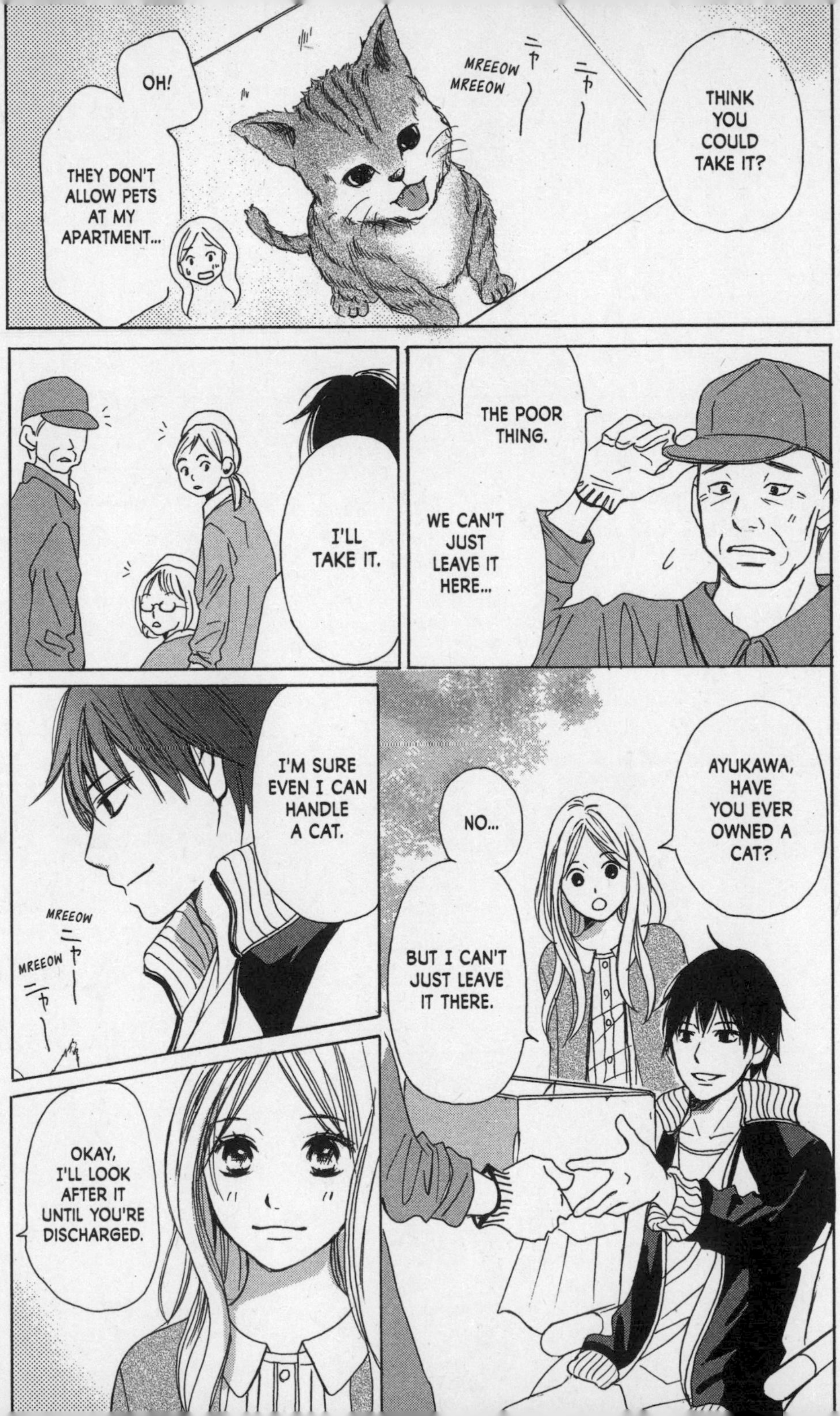
THINK YOU COULD TAKE IT?
MREEOW MREEOW
ニャ ニャ
OH!
THEY DON'T ALLOW PETS AT MY APARTMENT...
THE POOR THING.
WE CAN'T JUST LEAVE IT HERE...
I'LL TAKE IT.
AYUKAWA, HAVE YOU EVER OWNED A CAT?
NO...
BUT I CAN'T JUST LEAVE IT THERE.
I'M SURE EVEN I CAN HANDLE A CAT.
MREEOW
MREEOW
ニャー ニャー
OKAY, I'LL LOOK AFTER IT UNTIL YOU'RE DISCHARGED.

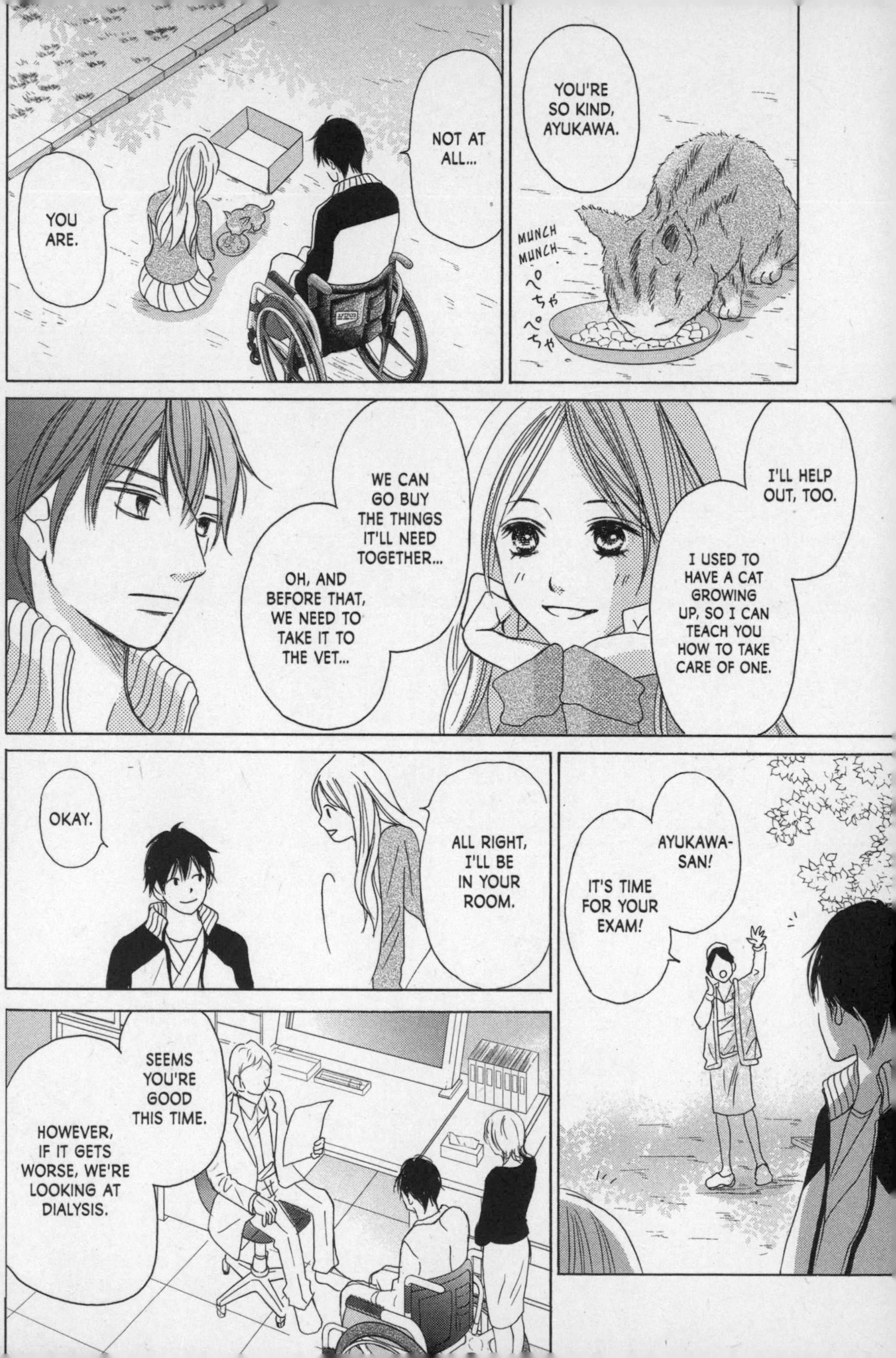
YOU'RE SO KIND, AYUKAWA.
MUNCH MUNCH
ぺちゃぺちゃ
NOT AT ALL...
YOU ARE.
I'LL HELP OUT, TOO.
I USED TO HAVE A CAT GROWING UP, SO I CAN TEACH YOU HOW TO TAKE CARE OF ONE.
WE CAN GO BUY THE THINGS IT'LL NEED TOGETHER...
OH, AND BEFORE THAT, WE NEED TO TAKE IT TO THE VET...
AYUKAWA-SAN!
IT'S TIME FOR YOUR EXAM!
ALL RIGHT, I'LL BE IN YOUR ROOM.
OKAY.
SEEMS YOU'RE GOOD THIS TIME.
HOWEVER, IF IT GETS WORSE, WE'RE LOOKING AT DIALYSIS.

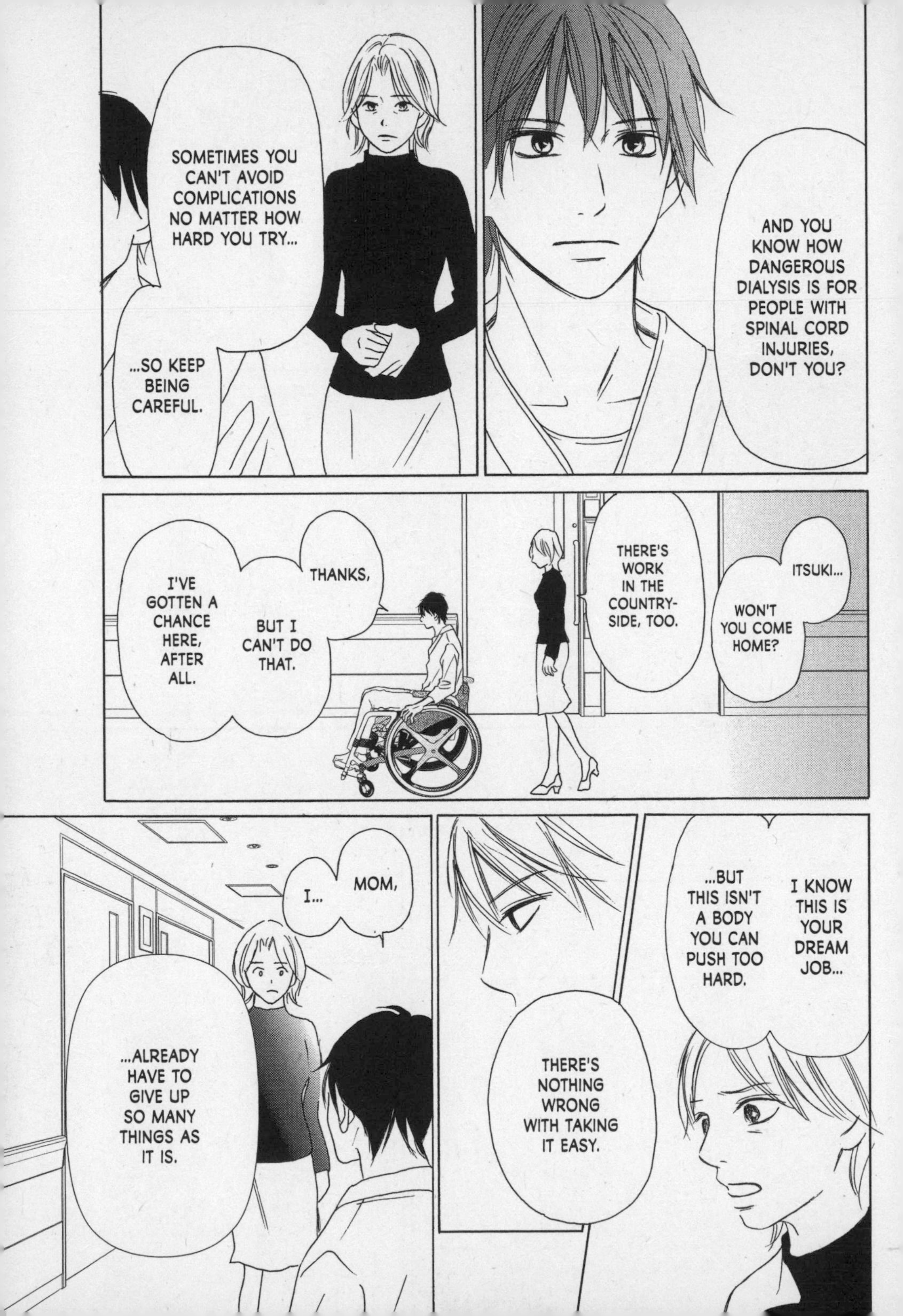
AND YOU KNOW HOW DANGEROUS DIALYSIS IS FOR PEOPLE WITH SPINAL CORD INJURIES, DON'T YOU?
SOMETIMES YOU CAN'T AVOID COMPLICATIONS NO MATTER HOW HARD YOU TRY...
...SO KEEP BEING CAREFUL.
ITSUKI...
WON'T YOU COME HOME?
THERE'S WORK IN THE COUNTRY-SIDE, TOO.
THANKS,
BUT I CAN'T DO THAT.
I'VE GOTTEN A CHANCE HERE, AFTER ALL.
I KNOW THIS IS YOUR DREAM JOB...
...BUT THIS ISN'T A BODY YOU CAN PUSH TOO HARD.
THERE'S NOTHING WRONG WITH TAKING IT EASY.
MOM,
I...
...ALREADY HAVE TO GIVE UP SO MANY THINGS AS IT IS.

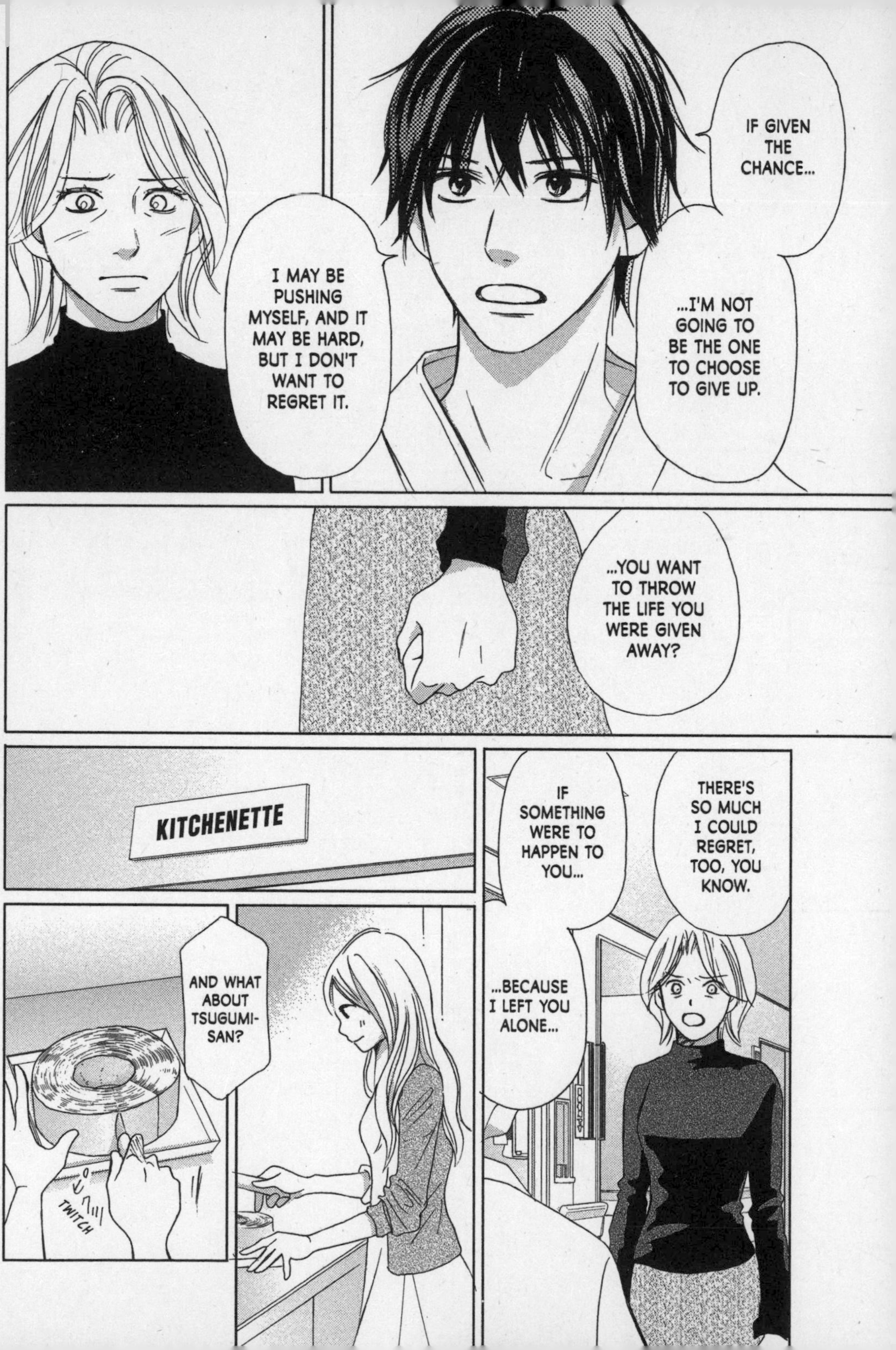
IF GIVEN THE CHANCE...
...I'M NOT GOING TO BE THE ONE TO CHOOSE TO GIVE UP.
I MAY BE PUSHING MYSELF, AND IT MAY BE HARD, BUT I DON'T WANT TO REGRET IT.
...YOU WANT TO THROW THE LIFE YOU WERE GIVEN AWAY?
THERE'S SO MUCH I COULD REGRET, TOO, YOU KNOW.
IF SOMETHING WERE TO HAPPEN TO YOU...
...BECAUSE I LEFT YOU ALONE...
KITCHENETTE
AND WHAT ABOUT TSUGUMI-SAN?
TWITCH

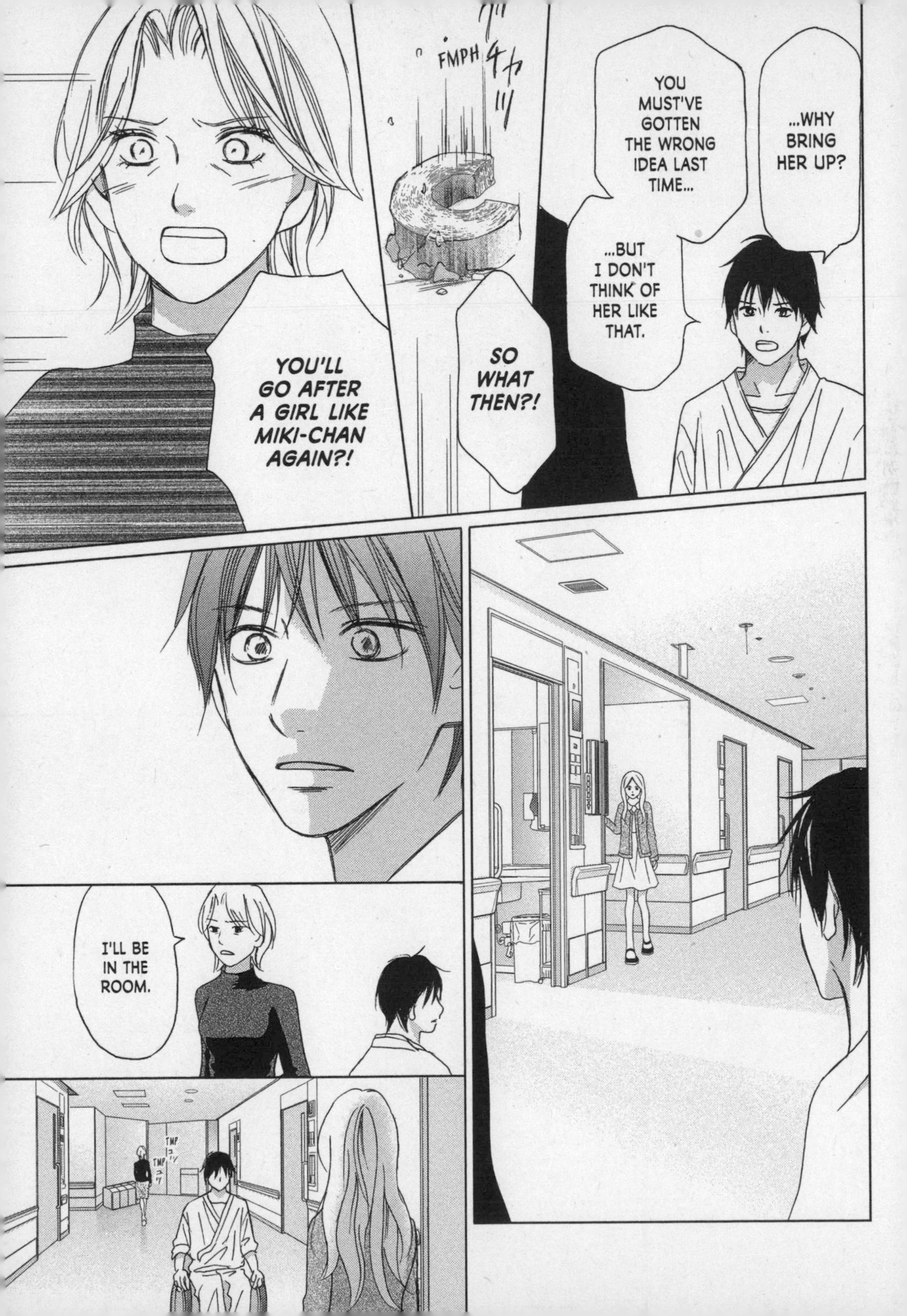
...WHY BRING HER UP?
YOU MUST'VE GOTTEN THE WRONG IDEA LAST TIME...
...BUT I DON'T THINK OF HER LIKE THAT.
FMPH
SO WHAT THEN?!
YOU'LL GO AFTER A GIRL LIKE MIKI-CHAN AGAIN?!
I'LL BE IN THE ROOM.
TMP
TMP

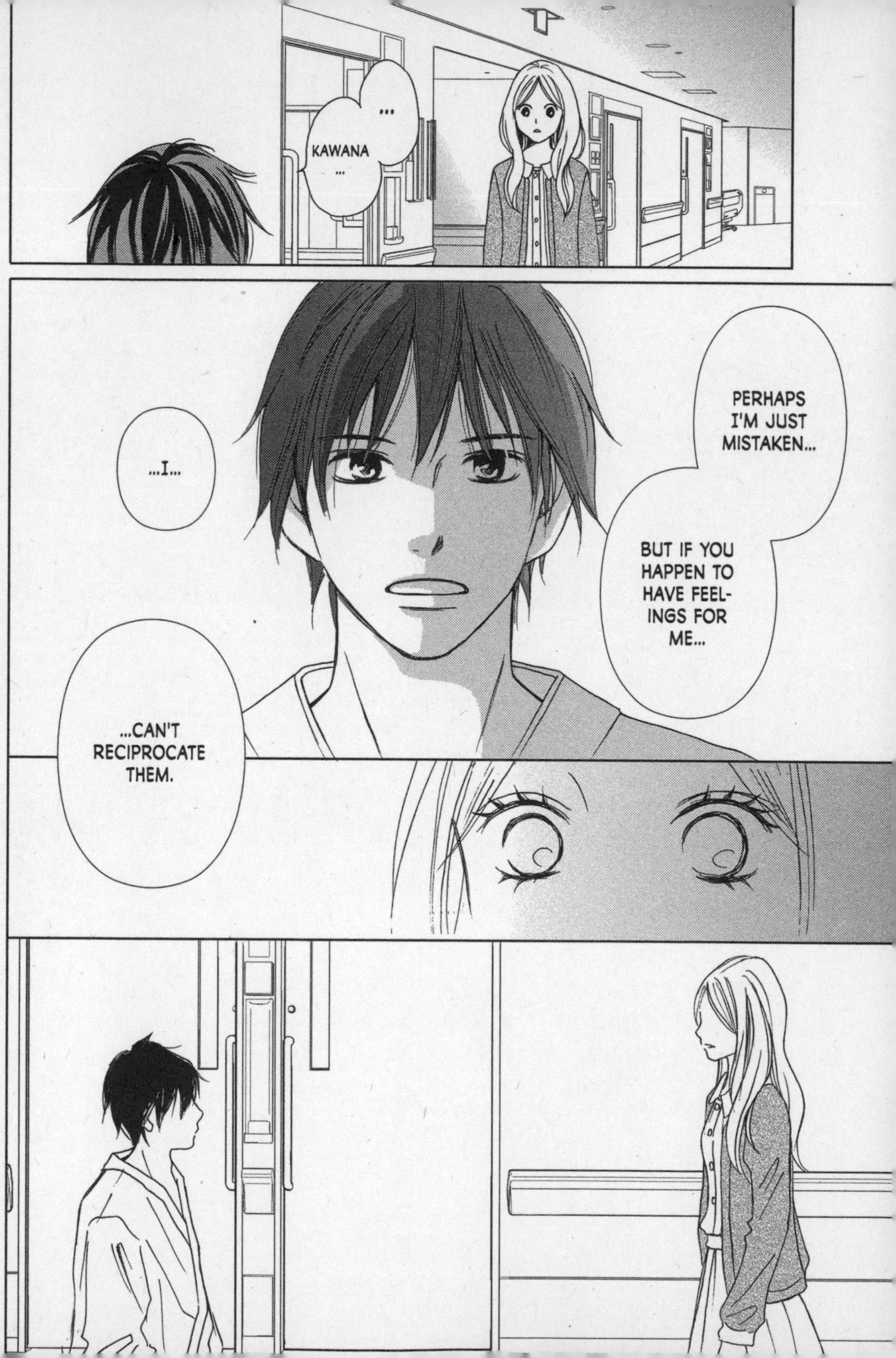
...
KAWANA ...
PERHAPS I'M JUST MISTAKEN...
BUT IF YOU HAPPEN TO HAVE FEEL-INGS FOR ME...
...I...
...CAN'T RECIPROCATE THEM.

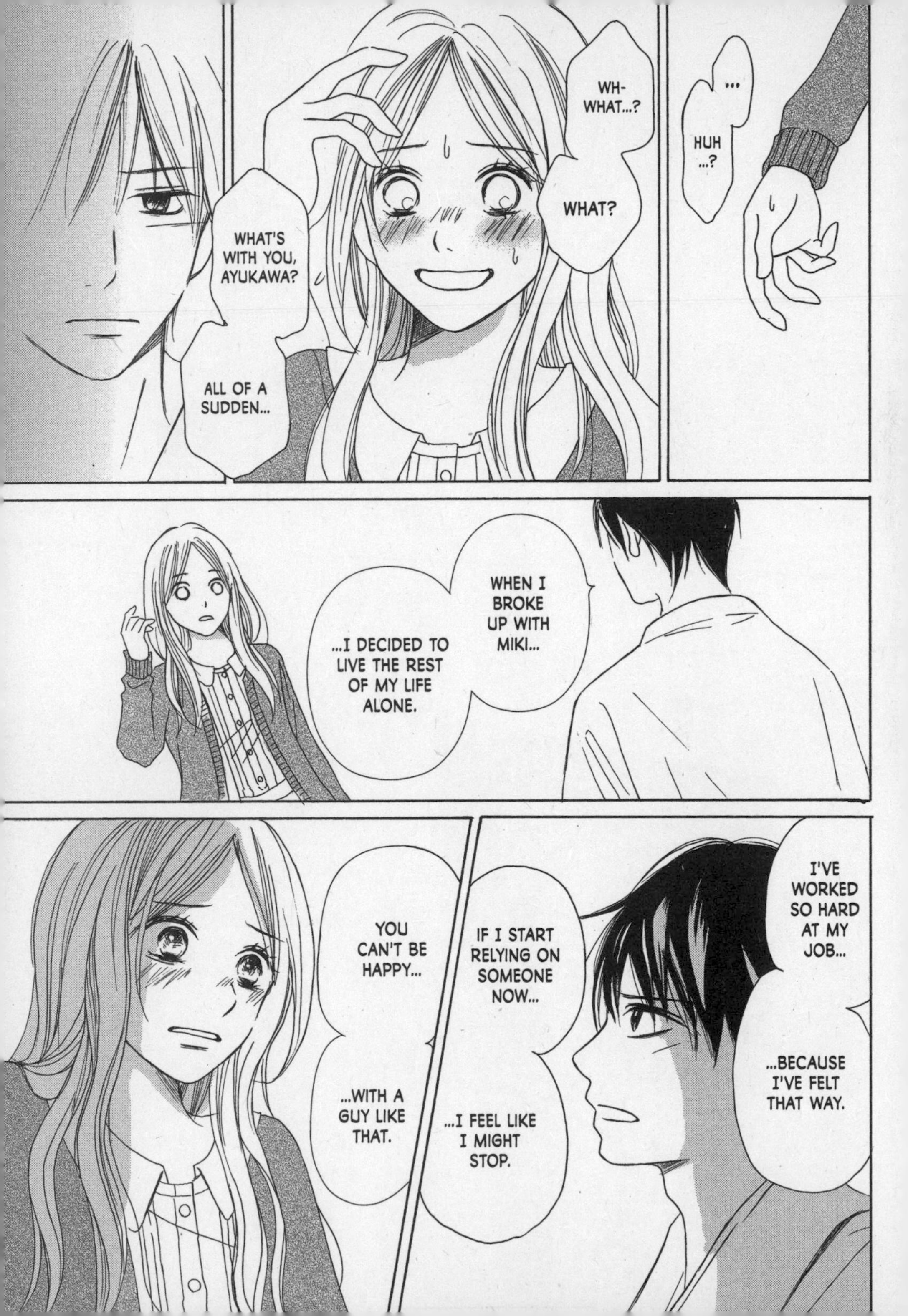
...
HUH ...?
WH- WHAT...?
WHAT?
WHAT'S WITH YOU, AYUKAWA?
ALL OF A SUDDEN...
WHEN I BROKE UP WITH MIKI...
...I DECIDED TO LIVE THE REST OF MY LIFE ALONE.
I'VE WORKED SO HARD AT MY JOB...
...BECAUSE I'VE FELT THAT WAY.
IF I START RELYING ON SOMEONE NOW...
...I FEEL LIKE I MIGHT STOP.
YOU CAN'T BE HAPPY...
...WITH A GUY LIKE THAT.

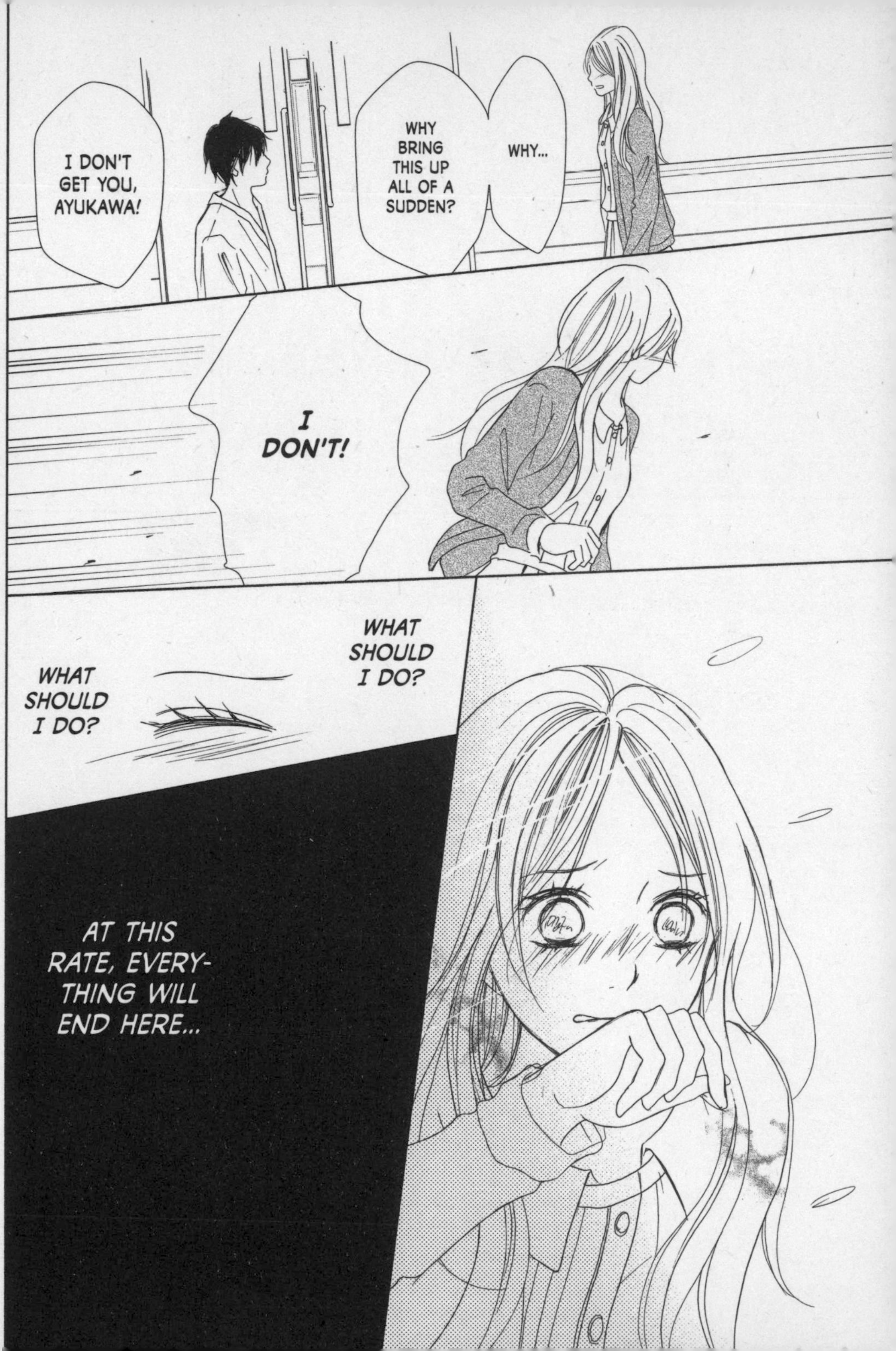
WHY...
WHY BRING THIS UP ALL OF A SUDDEN?
I DON'T GET YOU, AYUKAWA!
I DON'T!
WHAT SHOULD I DO?
WHAT SHOULD I DO?
AT THIS RATE, EVERY-THING WILL END HERE...

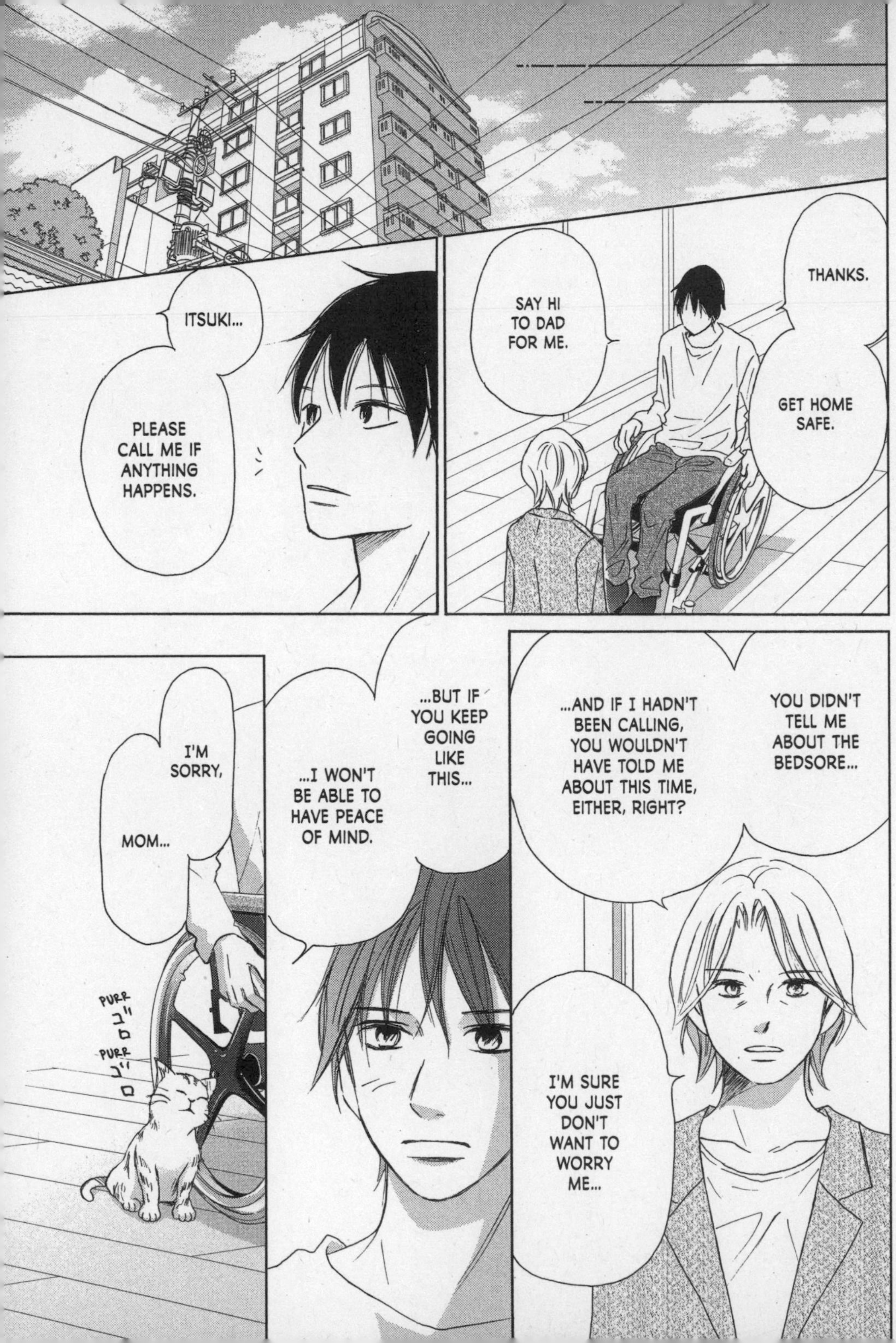
THANKS.
GET HOME SAFE.
SAY HI TO DAD FOR ME.
ITSUKI...
PLEASE CALL ME IF ANYTHING HAPPENS.
YOU DIDN'T TELL ME ABOUT THE BEDSORE...
...AND IF I HADN'T BEEN CALLING, YOU WOULDN'T HAVE TOLD ME ABOUT THIS TIME, EITHER, RIGHT?
I'M SURE YOU JUST DON'T WANT TO WORRY ME...
...BUT IF YOU KEEP GOING LIKE THIS...
...I WON'T BE ABLE TO HAVE PEACE OF MIND.
I'M SORRY,
MOM...
PURR ゴロ
PURR ゴロ

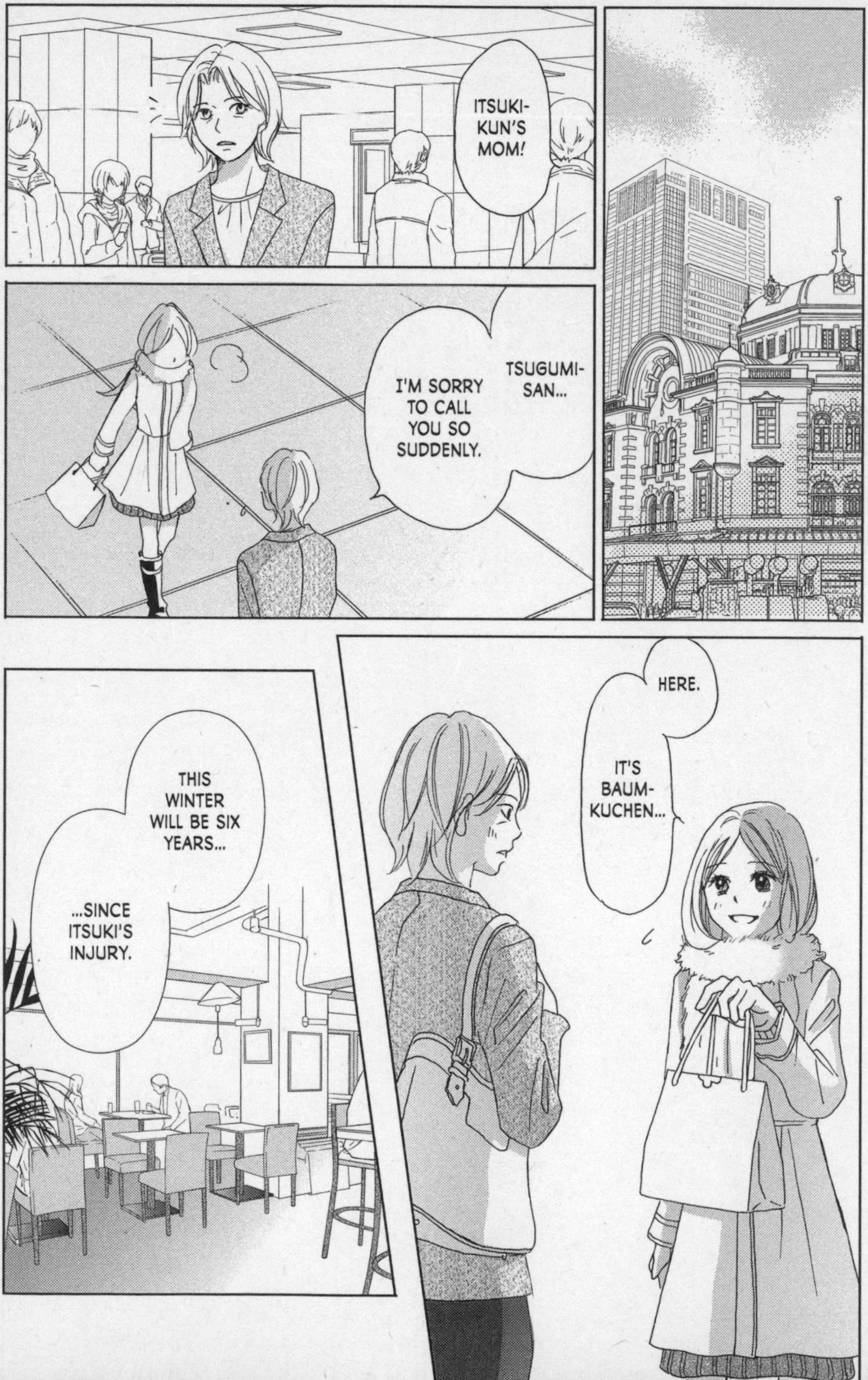
ITSUKI-KUN'S MOM!
TSUGUMI-SAN...
I'M SORRY TO CALL YOU SO SUDDENLY.
HERE.
IT'S BAUM-KUCHEN...
THIS WINTER WILL BE SIX YEARS...
...SINCE ITSUKI'S INJURY.

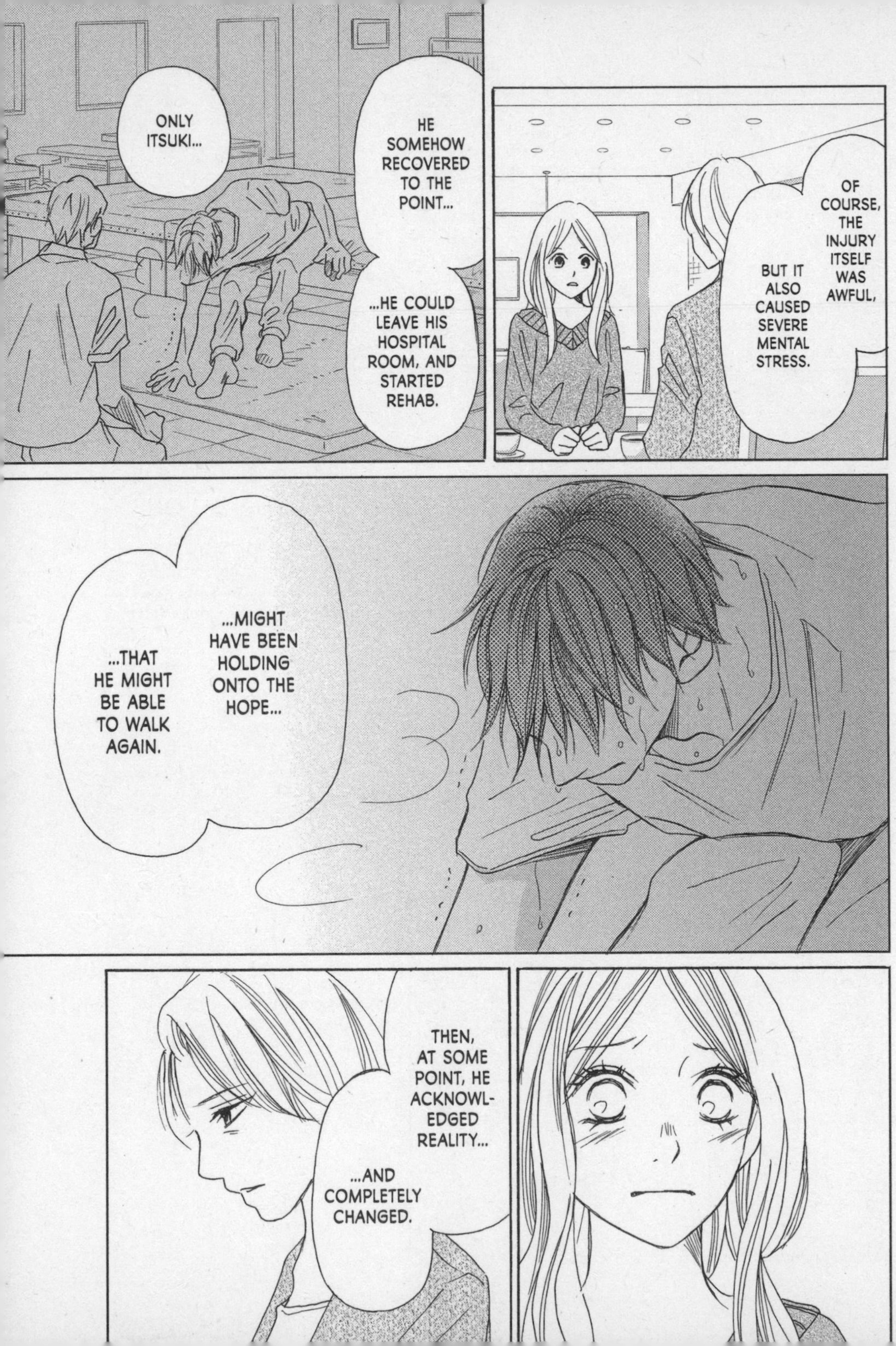
OF COURSE, THE INJURY ITSELF WAS AWFUL,
BUT IT ALSO CAUSED SEVERE MENTAL STRESS.
HE SOMEHOW RECOVERED TO THE POINT...
...HE COULD LEAVE HIS HOSPITAL ROOM, AND STARTED REHAB.
ONLY ITSUKI...
...MIGHT HAVE BEEN HOLDING ONTO THE HOPE...
...THAT HE MIGHT BE ABLE TO WALK AGAIN.
THEN, AT SOME POINT, HE ACKNOWL-EDGED REALITY...
...AND COMPLETELY CHANGED.

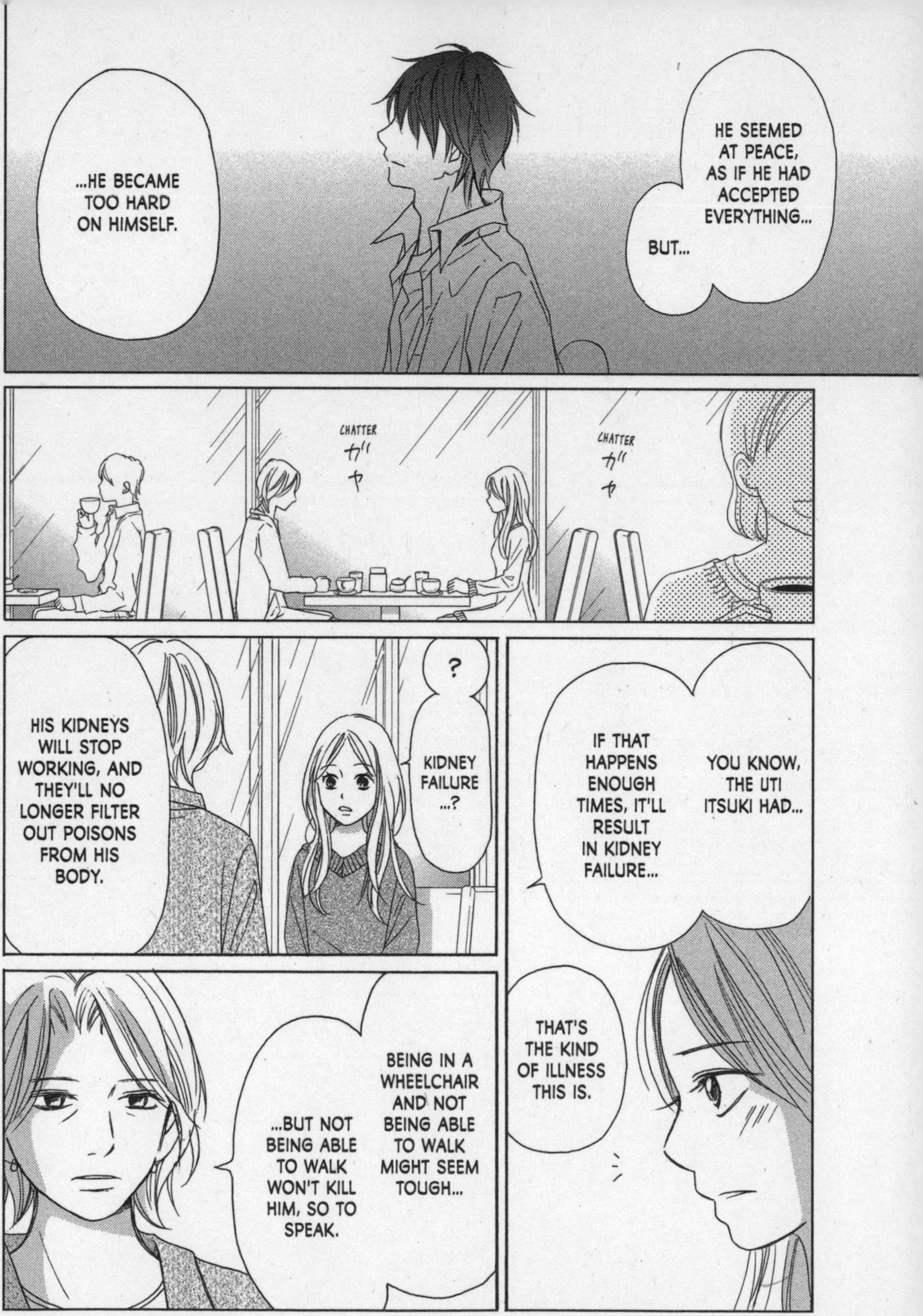
HE SEEMED AT PEACE, AS IF HE HAD ACCEPTED EVERYTHING... BUT...
...HE BECAME TOO HARD ON HIMSELF.
CHATTER ガヤ
CHATTER ガヤ
YOU KNOW, THE UTI ITSUKI HAD...
IF THAT HAPPENS ENOUGH TIMES, IT'LL RESULT IN KIDNEY FAILURE...
THAT'S THE KIND OF ILLNESS THIS IS.
?
KIDNEY FAILURE ...?
HIS KIDNEYS WILL STOP WORKING, AND THEY'LL NO LONGER FILTER OUT POISONS FROM HIS BODY.
BEING IN A WHEELCHAIR AND NOT BEING ABLE TO WALK MIGHT SEEM TOUGH...
...BUT NOT BEING ABLE TO WALK WON'T KILL HIM, SO TO SPEAK.

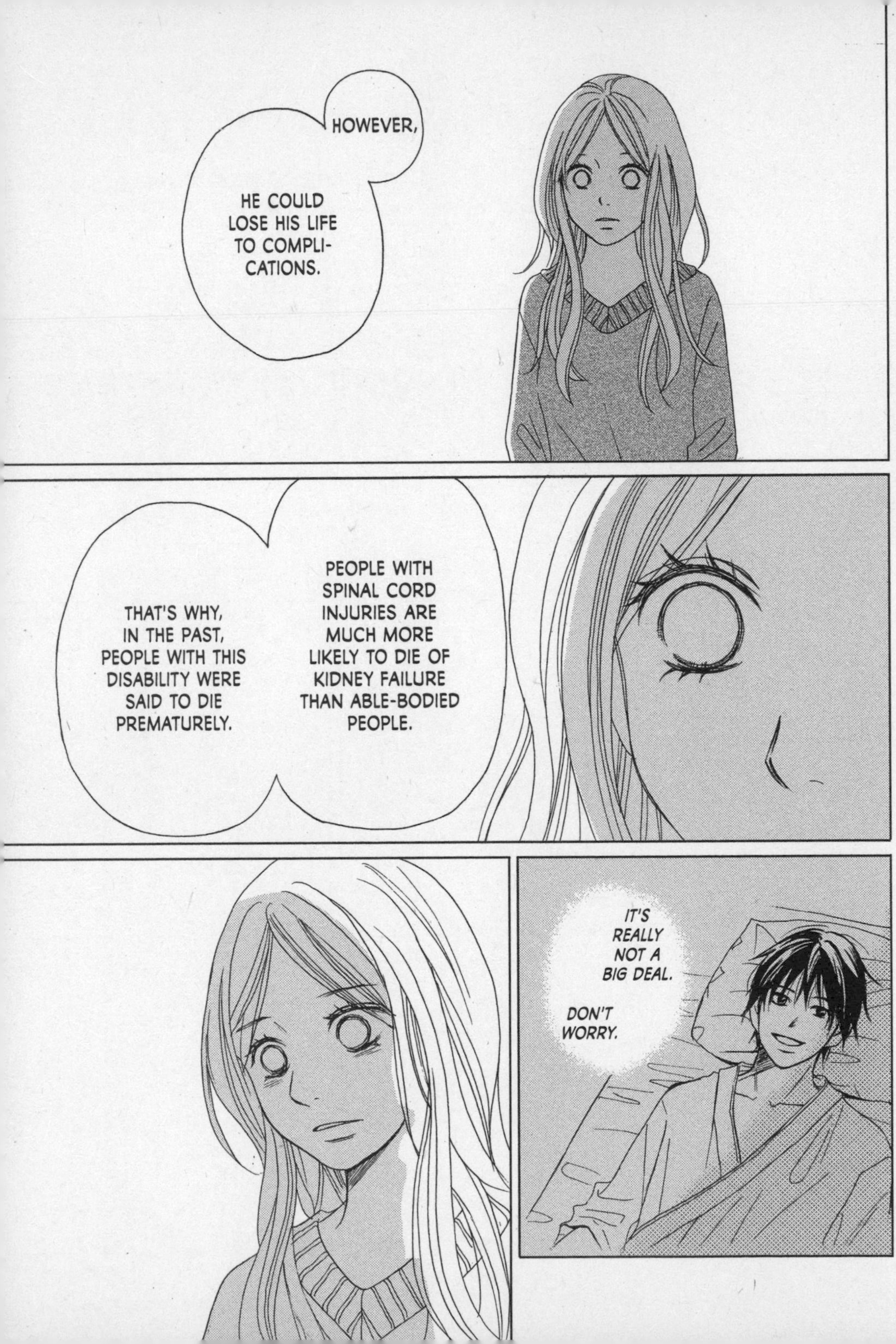
HOWEVER,
HE COULD LOSE HIS LIFE TO COMPLI-CATIONS.
PEOPLE WITH SPINAL CORD INJURIES ARE MUCH MORE LIKELY TO DIE OF KIDNEY FAILURE THAN ABLE-BODIED PEOPLE.
THAT'S WHY, IN THE PAST, PEOPLE WITH THIS DISABILITY WERE SAID TO DIE PREMATURELY.
IT'S REALLY NOT A BIG DEAL.
DON'T WORRY.

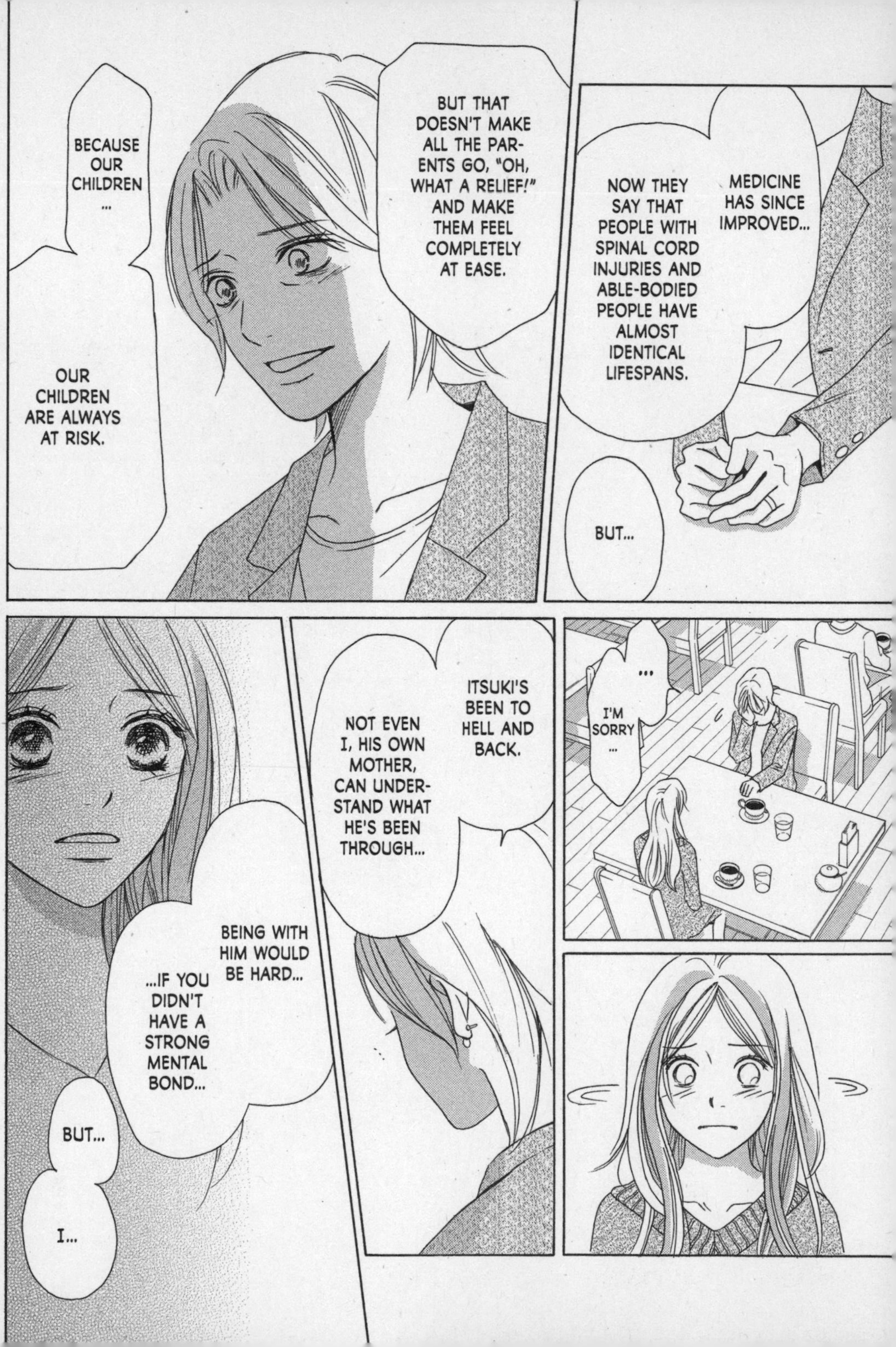
MEDICINE HAS SINCE IMPROVED...
NOW THEY SAY THAT PEOPLE WITH SPINAL CORD INJURIES AND ABLE-BODIED PEOPLE HAVE ALMOST IDENTICAL LIFESPANS.
BUT...
BUT THAT DOESN'T MAKE ALL THE PAR-ENTS GO, "OH, WHAT A RELIEF!" AND MAKE THEM FEEL COMPLETELY AT EASE.
BECAUSE OUR CHILDREN ...
OUR CHILDREN ARE ALWAYS AT RISK.
...
I'M SORRY ...
ITSUKI'S BEEN TO HELL AND BACK.
NOT EVEN I, HIS OWN MOTHER, CAN UNDER-STAND WHAT HE'S BEEN THROUGH...
BEING WITH HIM WOULD BE HARD...
...IF YOU DIDN'T HAVE A STRONG MENTAL BOND...
BUT...
I...

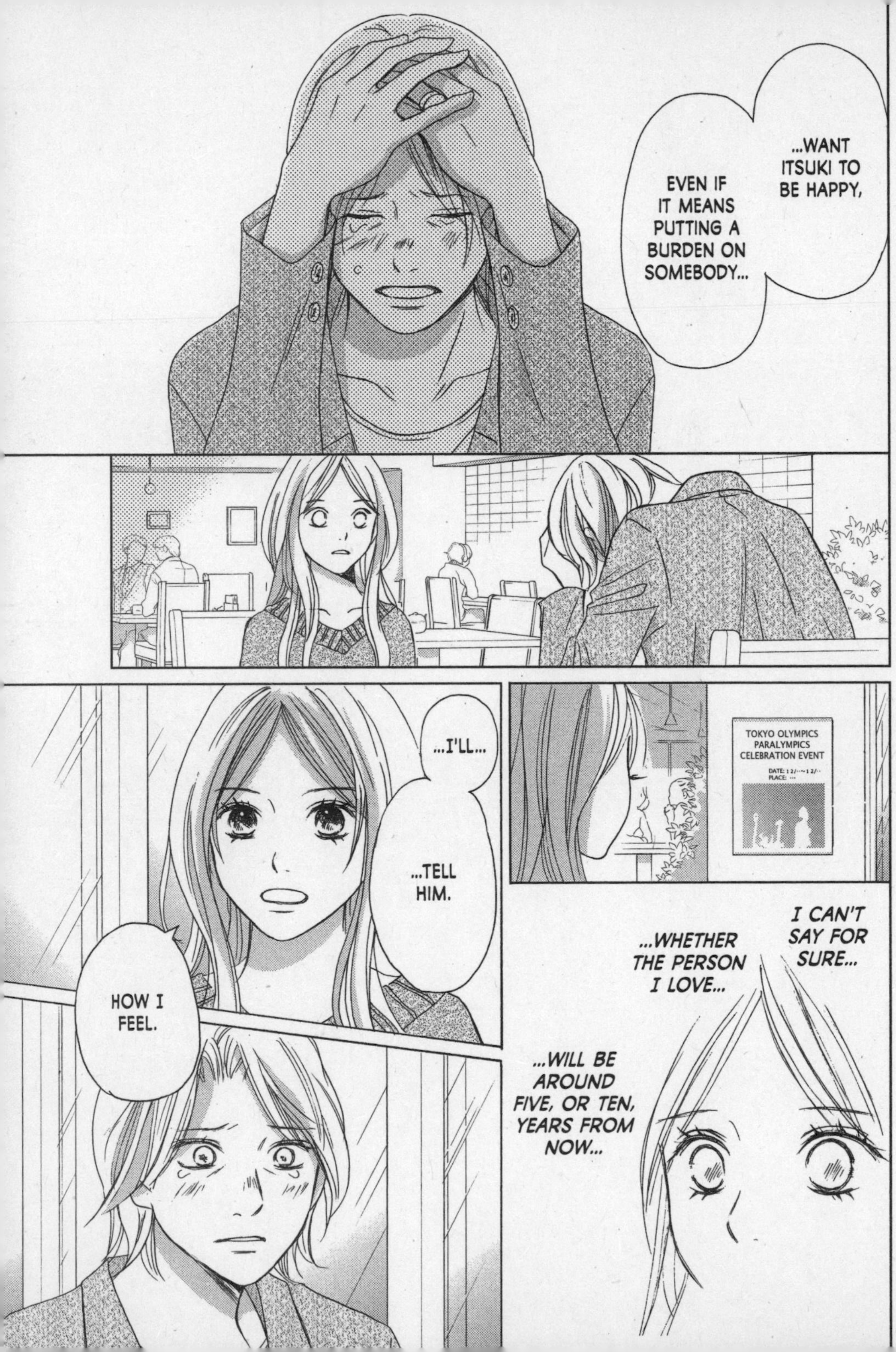
...WANT ITSUKI TO BE HAPPY,
EVEN IF IT MEANS PUTTING A BURDEN ON SOMEBODY...
TOKYO OLYMPICS PARALYMPICS CELEBRATION EVENT
I CAN'T SAY FOR SURE...
...WHETHER THE PERSON I LOVE...
...WILL BE AROUND FIVE, OR TEN, YEARS FROM NOW...
...I'LL...
...TELL HIM.
HOW I FEEL.

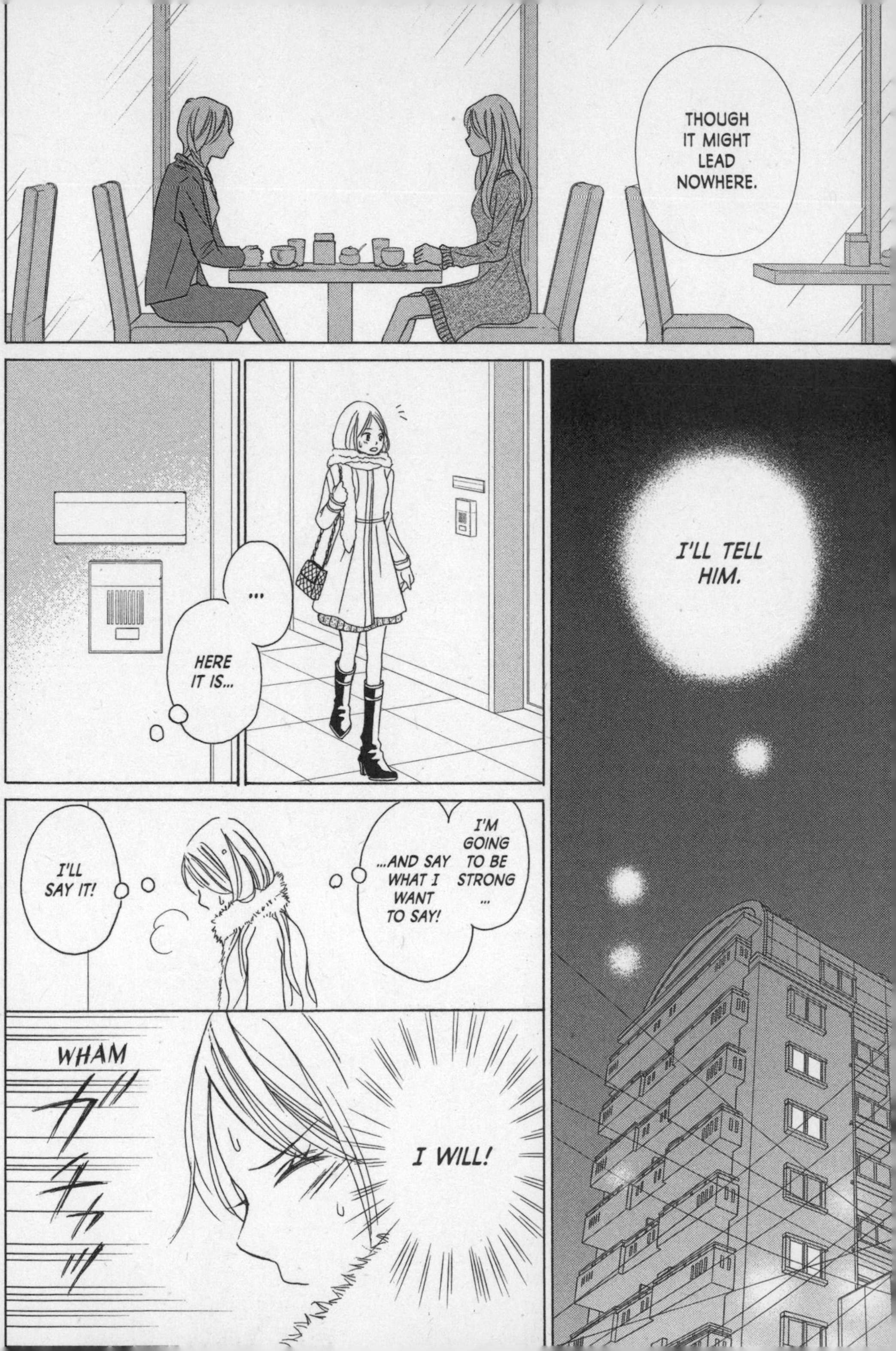
THOUGH IT MIGHT LEAD NOWHERE.
I'LL TELL HIM.
...
HERE IT IS...
I'M GOING TO BE STRONG ...
...AND SAY WHAT I WANT TO SAY!
I'LL SAY IT!
I WILL!
WHAM

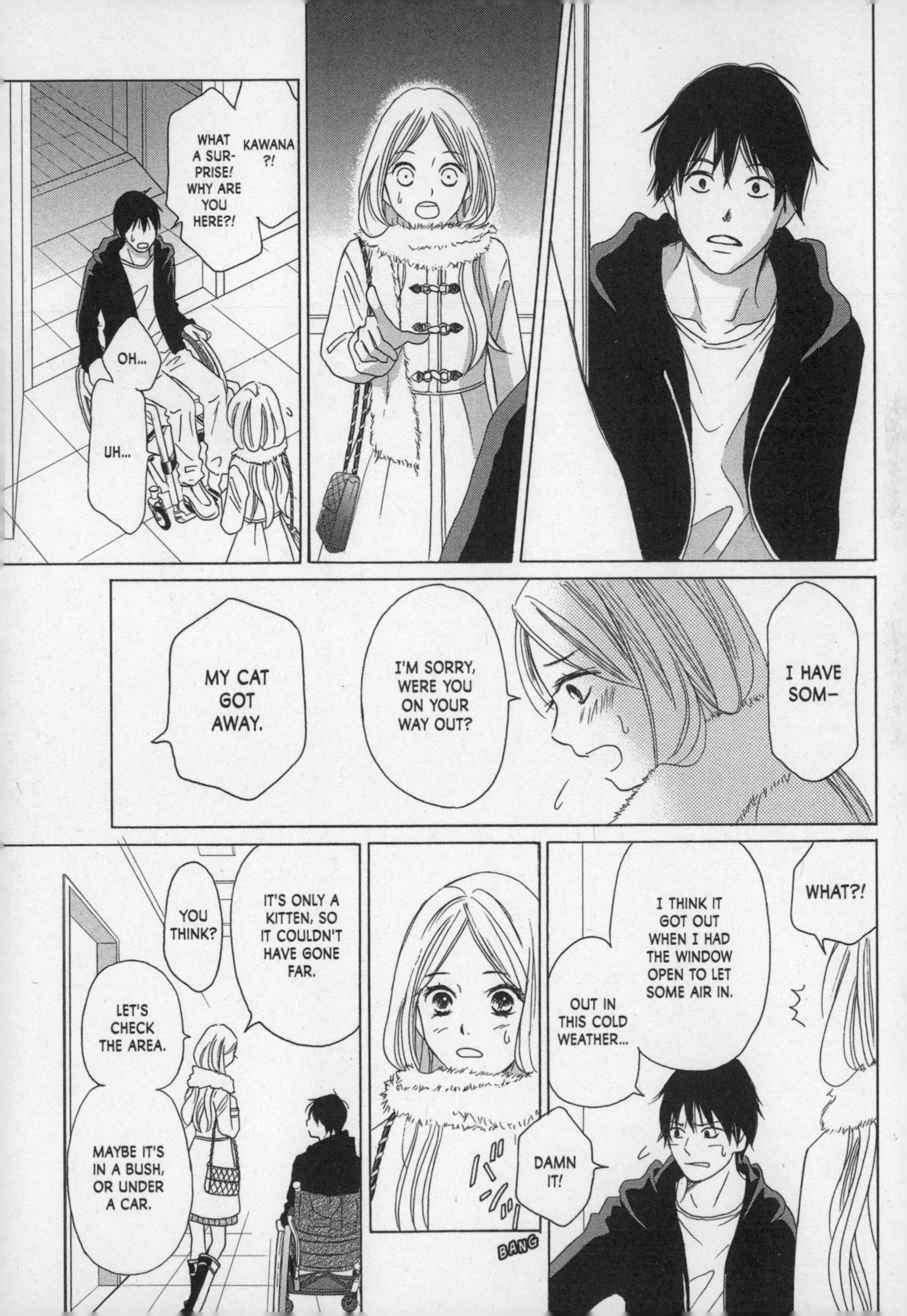
KAWANA ?!
WHAT A SUR-PRISE! WHY ARE YOU HERE?!
OH...
UH...
I HAVE SOM—
I'M SORRY, WERE YOU ON YOUR WAY OUT?
MY CAT GOT AWAY.
WHAT?!
I THINK IT GOT OUT WHEN I HAD THE WINDOW OPEN TO LET SOME AIR IN.
OUT IN THIS COLD WEATHER...
DAMN IT!
BANG
IT'S ONLY A KITTEN, SO IT COULDN'T HAVE GONE FAR.
YOU THINK?
LET'S CHECK THE AREA.
MAYBE IT'S IN A BUSH, OR UNDER A CAR.

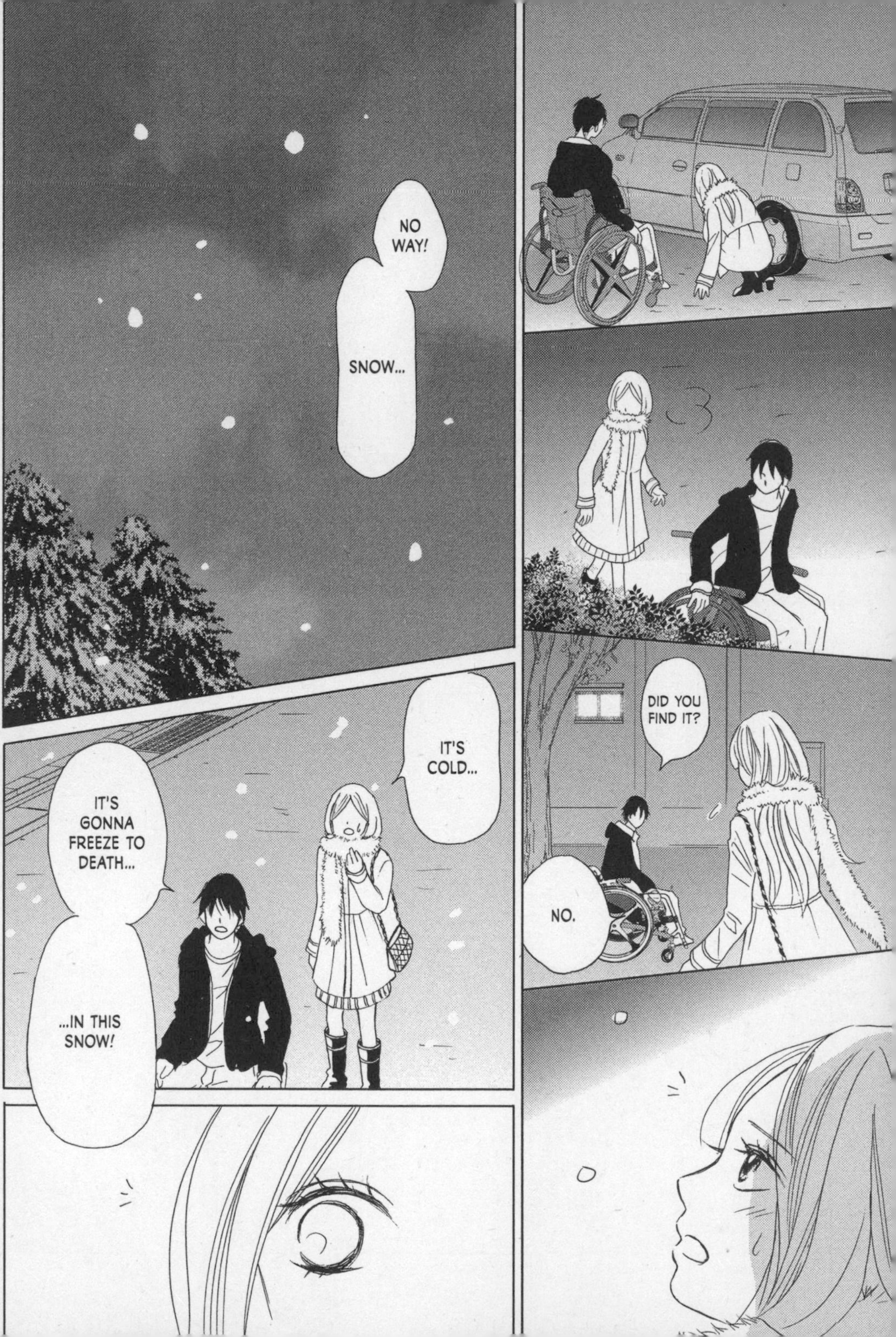
DID YOU FIND IT?
NO.
NO WAY!
SNOW...
IT'S COLD...
IT'S GONNA FREEZE TO DEATH...
...IN THIS SNOW!

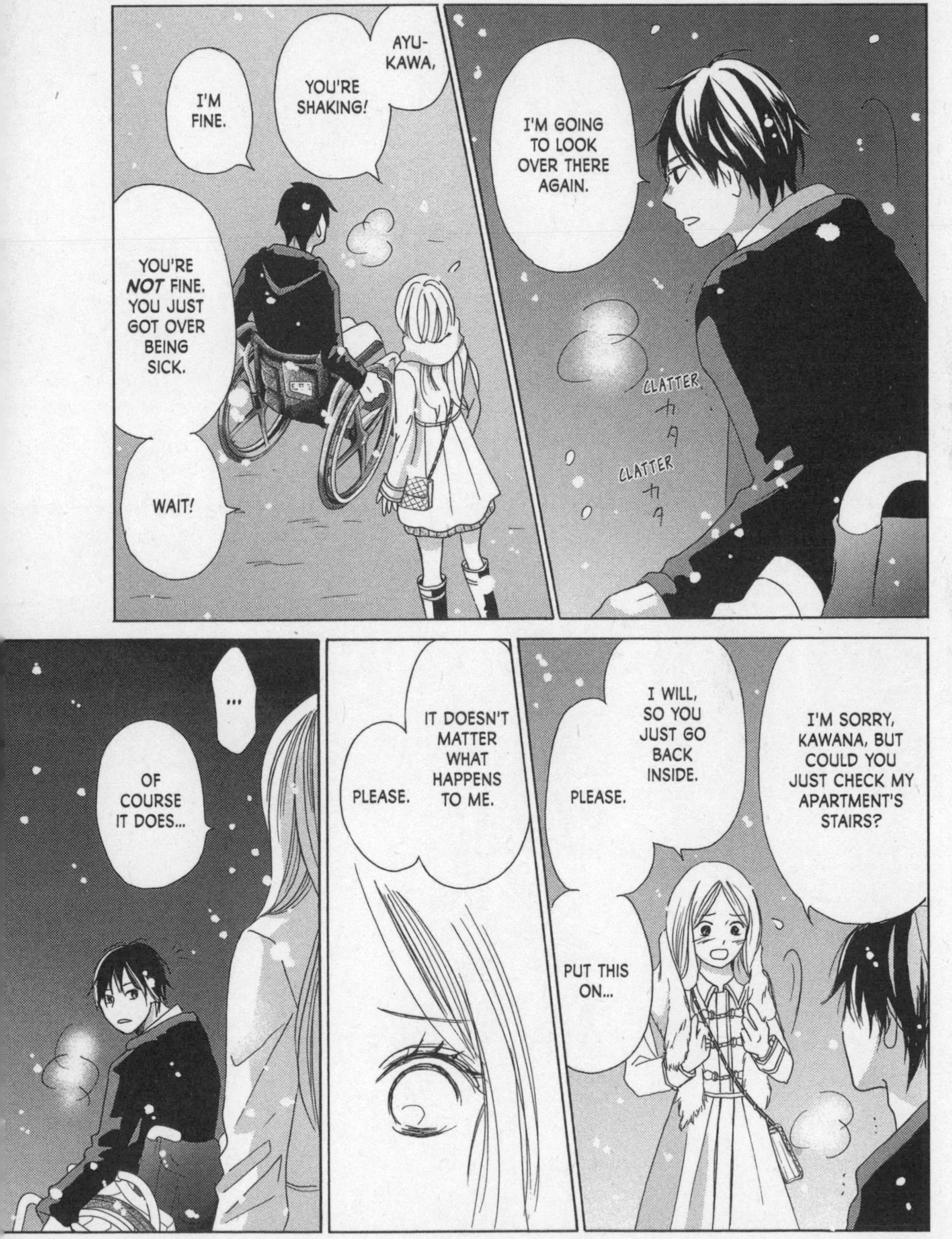
I'M GOING TO LOOK OVER THERE AGAIN.
CLATTER
カタ
CLATTER
カタ
AYU-KAWA,
YOU'RE SHAKING!
I'M FINE.
YOU'RE *NOT* FINE. YOU JUST GOT OVER BEING SICK.
WAIT!
I'M SORRY, KAWANA, BUT COULD YOU JUST CHECK MY APARTMENT'S STAIRS?
I WILL, SO YOU JUST GO BACK INSIDE.
PLEASE.
PUT THIS ON...
IT DOESN'T MATTER WHAT HAPPENS TO ME.
PLEASE.
...
OF COURSE IT DOES...

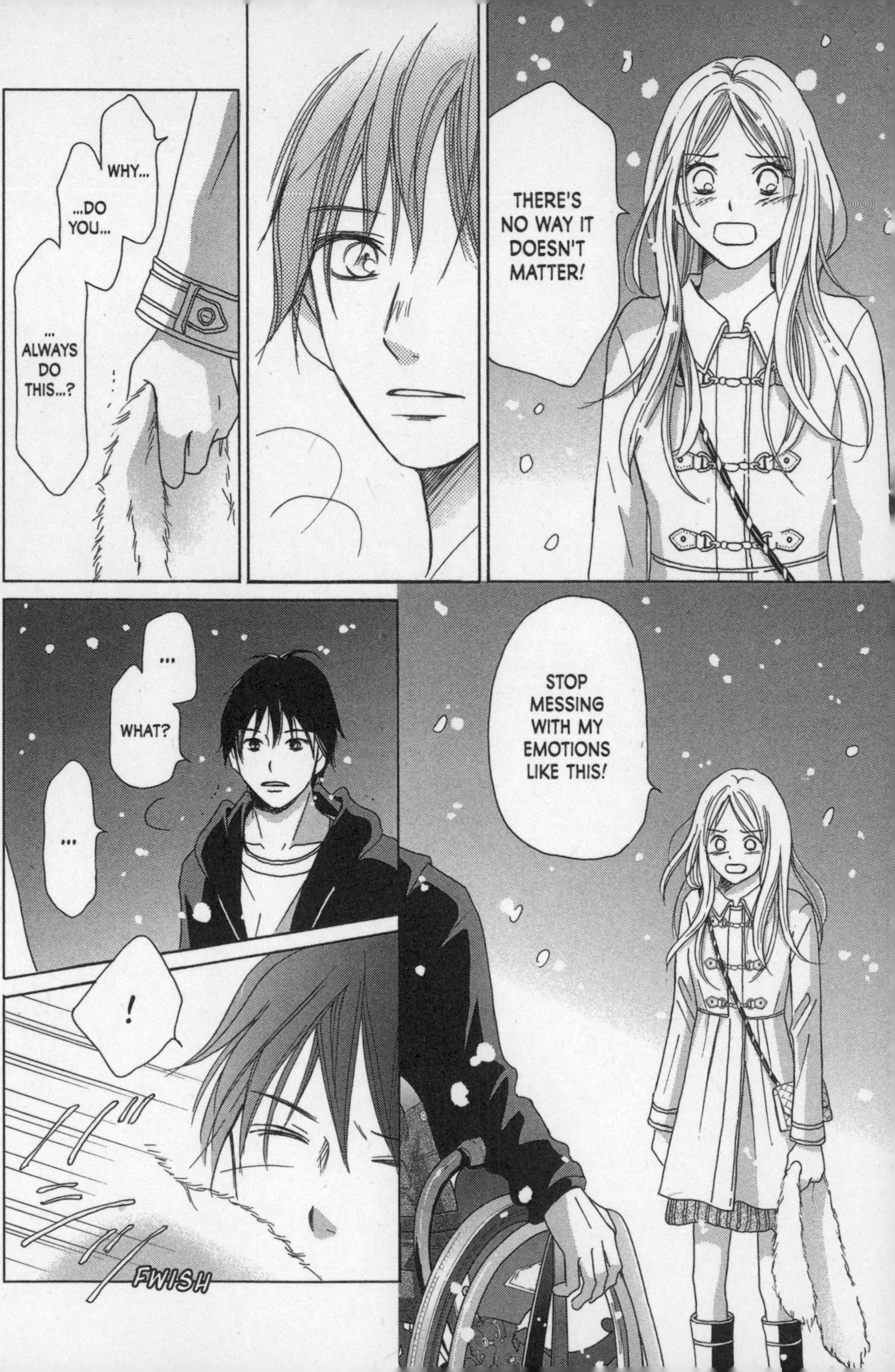
THERE'S NO WAY IT DOESN'T MATTER!
WHY...
...DO YOU...
...ALWAYS DO THIS...?
STOP MESSING WITH MY EMOTIONS LIKE THIS!
...
WHAT?
...
!
FWISH

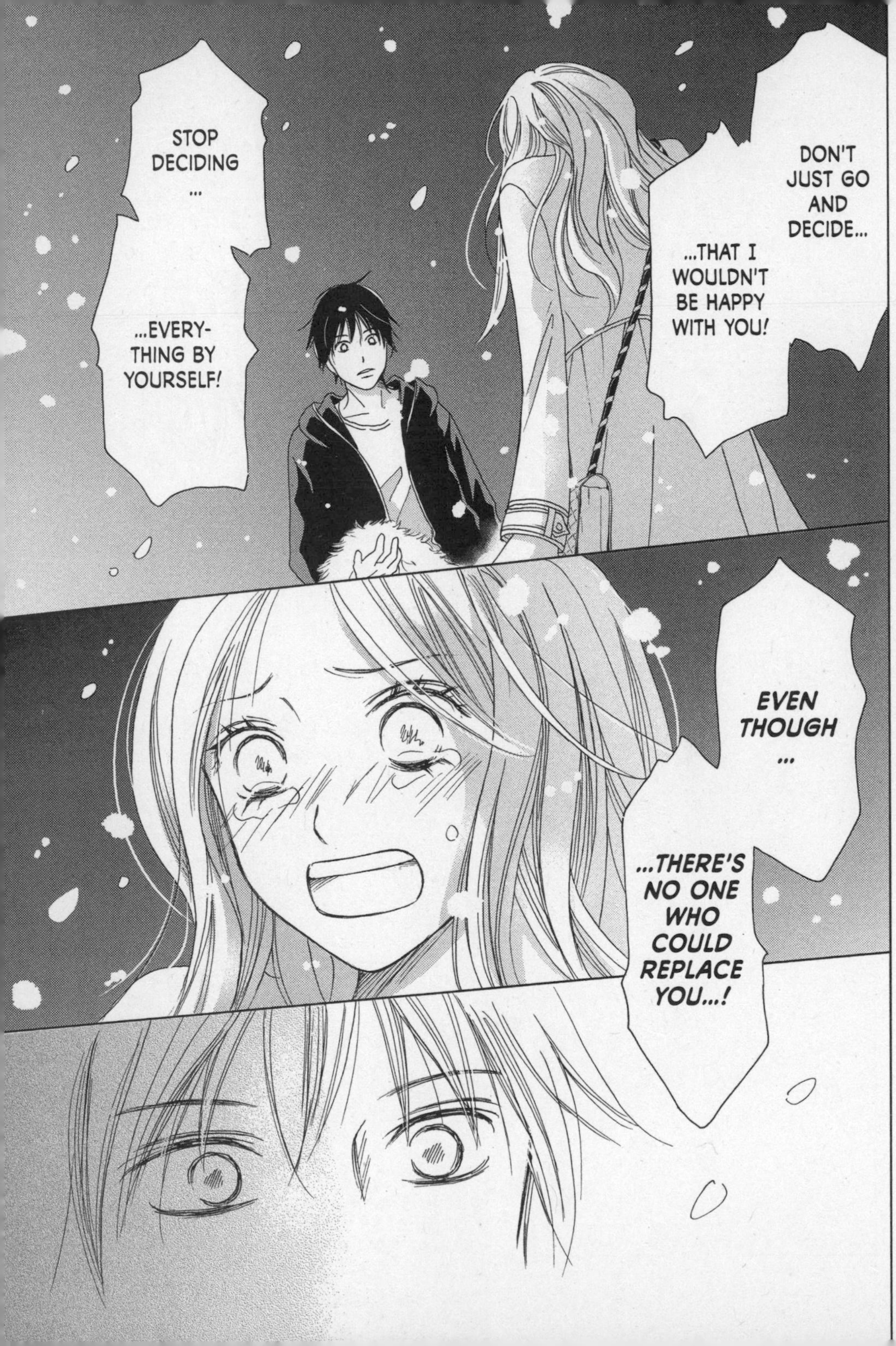
DON'T JUST GO AND DECIDE...
...THAT I WOULDN'T BE HAPPY WITH YOU!
STOP DECIDING ...
...EVERY-THING BY YOURSELF!
EVEN THOUGH ...
...THERE'S NO ONE WHO COULD REPLACE YOU...!

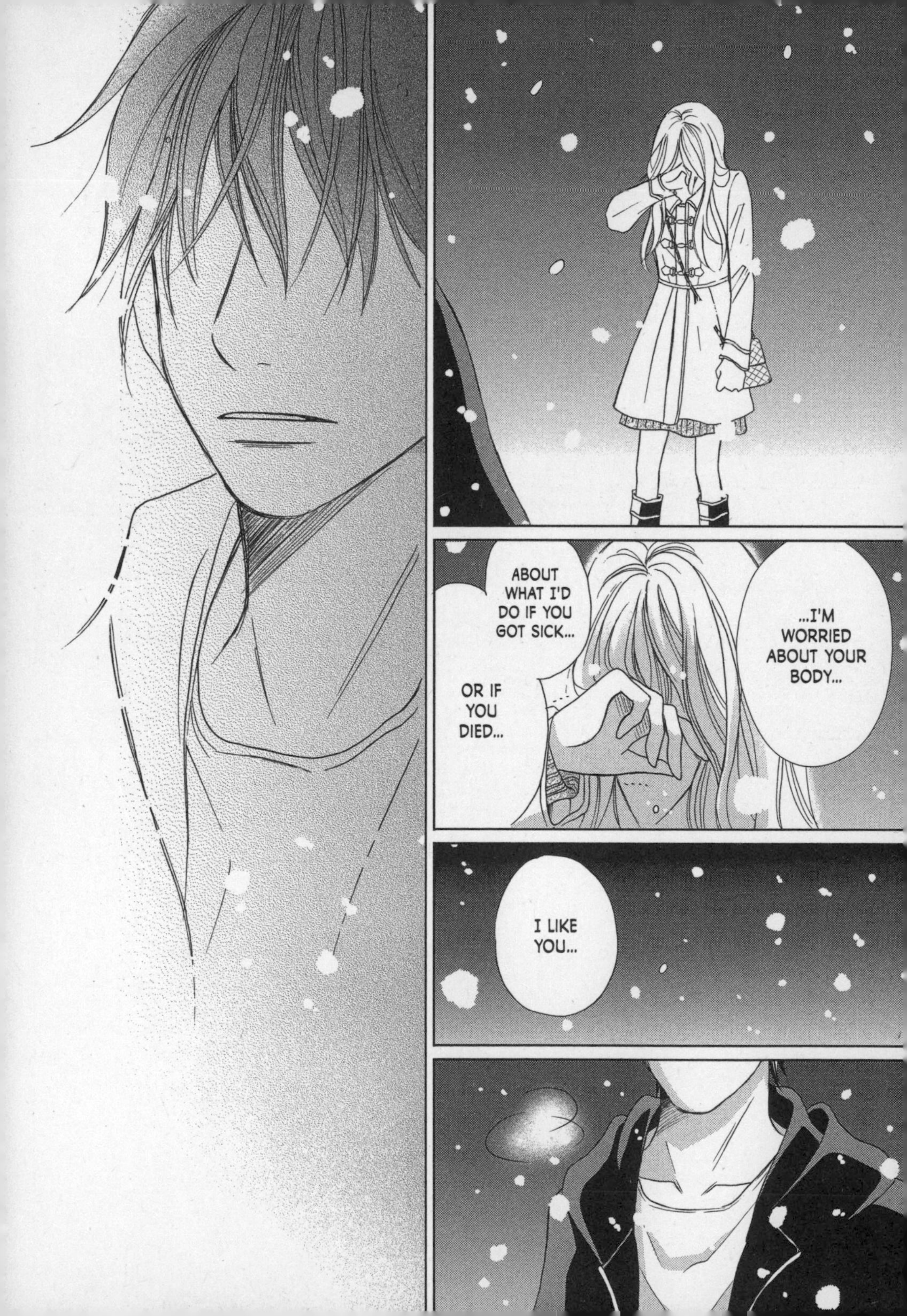
...I'M WORRIED ABOUT YOUR BODY...
ABOUT WHAT I'D DO IF YOU GOT SICK...
OR IF YOU DIED...
I LIKE YOU...

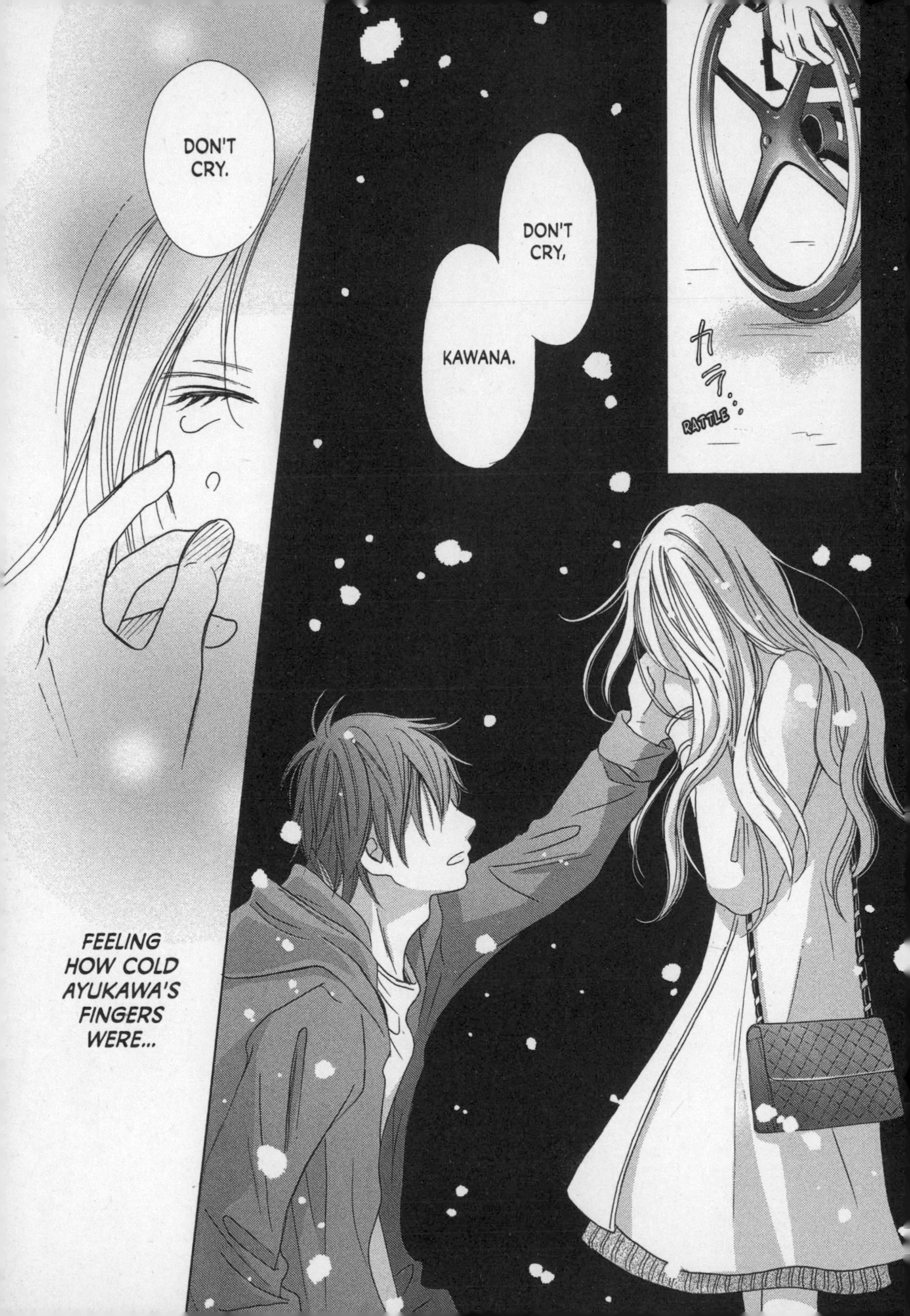
カラ...
RATTLE
DON'T CRY,
KAWANA.
DON'T CRY.
FEELING HOW COLD AYUKAWA'S FINGERS WERE...

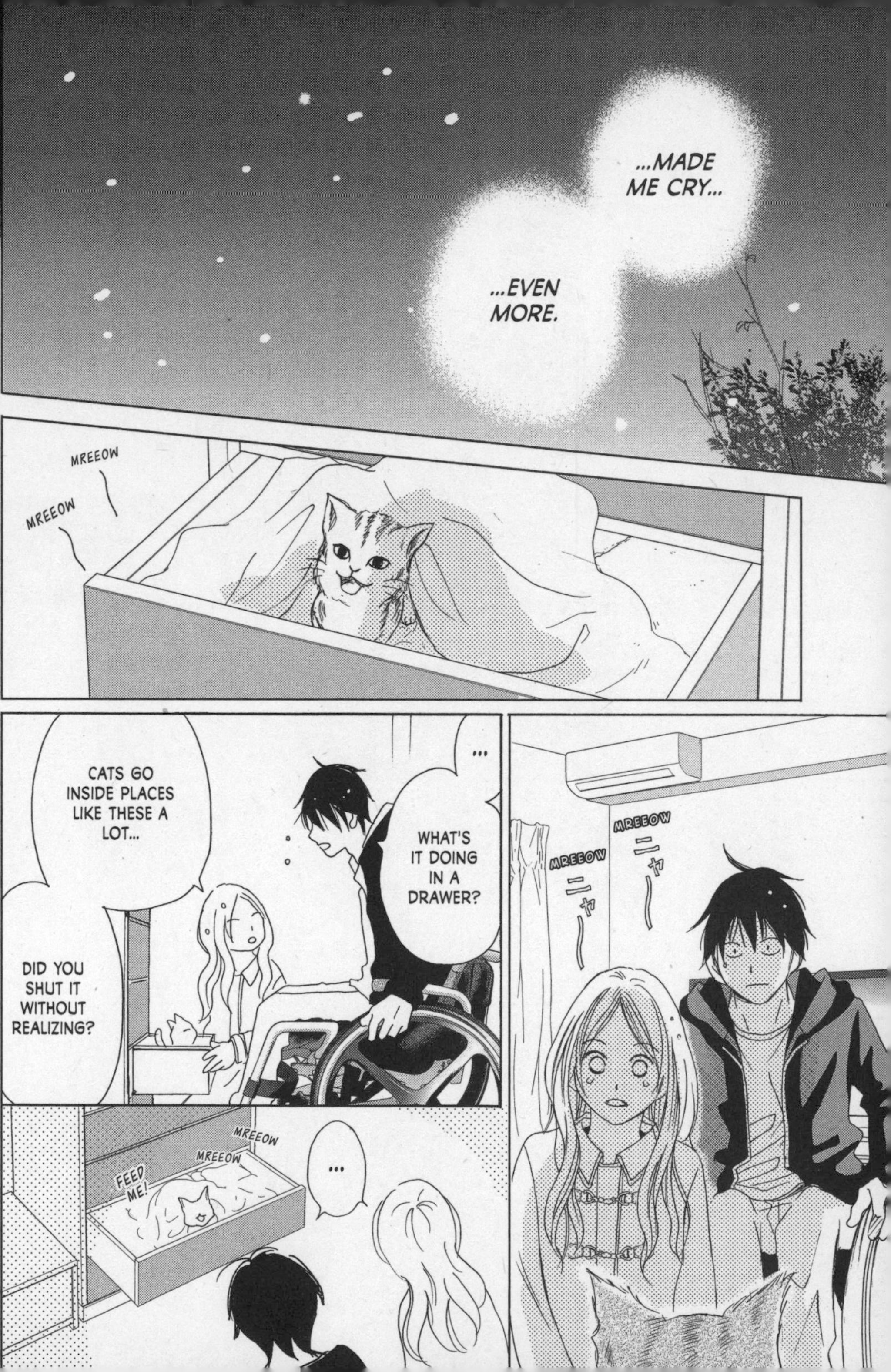
...MADE ME CRY...
...EVEN MORE.
MREEOW
MREEOW
MREEOW
ニャー
MREEOW
ニャー
...
WHAT'S IT DOING IN A DRAWER?
CATS GO INSIDE PLACES LIKE THESE A LOT...
DID YOU SHUT IT WITHOUT REALIZING?
...
MREEOW
MREEOW
FEED ME!

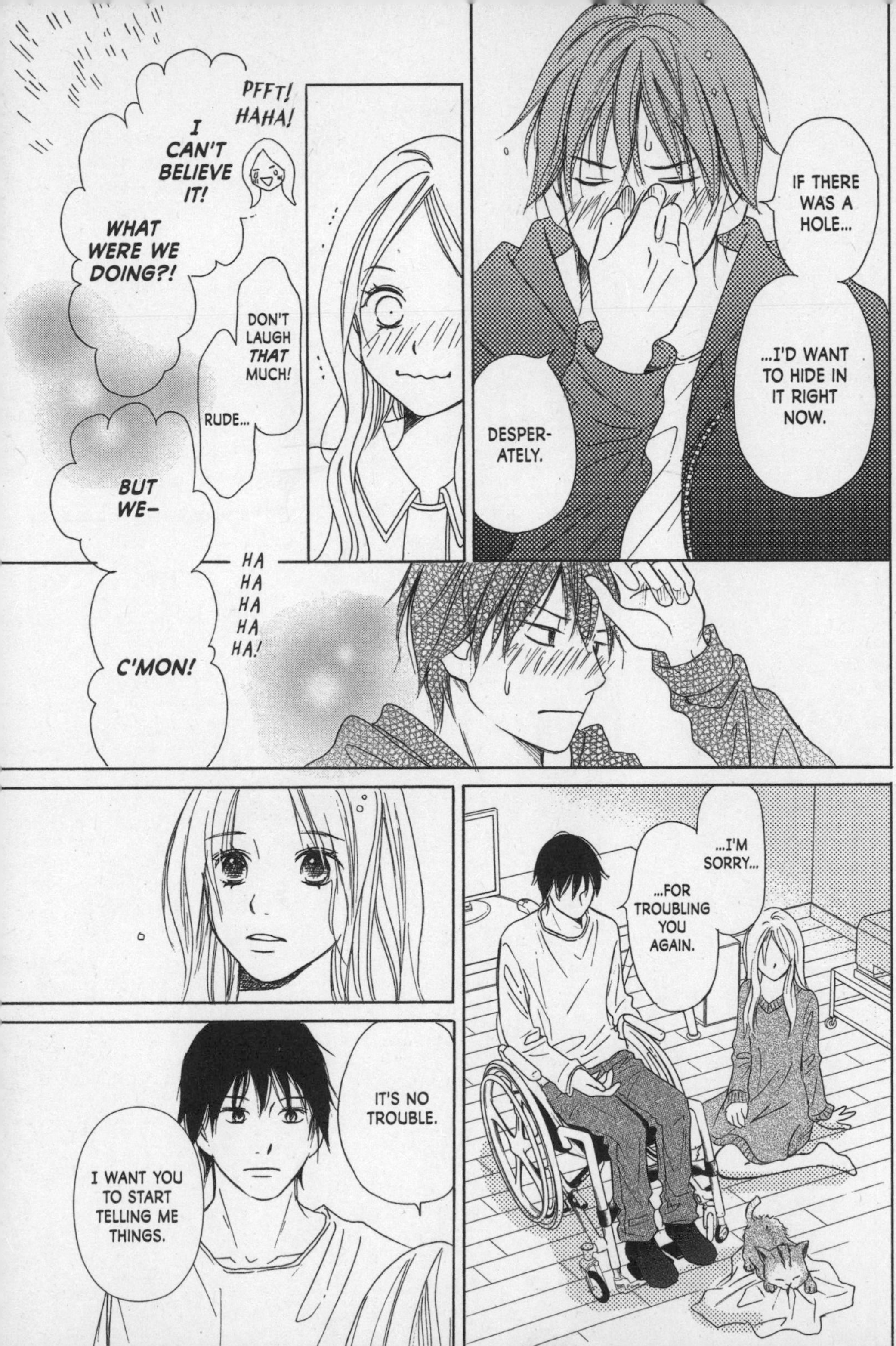
IF THERE WAS A HOLE...
...I'D WANT TO HIDE IN IT RIGHT NOW.
DESPERATELY.
PFFT! HAHA!
DON'T LAUGH THAT MUCH!
RUDE...
I CAN'T BELIEVE IT!
WHAT WERE WE DOING?!
BUT WE–
C'MON!
HA HA HA HA HA!
...I'M SORRY...
...FOR TROUBLING YOU AGAIN.
IT'S NO TROUBLE.
I WANT YOU TO START TELLING ME THINGS.

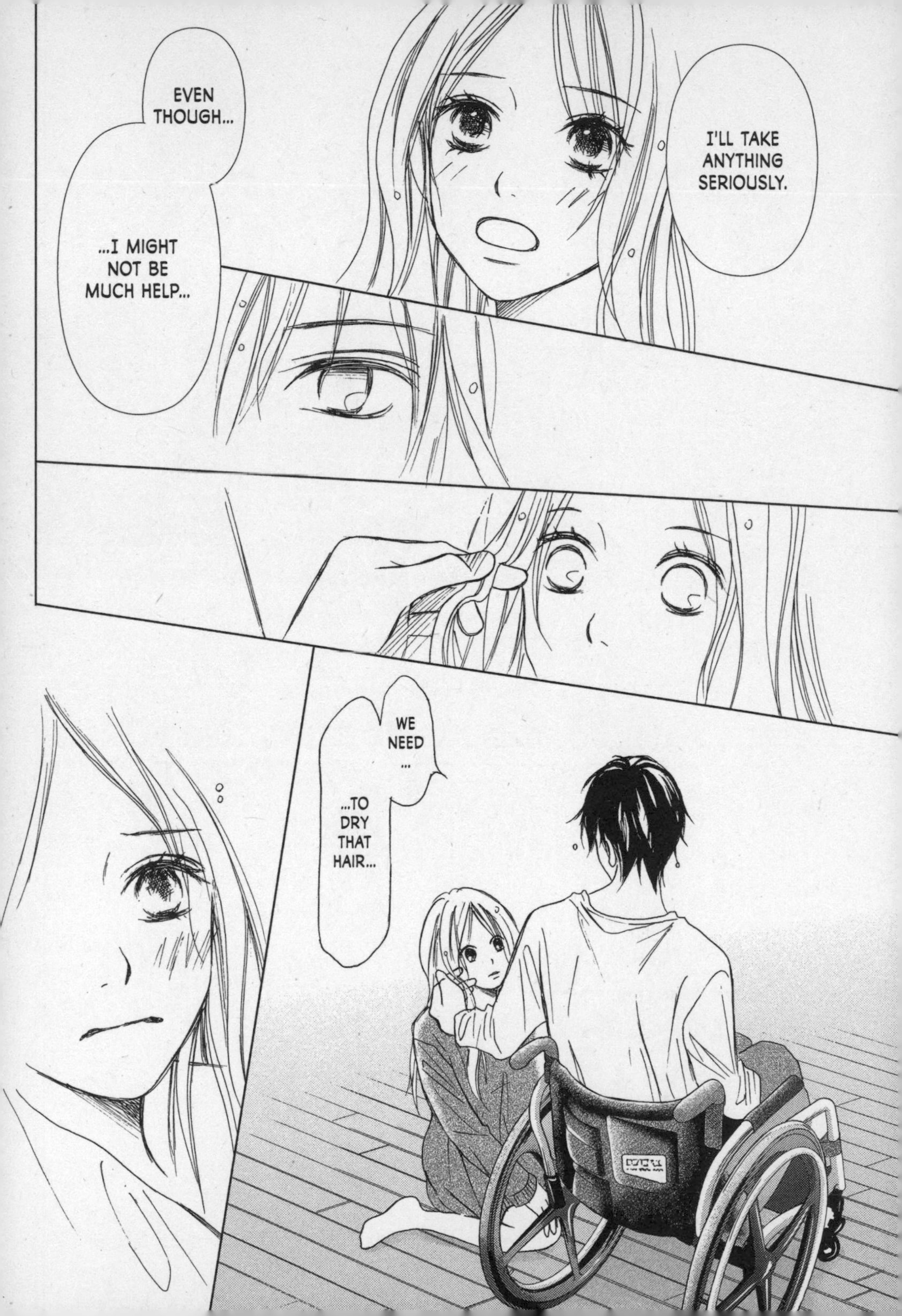
I'LL TAKE ANYTHING SERIOUSLY.
EVEN THOUGH...
...I MIGHT NOT BE MUCH HELP...
WE NEED ...
...TO DRY THAT HAIR...

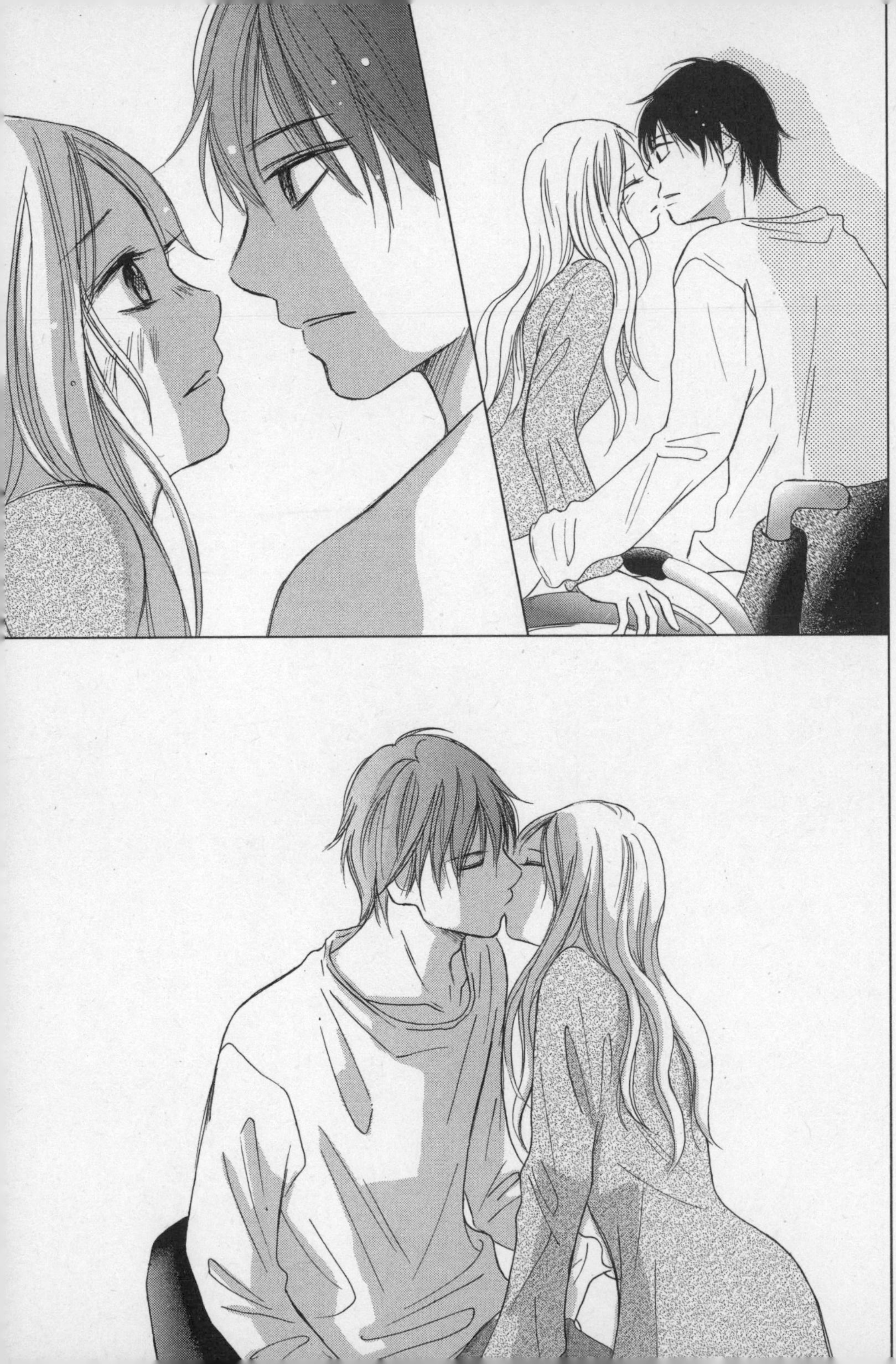

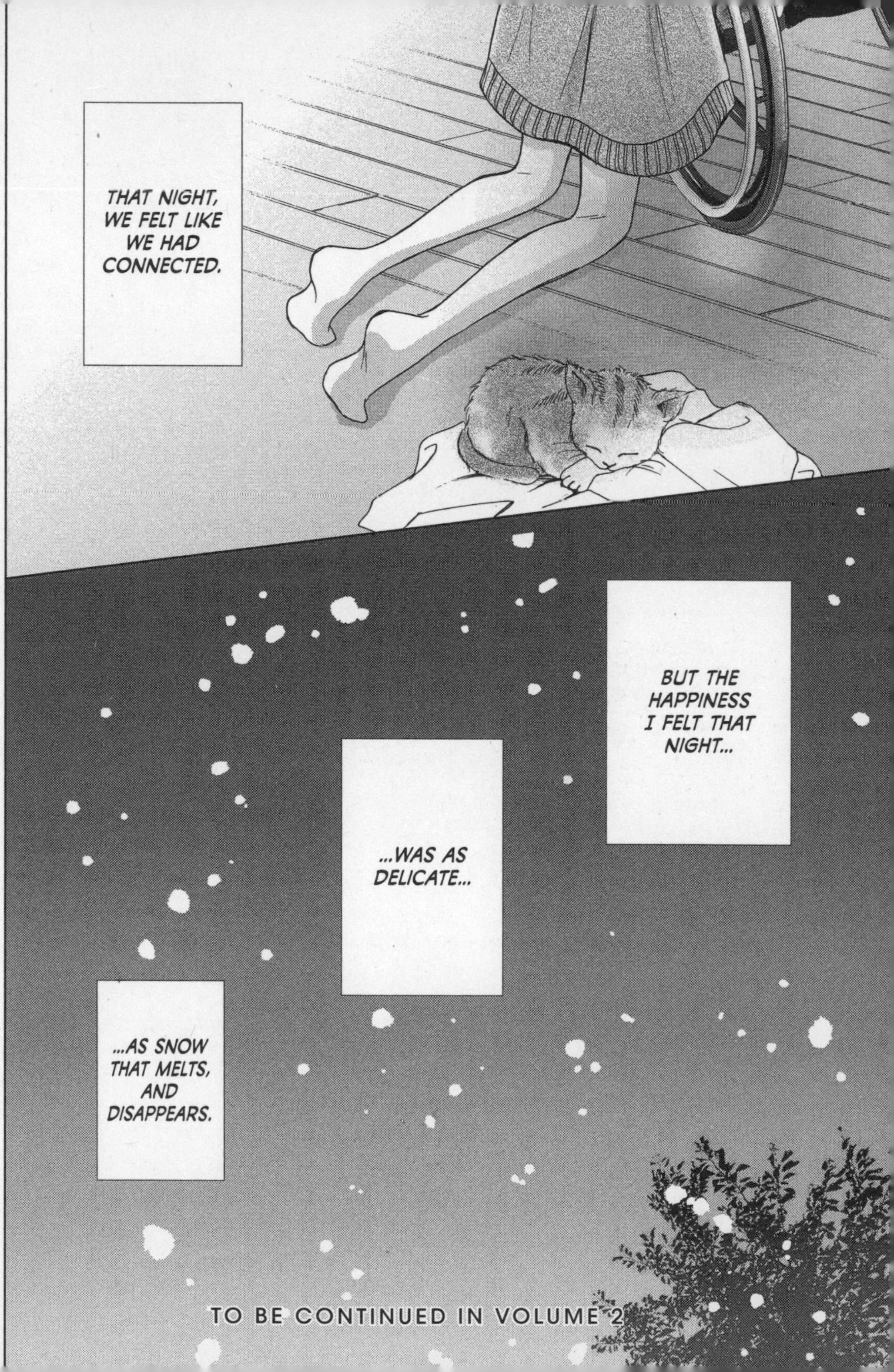
THAT NIGHT, WE FELT LIKE WE HAD CONNECTED.
BUT THE HAPPINESS I FELT THAT NIGHT...
...WAS AS DELICATE...
...AS SNOW THAT MELTS, AND DISAPPEARS.
TO BE CONTINUED IN VOLUME 2

Hello, I'm Rie Aruga!

Thank you for reading the first volume of *Perfect World*!
It was a one-shot at first, but thanks to the response from the readers,
it became a series.

I hope to grow alongside my protagonists in their struggles.
It's a juvenile first volume, but I hope you were able to enjoy it at least a little.

-Rie Aruga

— From the bottom of my heart, thank you to all of those who helped me. —

 * Kazuo Abe-sama from Abe Kensetsu Inc.
 * Yaguchi-sama * Sato-sama * Tomomi-sama * K-sama

 * My editor, Ito-sama * Everyone from the editorial department at Kiss
 * The designer, Kusume-sama * My assistants, T-sama,
                                        K-sama, and S-sama

My family, friends, everyone involved in getting this sold,
and also my readers.

TRANSLATION NOTES

KAZUO ABE, **PAGE 1**

ITSUKI AYUKAWA WAS MODELED AFTER KAZUO ABE, A CLASS-1 ARCHITECT WHO HAS A SPINAL CORD INJURY AND IS CEO OF ABE KENSETSU INC. IN NAGOYA, AICHI, JAPAN.

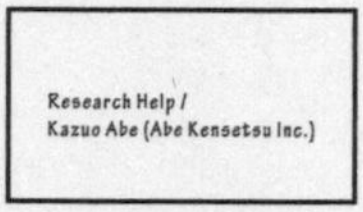
Research Help /
Kazuo Abe (Abe Kensetsu Inc.)

ADDRESSING SOMEBODY BY THEIR LAST NAME, **PAGE 5**

IN JAPANESE, IT'S POLITE TO ADDRESS SOMEBODY BY THEIR LAST NAME. AS TWO PEOPLE BECOME CLOSER, THEY MAY FEEL MORE COMFORTABLE ADDRESSING EACH OTHER BY THEIR FIRST NAMES INSTEAD, WHICH REPRESENTS A SHIFT IN THE RELATIONSHIP.

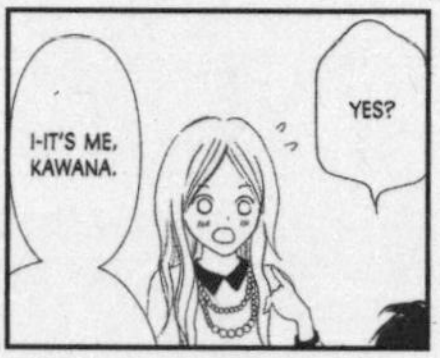
YES?
I-IT'S ME, KAWANA.

-SAN, **PAGE 8**

-SAN IS A GENDER-NEUTRAL SUFFIX USED TO ADDRESS AN ACQUAINTANCE IN A RESPECTFUL WAY.

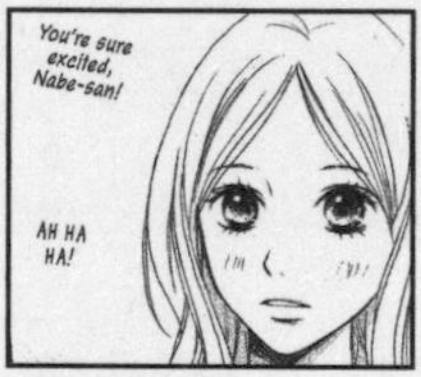
You're sure excited, Nabe-san!
AH HA HA!

SAILOR OUTFIT, **PAGE 16**

A SAILOR OUTFIT IS A KIND OF GIRLS' SCHOOL UNIFORM IN JAPAN INSPIRED BY THE UNIFORM TRADITIONALLY WORN BY ENLISTED SEAMEN. IT CONSISTS OF A BLOUSE ADORNED BY A SAILOR-STYLE COLLAR, AND A PLEATED SKIRT.

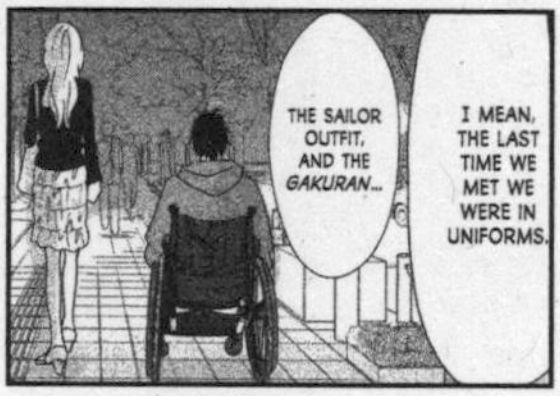
I MEAN, THE LAST TIME WE MET WE WERE IN UNIFORMS.
THE SAILOR OUTFIT, AND THE GAKURAN...

GAKURAN, **PAGE 16**

A *GAKURAN* IS A KIND OF BOYS' SCHOOL UNIFORM IN JAPAN INSPIRED BY THE UNIFORM TRADITIONALLY WORN BY PRUSSIAN CADETS. IT CONSISTS OF A WHITE SHIRT; A DARK, STRAIGHT-LINE JACKET; AND DARK, STRAIGHT-LINE TROUSERS. THE JACKET HAS A STANDING COLLAR, AND METALLIC BUTTONS RUN FROM TOP TO BOTTOM ALONG THE FRONT.

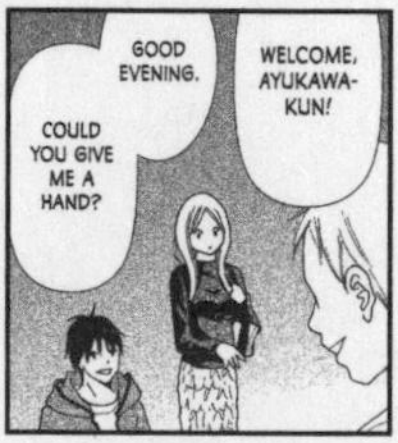
WELCOME, AYUKAWA-KUN!
GOOD EVENING.
COULD YOU GIVE ME A HAND?

-KUN, **PAGE 21**

-KUN IS A SUFFIX USED TO ADDRESS ONE'S JUNIORS, SUBORDINATES, COLLEAGUES, OR FRIENDS. IT IS MOST OFTEN USED TOWARDS MEN, OR BOYS, ALTHOUGH IT CAN ALSO BE USED TOWARDS WOMEN, OR GIRLS.

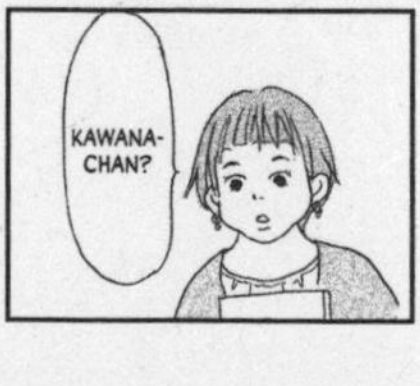
KAWANA-CHAN?

-CHAN, **PAGE 27**

-CHAN IS A SUFFIX USED TO ADDRESS CHILDREN. IT IS MOST OFTEN USED TOWARDS GIRLS, BUT IS ALSO COMMONLY USED TOWARDS YOUNG BOYS NOT YET IN SCHOOL. CLOSE FRIENDS, OR FAMILY MEMBERS WHO ARE ADULTS, MAY ALSO USE IT WITH EACH OTHER.

BARRIER-FREE, PAGE 53

THE TERM "BARRIER-FREE" REFERS TO A DESIGN CONCEPT IN WHICH BUILDINGS ARE ADAPTED SO THAT THEY CAN BE USED BY DISABLED PEOPLE INDEPENDENTLY. AN EXAMPLE OF THIS WOULD BE BUILDING A RAMP FOR WHEELCHAIR USERS.

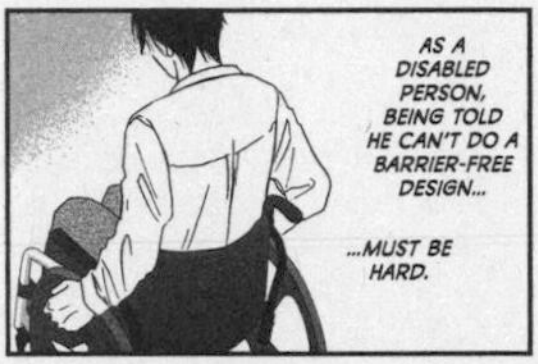
AS A DISABLED PERSON, BEING TOLD HE CAN'T DO A BARRIER-FREE DESIGN...
...MUST BE HARD.

YAKINIKU, PAGE 56

YAKINIKU LITERALLY MEANS "GRILLED MEAT." IT REFERS TO GRILLING MEATS SUCH AS BEEF, PORK, AND LAMB, BUT NOT FISH. IT IS AN EATING STYLE SIMILAR TO BARBEQUE, IN WHICH DINERS GRILL MEAT ON A GRATE, EATING THE MEAT GRADUALLY AS IT'S COOKED. AT A *YAKINIKU* RESTAURANT, DINERS ORDER RAW MEAT AND GRILL IT THEMSELVES ON A GRATE BUILT INTO THE TABLE.

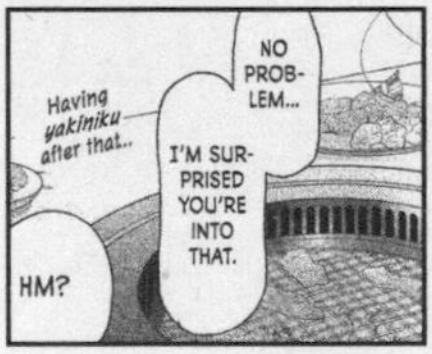
NO PROB-LEM...
Having yakiniku after that...
I'M SUR-PRISED YOU'RE INTO THAT.
HM?

ACCESSIBLE, PAGE 63

THIS IS AN ADJECTIVE USED TO DESCRIBE SOMETHING THAT WAS MODIFIED SO THAT IT CAN BE USED BY DISABLED PEOPLE INDEPENDENTLY. AN EXAMPLE OF THIS WOULD BE AN ACCESSIBLE PARKING SPACE, WHICH HAS AN AISLE ADJACENT TO THE PARKING SPOT SO THAT A PERSON IN A WHEELCHAIR HAS ENOUGH SPACE TO GET IN AND OUT OF THE CAR.

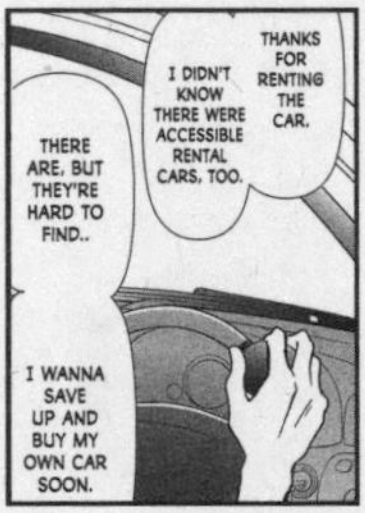
THANKS FOR RENTING THE CAR.
I DIDN'T KNOW THERE WERE ACCESSIBLE RENTAL CARS, TOO.
THERE ARE, BUT THEY'RE HARD TO FIND..
I WANNA SAVE UP AND BUY MY OWN CAR SOON.

ONIGIRI, PAGE 63

ONIGIRI IS A FOOD MADE OF WHITE RICE FORMED INTO A TRIANGULAR OR SPHERICAL SHAPE. IT IS OFTEN WRAPPED WITH DRY SEAWEED CALLED *NORI* AND STUFFED WITH INGREDIENTS SUCH AS TUNA OR PICKLED PLUMS.

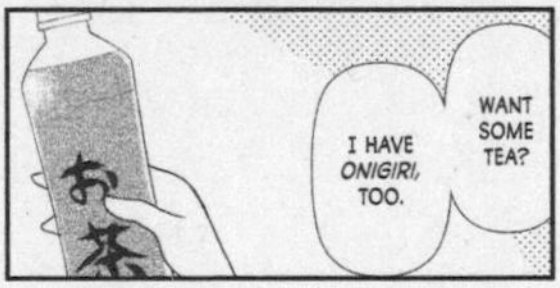
WANT SOME TEA?
I HAVE ONIGIRI, TOO.
お茶

KISS, PAGE 167

KISS IS THE MANGA MAGAZINE THAT SERIALIZES *PERFECT WORLD*. IT IS TARGETED TOWARDS WOMEN IN THEIR TWENTIES AND THIRTIES. IN JAPAN, MANGA ARE OFTEN SERIALIZED CHAPTER BY CHAPTER IN MAGAZINES BEFORE THE CHAPTERS ARE COLLECTED INTO A STANDALONE BOOK.

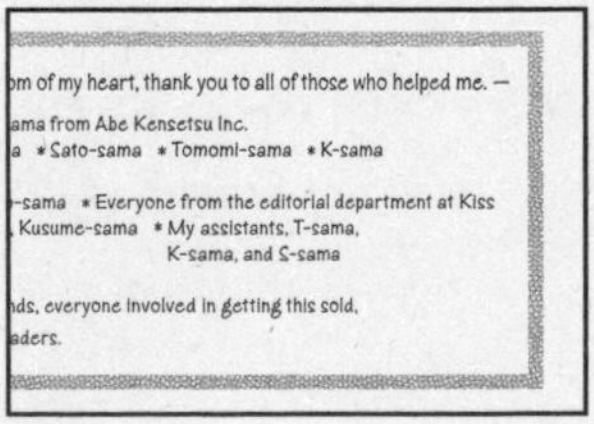
om of my heart, thank you to all of those who helped me. —
ama from Abe Kensetsu Inc.
a *Sato-sama *Tomomi-sama *K-sama
-sama *Everyone from the editorial department at Kiss
Kusume-sama *My assistants, T-sama, K-sama, and S-sama
nds, everyone involved in getting this sold,
aders.

A SMART, NEW ROMANTIC COMEDY FOR FANS OF *SHORTCAKE CAKE* AND *TERRACE HOUSE*!

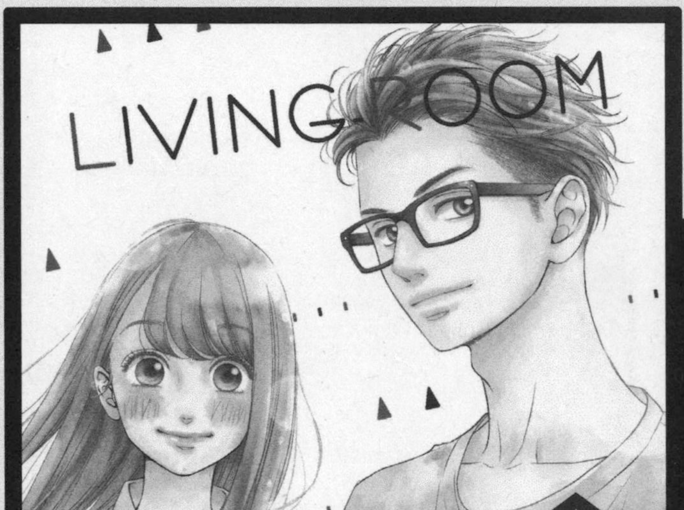
LIVING-ROOM
MATSUNAGA-SAN
1
Keiko Iwashita

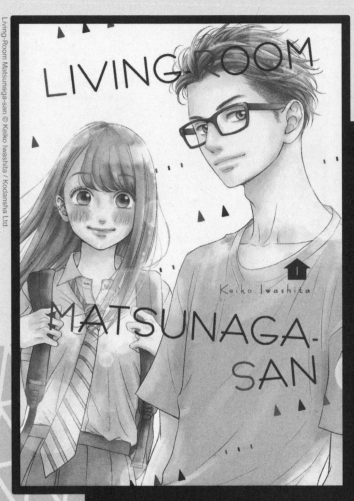

KC KODANSHA COMICS

A romance manga starring high school girl Meeko, who learns to live on her own in a boarding house whose living room is home to the odd (but handsome) Matsunaga-san. She begins to adjust to her new life away from her parents, but Meeko soon learns that no matter how far away from home she is, she's still a young girl at heart — especially when she finds herself falling for Matsunaga-san.

Knight of the ICE ©Yayoi Ogawa/Kodansha Ltd.

SKATING THRILLS AND ICY CHILLS WITH THIS NEW TINGLY ROMANCE SERIES!

A rom-com on ice, perfect for fans of *Princess Jellyfish* and *Wotakoi*. Kokoro is the talk of the figure-skating world, winning trophies and hearts. But little do they know... he's actually a huge nerd! From the beloved creator of *You're My Pet* (*Tramps Like Us*).

Chitose is a serious young woman, working for the health magazine *SASSO*. Or at least, she would be, if she wasn't constantly getting distracted by her childhood friend, international figure skating star Kokoro Kijinami! In the public eye and on the ice, Kokoro is a gallant, flawless knight, but behind his glittery costumes and breathtaking spins lies a secret: He's actually a hopelessly romantic otaku, who can only land his quad jumps when Chitose is on hand to recite a spell from his favorite magical girl anime!

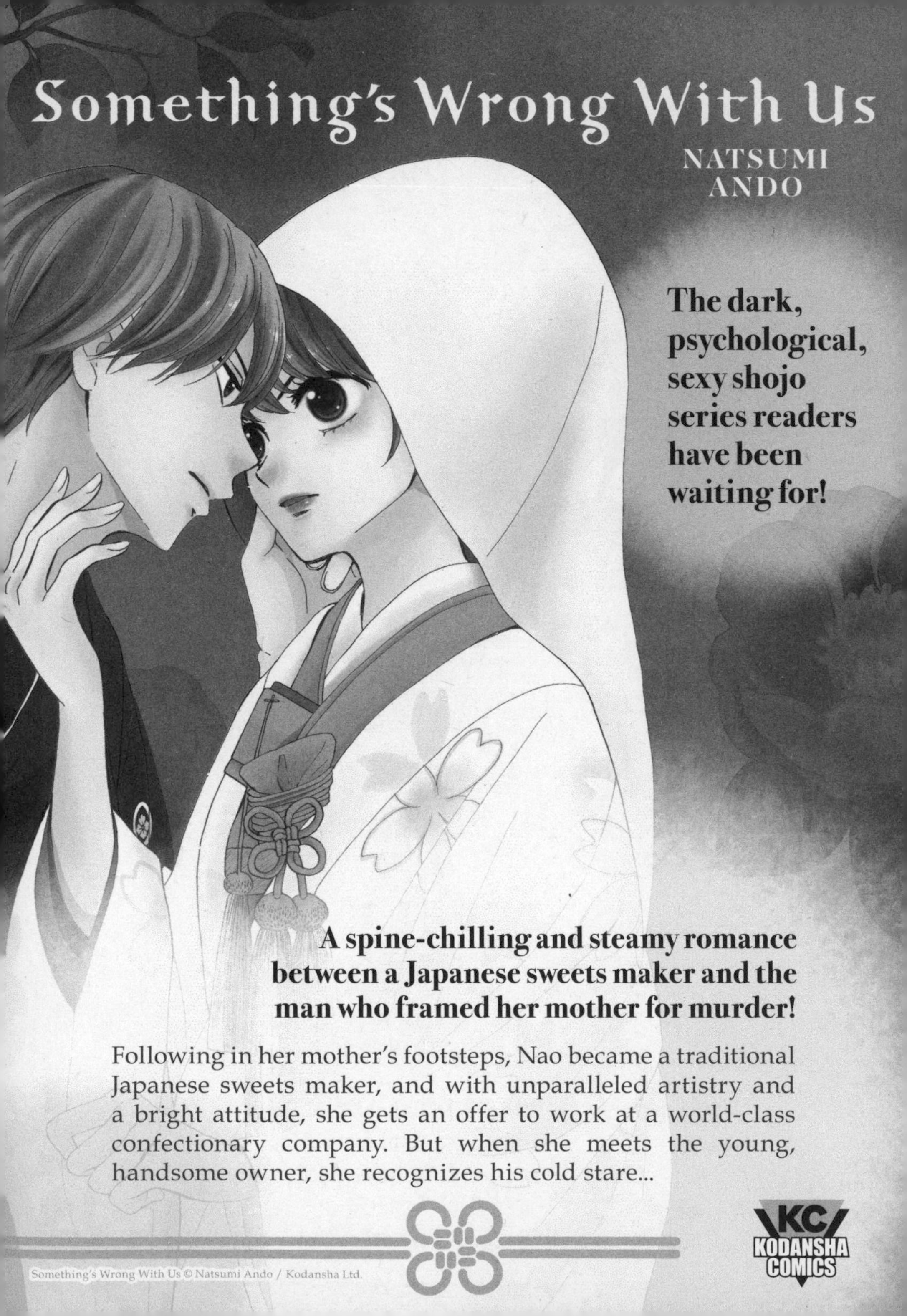
Something's Wrong With Us
NATSUMI ANDO
The dark, psychological, sexy shojo series readers have been waiting for!
A spine-chilling and steamy romance between a Japanese sweets maker and the man who framed her mother for murder!
Following in her mother's footsteps, Nao became a traditional Japanese sweets maker, and with unparalleled artistry and a bright attitude, she gets an offer to work at a world-class confectionary company. But when she meets the young, handsome owner, she recognizes his cold stare...
KC KODANSHA COMICS
Something's Wrong With Us © Natsumi Ando / Kodansha Ltd.

THE SWEET SCENT OF LOVE IS IN THE AIR! FOR FANS OF OFFBEAT ROMANCES LIKE *WOTAKOI*

VOL. 1

KINTETSU YAMADA

Sweat and Soap © Kintetsu Yamada / Kodansha Ltd.

In an office romance, there's a fine line between sexy and awkward... and that line is where Asako — a woman who sweats copiously — meets Koutarou — a perfume developer who can't get enough of Asako's, er, scent. Don't miss a romcom manga like no other!

KC
KODANSHA
COMICS

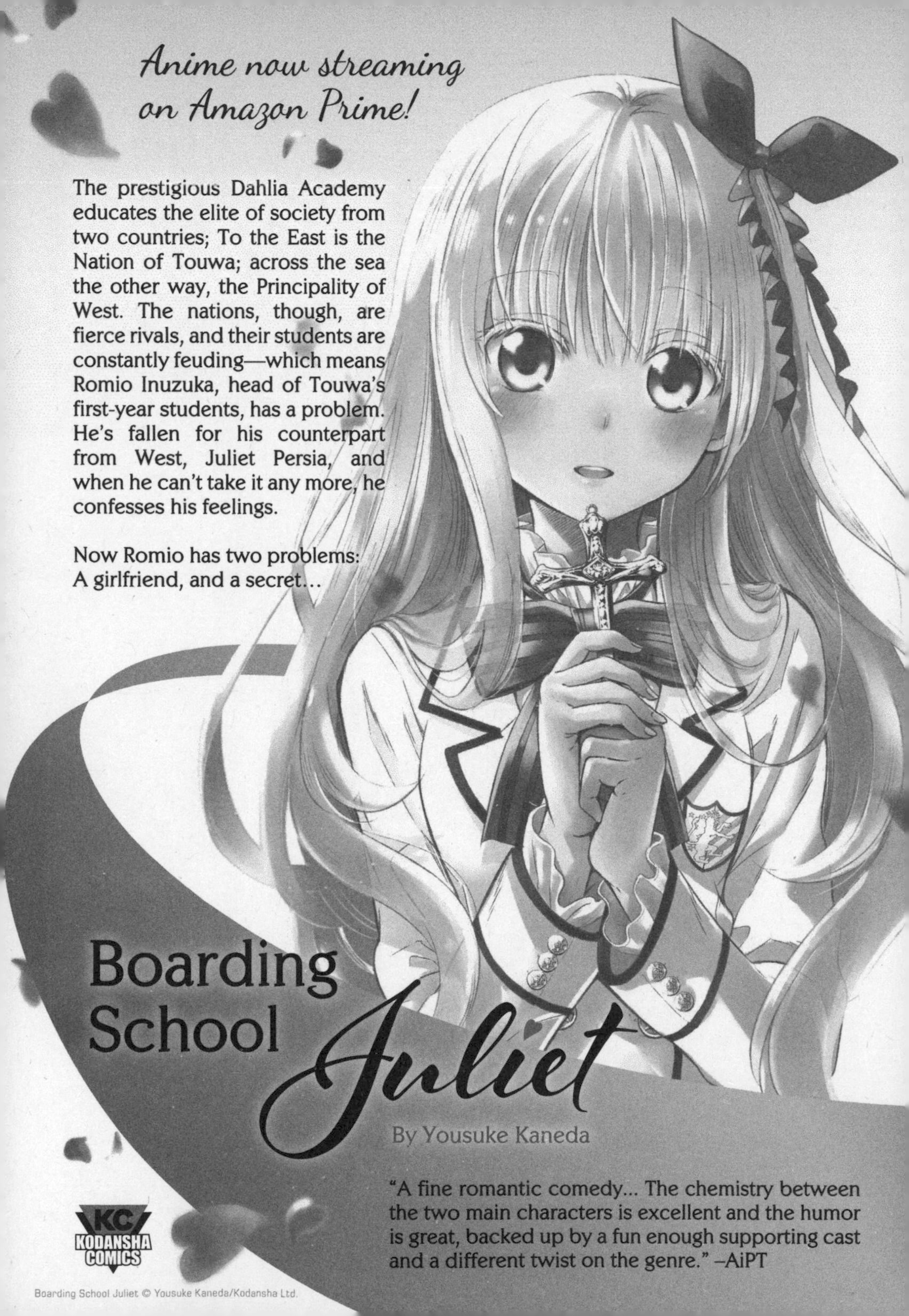

In love, there are
no save points.

NOW AN
ANIME!

ヲタクに恋は難しい

WOTAKOI:

LOVE IS HARD FOR OTAKU

by FUJITA

Narumi has had it rough: Every boyfriend she's had dumped her
once they found out she was an otaku, so she's gone to great
lengths to hide it. At her new job, she bumps into Hirotaka, her
childhood friend and fellow otaku. When Hirotaka almost gets
her secret outed at work, she comes up with a plan to keep him
quiet. But he comes up with a counter-proposal:
Why doesn't she just date him instead?

A Kodansha Comics Trade Paperback Original
Perfect World 1 copyright © 2015 Rie Aruga
English translation copyright © 2020 Rie Aruga

All rights reserved.

Published in the United States by Kodansha Comics, an imprint of Kodansha USA Publishing, LLC, New York.

Publication rights for this English edition arranged through Kodansha Ltd., Tokyo.

First published in Japan in 2015 by Kodansha Ltd., Tokyo as *Perfect World*, volume 1.

ISBN 978-1-63236-811-9

Original cover design by Tomohiro Kusume and Sayaka Mizui (arcoinc)

Printed in the United States of America.

www.kodanshacomics.com

9 8 7 6 5 4 3 2 1
Translation: Rachel Murakawa
Lettering: Thea Willis
Additional Lettering: Sara Linsley
Editing: Jesika Brooks and Tiff Ferentini
Kodansha Comics edition cover design by Phil Balsman

Publisher: Kiichiro Sugawara
Managing editor: Maya Rosewood
Vice president of marketing & publicity: Naho Yamada

Director of publishing services: Ben Applegate
Associate director of operations: Stephen Pakula
Publishing services managing editor: Noelle Webster
Assistant production manager: Emi Lotto and Angela Zurlo